P9-ART-555

Liberal City,
Conservative State

Liberal City, Conservative State

Moscow and Russia's Urban Crisis,
1906–1914

Robert W. Thurston

New York   Oxford
OXFORD UNIVERSITY PRESS
1987

Oxford University Press

Oxford   New York   Toronto
Delhi   Bombay   Calcutta   Madras   Karachi
Petaling Jaya   Singapore   Hong Kong   Tokyo
Nairobi   Dar es Salaam   Cape Town
Melbourne   Auckland

and associated companies in
Beirut   Berlin   Ibadan   Nicosia

Copyright © 1987 by Oxford University Press, Inc.

Published by Oxford University Press, Inc.,
200 Madison Avenue, New York, New York 10016

Oxford is a registered trademark of Oxford University Press

All rights reserved. No part of this publication may be reproduced,
stored in a retrieval system, or transmitted, in any form or by any means,
electronic, mechanical, photocopying, recording, or otherwise,
without the prior permission of Oxford University Press.

Library of Congress Cataloging-in-Publication Data
Thurston, Robert W.
Liberal city, conservative state.
Bibliography: p.
Includes index.
1. Moscow (R S F S R)—Politics and government.
2. Municipal government—Soviet Union—History.
3. Soviet Union—Politics and government—1904–1914.   I. Title.
JS6082.T48   1987   320.8′0947′312   86-28648
ISBN 0-19-504331-6
ISBN 0-19-504330-8 (pbk.)

Revised versions of the following articles appear in this volume by permission:

Robert W. Thurston, "Police and People in Moscow, 1906–1914," *Russian Review*
39, no. 3 (1980), 320–338.
Robert W. Thurston, "Developing Education in Late Imperial Russia: The Concerns
of State, 'Society,' and People in Moscow, 1906–1914," *Russian History* 11,
no. 1 (Spring 1984), 53–82.

All photographs in this volume appear by courtesy of the Library of Congress.

1 3 5 7 9 8 6 4 2

Printed in the United States of America

To my mother and the memory of my father

Acknowledgments

I want to thank many people and institutions for the help they provided in the making of this book. It began as a dissertation at the University of Michigan under the direction of William G. Rosenberg. At that point, he continually pushed me to improve my analysis and to sharpen the focus throughout. He made extremely valuable comments on early drafts of the manuscript as well. Beyond that, I owe him a huge intellectual debt, and I hope he realizes how much his assistance and support have meant to me.

Roberta T. Manning was amazingly generous with her time, comments, and support, to a person she did not even know when we began corresponding. Remarks she made about the section on education prompted me to rethink and rework the entire manuscript. She also went over an earlier draft with great care and attention to detail; her contribution to any quality this book may have is very substantial indeed. Her generosity can serve as a model to the entire field.

Michael Hamm and James Bater both read my dissertation and raised valuable questions about it. I hope they find this vastly revised product to their taste.

Cyril Black's incisive comments were a major contribution; they helped me to clarify some basic questions and issues of the entire study.

My parents-in-law, Theodore and Yetta Ziolkowski, provided a warm and challenging atmosphere during several summers. I am not sure I could have managed to complete the research for the book without their help and support, given steadily to a person who was sometimes frustrated and ornery.

My wife, Margaret Ziolkowski, has been involved in this project almost from the start. She read numerous drafts of the dissertation and the manuscript, and she made many important comments on organization, style, and substance. She took much time from her own intellectual concerns and work; I hope she derived satisfaction from watching this book develop. I wonder if there ever would have been a dissertation, let alone a book, without her.

My mother, Alice Thurston, gave me more than just a good start and intellectual curiosity; she humored and encouraged me in the lean years and made valuable comments on several sections of the manuscript.

Numerous institutions contributed money, a pleasant scholarly atmosphere, and resources. For work on the dissertation, I received grants from the Horace Rackham School of Graduate Studies and the Department of History at the University of Michigan, the Alvin Bentley Foundation, and the International Research and Exchanges Board, as well as a Fulbright-Hays Fellowship. A grant from the Kennan Institute for Advanced Russian Studies supported my work on the book. Awards I received from the Center for Slavic and East European Studies at Ohio State University and the University Research Institute of the University of Texas at El Paso (UTEP), primarily for work on other topics, also facilitated the completion of the book.

The staffs of the Library of Congress, the New York Public Library, the Lenin Library, and the Library of the Academy of Sciences in Leningrad, the Central State Archive of the City of Moscow (TsGAgM), Butler Library at Columbia University, the Law and Widener Libraries at Harvard, Princeton's Firestone Library, Michigan's Graduate Library, and the Hoover Institution were all extremely helpful. In particular I want to thank Hilja Kukk of the Hoover Institution for all her assistance. The inter-library loan personnel of the Universities of Vermont, California at San Diego, and UTEP did yeoman service in my cause.

Flo Dick of UTEP has been the ideal typist. She did a remarkable job of following my arrows, scribbles, and extended footnotes. She caught many an error and gave sound advice. All this she did quickly and cheerfully.

Every work of this sort is a collective effort in some fundamental sense, and perhaps my greatest debt is to all the scholars, Soviet and Western, who went over related ground before me.

El Paso, Texas   R.W.T.
September 1986

Contents

Note on Transliteration and Dates

The transliteration system used here is the one developed by the Library of Congress, with the exception of a few names widely known in the West; thus Tolstoy, not Tolstoi, for example. Most Russian terms are given in the new orthography: *gradonachal'nik*, not *gradonachal'nik''*, and *Russkie Vedomosti* instead of *Russkiia Viedomosti*.

All dates are given according to the Old Style or Julian calendar. In the early twentieth century, until the new regime changed it in 1918, this calendar was thirteen days behind the Western system. It was therefore a literal symbol of Russia's backwardness.

Liberal City,
Conservative State

Introduction

The Russian Revolution of 1905 reached and passed its bloody climax in the city of Moscow. During the ill-fated December Uprising, workers and other Muscovites set up barricades and battled government troops in the streets. The unequal contest was soon over, though soldiers took revenge on the rebels by executing dozens in factory courtyards.[1] Thus as the year 1906 began, Moscow had settled into an uneasy, forced calm. But the rubble in the working class districts caused by artillery shells and fires remained, a stark reminder of the questions the country still had to solve. What could be done to avoid another such upheaval? In particular, what policies could achieve social and political stability for urban Russia?

The Revolution of 1905, like its successor in 1917, began in the cities and hinged above all on urban developments.[2] Although the peasants certainly played a major role in each case, their opportunity to act developed on a broad scale only in the aftermath of the central government's weakness or downfall, brought about by events in the towns. Moreover, those peasants who had lived and worked in Russian cities were often central figures in rural disorders.[3] Thus the urban context was crucial in Russia's twentieth-century revolutions.

Even before the unrest of 1905 a general crisis of the country's cities should have been evident to any observant person. To give just one sign of the miserable urban situation, in 1904, of 1,084 Russian towns with more than ten thousand people, 892 had no organized water supply, and only 38 had city sewers.[4] What few municipal services did exist were often concentrated in the centers of the cities, which were inhabited by the wealthy elite, not in the poor outskirts populated by workers and other lower class people.[5] According to some Western accounts, this pattern, together with the traditional wide gap between Russia's educated elite (the *obshchestvo*, "society") and the common people (the *narod*), produced serious social tension. St. Petersburg workers were reacting by 1914 to "what appeared to them the indifference of privileged society."[6] It has been said that "as much as any other facet of Russian life, conditions in the cities blatantly manifested this indifference."[7]

Yet most members of the educated stratum were not stupid or unobservant regarding the milieu of the urban poor. Moscow's leading industrialists and city officials, for example, were deeply concerned about the events of 1905. They could hardly avoid paying attention, for the members of the city duma (council) were literally caught in the middle of the trouble. The tension was so great that the mayor, Prince V. M. Golitsyn, lost his nerve when a threatening crowd formed around the duma's building in October. Reduced to a quivering, incoherent wreck, he could barely stammer out his desire to resign to the sorrowful deputies before him.[8] Sympathetic and respectful toward Golitsyn and frightened themselves by the situation, the members accepted his resignation. Naturally, the council could hardly be indifferent to what was happening around it, and indeed it debated the causes of the unrest and what to do about them. As trouble mounted, Moscow's elite in and outside the duma produced a flood of writings and speeches about Russia's problems and offered many suggestions for their solution.[9]

The entire country's business class, like all of its educated stratum, was thoroughly engaged in considering the roots of social unrest in 1905. It was hardly possible to remain aloof from the programs, debates, and pressures for change in that year.[10] The attitudes of the upper classes toward the urban poor after the return of order in 1906 should be characterized not as indifference but as a search, desperate at times, for a solution to unrest. This quest occupied thinkers and activists across the political spectrum.

Given this acute awareness of the perilous situation in at least some sectors of "society," why wasn't more done to improve the conditions in the cities? A central question about the Old Regime arises at this point, one not widely explored in the existing literature. What were the towns' possibilities for reform? In everything they did, Russian municipalities found themselves under the tutelage of the state. Most towns really had not one but two local governments, very much intertwined and mutually responsible for municipal life. These two aspects or branches of urban administration were the locally elected officials (the *obshchestvennoe upravlenie*) and the tsarist authorities (*administratsiia*), appointed of course by the central government. The complexity of the situation is illustrated by the fact that both *upravlenie* and *administratsiia* may be translated into English as administration. Certainly any examination of Russian urban affairs before 1917 must cover municipal government in depth; yet it is impossible to understand what was going on in the cities without looking carefully at the state's policies and attitudes toward the towns, the powers of the tsarist administrators on the scene, and what those officials did with their authority. To date, little has been written about the great scope of the central bureaucracy's power in the towns and how it affected their governance, as well as their ability to bring about improvements in local life. What problems or opportunities for change did this situation create?

There are some discussions of central government policy toward local affairs, centering on the importance of the Extraordinary Measures of 1881. These laws granted certain tsarist officials at and below the provincial level the right to dominate local elected governments or to issue their own sweeping regulations. However, few works explore the application of these laws.[11] In general, there are few studies of Russia in this period that look carefully at the way policy worked out in practice on the local level, where it affected most people. How did the Extraordinary Measures and other similar laws affect Russian life? How were they received by the public? What role did such statutes and their application play in preparing the way for the revolutions of 1917?

Considering the explosion of so many towns once more in that year, and the obvious lack of significant improvement in many locales by the eve of World War

I, the role of the state in producing the situation must have been significant, and needs to be examined. On the other hand, Russian poverty pure and simple, the massive influx of peasants into the towns, which exacerbated all problems, or the indifference of municipal leaders might also explain a great deal. Where does the responsibility lie?

In reforming Russia on any level, many moderates were willing after 1905 to cooperate with the central government. This position was typified by the Octobrist party. Its official title was the Union of October 17, commemorating the October Manifesto, a statement issued by the tsar on that day in 1905, which promised basic civil liberties and a national legislative assembly to the population. This was the foundation on which the Octobrists expected to cooperate with the government. But by 1914 many such moderates had turned completely away from the state and virtually given up hope of avoiding another revolution. Why did this divergence occur, and why was so much of the new opposition centered in Russian cities, above all Moscow? What relation did this trend have to local conditions? Moreover, this new mood developed despite the facts that the central government allowed many reform efforts to proceed in the city, that the municipality's financial situation was improving, and that Moscow's elected officials were frequently able to find ways around central government restrictions. So why did mutual antipathy grow between city and state, when many things appeared to be getting better? One answer lies in an ideological crisis of the Old Regime: educated urban dwellers saw the vital necessity to develop their country in one way, but the dominant group among the central authorities envisioned a very different future. This ideological disagreement and its importance need to be examined more thoroughly than the literature has done to date. In this regard, a detailed investigation of one urban center can serve to illuminate matters in a way that studies of national parties and politics cannot.

Recent Western literature on Russia's business classes speaks of their ideological and social fragmentation on the eve of World War I.[12] This may have been so, yet at least the leading segment of Moscow's business group had enough flexibility and pragmatism to promote a series of local policies that were promising and coherent steps toward stability. This cohort was also willing and able to work with Moscow's intelligentsia and progressive nobles in order to achieve change. What was ultimately most important in splitting the business or any other elite was its relation to the state and its policies; here ideology again assumed great significance.

The ideological issue bears on another question about the tsarist regime after 1905: why did it develop and partially implement a broad program of change in the countryside, while it had almost no idea of what to do for the cities, despite the extensive upheavals there? Prime Minister P. A. Stolypin presented broad reform proposals to the newly created Russian parliament (State Duma) in 1907, including changes in the laws on religion, peasant life, the court system, and agriculture.[13] But his ideas contained very little for the towns. He told the Third Duma in November 1907,

> The organization of the country demands great transformations, but all improvements in local routines [*rasporiadakh*] in the courts and in administration will remain superficial, will not penetrate deeply, until [we have] raised the well-being of the basic agricultural class of the state [. . . and that is] the

basis on which the transformation of the Russian state structure will be firmly created.... Therefore the essential concern of the present Government, its guiding idea, is always the agricultural question.[14]

When Stolypin outlined his proposals for local government reform to the State Council in 1907, he mentioned the towns, but all of his detailed plans related only to the countryside.[15]

The premier's emphasis echoed his sovereign's. On April 17, 1906 Nicholas II addressed the members of the State Council and the First Duma.

I will unshakably uphold the institutions which I have granted, with firm confidence that you will devote all your strength to selfless service to the Fatherland for the clarification of the needs of the peasantry, so close to my heart, of the education of the people, and the development of their well-being.[16]

The tsar mentioned no other group in the population besides the peasants. Thus the stage was set for Stolypin's major reforms, which attempted to end the control of the village communes over peasant agriculture in favor of individual farming. Even these changes were not originally passed through the State Duma, but around it.[17]

In this way, the tsarist government tipped its hand; it had almost no new policies to offer to the cities. While it considered various projects for the reform of local government after 1905, it focused its attention here, too, almost exclusively on the *zemstva*,[18] the organs of rural self-government. Why did the regime respond to urban and rural problems so differently?

At the same time, the regime did have a policy of sorts for the urban working class after 1905. For a certain period, roughly 1906 to 1912, this policy appeared to succeed, and it had some elements that appealed to workers and others that appealed to employers. The other side of the coin was that the policy could not strongly satisfy either group and thus contained the seeds of its own collapse. Ironically, the defects of the tsarist approach helped to push liberal industrialists and some workers closer together, at least on paper, when a new mood developed that was evident by 1912. The story of this alliance has not yet been told, though it forms a central part of the liberal movement in this period and can offer new perspectives on the revolutions of 1917.

Given the liberals' approach to the labor movement and many other aspects of lower class life in Moscow, can it be said that the city fathers (and they were all fathers—no mothers were allowed in council seats) displayed the "indifference" of the privileged classes noted in the Western accounts cited earlier? If not, it will be useful to know why the Muscovites were different in outlook and programs. Conclusions may be drawn from this study about the prospects for Russian urban reform in general: what preconditions did it require? What were the factors whose presence in Moscow conditioned the course of reform there and whose absence elsewhere meant that at best change would be much slower? One significant aspect of this question is the financial position of the towns in law and in practice, something that has not yet been examined in any detail.

The connection between class and policy is an issue of Russian urban affairs to which Soviet and Western scholars have paid particular attention. One might assume a strong correlation between these two things in Moscow, since by law its city duma deputies were almost all propertied men. Works on urban affairs in other settings have concluded that love of private property and wealth greatly hampered ameliorative efforts. In Philadelphia during the 1920s, this sentiment among municipal leaders helped produce what Sam Bass Warner, Jr., has called the "private city." A lack of public spirit and concern resulted in "the notorious failing of the modern American city," in which many more people lived at an inadequate level than was necessary, given the wealth of the society.[19] Enid Gauldie has similarly explained the failure to regulate housing conditions in nineteenth-century Britain.[20]

Observers of Russian life before 1914 were well aware that the urban franchise was undemocratic and that as a result the municipal council was dominated by certain social groups.

> According to the active City Statute of 1892, city self-government as we understand it does not exist in Russia, for the conduct of all city affairs is given not to the urban citizens, not to a majority of them, but to a small, privileged group of rich merchants and property owners.[21]

However, the author of these lines worked closely with the Moscow city government and in 1913 edited an official account of its activities that was extremely favorable and contained no hint that class bias affected policy decisions.[22]

Nikolai Astrov, a leading member of the liberal Constitutional Democratic (*Kadet*) party and for many years a Moscow city duma deputy and municipal secretary, also believed that class origins did not affect the council's performance.

> The privileged city Duma did not maintain distance and isolation from the population, for the principles of its work were not opposed to the interests of the population. On the contrary, they fully coincided with its goals and needs ... and the city duma carried out work for all that was above class considerations.[23]

However, another writer took the opposite view during the turbulent year 1917.

> The reason for the inadequate facilities of our cities, for the mess that dominates their sanitary arrangements, lies once again in the composition of the city Duma delegates, chosen from the property owners and shopkeepers, who are interested in seeing that the sanitary regulations are not put into effect.[24]

Some Soviet historians have also described the city's duma in these years as class-bound and pathetically ineffective. For instance, B. V. Zlatoustovskii has written,

> Finally, the third [and last tsarist] period in Moscow city government came about as a result of a reactionary counterreform, that is the law of June 11, 1892, which decisively changed the organs of city self-government into an appendage of the state bureaucratic institutions, ruled by a handful of rich men as a firm bulwark of autocracy and reaction.[25]

In recent Soviet work a somewhat more favorable view of the municipality has begun to appear. For example, the third edition of *Istoriia Moskvy; kratkii ocherk* (The History of Moscow: A Short Outline) discusses the programs and accomplishments of the city duma much more positively than did older Soviet studies, though there is still a strong note of condescension.[26]

For an investigator of the Moscow city government who operates across a considerable expanse of time and space, the question of its members' class orientation and its impact on policy formation is a difficult one. To what extent did municipal leaders attempt to implement a "bourgeois" philosophy, and if they did that at all, were they shortsighted or visionary in their choices? A decision to protect their fellows' pocketbooks in the short run by skimping on city services might have the long-term result of producing great dissatisfaction and dangerous unrest; thus the interpretation and protection of "class interests" could take widely varying forms. The ready identification of social background with certain municipal policies or lack thereof really explains nothing at all. A more detailed investigation of what took place on the urban scene and why is in order.

Moscow from 1906 to 1914 is particularly well suited to this kind of study, for several reasons. First, it had all the typical Russian urban problems of the day: unhealthy and overcrowded housing; a very low level of education among the lower classes; widespread poverty; severe defects in sanitation, cleanliness, and health care facilities; and inadequate municipal services in every category. A steady, massive influx of peasants into the city greatly exacerbated all these problems. Moscow was the second largest city in the Russian Empire before 1914 but the fastest-growing.

The second major reason the city lends itself well to a study of Russian urban life is that its local government was, by general contemporary acknowledgment, the leader in the country's efforts to improve the situation. Moscow had model programs in a number of areas. Part of the reason for this distinction was the city's greater wealth compared to other towns. Even St. Petersburg, the only larger city in Russia, was not so well favored financially: a lot more property there than in Moscow was owned by the central government, and such property was kept from local taxation. This fact also underlies the St. Petersburg duma's greater dependence on the state; Moscow's council was more independent and thus freer to seek its own path of development.

In making that path, the Moscow city government stands out as a generally liberal body interested in modernization, an approach that frequently brought it into conflict with the conservative state. The key terms in this statement require some elucidation. *Liberal* is often a slippery word, one that is of course relative and largely tied to a specific political context. The liberals of Berlin in 1848 did not want the same things for government and society as the liberals of Washington in 1960, for example. The Russian Kadets were liberals before 1917; after the February Revolution produced the collapse of tsarism, they found themselves on the right, even though their central goals had not changed. In a few weeks the changing context propelled the same platform from liberalism to conservatism.

Russian liberals before 1917 are usually characterized as focusing their attention on political rather than social improvements.[27] This concentration certainly appeared in Russians' own definitions of *liberal* and *liberalism* in the late nineteenth and early twentieth centuries.[28] One central concern of Russian liberals was for "legality, the juridical guarantee of individual and property rights." Liberalism "could be opposition to the government, or rejection of state authority. . . . Liberal was anything that meant or led to a decrease in state power."[29] Yet in Moscow the liberals were acutely concerned about social change and improvement; their milieu absolutely forced them to be.

Liberals anywhere are generally interested in gradual change that will preserve the basic outlines of their society. The same might be said of some conservatives. While liberals usually emphasize the change, conservatives usually stress the preservation. Moderate liberals and moderate conservatives hold views that shade into each other. This occurred in Russia with right Kadets and left Octobrists, and it is one reason that historians have not been able to agree on a convenient label for the Octobrist party.[30]

Russian conservatives believed in the necessity of upholding the country's greatness and stability through appealing to traditional values and institutions. They emphasized loyalty to tsar and fatherland, Russian nationalism, and Orthodoxy. These beacons of virtue should shine upon a rigid social structure. Any deviation from this model or any questioning of the secular and religious authorities supporting it could cause the whole edifice to shatter, precipitating chaos and the ultimate horror, revolution. The best guarantee that this would not happen was to encourage the state to exercise its broad powers in favor of the conservative view.

The important point to bear in mind is that we are speaking of a spectrum of views on the necessity, nature, and scope of change, ranging from radicals on the left to reactionaries on the right. It was clear to contemporary Russians who stood where in relation to whom; the words *left* and *right* were part of everyday political discourse, and there seemed to be no mystery about them. This work employs the labels *liberal* and *conservative* because the equivalent terms in the years 1906–1914 are more cumbersome and much less meaningful to present-day readers.

Members of the Moscow city government did not describe themselves with the terms liberal or conservative, although in 1905 the duma pointed to the necessity for "liberal reforms . . . which alone can put the country on the path of peaceful development."[31] However, council members did identify themselves as progressists or moderate-rights, terms that of course also describe relative positions on a political spectrum.

I describe the Moscow city government as liberal in this period because it strongly promoted change in the city. It worked for improvements for the lower classes in many respects, while calling for expanded civil rights, political liberty, and political participation. The city duma on a number of occasions found itself in opposition to the government and engaged in rejection of state authority. This tendency became more pronounced as Russia drew nearer to the war; the municipality clearly became more liberal as time went on. However, this process was sometimes hesitant, uneven, or contradictory. The city government's liberalism represents a trend, not an absolutely set position, but a readily discernible trend nonetheless. The state's conservatism was also hesitant and uneven, but it too was a deepening tendency after 1907.

Much of the conflict between city and state arose from the former's attempts to modernize in its jurisdiction. To use the word *modernization* is undoubtedly to wave a red flag before the eyes of many readers. But any substitute term seems even more problematic. A phrase penned by Marion J. Levy, Jr., is appropriate here. Speaking of his own work, he wrote, "Anyone who feels strongly that the term modernization *must mean* something other than its explicit definition here should feel free to substitute any other term or symbol provided he does so consistently."[32] Cyril Black also expressed diffidence about the term when he prefaced a discussion of it with the phrase, "If a definition is necessary."[33]

For the purposes of this work, *modernization* means the attempt to adapt historically evolved institutions or to create new ones to meet the demands generated by rapid economic, social, and political change.[34] The word thus refers to a vast set of changes and attempts by societies to keep pace with them. What happens is a "holistic process affecting all aspects of society."[35]

It may be valuable at the outset of this study to clarify which aspects of modernization will be emphasized here and which will not. What various authors have called *social modernization*, which refers to changes in social structure and relations, will be more or less a fundamental but background concern throughout. It will not be directly covered except as some of its features relate to the greatest social change of this period in Russia, the massive migration of peasants to the cities. Otherwise, the social, together with the economic, technological, and psychological aspects of modernization, will not figure prominently in this book.

Instead, the central focus will be on what might be called *institutional modernization*, as the definition given above implies. How did Russian urban institutions respond to the very serious problems the cities faced after 1905? Of course, *institution* is also a broad term; what is meant here is largely features and programs of public life as provided by government. In order for institutions to change, concerns and attitudes have to change first, and the resources for new programs have to be available.

Institutional adaptation is perhaps the most important aspect of modernization for a historical inquiry. Technological change, industrialization, urbanization, and a host of other processes have taken place in many societies over a long period of time. Those societies have responded in many different ways, by doing very little or by revamping or abandoning old institutions and creating new ones. Societies that follow the latter course quickly and flexibly in the face of great stresses are successful and achieve a reasonable degree of social and political stability. Societies whose institutions do not adapt successfully in such a situation are likely to undergo serious unrest.

The nature, weight, and flexibility of tradition are key factors in determining any society's response to new conditions. What seems particularly striking about the history of Russian modernization in the early twentieth century is the difference in the importance of tradition to the various branches or levels of public administration.

Most of the historical literature on the Russian Empire in this period concentrates on national political life, though in recent years much work has been done on peasants entering the urban environment and on the workers' movement. In these and other areas Moscow has been the subject of important contributions to our knowledge. Usually, such works concentrate on one specific group in the population: the workers, the peasants, or the bourgeoisie, for example.[36] There is no detailed study of a Russian city, in the interrevolutionary or any other period, that examines the complex whole of urban problems and the approach to them taken by local and state agencies.

I have tried to draw a broad picture of one of the major Russian centers, Moscow, in a period of great challenge and innovation. My object has been to describe and analyze the major currents acting upon the lower classes, "society," and the central government alike. This book is therefore partly social history, partly institutional and political history, and partly urban history. There is no better place than the Moscow of 1906–1914 to examine the interaction between the various forces of tsarist law, traditional attitudes, Russian liberalism, the process of modernization, and the effects of rapid economic and demographic change.

The stakes were high in this interaction. After the scare they experienced in 1905, the leaders of the conservative state and of the liberal city were both groping for ways to avoid another, greater catastrophe. For both sides, the year 1906 and the quest for a stable Russia began at the same time.

1

The Character of the City, 1906–1914

For five or six years the proletariat of the capital has doubled and trebled and it can be imagined what material this will offer for rebellion.

M. Menshikov, 1907[1]

The layers of refuse that had been deposited under successive snows during the winter all appeared on the surface now and gave off odors beyond description.

Samuel Harper, describing March 1904[2]

A newcomer to Moscow in the year 1906 would have gone to the Sparrow (now Lenin) Hills, located on the southwestern outskirts, for the best view of the city. At the base of the Hills, the new arrival would have seen the Moscow River; it runs north to south there, before making a tight loop back to the north in the center of the city, where it passes beneath the Kremlin. Finally the river bends back upon itself yet another time, resuming its north-south course before passing out of Moscow on the southeast side.

Beyond the river, the gazer on the Sparrow Hills would have seen flat, open fields, then a jumble of one- and two-story buildings, and finally four- and five-story structures in the city center. One's eye would have been caught, especially on a sunny day, by the brilliant gold domes of many of the city's churches. Above all, the newcomer would have remarked two sights. The first was the huge Church of Christ the Savior, southwest of the city center. Built between 1839 and 1883, this edifice covered an area of 8,020 square yards and had five gilded domes, forty-eight exterior marble reliefs, and extensive decorations in gold and marble inside.[3] (Sadly, the new regime blew it all up in the 1930s, with the intention of putting an equally huge Palace of Soviets in its place. The ground proved too weak to support such a structure—leaving the question of how the church stood there in the first place—and today the site holds a swimming pool.)

The most arresting point of interest visible in 1906, still very much there today, was the Kremlin. It was then not an administrative center but a complex of churches, monasteries, and palaces. The tsars came to Moscow to be crowned in one of the Kremlin cathedrals, returning from the more westernized St. Petersburg to the heart of old Russia, where presumably they imbibed the true spirit of their country before setting out to rule.

After absorbing the view of Moscow from the Sparrow Hills, the observer could have descended to the river and taken the ferry across. Walking or riding

Moscow in the early twentieth century. The view is from the southeast. The Kremlin, dominated by the Bell Tower of Ivan the Great, is in the center of the photo; Zamoskvorech'e is to the left.

the distance of about 7.2 kilometers to the center of the city, the newcomer would have encountered a teeming urban scene that combined the East and the West. Moscow was a place as vital and exotic as Istanbul or Cairo today, where for a price, anything was possible. It was a city with pockets of great wealth and luxury, yet overwhelmingly noisy, dirty, and poor, even by contemporary European standards. It was a religious center said to have "forty times forty" churches, though in reality there were 450 in 1914.[4] There were also more than eighty monasteries and nunneries. The city was sometimes sophisticated and polished, but as one observer wrote in 1915, "In general it is possible to call Moscow a peasant city."[5] This was long an appropriate characterization because the majority of the population at any given time had recently left the countryside. The peasant flavor was strengthened after 1906 by a steady influx of rural job-seekers.

Within Moscow thousands of street vendors sold household goods, pies, cakes, fish, toys, and drinking water. The shabby lower trade rows on Red Square catered to anyone, but the city's elite preferred the elegant shops of Kuznetskii Most. Expensive restaurants such as the Hermitage or Slavianskii Bazar were famous for their cooking, but the poor ate in cheap dining rooms where they could fill up for twenty or twenty-five kopecks. The menus included cabbage soup, porridge, and roasted and boiled fish. Portions were large, but these places were often absolutely filthy, with layers of grease and dirt everywhere, and roaches that crawled around unhampered and fell into the pots.[6]

There was another Moscow, too, one that had begun to overshadow the old traditions and chaos. In the past few decades the city had grown into an industrial giant, second in the empire only to St. Petersburg.[7] For generations the center of the Russian textile industry, Moscow had recently begun to diversify and expand its heavy manufacturing. As a banking center it ranked well below St. Petersburg but, in contrast to the capital, its money was proudly Russian. In the years before World War I the city's large banks began to finance the development of projects in central Asia and southern Russia, extending Moscow's influence over a huge area.

The city was also a cultural center that in some ways surpassed St. Petersburg. The Bol'shoi Theatre was magnificent, and the young Moscow Art Theatre was the most dynamic arena for plays in the country. Symbolism and Futurism, to name only two of the contemporary movements in art and literature, were well represented in the city. Among others, Mayakovsky, Repin, Vrubel, and Blok worked there.

Art had to coexist with sin and crime. On the boulevards that curved around the center of Moscow, the elite of the town took their evening walks. On such strolls they had to weave among the many prostitutes and their pimps, for whom the boulevards were a favorite hunting ground. Anyone who lived in the city had to watch out for drunks as well: 4,394 unconscious inebriates were taken to police clinics in 1909, and 5,620 the following year.[8]

There were also many beggars, who sometimes became aggressive. If they were not begging they might be picking someone's pocket. Occasionally the police swooped down and made massive roundups of such people. On the night of May 23, 1912, for example, police arrested 3,145 beggars and measured their bodies for departmental files, a fashionable European police practice of the period. Of those caught, 1,103 were pronounced to be recidivist thieves, and 1,025 had no identification. Some were released, but the "majority of those arrested were exiled administratively to their birthplaces or elsewhere."[9] This expedient was a favorite police solution to the city's problems, yet there were always many to take the places of those who were thrown out.

Coming or going, rich or poor, Muscovites could find a few peaceful spots. Well-developed parks and squares were scattered throughout the city, and it was a quick and fairly inexpensive tram ride to the quiet of the Sparrow Hills or Sokol'niki Park, also located on the outskirts. However, the scene included other aspects, as a report to the city stated in 1913.

> Street dust and dirt lead to the spread of all sorts of infectious diseases and tuberculosis, which claim thousands of lives every year. The constant noise of carriages, the clang of iron, the rumble of automobiles, in general terrible noise and racket, occurring day and night on Moscow's streets, are reflected in the significant increase of nervous and psychological illnesses and thus in an indirect fashion contribute to the growth of suicide, which is taking on horrifying dimensions.[10]

Industrialization meant the growth of such conditions, along with the rapid expansion of Moscow's economy and population. Immigrating peasants went to work in factories, if they could, though more often they took jobs as apprentices to artisans, day laborers, or in any of a host of other semi- or unskilled trades. Increasing population meant in turn that existing overcrowding in housing would worsen, the already high death rate would climb, more beggars would appear on the streets, and a smaller percentage of the people would be educated—unless large-scale efforts were made to improve Moscow's facilities. This was the challenge facing the city government. In attempting to meet that challenge, the municipality set great changes in motion. This chapter outlines the physical and social setting in which those processes took place.

Moscow was, and is, laid out in concentric circles around the Kremlin. Contemporary descriptions identified three sections of the city: the center, reaching to the boulevards, which went along the path of an old city wall; the area between the

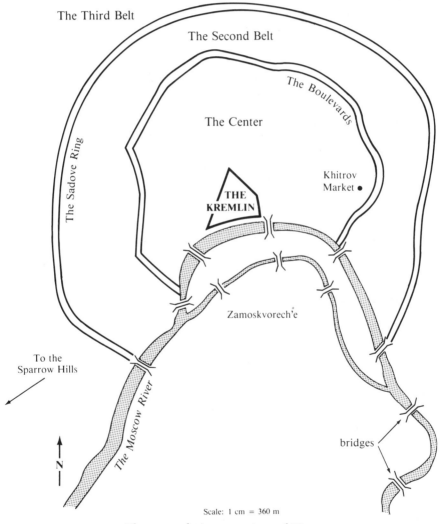

The prerevolutionary regions of Moscow

(*Source:* Moskovskaia gorodskaia Uprava, *Sovremennoe khoziaistvo goroda Moskvy,* ed. Ippolit Verner [*M.:* 1913], map following p. 416.)

boulevards and the broad circular road called the Sadovoe Ring; beyond Sadovoe, or the outskirts. These were also designated the first, second, and third belts. The region known as Zamoskvorech'e (literally "beyond the Moscow River"), a section south of the Kremlin almost enclosed by a sharp loop of the river, was often mentioned separately.

These parts of the city differed from each other in their general characteristics. The center included the Kremlin, and on its side of the river, to the boulevards, commerce predominated. This area was no longer losing population as in previous years, but it was growing very slowly.

Also in the center, about 1.3 kilometers east of the Kremlin, was Khitrov Market. Not really a market at all, this complex consisted of a group of flophouses that were home to the poorest people of Moscow. Khitrov was infamous in its time as a breeding ground for crime and infectious disease. The municipality was constantly preoccupied with the Market and began or planned many times to alleviate the situation there. However, little had changed by the start of the First World War. Khitrov was the unhealthiest place in Moscow, but men, women, and children jammed into it because there they could get a space on two narrow boards for seven kopecks a day. It was especially attractive to immigrants.

> [They] end up for the most part in Khitrov Market or other places where the dregs of the population crowd together, carrying with them all sorts of diseases or themselves becoming the victims of them. The masses spend time looking for work in vain, and workers go from one factory to another or one subcontractor to another, without places to lay their heads, sleeping in summer under fences and in ditches, the money they brought with them quickly disappearing.[11]

Outside Khitrov's flophouses men sat and tried to sell their shoes for a few kopecks. Inside they gambled, drank, and fought. People were packed into large rooms with little or no bedding, so they used their clothes or each other for warmth. Men and women slept together everywhere, though the law said they had to be quartered separately. The whole Market was a school for young criminals, and it served well as the model for the setting of Gorky's *Lower Depths*. Khitrov's flophouses were the most crowded and notorious in Moscow, although similar, only slightly better quarters existed in other parts of the city.

Areas like Khitrov Market were common to all large Russian cities and to many in the West in this period; similar scenes can be found today in numerous cities of the developing world. It is difficult for comfortable Westerners to imagine the depth of the need that drove people, and still drives them, from their villages to such places. Of course, not only poverty at home moved them to leave, but also the attraction of city life and pay. Wages were generally higher in Moscow than in the countryside, work was often more plentiful, and those who planned to beg for a living could also expect to do better.[12] Despite the difficulties of getting a foothold in the city, urban migration also attracted young people because it offered both a way to escape the domination of their families and more stimulation than the fabled boredom of Russian villages, a product of the long winters, tedious work, and lack of culture.

Adjacent to the skid row and commercial districts of the center was the most desirable residential area of Moscow, the second belt. Lying between the boulevards and the Sadovoe Ring, it sheltered the "pretentious houses of capitalist magnates and simple houses of the large and middle merchantry and bureaucrats."[13] Among the mansions were the elegant and sometimes startling homes of industrialist clans like the Riabushinskiis and Morozovs. Here too were many nobles' houses, surrounded by gardens and fences. Yet in the second belt, as everywhere in the city, there were also many poor people.

Further out, past the Sadovoe Ring, lay the factory districts of the third belt. Here most of the fighting of December 1905 had taken place. In this area lived anyone who worked in the city but could not afford the high rents of the inner districts. From there, Moscow gradually faded into open fields and small villages. Beyond the third belt there were also some lively and fast-growing suburbs. These outposts of the city were receptacles for its overflowing population. They were neglected stepchildren, generally lacking clean water supplies and adequate means for removing waste, which was routinely dumped in ravines or pits. In the words of a city doctor, the result was a "belt of maximal infectious disease." He also claimed that as a source of such disease Khitrov Market was "immeasurably less dangerous" than the suburbs.[14]

A description of housing patterns by occupation, based on the census of 1902, was published by the city in 1912. It reported that factory workers lived mostly beyond Sadovoe, where they comprised 18.5 percent of the population, and in Zamoskvorech'e, where they were 28 percent. Other workers, such as artisans and construction laborers, were spread fairly evenly throughout the city, ranging from 12.6 percent of the population in the center to 16.4 percent beyond Sadovoe. Tavern and trade workers were also spread across the city, though their greatest concentration was in the center. Servants were naturally found above all in the wealthy second belt.[15]

While some areas of the city, for example Arbatskaia district, were unquestionably posher than most, the population was generally well mixed, in terms of social standing and wealth. Indeed, different strata sometimes lived literally on top of each other. Throughout the city were many recently constructed apartment houses in which the "big wheels" (*verkhushki*) of the free professions and the highest employees of government and industry lived on the lower floors; above them lived people in the same professions but in lower positions; last came minor employees, artisans, students, and pensioners. The further away such buildings were from the center, the more likely they were to house factory workers on their upper floors or in their basements.[16] The occupational heterogeneity of the city may have had important ramifications for its political and social development. Since the various strata lived among each other, they had less reason to develop the abstract generalizations about class behavior that seem so necessary a basis for intense social antagonism.[17]

Mixed in or separated, the poor often lived in atrocious housing. About one-third of Moscow's people, not counting those in the suburbs, lived in basements, semibasements, or what were called cot-closet apartments. All three types were likely to be cold, damp, dark, filthy, and overcrowded. The cot-closet apartments were usually rented by a poor person who in turn rented out space wherever possible, setting up cots or simply assigning part of the floor to subtenants.

In 1899 the city government surveyed many of the cot-closet apartments. Officials registered 16,140 of them, in which 171,000 people lived. No one knows

Women selling dry goods at an open-air market, early 1900s.

how many similar apartments were not registered. About nine-tenths of the tenants lived in damp conditions, more than one-third in cold quarters. By 1912 the situation had worsened in absolute terms: there were 23,322 of these apartments in Moscow with 275,959 residents. In the same year 124,561 people occupied basements or semibasements.[18]

The 1899 survey included descriptions of some of the worst apartments. Since such housing certainly had not improved overall by 1914, these statements are typical of the later period as well.

> The stuffiness is insupportable because of the dense population. In a closet where there are three cots altogether, thirteen people live.

> Upon entering the apartment, it seems that one has gone into an outhouse, the stench is so strong . . . all the children are sick.

> The ceiling is covered with mold, the apartment is cold, there is a stench from the slop pit.[19]

Housing in the Russian capitals, as Moscow and St. Petersburg were called together, was much more crowded than in western Europe. While Berlin averaged 3.9 residents per apartment and London 4.5, Petersburg and Moscow had 8.4 and

8.7 respectively. Besides those who had permanent cramped quarters, there were an estimated 15,000 homeless people in Moscow. About six thousand stayed each night in the flophouses of Khitrov Market.[20]

One other statistic suggests that relatively few Muscovite families in these years lived in quarters conducive to a healthy, productive existence: in 1912 only 29.3 percent of the population lived without unrelated persons.[21] That is, all others who rented flats, except those with servants, took in subtenants. This practice often led to overcrowding. Life in such cramped, shabby conditions often produced a high level of friction between residents.[22]

Moscow's housing problems were worsening before the war. Between 1907 and 1912 the number of housing units (*zhilye kvartiry*) rose by 8.8 percent, but the population rose 16.1 percent.[23] In this regard the city was losing the race with immigration.

Altogether, more than four hundred thousand Muscovites lived in conditions that even at the time were considered unacceptable. However, even a large number of "good" apartments lacked modern amenities. Only 36.4 percent of the population of rented quarters had complete plumbing. For another 41.5 percent running water was available, but not sewerage.[24]

There are no data on the number of workers living in factory housing. This traditional arrangement for Russian workers had begun to disappear by 1906, though more slowly in Moscow than elsewhere. Conditions varied widely in such quarters, from workbenches doubling as beds to individual rooms.

In sum, the city of Moscow in the years 1906–1914 faced a huge housing problem, characterized by overcrowding, lack of sanitary facilities, and high prices. The burgeoning poor population, strangled by its own growth, was at the mercy of the landlords. Despite a tentative effort to improve housing by the city government, matters were worse when the period ended—a story to be told in a later chapter.

Poor living conditions had a great influence on other problem areas of city life, especially public health. Almost every year Moscow endured one or more epidemics of typhus, typhoid, diphtheria, scarlet fever, measles, or cholera. These and other factors made one's chances of dying greater in Moscow than any other large European city. Here Moscow surpassed even St. Petersburg, whose reputation for high mortality has been well established. For example, the toll across Europe for tuberculosis, always an indication of crowded housing, shows Moscow's deadly position.[25]

Overall, the city could have laid claim to the title of Europe's deadliest metropolis in the entire span from 1881 to 1910, as shown in Appendix A. Its death rate at the end of that period, as well as its average rate for the years 1906–

TABLE 1-1.   Death Rate from Tuberculosis, 1911, per 100,000 Population

London	17.6	Vienna	42.7
Rome	18.6	St. Petersburg	44.1
Berlin	20.0	Moscow	45.6
Paris	38.7		

1910, was higher than the average rate for almost all the other major European cities in 1881–1885, twenty-five years earlier. Even St. Petersburg improved more than Moscow in the decades before World War I. Especially compared to cities like Berlin and Vienna, Moscow between 1881 and 1910 did not make great progress in its attempts to achieve a high level of public health.

In 1906, therefore, the municipality faced a situation in public health that had not changed substantially, compared to the very low level of 1881. Despite the expenditure of large sums and the expansion of its health programs in various directions, the city had not succeeded in significantly improving this picture by 1914.

Public health in the city was intertwined with other major problems, as is true in the developing world or in urban America today. The state of the citizenry's health depended to a great extent on the water and sewer systems. Education could not alter many people's lives until their health and housing were better, and so forth. These interconnections between Moscow's problems made the municipality's task in solving them considerably more difficult.

One other factor, also common to cities in less developed countries today, aggravated all of Moscow's defects. This was population growth. It was the most important single characteristic of the city at this time and will be emphasized throughout this work. Not only did the city grow, but every year the rate of growth increased.[26]

All parts of the city were growing from 1907 to 1912—the farther out, the faster. Rents and real estate prices rose more rapidly in the central districts than outlying areas, which meant that people often had to keep searching farther out until they found something they could afford. Immigrants, in particular, if they could rise above the level of Khitrov Market, usually had to live on the outskirts to find housing within their budgets. The result was population growth of only 3 percent in the center, with a rising curve outward to 14.6 percent in the third belt, 19.2 percent in Zamoskvorech'e, and a staggering 41 percent in the suburbs.

Within the Russian Empire, Moscow was smaller only than St. Petersburg, which had 1,907,708 people in city and suburbs in 1910. It was much larger than Warsaw or Odessa, which had about 500,000 people each at this time.[27] No other Russian city approached these population figures. Foreign cities comparable in size to Moscow were Philadelphia, with 1,549,008 people in 1910, and Vienna and Berlin, each with slightly over 2,000,000 in the same year.[28]

TABLE 1-2.   Moscow's Population, with Suburbs 1897–1917

			Percent Growth Per Year
	1897	1,038,591	
	1902	1,174,673	2.62
	1907	1,345,745	2.92
	1912	1,617,700	4.04
1 Feb.	1917	2,017,173	4.94

For much of this period only New York among European and American cities grew faster than Moscow, and by 1912 the latter's rate of increase was higher. Some of this growth was natural, that is, from births in the city, but most of it was a result of immigration. Newcomers made up 10.49 percent of the population increase between 1897 and 1902 and 14.67 percent by 1907–1912.[29]

On the other hand, a significant number of people left the city each year; one author has estimated this outflow for the year 1902 at ninety thousand.[30] In all likelihood this movement increased from 1906 to 1914. All population growth figures presented here are net increases: immigration plus natural additions minus emigration and deaths.

In 1912 the city reported that as of 1902, 80 percent of those who had lived in Moscow for less than two years were peasants. Over 80 percent of all immigrants had come from the surrounding provinces of Moscow, Tula, Riazan', Kaluga, Smolensk, Tver', Vladimir, and Iaroslavl'. This trend had evidently continued to 1912, the report suggested.[31]

The huge influx of peasants had important implications for social relations and structure in the city. A few aspects of this issue are important here. To begin with, those peasants who had most recently arrived in Moscow were, naturally, least likely to have broken their ties to the villages. For example, of 15,992 people enrolled at the city employment bureaus from February to May 1914, 11,498 had homes and land in the countryside.[32] The unemployed would generally have arrived more recently than the employed. In the years 1906 and 1907, the city purchased tickets for unemployed people to their home villages, which suggests that their ties had often been maintained.

Yet even workers who had been employed in Moscow for fifteen years or more, and who had remained in the city year-round, preserved strong ties to the countryside. So-called hereditary workers, those whose parents had worked in factories, were often born and raised in villages, followed in their parents' footsteps to work, and returned to the countryside in later life. This was true of a majority of Moscow print workers in a survey discussed later; this group was relatively highly skilled and paid, which would ordinarily lead one to believe that they were well rooted in the city.[33]

Despite such patterns, it seems that in general Moscow's population was becoming more firmly tied to the city than previously. There are three indications that this was so. First, the percentage of males living in Moscow who were born there was rising, from 20.8 in 1882 to 25.4 in 1912.[34] Men were increasingly likely to grow up in the city, though this group was still relatively small. Second, as early as 1905, children of the peasant *soslovie* predominated in the elementary schools; they were 62.3 percent of all female and 61 percent of all male pupils.[35] This suggests that parents were bringing their children with them to Moscow more often and were settling there permanently as families. Third, the number of women relative to the number of men was increasing. In 1871 there were only 700 women for every 1,000 men in Moscow; by 1912 there were 839. This change, an official review of the city government's activities commented, "reflects the growing tendency of the incoming laboring population to settle permanently in Moscow." Among the reasons cited by the report were the increasing scarcity of land in the countryside, the growth of industry in Moscow, higher wages, and the attractions of city culture.[36]

It should be noted that Moscow was unusually imbalanced in its male-to-female ratio, both in comparison to other Russian cities, where there was an average of 910 women per 1,000 men,[37] and abroad. By comparison, Berlin in 1910 had 1,083 women per 1,000 men, and New York 1,015. Among the cities for which data are available, only St. Petersburg (843 women per 1,000 men in 1900) showed a comparable imbalance.[38]

Sexual ratios also varied across Moscow. By 1912 the Prechistenskaia and Arbatskaia districts, where the inhabitants were generally wealthier, counted 1,254 and 1,190 women respectively for every 1,000 men.[39] More complete families could be found here than among the poor, especially the recent immigrants. Such ratios also developed partly because of the more settled quality of life in these districts, so that a demographic tendency of Western societies, in which women often live longer than men, manifested itself. The greater number of women in these districts also reflected the fact that wealthy families often kept many female servants.

In the central district, Gorodskaia, in 1912 largely a commercial area, there were only 483 women for every 1,000 men. In the regions more heavily populated by workers beyond the Sadovoe Ring, there were also far fewer women than men. The number of women per 1,000 men ranged from 922 in Presnenskaia, an older workers' district with long-established factories and the scene of the heaviest fighting of 1905, to 770 in the Serpukhovskaia district,[40] which was more outlying. This pattern, too, suggests that workers' families were settling more frequently in the city than in previous years. Of course, this did not exclude their maintaining ties to their home villages.

The disequilibrium in the number of men and women, still pronounced in 1912, had important consequences. For example, there was very probably a higher tendency to drunkenness and violence than under more balanced conditions, stemming from the frustration of forced separations. Certainly prostitution was more highly developed than would otherwise have been the case.

Familial dislocation is also evident in data on the *samodeiatel'nyi* population, those not basing their livelihood on another's earnings. In the census of 1902 almost 70 percent of the inhabitants were *samodeiatel'nyi*. Thus only about 30 percent of all Muscovites were family members living with and drawing support from the head of a household.[41] The high percentage of self-sustaining residents again indicates that the city had a large number of immigrants who had not yet established their families there.

One Soviet author gives the *samodeiatel'nyi* figure for 1912 in Moscow as 65 percent.[42] The decrease from 1902 is not great, but it does match the other trends mentioned above. In other words, the number of dependents in the city grew from 1902 to 1912, indicating that more families had come to Moscow.

Even in 1914, however, many more residents had been born outside the city than in it, and the problems created or aggravated by this flood of immigration were severe. Only in regard to elementary education, as later chapters will show, could the city keep up with the tide. In other services, expansion did not stay abreast of population growth. (Moscow's spectacular growth has continued to the present day, and the authorities are still not able to limit effectively the number of people living there.)

Turning to the city's social and occupational structure, several characteristics

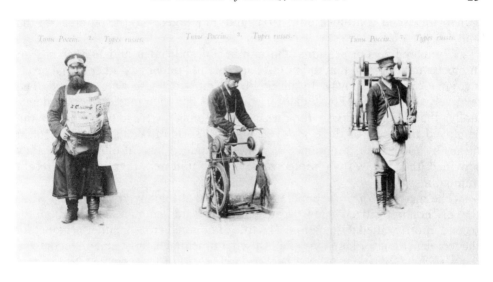

"Russian types." Street vendors and service people common in Moscow before World War I.

and trends stand out. (See Appendixes B and C for detailed information.) First, the increase in the absolute and relative numbers of peasants in the population between 1871 and 1902 is striking. Urban-born people were also designated peasants by *soslovie* if their fathers were in that legal category, so that the increase of peasants is not an infallible indicator of migration to the city. However, as the descriptions of immigration given above indicate, Moscow's peasant population grew overwhelmingly from immigration. The city's "peasantry," whose members worked at every conceivable kind of job and could be found at almost all social levels, though mostly the lower ones, increased more than threefold in thirty years. Their relative size in the population rose one and a half times. As noted earlier, this trend continued until 1912, and undoubtedly to the outbreak of the war.

Compared to the peasants, the number of guildsmen and *meshchane*, an imprecise urban group that did not fit conveniently under any other tsarist heading, grew only very slowly. In all likelihood most of these were cityborn. The relatively slow growth of these categories suggests that their increase occurred naturally, that is, as births to families already living in the city. Although the employed members of these *sosloviia* filled all sorts of occupations and social niches by 1906, their importance as groups remained high, if only because they provided the city with a more stable urban tradition than did the recent immigrants.

The merchant *soslovie* population decreased absolutely and relatively while that of "honored citizen" grew because the crown granted many businessmen the second, more exalted designation. The title of honored citizen, either personal for the recipient alone or hereditary for himself, immediate family, and direct descendants (*lichnyi* or *potomstvennyi pochetnyi grazhdanin*), was created by the government in 1832 so that it could bestow special status on successful businessmen. In this sense, these ranks were the rough equivalent in the business world of conferred nobility, granted for government or military service. They were also occasionally given to lower categories of state officials, nonnoble persons with university educations, and children of personal nobles.

The great increase in the number of Moscow's "honored citizens" took place between 1882 and 1902 when they reached 3.5 percent of the population, during the period of Russia's first industrial spurt. The nature of business began to change in the city, as the old merchant function of commerce came to be overshadowed more and more by manufacturing. Following this trend, many of Moscow's *kuptsy* became honored citizens, which the government considered a more appropriate title for manufacturers.

By the early twentieth century these conferred titles had come to mean very little in practice. Originally they had provided freedom from corporal punishment, recruitment, and the direct poll tax, but the recruitment exemption had disappeared in 1874, the poll tax had been abolished in 1886 for all citizens, and corporal punishment had greatly declined after the emancipation of the serfs in 1861. "Honored citizens" still had one meaningful privilege, however: they held permanent internal passports, enabling them to travel within the country whenever they pleased.

In any event, tsarist Russia was extremely status-conscious, and it meant a great deal to people to be able to write something more elegant than "peasant" beside their names. Such status often counted for much more than money. One's access to and treatment by officials, ability to get credit, and acceptance by society, for example, all depended more on status than on wealth. A similar situation prevails in the Soviet Union today. Privileges have long mattered in Russia and the USSR more than the financial ability to buy things. One difference between the pre- and postrevolutionary situations in this regard is that status and privileges were more easily passed on before 1917, though in recent decades the same tendency has appeared in Soviet life.

Tsarist *soslovie* data, as the preceding discussion has shown, must be treated with great caution. Appendix B serves only as a very rough description of classes in Moscow because a very wide variety of occupations and degrees of wealth could be found within each *soslovie*. It was entirely possible, for instance, for a noble to be completely impoverished, or for a peasant to become a cultured millionaire, as sometimes happened in the city. Almost all workers had "peasant" entered in their passports as their *soslovie*, even though a given family might have been urban dwellers for generations. The increasing irrelevance of *soslovie* designations for Moscow's life had important implications for politics and ideology.

Information on occupations, as outlined in Appendix C, provides a better description of Moscow's social structure than do the *soslovie* data. Factory workers formed by far the largest single component of Moscow's laboring population, though not a majority of it. Although the number of factory workers increased between 1902 and 1912, they actually lost ground relatively. A. G. Rashin estimates the size of Moscow's industrial working class in 1912 at 165,000, or 37 percent of all workers in all branches of trade and production.[43] The factory people of the city were a distinct minority of its working population; however, their influence belied their numbers. Partly because they worked in larger groups than others did, industrial workers found it easier to organize and communicate than did their counterparts in small workshops. They tended more to act in unison, for example in their angry reaction to a massacre of striking workers at the Lena Goldfields in 1912.

Substantial growth also occurred among employees (*sluzhashchie*, white-collar workers) in business and administration. The "administrative employees and aides" category in the 1902 statistics was apparently divided into the "administrative employees" and "auxiliary personnel outside production" categories in 1912. If this division is taken into account, their growth was 14,000 over the ten years, or 34 percent. The rise of the employees can be explained by the expansion of business and its increasing sophistication, especially in terms of trustification and stronger connections with the local banking community.

A related development was the growth of free professions by 17,200 members, or more than 42 percent. More engineers and lawyers were needed to serve the larger and more complex economy. In addition, more doctors worked for the city and privately, and more teachers taught in public and private schools. The population as a whole increased slightly less than 38 percent between 1902 and 1912. Thus the faster growth of the free professions may be taken as a sign of modernization: an ever-larger part of the work force was employed in meeting the city's new, more demanding needs. Moscow was beginning to develop a sizable middle class.

The artisans were also increasing in numbers, though just barely in relative terms. In 1912 their enterprises still constituted a highly important sector of the city's economy.

One other major expanding category was "persons on public welfare." In 1902 they numbered 67,800, or 8.3 percent of Moscow's population, already a substantial segment. By 1912 they had increased by almost one-third, to 99,200 or 9.4 percent of the inhabitants. Though the growth of this group fell short of overall population growth by a narrow margin, the improvement in the capacity of welfare programs in the city was significant. The number on welfare over the ten years illustrates the way that rapid population growth complicated all the city government's efforts to deal with social problems.

The changes in the occupational structure of Moscow's population between 1902 and 1912 reflect the overall economic upswing of the period, which occurred despite stagnation or slow growth from about 1904 to 1910. As it expanded and continued on the path of industrialization and greater sophistication in business, Moscow was modernizing in key respects. Thrown into this process were vast numbers of rural people, who dominated the population and helped to maintain many aspects of the city's old character as an overgrown village.

Occupational data also shed some light on the position of women in Moscow. They occupied far fewer jobs requiring skill or education than did men, as the figures on employees in production show, for example. Only in the professions do they seem to have fared better, but this is because more women than men were city elementary school teachers, positions with very low pay.

Women also worked more commonly than men as domestic servants, often a particularly undesirable job. Even if a female servant had free room and board, her pay was frequently only enough to buy the "proper" clothing required by her employers. M. N. Gernet, a leading jurist of the day, described the working conditions that predominated for a woman in this position:

> her work day, starting in the early morning, ends late in the evening and very often comprises a period of sixteen or more hours. She does not know rest in the course of the day and rarely receives a vacation.[44]

Such women were often at the mercy of their employers, especially the males, and were physically or sexually abused. If they became pregnant by a master they were almost invariably turned out immediately. They put up with such conditions only because competition for the work was extremely intense. It was often the only thing a woman fresh from the countryside could hope to do in a large Russian city, coming as she usually did with no marketable skills or experience. In the years just before the First World War, the requests for female domestic servants at Moscow's public labor exchanges far exceeded the demand for women in any other category.

Working conditions in other jobs were often quite onerous.

> The labor of the bakery workers' guild is one of the most difficult, in the duration of the work as well as in its character. The length of the working day reaches seventeen hours, and the majority of workers do not sleep enough because of this. They are forced to sleep in these circumstances in extremely crowded conditions, often two, three, or four in a bed. The usual quarters— underground, dirty, dusty, stuffy, damp. Bakery workers rarely go to the baths because of lack of time. There are no holidays for them; before holidays the work increases. The last days before Easter and Christmas are almost without sleep. In such circumstances there can be no thought of the satisfaction of any kind of spiritual needs. It is necessary to refrain from having families; bakery workers live in quarters provided by the employer.
>
> The exhausted, sleepless man has no appetite, and we see that the majority of bakery workers are pale, haggard people. The sleepless man cannot be attentive, and therefore we should not be surprised that in bread and rolls we often find cockroaches, flies, pieces of wood, and so forth. The consumer does not think that with his bread he is eating the sweat and blood of the bakery workers.[45]

One case from Moscow that reached the attention of the Ministry of Trade and Industry involved a woman who ran a small bookbindery. She kept her apprentices on the job from 6 or 7 A.M. until 9 or 10 P.M., with only a half-hour break. On Sundays and holidays the apprentices worked a half-day.[46] Here and in most small businesses, apprentices slept at the workplace, often in the same rooms in which they toiled. The laws required separate sleeping quarters for all jobs, but many employers ignored this provision.

A survey of print shops in Moscow in 1910 revealed that sixteen of forty-six had no ventilation and that 13 percent had only small windows. In 67 percent the floors were seldom or never washed. Half of the shops had no guards on dangerous parts of machines, and in eleven the guards were insufficient.[47]

There are many other contemporary descriptions of terrible working conditions, apprentices forced to sleep on floors covered with filthy rags, dust and damp in the air, and long hours with low pay. In 1910 women candy makers, for example, received a cot, their food, and three rubles per month.[48] The maximum wage a female laundry worker could hope to earn was fifteen rubles a month, enough to maintain only a miserable existence. The laundries were filthy and wet; temperatures sometimes reached thirty degrees Centigrade.[49]

The wages of Russian industrial workers were notoriously low, and Moscow's were no exception. Among factory hands pay was higher in Moscow than the Russian averages, but lower than in St. Petersburg. In 1913 the average pay of a factory worker in all Russia was 22 rubles (worth $11) per month; in Moscow it was 27.1 rubles and in St. Petersburg 34.7. For 1914 the range was even wider: the averages were 21.3 in Russia, 26.1 in Moscow, and 37.6 in St. Petersburg.[50] The differences reflect the fact that Moscow's industry was often light. Moscow had long been and still was the center of the Russian textile industry. St. Petersburg had tended to develop more heavy industry and machine-building, which required more skilled labor than much of Moscow's industry.[51] However, heavy industry was also developing in Moscow before the war, and this helped to push pay there above national averages.

In general, pay in the city was much lower than the factory wages alone would suggest. The average monthly pay for workers of all categories in "the Moscow region" in 1908 was only 11 rubles 89 kopecks. The Moscow region included the city and the enterprises in its immediate vicinity, in which pay tended to be lower. This average wage compares extremely unfavorably with pay in England, where the average wage was equivalent to 26.64 rubles, and in North America, with an average of 56.97.[52]

Women were paid much less than men for the same work in Moscow, as they were across Russia. In printing establishments, for example, women's pay averaged 40 percent of men's.[53] Moreover, tradition and male prejudice usually relegated women to low-skill, low-paying occupations such as the candymaking, laundering, and serving positions mentioned earlier. In this respect Russia was no different from Western Europe or America.

The combination of low pay and high rents meant that Russian workers could afford little beyond the bare necessities. In 1911 one writer estimated that they spent from 55–88 percent of their budgets on essentials, while American workers spent 42–45 percent and French workers 40–45 percent for the same purposes.[54] Two detailed surveys of Russian workers' budgets, including married and single workers in Moscow and St. Petersburg, confirm the picture of a struggle for mere existence. (These studies are illustrated in Appendix D.) Of the married workers surveyed, 63 percent in St. Petersburg and 45.2 percent in Moscow could not make ends meet from their own pay. Among the single workers, 35 percent of the St. Petersburg budgets were not self-sufficient and 12.1 percent were inadequate in Moscow.[55] Workers attempted to survive financially on borrowing, moonlighting, or the limited public and private charity available to them.

The percentages of these budgets spent on essentials are very high—of the married workers' outlays, 85.31 percent in St. Petersburg and 81.65 percent in Moscow. Often little was left over for entertainment or cultural pursuits. This is reflected in the relatively low percentages of income spent on alcohol: in St. Petersburg, 2.99 among married workers, 10.2 among single people; 2.64 for married Muscovites, 2.3 for single people.[56] However, workers may not have reported expenditures on alcohol truthfully, out of a desire to make a good impression, denial of drinking problems, or fear that the information might be used against them. The figures given here for alcohol purchases seem unrealistically low.

The surveys suggest that Muscovites maintained closer ties to their villages than their St. Petersburg peers. Workers surveyed in Moscow regularly spent more money returning to the countryside and sent more money to relatives there than did St. Petersburg workers. This is probably due partly to the fact that Moscow was much more centrally located than St. Petersburg; immigrants often came shorter distances to the former.

Both surveys indicate a higher standard of living for single St. Petersburg workers, who were paid more than their counterparts in Moscow, in terms of the portions of their budgets they could spend on nonessentials. Married workers in both cities, however, spent much more of their money on essentials than singles did, largely because of the much greater cost of housing for families. Single workers and people in all job categories could and did rent spaces to sleep anywhere, in closets or corners, if need be. It was much more difficult and expensive to rent enough space for a family.

A study of Moscow print workers in 1908 illustrates the problems of the housing situation. Of 3,772 respondents, 38 percent slept in "corners or cots," 41 percent had rooms, 15.5 percent had apartments but took in boarders, and only 5.5 percent had apartments to themselves.[57] The workers paid an average of nineteen rubles a month for an apartment, eight rubles for a room, and three rubles for a cot.[58] These prices demonstrate the differences in costs faced by married and single workers.

Print workers lived in such conditions despite the fact that they were paid about twice as much as the average Russian worker. Compared to the general standards of Moscow's laboring people, they lived well; indeed, they were among the elite of the city's working class. The print workers' situation illustrates the depth of the housing problem in Moscow: the city's poor desperately needed help with housing, as with many other social problems.

Were standards of living among Moscow's lower classes rising or falling in the decade or so before World War I? It is difficult to tell. Wages were going up, but in general so were prices, although it is not clear that this was true for food. The pattern of price changes for rye flour from 1900 to 1913 suggests that food did not increase greatly in cost. Rye bread, for centuries an essential component of Russian diets, was extremely important to the city's population. While the price of rye flour varied widely, it showed no clear tendency to increase, at least after 1906. Official statistics on the prices of bread and meat show the same absence of a trend. For example, white bread cost virtually the same in June 1914 as in 1907. (See Appendix E for movement of food prices in the city.)

In contrast, apartment costs did rise, as a result of population pressure. Inside the boulevards, rent rose an average of 30.3 percent from 1902 to 1912. Between the boulevards and Sadovoe, the second belt, prices went up 38.1 percent; the third belt saw an increase of 19 percent.[59]

Figures are available for wages over time in four job categories, all of which show increases. Carpenters, for instance, earned an average of 129 kopecks a day in 1902 and 190 kopecks in June 1914. (Appendix F shows wage trends in detail.) Pay patterns reflected the city's economic situation: decline or only slow growth occurred from 1904 until 1910 or 1911, when business began to improve much more rapidly. Unemployment was especially heavy in the city in 1906 and 1907 but was always a problem during this period.

One Soviet publication claims that real wages in 1913 in Moscow were 97.5 percent of what they had been in 1906, based on the "rise in prices for foodstuffs."[60] The municipal data presented above do not reveal such a rise; on the other hand, the increase in housing prices could account for this difference and more. Yet as the economy improved in the years after 1910, so did wages, and most inhabitants who had marketable skills or experience probably did not suffer greatly from inflation.

Most peasants fresh from the countryside, however, lacked such a background. They were still involved in strong competition for low-paying, low-skill jobs. The presence of a "reserve army of the unemployed" kept wages down for the unskilled. Between 1904 and 1914 average daily pay for carpenters went up 52 percent, but average pay for day laborers rose only 27 percent for males and 33 percent for females. The people at the bottom of the economic scale were losing most to inflation.

The flow of peasants into Moscow exerted steady pressure on housing prices. Yet inflation was certainly not runaway in the city just before the war, and wages were at least not lagging far behind price increases. In this sense, there was a certain stability in Moscow. However, the uncertainty of business cycles and the intense competition for many jobs made it all too easy for the lower classes to be thrown out of work.

We can draw a very rough overall picture of the Muscovites' standard of living between 1906 and 1914. To begin with, it is possible to isolate certain occupations whose pay was generally low: artisans, workers and apprentices in industrial production, persons on public welfare, and domestic servants and day laborers. While some people in these categories, for example a number of the artisans who hired labor, undoubtedly were living fairly well, they are probably more than balanced here by poor people in other groups. Nor is the designation of employees considered here, despite the fact that a good many of them were clerks or salespeople who did not earn much. Elementary school teachers are also excluded, though they earned less than some factory workers. Therefore it seems conservative to estimate that in 1902 about 77 percent of all Muscovites lived as well or worse than the elite print workers; the figure for 1912 is 73 percent. This conclusion is not meant to suggest a trend, as the time span is much too short and the method too rough. Rather, it suggests the existence of a condition which would be very hard to change.

Observers of urban life, particularly a school of American sociologists who began publishing in the 1920s, used to believe that the kind of human flood that inundated Moscow in the early twentieth century automatically created severe personal and political distress. Such immigration supposedly led to the rupture of most close human ties, the rejection of tradition and religion, increased isolation and loneliness, and economic frustration. As a result, a greater tendency to violence and political radicalism would develop among newcomers to the city.[61] This set of ideas grew out of the facts that numerous upheavals and revolutions had taken place in cities and that these usually involved the lower classes above all.

In recent years this theory has come under withering fire. The first and most obvious objection is that such upheavals have *not* occurred in many cities, including a large number where massive immigration has occurred. Second, various scholars have demonstrated that in both the recent and more distant past, it has not been largely the newcomers to the urban world who have turned radical and rebelled against the strictures of their new environment. Arrivals in big cities often tend to hold on to tradition, to find networks of people to enter, to be less radical than long-time city dwellers, and to be fairly satisfied with their existences.[62] Thus it seems rather clear today that we cannot generally pin the blame or the praise for revolutionary sentiment on migrants to the cities. Nor is it by any means evident that poverty plain and simple makes for mass discontent, now or in the past. Lord John Russell observed in 1840 that London had a larger population than any other British town, and that its slums were more extensive if not necessarily worse than elsewhere. Yet London's people were "an example of an orderly population conducting themselves as well if not better than any other population of the same extent."[63]

In 1905, Moscow's lower classes did not conduct themselves in an orderly manner. So far as we can trace the unrest in the city, it seems to have been the older, more skilled and established workers and artisans who led their fellows. It may well be that their dissatisfaction was rooted above all in declining status and independence as large factories took work away from them or even absorbed them into the plants.[64] But lower class Muscovites—workers or not, newcomers or established residents—had displayed serious dissatisfaction with the existing state of affairs, even after the tsar issued the October Manifesto. What could be done to make them feel that Moscow was their city, a place in which they had a stake and could expect decent lives for themselves and their children? In short, how could the poor be integrated into urban life? This was an old Russian problem,[65] recast now with greater urgency than ever before. If unrest grew primarily at the workplace, that effect might be balanced by other, positive spheres of urban life, if they could be developed. A sensitive urban elite might also find ways to reduce class tension at the workbench.

In attempting to solve these questions after 1905, the Moscow city government faced most of the difficulties that plague developing cities today: a generally poor and uneducated population, terribly overcrowded housing, sewerage and sanitation facilities that did not begin to meet people's needs, yearly epidemics and other constant public health problems, and inadequate transportation and welfare systems, all worsened by ever-faster population growth. Many residents had little chance for the pursuit of anything beyond subsistence, a fact that by itself could have prevented many of them from feeling that they had a stake in the existing order.

The municipal duma, comprised largely of men from the upper classes, had started to work on Moscow's problems in 1870, the date it gained the right to allocate resources and make policy. By 1906, although some progress had been made, the city's difficulties had far outdistanced the elected government's efforts to deal with them. Thus the challenge to municipal officials remained immense.

2

The Elected City Government: Legal Competence and Financial Position

In those cases . . . where the salvation of the motherland is concerned, then it is necessary to adopt measures that do not apply in the normal course of life.
Prime Minister P. A. Stolypin to the Third State Duma, November 1907[1]

There is not a single important country that is as backward as Russia in the matter of local budgets.
A. I. Shingarev, a leading Kadet, 1912[2]

The quest for control and concentration of power in the hands of the state were essential features of tsarism, with several exceptions, from medieval times to 1917. The state's power had originally developed out of the need for simultaneous, centralized direction of defense on widely separated frontiers and the hope shared by many Russians of ensuring an end to the country's perennial fragmentation and civil strife. Strong regional or social forces capable of checking the state's power did not arise. Because of this perceived need for a strong central government, and the slow economic development of towns and trade, the central government was able to crush local privileges by the sixteenth century at the latest. In western Europe the privileges of nobles, towns, and regions often served as starting points for the growth of democracy on a national scale. There was no such possibility in Russia.

For various reasons, however, the tsarist state never succeeded in establishing the thorough control over its citizens that it sought. First, it could never find enough money or trained administrators to rule efficiently. Second, it never quite trusted law, which is essential for systematic government. Law, the state seemed to believe, could interfere with its right to do exactly as it pleased, for law is a set of rules to be applied indifferently in any situation. Tsarism, by contrast, was a personal system that could admit no limits on its right to act. This approach extended even to Nicholas II's attitude toward the State Duma and the Fundamental Laws, the quasi-constitution adopted after 1905. When the tsarist regime did turn to law, it often produced vague statutes such as the Extraordinary Measures of 1881, full of provisions that allowed great arbitrariness and freedom of administrative action. To govern the country the tsarist system came to rely heavily on administrative measures, the decisions on the spot of appointed officials without reference to the courts. Especially after 1881, the regime frequently bypassed the civil courts and the "ordinary" laws, which specified due process in them.[3]

Tsarist ideology played a very important role in the state's attitude toward law and its quest for control of local affairs. Developed in the 1820s by Count Sergei Uvarov, the Old Regime's ideology was called Official Nationality, comprised of Orthodoxy, Nationality, and Autocracy.[4] The first and last of these terms are reasonably clear: they refer to the spiritual preeminence of the Orthodox Church, whose role was partly to preach obedience to the authorities and acceptance of one's lot on earth; and to unlimited power in the hands of the monarch. *Nationality* is a much more difficult concept: it had "reactionary, dynastic, and defensive connotations" and was intimately related to European romanticism of the early nineteenth century.[5] It led thinkers either to an intense glorification of all Russians and their equality in brotherhood, the "nationalistic" view, or to a similar elevation of the tsar as the head of the Russians, the "dynastic" approach. Naturally the regime preferred the second tendency.

Either way Nationality was interpreted, Official Nationality served as the foundation of tsarist policy in the reign of Nicholas I (1825–1855), and it continued to have major influence until 1917. According to this system of ideas, God fixed a place for every Russian at birth. Only the tsar stood above it all, able to see clearly the needs of the whole nation and to act upon them. To keep order and control man's natural, base instincts, careful organization of society was necessary. Russian subjects were therefore divided into legal categories, the estates (*sosloviia*), each of which had some organizations and elected officials responsible for maintaining order within the given group. The major *sosloviia* were the nobles (*dvorianstvo*), the peasants (*krest'ianstvo*), the clergy (*dukhovenstvo*), and various categories of townspeople. The estates were ranked in order of status and service to the state, with nobles at the top and peasants at the bottom.

For centuries the *soslovie* system had worked, after a fashion, in the countryside, where the division between gentry and peasantry was clear before the emancipation of the serfs in 1861 and remained generally quite distinct afterward. Since social and legal status in the Russian system continued to depend on land ownership as well as estate, the gentry could be sure that as long as it held a considerable portion of the land, its privileged position could be maintained. *Sosloviia* had real significance for rural gentry.

On the other hand, the estates never meant very much in the towns. Urban life is simply too fluid to be categorized in such terms. As early as the seventeenth century, tsarist officials were looking the other way when serfs fled to urban settlements; the need for labor overrode social demarcation. The anomaly grew more pronounced in the eighteenth and nineteenth centuries as peasants went in ever-growing numbers to work and settle in the towns, where they were typically denied citizenship and access to municipal services.[6] The new town dwellers, and even many of the hereditary townspeople, did not fit into the established *soslovie* system; the state's response was to ignore them or hope that eventually they would reinsert themselves into that system by returning to the countryside. The regime thus demonstrated a failure to modernize regarding the towns or even to recognize the preconditions for a modern policy; its ideology was never particularly well suited to the development of a coherent approach to urban life. This problem worsened as Russian urban growth accelerated. In Moscow only the municipality, not the state, seriously attempted to deal with the issue of city dwellers' integration into their community.

If it failed to address Russia's town life, Official Nationality nonetheless remained the underpinning of the regime's political and social policies until the very end. Only this kind of ideology could serve to justify the landlords' position as owners of the land and overseers of the peasants, roles the state tried to prop up after the late 1880s. Only this sort of reasoning could justify the tsar's autocratic power: he was born to it as God had willed, and no person could step out of the role God had assigned. The *soslovie* system was merely the legal recognition of this principle, so vital to the regime.

Official Nationality's precepts were restated at the highest levels of government into the twentieth century. Konstantin P. Pobedonostsev was the most prominent and articulate conservative thinker of the Old Regime's final decades. He served as tutor and advisor to both Alexander III (1881–1894) and Nicholas II (1894–1917); as Procurator of the Holy Synod, he was lay head of the Orthodox Church and a member of the Council of Ministers from 1880 to 1905. His influence on the last two tsars, from their adolescence forward, was great. Although he specifically disdained the *soslovie* system in favor of an aristocracy of merit, his views on how to organize Russian society and education pointed in the opposite direction and echoed Official Nationality. "Do not trespass beyond the limits of thy destiny" was one of his favorite phrases.[7] Every person should remain "in that place, in that area, in that corner where fate has placed him."[8] Above everyone was the tsar, the "servant of all," charged with upholding tradition.[9] Add to this Pobedonostsev's view that the land-owning nobility was more loyal to the tsarist state than other groups,[10] and the essential conservative platform is complete.

Thus only the gentry landowners could find much of tangible value in tsarist ideology. Of all Russia's social groups, they had the only desirable status that depended in large measure on the estate principle. Many rural gentry therefore felt that the regime's ideology gave them the most substantial promise available of a secure, privileged future, and they defended it in all areas of Russian life, from politics to religion and education.

Conservative nobles often phrased their political positions in terms of *soslovie*. To them, landowners who joined the Kadet party, which called for compulsory alienation of land in favor of the peasants, were traitors to their estate. Influential nobles and bureaucrats often called for a *zemskii sobor* (assembly of the land), patterned after meetings of representatives chosen from the estates in the sixteenth and seventeenth centuries, to replace the State Duma.[11] A new *zemskii sobor* would have been dominated by the nobles and would have had the right only to advise the tsar, not make law. The Union of the Russian People, an archconservative, anti-Semitic organization that Nicholas II endorsed, also called for a *zemskii sobor*. It is no accident that this group was also antiindustrial and in favor of keeping Russia agricultural.[12] In June 1905 Nicholas himself stated his approval of voting by *sosloviia*, especially the two landed categories of nobles and peasants, for the advisory State Duma he had ordered created in February.[13]

Town dwellers and officials had little reason to expect benefits from either a *zemskii sobor* or the prevailing ideology. In fact, the regime's view of the ideal society ran counter to the necessary approach for the prevention of urban revolution. The fluidity of town existence had to be recognized and supported; anything else would be counter to reality, would be working against trends in Russian life that were deepening as the cities grew, and would not be modern but backward and potentially dangerous. To try to maintain the estate system in the towns was to attempt to keep people in artificial boxes, or in the case of peasant immigrants, in a kind of unrecognized limbo, for which the state offered only the erratic ministrations of paternalism. In the urban context *sosloviia* did not do what they were supposed to: order people's lives. This failure called the whole political system into question, for the tsar's role depended on his being above the other categories in a class by himself.

This stress on the monarchy as the pivotal controlling force in society, found in other Old Regimes as well,[14] helps explain the state's virtually constant efforts to dominate local government. Given its striving for centralization, the Russian imperial government found it possible to grant real powers of self-rule to the country's cities for only a brief period, 1870–1881. Beginning in the sixteenth century, and continuing under Peter the Great and more seriously under Catherine the Great, the state made a number of tentative moves in this direction but always stopped short of permitting significant local autonomy. In the eighteenth and early nineteenth centuries the central government hoped to lighten its administrative and financial burden by attracting capable men to run the cities. Such local additions, either appointed or elected, were expected to serve at minimal pay and to supplement the small number of effective administrators at the state's disposal. But the efforts to bring local men into urban government were never very successful, largely because the regime could not bring itself to relinquish its traditional control over localities. Except for the years 1870–1881, this need for control remained the central principle of its attitude toward the towns. And so urban citizens persisted in regarding their participation in city government as an onerous duty and did not come forward willingly or in large numbers to take up the available positions.[15]

Prior to 1870, the year of passage of the first City Statute, the franchise for urban elections was based mainly on *sosloviia*. Catherine's Charter Granted to the Cities of 1785, which regulated municipal government until 1870, recognized six electoral groups or curiae of urban residents. These followed *sosloviia* or socioeconomic lines, though purely economic qualifications for the franchise applied only to those who owned urban real estate or had more than fifty thousand rubles in capital, certainly not a large percentage of any town's population. Women and serfs were completely excluded from voting. When Nicholas I granted a highly limited form of self-government to St. Petersburg in 1846, he organized the franchise even more closely on the basis of *sosloviia*. Thus peasants residing in the towns gained the right to participate in urban elections for the first time in 1870. Women were allowed to vote directly in local elections only with the February Revolution of 1917.

The statute adopted in 1870, though still based on "privilege,"[16] the idea that some citizens had more rights than others, represented a slight liberalization of earlier franchise requirements. The right to vote now depended only on payment of municipal taxes. All persons or institutions who paid any city taxes, duties, or fees, even as little as one ruble for a street vending license, were entered on a list in the order of the amount rendered. That is, the one who paid the largest tax was listed first on the roll of voters, the one who paid the second largest amount was second, and so on down to the person who paid the least.

The taxpayers at or near the top of the tax rolls, whose payments together amounted to one-third of municipal collections, formed the first city curia, with the right to elect one-third of the city duma delegates. The same system applied to the second and bottom thirds of the tax roll. Women and institutions voted by proxy through males. Under this system, Moscow in 1884 had 222 electors in the first curia, 1,360 in the second, and 18,310 in the third. That is, 2.6 percent of the population of 753,500 could vote, and about 1.1 percent of the voters elected one-third of the duma deputies. The central principles of this system were:[17] (1) only those who contributed to the city's finances were allowed to vote for delegates to the municipal policy-making body and (2) the very wealthy had an overwhelming voice.

Only a brief sketch of the system of city government created in 1870 will be offered here, as fuller treatments have been presented elsewhere,[18] and because there were changes later that profoundly affected the rights and nature of urban government. However, it is important to note that despite much public pressure for reforms the basic municipal structure of 1870 lasted until 1917.

The City Statute of 1870 was a key part of the "Great Reforms." These changes included the emancipation of the serfs in 1861, the creation of organs of rural self-government (zemstva) in 1864, judicial reforms, the new municipal structures, and army reforms in 1874. Russia's humiliating defeat in the Crimean War of 1853–1856, lost on her own soil to Britain and France, had helped spread the realization that fundamental changes were necessary to develop the country and to reclaim its Great Power status. Coupled with a long tradition of social criticism, especially of serfdom, and the personal commitment to reform of the new tsar, Alexander II, the stimulus of the Crimean defeat had produced irresistible pressure for improvement. The need for change overrode the resistance of conservatives, particularly among the nobles.

As part of the Great Reforms, the 1870 City Statute created a fundamentally new kind of local government. The law provided for elected municipal organs (gorodskie obshchestvennye upravleniia) in 423 towns, mainly in European Russia. A large duma, consisting of 250 delegates in St. Petersburg and 180 in Moscow but much smaller elsewhere, made municipal policy. It determined what services were offered to the local population and how city revenues were allocated. From either within or outside its membership each duma elected a mayor and a small executive board called the uprava.

City governments were supposed to care for the needs and well-being of urban residents. The law listed specific areas of municipal responsibility, which were very similar to the ones given below for the 1892 City Statute. However, one section sharply distinguished the earlier from the later law, and that was the passage that contained the so-called golden words:

> The municipal public government, within the limits of authority granted to it, functions independently [samostoiatel'no]. The instances and procedures in which the actions and decisions of the government are subject to the confir-

mation and supervision of the state authorities are indicated below [in specified] articles.

There followed a list of clearly defined cases in which the central authorities might intervene in urban affairs. Interference in other areas was forbidden, providing the cities some legal protection for their self-government.[19]

This degree of independence did not last long. Following the assassination of Alexander II in March 1881, the government promulgated the Extraordinary Measures, which provided for two degrees of martial law in the areas where they were applied. These laws gave leading state authorities—governors, governors-general, and *gradonachal'niki* (city governors or prefects)—extremely wide power to control organizations and individuals.

The weaker of the two measures was called "strengthened security" (*usilennaia okhrana*). It gave these state officials the right, among other powers, to

1. decide in administrative fashion cases of violation of the obligatory regulations issued by them
2. forbid any popular, public (*obshchestvennye*) and private gatherings
3. close any trade or industrial enterprise temporarily or for the duration of the strengthened security
4. forbid individuals to be in places declared under the statute.

These officials could also transfer criminal cases to military courts when they felt it necessary to protect public order and calm, and they could order closed trials. Under this law, as at all other times, administrative exiles, either banning a person from a given area or limiting residence to a specific place, had to be cleared with the minister of internal affairs.[20]

The stronger of the two statutes was called "extraordinary security" (*chrezvychainaia okhrana*). When it went into effect, all the rules of the first law remained in force. In addition, any case could be decided administratively, special military detachments could be set up to aid police, and property or income could be sequestered if they were being used for criminal purposes or had "dangerous consequences for public order." Furthermore, governors, governors-general, and *gradonachal'niki* could postpone or close regular or special sessions of *soslovie*, city, or *zemstvo* organizations. They could remove matters from their agendas. Periodicals could be closed for the duration of the extraordinary security, and educational institutions could be shut down for as long as a month.[21]

The tsarist authorities in any area placed under these statutes could issue regulations with the force of law on matters of well-being (*blagochinie*), order, and security. These could refer to a "series of specific and unique cases or be designed to prevent or end violations of the laws securing public order." The word *blagochinie* implies a concern for the welfare of the people, an idea the Moscow tsarist administration pursued from time to time. Such regulations could not in any event contradict existing laws or statutes,[22] a provision of the new regulations that was clearly contradicted by their "extraordinary" nature. In practice, they frequently replaced previous statutes.

The breadth and vagueness of these laws are immediately apparent. They gave local tsarist officials the power to rule by decree and administrative action, as they saw fit. The Moscow *gradonachal'nik* decided what had "dangerous consequences for public order," including questions scheduled for discussion by the city duma. The elected government might also find that the tsarist administration had preempted it to issue regulations covering some area of city life—this happened numerous times in Moscow. The Extraordinary Measures were so broad that the administration could have ruled the city without the duma; the vagueness of the laws supplied the legal right to do so. The duma, on the other hand, could not make a move that was not subject to the administration's scrutiny and review. In 1907 the Council of Ministers stated, "In existing law there is no special limitation on the right of governors [or *gradonachal'niki*] to oversee [*proizvodit' reviziiu*] these institutions [cities and *zemstva*]."[23] That was exactly the way the state wanted it to be.

The central government applied the Extraordinary Measures extensively: by 1912 only 5 million of 157 million Russians did not live under one of them.[24] A. A. Lopukhin, head of the Ministry of the Interior's Department of Police from 1902 to 1905, wrote after his retirement that these laws made the "entire population of Russia become dependent on the personal opinions of the functionaries of the political police."[25] The statement seems questionable only in that the regular police, nominally responsible only for everyday law and order, often had more to do with enforcing the statutes than did the political police. At least, this was the case in Moscow (as Chapter 4 will show). In any event, the importance of these laws was immense.[26]

The immediate reason for their passage was to repress terrorism after the assassination of Alexander II. Of course, they recalled the old tradition of attempts by the state to control its people and localities. But by 1881 the issue of central versus local control had assumed new urgency. Before the emancipation of the serfs twenty years before, all but a small minority of Russians lived in the countryside and were ignorant, unable to communicate with each other, lacking in any political perspective on their existence, and oblivious to connections between the government and their socioeconomic position. In that context the government was relatively secure. The gentry had been bought off with positions in state service or by receiving the right to control the peasantry; no other groups were sufficiently large, educated, or organized to offer any resistance to the regime. Peasant rebellions had occurred, of course, but the large ones were disorganized affairs in the borderlands, where state control was much less well-established than in areas settled earlier. The groundwork for organized protest against state tutelage was laid when the lower classes began to receive some education, to learn about alternate forms of government and social relations, to gather in large numbers and concentrations in cities and factories, and to have sustained contact with revolutionaries.

By 1881 very little organized protest had taken place among workers or peasants. But the government, having followed revolutions in western Europe with fear and great interest, realized that the potential for disturbances was large, especially in the cities.[27] Top officials were also naturally very anxious to combat the terrorist threat. The sweeping provisions of the Extraordinary Measures testify to the extent of the state's concern about the situation. Also in 1881 the government revitalized and reorganized the political police, now called the *Okhrana*, and another branch of the police often used for political work, the gendarmes.

The new emperor, Alexander III, and his closest advisors considered the new laws and police bodies necessary to control the population as a whole, for on some occasions the public had given its tacit approval to the anti-regime violence. In one famous example, a jury acquitted the terrorist Vera Zasulich in 1878 after she shot and severely wounded the *gradonachal'nik* of St. Petersburg. There had been other indications that public opinion was turning against the autocracy; yet the overwhelming response to the assassination of Alexander II was shock and outrage. Despite this sign of fundamental public loyalty to the government, Alexander III chose to return to old traditions. Not for him the reform impulse: he would rule Russia in the ancient, autocratic fashion. Nonetheless, it was not easy to undo all that had been done, and the attempt might further provoke his subjects. Therefore his regime found ways to leave the new institutions basically intact in form while creating means to circumvent them and rule by personal decision. Nicholas II followed his father's lead after 1905 in regard to the State Duma.

The Great Reforms had gone only a certain distance in drawing citizens into participation in public affairs. Cities had their dumas and the countryside its *zemstva*, but there was no national parliament. And what the tsar had granted, he or another tsar could take away or bypass. The essence of tsarism, personal rule, remained intact. However, new efforts were required to protect that essence, and nowhere was the problem outlined more clearly than in the cities.

The government took yet another step to ensure its control over the towns in 1892, when it adopted a new City Statute. Evidently considering that even the Extraordinary Measures were not enough, the government reversed many of the liberal provisions of the 1870 law. The franchise was severely cut back; it was limited in the capitals to those who owned property assessed for tax purposes at more than three thousand rubles, which reduced the previous electorate in Moscow by almost 75 percent. The tsarist administration now held veto power over appointments of city *uprava* members. If administrators rejected two candidates for the same position, the state appointed its own choice. The 1892 City Statute viewed mayors and *uprava* members as civil servants subject to ordinary legal proceedings. Cases involving them came under the jurisdiction of the civil service disciplinary courts.[28] In other words, the bureaucracy, not the regular court system, tried city officials, which gave the government another means of exerting pressure on municipalities. Overall, the 1892 law did for city government what the *zemstvo* counterreform of 1890 did for rural self-government.[29] The latter law curtailed the rights of the *zemstva* and placed them firmly under the control of tsarist administrators.

After 1892, any Moscow duma resolution which the *gradonachal'nik* thought "did not correspond to the general well-being and needs of the state or clearly violated the interests of the local population" could be blocked with a temporary veto and referred to a state office in the city.[30] This body, the Special Office for City Affairs, included the mayor, the president of the provincial *zemstvo*, and one person elected from the city duma, but was headed by the *gradonachal'nik* and dominated by tsarist administrators. It was possible for the city to appeal the Office's rulings to the Ministry of Internal Affairs or in some cases to the Senate, the rough equivalent of a supreme court, but this process rarely overturned the *gradonachal'nik*'s original vetoes. In cities not designated *gradonachal'stva*, this veto power belonged to the provincial governor or the governor-general, if there was one.

The "golden words" of the 1870 City Statute did not appear in the 1892 law. After that date the tsarist administration was not required to use legality as a criterion for vetoing city council resolutions; intervention was left to the judgment of the heads of tsarist jurisdictions. The way was clear for renewed arbitrariness and thorough supervision by the administration.

Like the Extraordinary Measures, the controls and checks on municipal government of the 1892 City Statute represented not a new direction in imperial policy but a return to previous patterns. The old *Uprava Blagochiniia* (literally Board of Good Order), which remained nominally in charge of administering many Russian cities from Catherine the Great's time until the 1860s, was partly an elective body. However, the local chief of police, a government appointee, controlled the board and had veto power over its decisions. Before Catherine's Charter Granted to the Cities in 1785, municipalities had had even less say in their own affairs.

After the adoption of the Extraordinary Measures and the 1892 City Statute, Russian city governments operated largely at the grace of the local tsarist administration. This administration frequently stymied municipalities' efforts to improve local conditions. The issue was usually not change per se, but the extent of the state's control.

The 1892 law began, "The public administration of municipal jurisdictions has charge of affairs relating to local well-being and needs." The statute then specified the following areas of activity:[31]

1. Collecting established taxes and duties for city use.
2. Administering capital funds and other city property.
3. Taking measures to prevent food shortages "by the means available to it."
4. Construction and maintenance of roads, squares, quays, sewers, water supply, lighting, and so forth.
5. Supervision of the poor, prevention of begging, construction of charity and health care institutions.
6. Participation in measures to protect public health, development of means of medical help for the city population, improvement of sanitary conditions.
7. Concern for the better construction of the city according to established plans [i.e., established or approved by the emperor, in the case of Moscow], and also for preventive measures against fires and other calamities.
8. Participation in running city societies for mutual fire insurance.
9. Concern for the development of means of public education and participation in the administering of educational institutions according to law.
10. Concern for the construction of public libraries, museums, theaters, and other similar sorts of generally useful institutions.
11. Development by the means available to it of local trade and industry, construction of markets and bazaars, correct conduct of trade, establishment of credit institutions, and support for the establishment of stock exchange institutions.

12. Satisfaction of the lawful demands placed on it by military and state institutions.
13. Action on cases given to it on the basis of special laws and statutes.

The law thus assigned the cities a wide range of activity, but its language permitted many restrictions on their work. For example, towns could develop and administer educational institutions "according to law," which meant that almost every phase of their efforts in this regard was open to review and rejection by tsarist authorities. The latter passed judgment on curricula and even the hiring of teachers. Cities received the right only of "participation" in efforts related to public health; the local state administrations also had broad responsibilities in this area.

The law further charged municipalities with constructing and maintaining Orthodox churches. Towns were to support institutions that "have as their goal strengthening religious feelings and raising the morality of the city population."[32] Such concern for Orthodoxy had long been a responsibility of urban police and governments.

The 1892 City Statute was notable as well for omissions in the towns' rights. Most important among these was the police, left under the administration's control, although the cities paid all costs of law enforcement. The Moscow *gradonachal'nik* was also chief of police in the city, which made his power quickly and effectively realizable. This concentration of power in one office was a long-standing tsarist device.

The new law allowed the central government to interfere even in seemingly innocent, purely local affairs. Moscow's duma could "guard public health," for instance, but could not regulate flophouses. In 1898 the city government established a commission on Khitrov Market. This body presented a petition in 1903 to the Ministry of Internal Affairs asking for authority to establish firm rules on the construction and management of flophouses in the Market, as well as standards for fire protection, safety and health, and taxes on the houses. The city also wanted the right to ask for court orders to close buildings that did not comply with existing or future rules.

The municipality repeated the petition in 1907 because it had not received a reply to its original request, a rather typical instance of the slowness of the tsarist state apparatus. However, on the second try the answer came quickly: rejection. The ministry stated that this "widening of the rights of a city administration" could take place only after the whole City Statute had been changed,[33] which never occurred.

Vagueness in other tsarist laws also created problems for cities. For example, towns and *zemstva* had the right to issue rules on the construction and maintenance of sanitary conditions in factories. However, the state's Main Office for Factory and Mining Affairs had the right under an 1899 law to regulate safety, health, workers' morals, and medical aid.

In 1906 this office, which was under the Ministry of Internal Affairs, complained in a circular to military governors, governors, and *gradonachal'niki* that the "lack of clarity in the limitation of local rights has led to different local practices." The circular asked if any petitions for the "widening of local powers in this respect" had come to the above officials and requested their comments and copies of the documents, along with all local regulations on factories.[34] Such confusion was typical of the state's relations with localities. A city or *zemstvo* might try to act on its legal right to regulate some aspect of local life, only to find that a state agency had the same right and had overruled it. Or different sets of regulations might exist side by side, as in the above instance, and the courts would have to try to sort out the tangle. Central officials' aversion to any "widening" of local rights, as illustrated in the two cases just reviewed, demonstrates their overriding attention to state power.

Even on relatively minor points the city could not escape government supervision. For instance, the Ministry of Internal Affairs had to approve any Moscow duma resolution on collections for cleaning chimneys, the removal of night soil, or the construction and maintenance of sidewalks and pavement. In 1913 the Council of Ministers, the cabinet, itself ruled on whether or not a Moscow firm could produce margarine.[35] All resolutions on health, charitable, and other "generally useful" institutions had to be cleared with the head of the Main Administration for Affairs of Local Government,[36] which was part of Internal Affairs. The tsar personally had to approve any proposal of the Moscow duma to change the official plan of the city, which established the location and size of streets, squares, and parks.

The degree of government control over Moscow's affairs was typical for all Russia. The Council of Ministers spent considerable time on such weighty concerns as the expenses of a police captain in a small town and a bill for the State Duma to establish a tax on carriages and cattle crossing a railroad bridge over the Dnepr river at the village of Kichkas.[37] While some such matters might have had significance as national precedents, most did not. It seems that the conservative state did not trust localities to do the simplest things. Even the records of 1914 have the feeling of the seventeenth century, when the tsar's officials galloped back to Moscow to report on local events and obtain a decision.

In relation to local government, the Russian legal structure after 1892 or even 1881 was designed to ensure that the national authorities could act flexibly and without restraint to uphold tsarism as a system. Especially after 1905 and the tantalizing promises of the October Manifesto for a new era of political freedom, liberals often found the administration's powers under the old laws intolerable. Conservatives, however, especially rural ones, who stood to lose their whole way of life in another massive upheaval, could still support the government's reliance on laws like the Extraordinary Measures.

In 1908 the debate between the two political groups over this issue flared up in the State Duma, after the government announced yet another broad extension of the Extraordinary Measures. Members of the Octobrists were angered because they predicated their cooperation with the government on the belief that it would change its old ways and habits; the extension was a signal that would not happen, so that party spokesmen took it as a slap in the face. Prince A. D. Golitsyn, an Octobrist from Kharkov, but whose family had been connected with Moscow for centuries, attacked the regime on this issue in broad and bitter terms. "Do we have," he asked the Duma, "a representative system of government based on law, or do we have reigning in full strength to this moment arbitrariness and personal discretion, relying on something ranging outside the law and the legislative institutions of the country?" He concluded that the latter, not the former, existed in Russia.

> Before our eyes an entire system of separate satrapies is unfolding, not subject to any law or authority, but within the limits of its territory ruling the courts and issuing special legislation, directed only by its own outlook.... I state loudly and directly that the Minister of Internal Affairs does not have the power to subordinate to himself any governor-general, whose name in Russia is now legion.

This opinion provoked applause, presumably from the left benches.

Prince Golitsyn added that the Octobrists found the "endless extension" of the Extraordinary Measures "completely unacceptable." He went on to state his belief that many in the government found ruling by (personal) discretion much easier than adherence to written law; the "situation of complete lack of responsibility is much more pleasant for many than strict responsibility before the law."[38] In his anger the prince ignored the fact that it was pointless to charge the regime with bending the law, since the vagueness of the statutes made many infringements of civil liberty perfectly legal.

Golitsyn's remarks were surpassed in precision and intensity by those of V. A. Maklakov, a moderate Kadet (Constitutional Democrat) from the city of Moscow and one of the country's most prominent trial lawyers. Kadets placed much less reliance and hope than the Octobrists in the possibility that the regime would change fundamentally. Maklakov therefore pointed to the "great danger" in the "basic division corrupting our state organism": that at the national level representative government existed, while at the local level nothing had changed. There was no rule of law in the localities, a problem existing across Russia. Most of the country "found itself under a regime of legal lawlessness, under the regime of the extraordinary statutes." Maklakov informed the deputies that in Moscow those laws had been in effect continuously since 1881. Application of the statutes had "ceased to be a means of struggle against terrorism but had become the means of normal administration." Today "the reason for their existence is not sedition, which they were supposedly introduced to combat, but the most common phenomena, for which, if it is even necessary to struggle against them, there are ordinary means."

Maklakov continued by complaining about restrictions and fines on the press and government interference in the last Duma elections. "Where there is authority and its arbitrariness," he said, "there is also malfeasance." He concluded by warning the deputies that the Extraordinary Measures were "directed not against us [the Duma] . . . not even against Moscow, but are directed against the October Manifesto itself." Applause broke out among the left benches.[39]

The speeches of Prince Golitsyn and Maklakov evoked a warm response among their own liberal parties and on the left but were anathema to the right side of the State Duma. G. G. Zamyslovskii, a Rightist landowner from Vilensk province, rose in the chamber later in the year to offer a concise outline of his party's attitude toward the Extraordinary Measures. The Rightists were the most diehard conservatives in the Duma, men dedicated to tsar, country, and their own social positions as they existed before 1905. Zamyslovskii told the assembly, "Extraordinary security is introduced on the basis of His Majesty's will; therefore we cannot judge whether it is correctly applied or not." The statute is put into effect because an area is "beset with trouble." In such cases the administration, "on the precise basis of law, is presented with powers that place the average citizen at the whim [*proizvol*]" of the authorities. "Yes, that's the way it is," Zamyslovskii ended, "but it is on the basis of law." No one could consider the "colossal powers" granted by the statutes illegal. Applause followed from the right benches.[40]

Thus Russian conservatives could endorse the efforts of the tsarist regime to preserve itself through extraordinarily vague measures; these laws served to uphold the position of the old upper classes as well. On the other side, Russian liberals greatly valued political freedom and civil liberties and thought that their protection was the key to defusing tension in Russia. This outlook is reflected in Maklakov's stress on the "great danger" in the lack of such freedom anywhere but the State Duma chamber itself. The same reasoning is evident in the repeated calls for political liberties issued in 1905 by the Moscow city duma and numerous groups of industrialists. Liberals and radicals had no chance, of course, of removing the Extraordinary Measures by working through legal means; even if the State Duma had passed a bill to that effect, it would have failed in the State Council (*Gosudarstvennyi Sovet*). This upper chamber of the legislative system received half its members as appointments from the tsar. The other half were elected by various organizations, for example the universities and the *zemstva*. The result was a highly conservative body.[41]

Moscow's Financial Position

If the tsarist state was determined to limit the towns' general legal competence, it was almost equally dedicated to controlling their financial powers. Always short of money, the regime was loath to see much of it diverted for local needs. According to one calculation, 89 percent of all "budgetary means" were in the hands of the central government in 1908, compared to 46 percent in Great Britain and 28 percent in France.[42]

Certainly Moscow's tax receipts did not compare to those of large foreign cities. In 1910 its taxes brought the municipality only 6.73 rubles per capita, while Berlin collected the equivalent of 21 rubles and Paris the equivalent of 25 rubles per person.[43] Of course, Moscow was poorer than the other two, but not three times as poor. Moreover, at least one remedy, changing the way property taxes were collected, was available to the city government, as shown below.

The law codes gave Russian towns the right to impose various kinds of taxes, on items ranging from cab drivers to taverns to truck gardens.[44] However, for most cities only the real estate tax produced much revenue. A municipality had to use net income from property as the basis for this tax unless it proved to the central government that income could not be determined for a substantial amount of real estate within city limits, in which case value became the basis for the levy. In any event, the tax could not exceed 10 percent of the net income or 1 percent of the value.[45] Income-producing potential (*dokhodnost'*) could be taken as the basis of assessment for private homes or vacant land that produced no actual revenue. Most towns used the income method, which meant that wealthy people who lived in their own homes frequently paid little or nothing in property taxes; *dokhodnost'* was often assessed quite low for private houses.[46]

Until 1915, the tax was figured in Moscow on the basis of income. Various writers at the time and since have charged the city duma with making the property tax much lighter than it might have been. For instance, one Soviet author believes that the opportunity to deduct expenses allowed owners to pad their bills and thus underreport their net profits. Furthermore, reassessments were made only every ten years, which meant that the rise in property values kept the real amount of the tax well below 10 percent.[47]

These criticisms miss their mark. Of course, the Moscow duma had no stated policy of allowing property owners to cheat on expenses; this problem could have been a matter more of enforcement than policy. Lax enforcement may be a policy itself, but the problem here was more likely the difficulty of checking on each owner. And it was a monumental task to reassess all property, not one the city could easily undertake every few years.

In fact, the duma did move, albeit slowly, to alter the property tax situation. In 1907 it directed the *uprava* to prepare for a reassessment. The preliminary work dragged on until 1913, partly because of the *uprava*'s immense workload and the duma's lack of desire to push its executive board to faster action. However, another factor was involved in the council's reluctance to reassess property. By law, the city of Moscow constituted a separate *uezd* (county) under the provincial *zemstvo*, having equal weight there with thirteen other *uezd zemstva*. The provincial *zemstvo* had the right to tax real property in the city, which it exploited fully: in 1908 Moscow property owners contributed 1,061,000 rubles to the provincial *zemstvo*, while the other *uezdy* together were taxed only 760,000 rubles.[48] The *zemstvo* used the municipality's assessments to set its taxes on real estate in the city. It could and did use money collected from Moscow under this system for purely rural purposes, which naturally increased the city government's reluctance to raise assessments and thus contribute to an outflow of money from its territory. The provincial *zemstvo* collected over 1.5 million rubles in real estate taxes from the city in 1913, for example, and contributed only 186,469 rubles to the municipality's expenses.[49] State law had created this situation, and only the state could change it, something the city ardently desired.[50] This may also be a case of the regime's rural bias; in any event there is no record that it responded to the city's requests for liberation from the provincial *zemstvo*.

The central government also relied on city assessments to set taxes on property in Moscow until 1910, when it began to make its own evaluations of real estate.[51] It is surely no coincidence that in the same year the Moscow duma moved to adopt a system of assessing real property according to its value and in the next year decided to reassess every seven years instead of every ten.[52] Now the municipality could raise its tax rates without fear that the result would automatically be a greater outflow to the state.

The switch to a tax on value provoked sharp debates in the council over the question of its legality, as previously there had been no evident difficulties in calculating a tax on income. Nonetheless, the value basis was adopted in 1913. It took still more time to work out exact instructions for assessment, and the city did not actually use the new method until 1915. There is no record of the state's opposing the change, though it could easily have done so with the same criticism made by many city duma members, that income could readily be determined.

The Moscow duma's tax policy did have the effect of protecting its members' financial position before 1910. But the changes begun then were undoubtedly a recognition that the achievement of stability required more attention and more money for the city's urgent problems. Property tax receipts then increased sharply, as follows:[53]

1914	7,565,000 rubles
1915	10,060,000 rubles
1916	11,400,000 rubles

The rise after 1914 was due much more to the new system and higher assessments than to wartime inflation.

The levy on value meant that some kinds of property were now taxed for the first time. Many wealthy homeowners paid little in property taxes before 1915; quite a few duma delegates were among them.[54] Property that was not built up had previously borne only light taxation, since it produced no income. Speculators had thus been able to hold land with no tax obligation.

It took many years, and the circumvention of tsarist law, which obviously the duma could not take lightly, to change the property tax structure. In this case the council's desire to raise municipal income overcame whatever desire it may have had to protect the short-term financial interests of the propertied classes. Without the various state restrictions on its ability to raise taxes, even the privileged Moscow duma might have found more ways to increase revenue.

Besides these indirect taxes, Russian municipalities collected two direct taxes established by the state. One was a fee on passports; the other was the hospital tax, which after 1890 was set at 1.25 rubles per person per year. Liable for this payment were males and females of any title or rank (*zvanie*) who worked within city limits as domestic servants, artisans, apprentices, or workers. Theoretically, those who paid the tax received free medical care in city hospitals. Collection of this tax in Moscow was not systematic: in 1901 it brought in 666,435 rubles, but receipts fell to 398,203 rubles in 1909 and 344,835 rubles in 1911.[55] A city publication commented in 1912 that the decrease occurred because "many refused to pay."[56] Obviously the municipality was not particularly interested in enforcing payment of this archaic levy; the duma recognized that the bulk of the hospital tax fell, as it said, on the "most needy" strata of the population.[57] On other occasions the council expressed the idea that the lower classes should not be taxed heavily, either directly or indirectly.[58]

The city could also petition for the establishment of other taxes. For example, it asked the government to allow it to tax renters of apartments and other buildings used for living quarters. The state never granted this request. For years Moscow petitioned the government for the right to tax freight coming into the city, a privilege forty-seven other cities received. In 1906 the government hinted that it would agree to the proposal, but it continued to stall, bowing to pressure from some Moscow industrialists. Four years later both state legislative houses passed a bill authorizing the tax, and the emperor affirmed it, which should have made it law. Yet the government delayed implementation of the tax. Just before the war it seemed again that the government would approve the request, but the outbreak of the conflict buried the question forever.[59] Had the city ever received money from such a tax, by law it could have been used only for the construction and maintenance of roads and bridges leading to port facilities or railroad stations.

Besides taxation, Moscow had still other sources of revenue: it collected fees from property owners for maintaining pavement and sidewalks, cleaning chimneys, night guards to protect against fire, and removal of garbage and waste.[60] The city also charged for connections to its sewer and electrical systems. However, for many years the state did not allow it to require property owners to make such connections and to pay for them. The state saw the issue as a national one; in May 1911 the Council of Ministers agreed that a bill should be sent to the legislative chambers giving local governments the right to require sewer connections.[61] But there is no record that such a bill ever became law. Given its acute distress over problems of public health, the Moscow city duma would certainly have acted to require sewer connections had it been allowed to.

Another steady source of income for the city was bond issues, which it floated on both domestic and foreign markets. This was sometimes a slow process, as each issue by a municipality had to have the tsar's approval. In some cases Moscow's city government waited several years for his permission, which meant that the estimates on which the need for the loan had been based were no longer valid.[62] Nevertheless, Moscow was generally fairly successful with bonds: city debt grew from 27,243,700 rubles in 1901 to 112,538,078 in 1912.[63] Yet in general, Russian local governments borrowed far less than did those of France or England. According to G. G. Lerkhe, chairman of the Finance Commission of the State Duma, the indebtedness of local authorities in England in 1907–1908 was 3.5 times their annual revenue, and the indebtedness of the French communes was 4.5 times annual income. In Russia, however, 1,120 towns owed less than twice their revenue, while 393 *uezd* and provincial *zemstva* had debts that did not even equal their income. While such indebtedness can be a sign of financial trouble, Lerkhe felt it was more a measure of ability to raise capital for beneficial projects.[64]

In Moscow the income from bonds was used exclusively for city enterprises, and almost all the money obtained was invested in their expansion and improvement rather than in operating expenses. In this use of its loans Moscow was more efficient than several other Russian and European cities; 98.4 percent of its borrowing went for such so-called productive purposes, while 63.3 percent of Berlin's loans and 20 percent of Paris' went in that direction.[65]

Moscow's city government was able to borrow money because its enterprises were quite profitable. This made potential investors feel that the city was well run and would have the funds necessary to pay interest on loans and retire the bonds when they came due. Income from Moscow's enterprises grew from 4,090,904 rubles in 1901 to 21,401,360 in 1911. These figures represented 27 percent of all city income in the first year and 54 percent in the second. Net income from the enterprises increased from 394,487 rubles to 3,823,482, or almost ten times.[66] St. Petersburg followed the same pattern: in 1901 its enterprises brought in 31.3 percent of all city income, in 1912, 57.2 percent.[67]

Moscow's biggest money-maker was its tram system. In the early 1900s the

city began to buy the horse-drawn lines from their Belgian concessionaires, com-
pleting the acquisition in 1911. The municipal government invested substantial
amounts in the trams every year to extend the lines and convert them from horse
to electric traction. Partly because of these expenses the city showed a net loss on
the trams from 1905 to 1907. In the next year, however, the investment began to
pay off, and in 1912 the streetcars produced a net income of 3,296,000 rubles.[68]
The city often made money on other services as well, ranging from hospitals to
pawn shops.

In this period the Moscow duma was determined to earn income from most
of its enterprises. (This will be shown later for transportation and housing, for
instance.) Service to the population in any given program was usually a somewhat
lesser consideration, except in areas like education, which could not be expected
to show a profit under most circumstances. However, this philosophy began to
change in the years just before the First World War. For example, in 1914 the city
began to operate bakeries that sold directly to the public at prices below commercial stores. Enthusiastic response prompted the duma to plan four more bakeries in April 1914.[69] During the war the council considered lowering the price of
municipal water, on which it made a profit, but decided that the conflict made
that impossible.[70]

Contemporary writers criticized Moscow's profit-making on several grounds.
In the liberal journal *Gorodskoe Delo* (City Affairs), one author wrote,

> The property-owning duma, it is self-evident, has tried with all its might not
> only not to develop, but on the contrary to limit the role of the first of these
> sources of city income [the property tax] and to transfer the whole weight of
> the budget onto the city enterprises, establishing in this way indirect taxes.[71]

As noted earlier, the duma eventually raised the property tax. However, this
writer correctly described the city budget in the sense that an ever-greater portion
of municipal income in this period came from its enterprises. (Appendix G outlines city revenues and expenditures for the years 1901 and 1909–1912.)

Another writer for *Gorodskoe Delo* criticized the city of Moscow for operating contrary to all theories of public enterprises by taking huge profits from them.
There should be no profits, he maintained, or only very small ones. Yet he also
remarked that sources of income for cities were quite small. As in many Russian
towns, Moscow's financial position was difficult, and profit-making could not be
considered "so terrible" there.[72] He understood that the municipality had little
choice about its sources of revenue.

It should be noted that *Gorodskoe Delo* was generally a staunch supporter of
the Progressive Group of the Moscow duma, the more liberal wing, whose platform included operating city enterprises to make money. In Moscow and other
Russian cities, liberals and conservatives alike found their local governments in
a financial bind. Given the legal restrictions on their ability to tax, the Russian
capitals and some other towns naturally turned to their enterprises for income.
In Moscow this revenue was reinvested in services that did not make money, for
example education and parks. The fees charged for trams and other enterprises
were indirect taxes but were used largely for the benefit of the population. Considering the entire situation, it is difficult to accept the criticism of *Gorodskoe
Delo* or of various Soviet writers that profit-making from enterprises was in any

sense terrible. Moscow's government felt a strong need to look for money wherever and however it could. Writing in 1912, Lerkhe fully endorsed profit-making by localities. "In view of the poverty of the finances of local governments," he believed, "one must expect them to undertake on a large scale only revenue-producing works."[73]

Unlike most Russian towns, Moscow and St. Petersburg were in a position to earn revenue from their enterprises.[74] The capitals were large enough to attract foreign investment, in bonds or in enterprises as concessions, and were also wealthy enough in their own right to generate large—though still inadequate—tax revenue, which could be invested in services. The combination of poor economic development and tight state restrictions on taxation made it very difficult for most municipalities to collect the funds necessary for such investment. Other Russian towns simply did not have the resources to develop their own enterprises in the first place and were thus caught in a vicious cycle: they could not raise loans on the basis of profits from enterprises. St. Petersburg also suffered financially because the state owned a good deal of property, which could not be taxed, within the city. Moscow, wealthier in the first place, was therefore in a better financial position to modernize services than any other Russian town.

How could modernization occur in most Russian cities when they had so few funds to put into improved schools, hospitals, and the like? While a national government might produce liberal change by deficit spending, local bodies find that difficult to do. Urban Russian liberalism was very much bound by its financial possibilities; it was easier and much cheaper in many cases to limp along with traditional inadequacies. Moscow was the country's leading city in terms of both resources and progressive policies;[75] the municipality's relatively good income facilitated its liberalism.

Another source of income for Moscow's government was donations. These were usually made for some specific purpose such as construction of a new clinic or a city nightlodging house, an overnight hostel for the poor. In other cases the municipality could not touch the capital of a gift but could use income from it to operate designated institutions. Donated capital held by the city totaled 12,633,811 rubles in 1902; by 1912 it had grown to 20,035,982 rubles.[76]

Each year the city received subsidies from the central government for various purposes. In 1901 these payments amounted to 433,546 rubles; in 1911 they reached 932,152 rubles, an increase of 115 percent. The latter sum represented 2.3 percent of city income. Part of this money was granted for education, but the bulk of it, 65.7 percent in 1911, was for quartering troops in the city.[77] The municipality usually paid much more to the government for various services than it received. The city referred to these payments as "general state requirements"; they covered the maintenance of state institutions in the city, the police, and the quartering of troops. (Thus for this last purpose the city government both paid and received money. In some years it appears that Moscow profited from this exchange; for example, a positive balance of 138,179 rubles occurred in 1911.[78]) Some of these payments were downright silly and reflected only the state's inertia. Until at least 1910 the city had to pay for the chancellery of the Moscow governor-general, though none had existed since 1908. It also had to pay for special envoys and bureaucrats assigned to the city early in the nineteenth century, despite the fact that the papers authorizing these posts had burned up in 1846.[79]

These expenditures were the only ones required of Moscow by law. The state, not the city, determined their size. In 1909 the Special Office on City Affairs protested the city budget and delayed its implementation. The dispute developed because the office had introduced an item of 290,000 rubles into the budget to cover the cost of housing for police sergeants for the preceding three years, and the municipality had refused to pay this sum.[80] Thus the government acted to ensure that cities or *zemstva* made the payments it demanded.

In 1901 the state requirements comprised 17.7 percent of Moscow's budget; by 1911 this portion had fallen to 12.8 percent.[81] This was because the government increased its demands only slightly over time. In 1909 it asked the municipality for almost 2.7 million rubles; by 1912 the required sum had risen only 280,000 rubles.[82]

Some relief from state expenditures seemed imminent in 1912, when the central government passed a law obligating itself to assume one-half of all urban police costs, starting January 1, 1914. The state would also pay, starting in 1913, for the Special Office on City Affairs and for the salaries, housing, and food of court employees.[83] The newspaper *Russkie Vedomosti* (Russian News) reported that in addition the treasury would help defer Moscow's costs of maintaining mentally ill criminals, curing the mentally ill in general, and providing water for troops quartered in the city.[84] The *uprava* projected a savings of 1,350 to 1,400 million rubles a year from these subsidies.[85] The minister of finance, however, protested this law on the grounds that it was meant to apply only to *zemstva* and not to cities. When the case reached the Senate, it decided in favor of the municipalities. Yet by the end of 1916, St. Petersburg and "presumably other cities" still had not received this revenue, because government officials could not agree on the size of the subsidies.[86] There is no record of Moscow's having received such payments before the war.

A law enacted in December 1913 promised the cities that 1 percent of state property tax revenue from them would be returned to them. This item also did not appear in Moscow's budget in 1914. Despite these delays, city finances were improving in virtually every respect on the eve of the war.

The city was also able to float bond issues without serious difficulty, though the requirement of imperial approval made this a slow process. Moscow's costs were not rising in this respect: in 1883 the city borrowed at 4.5 percent interest; in later years it paid as little as 4 or as much as 5 percent, but in 1910 it was again paying 4.5 percent.[87]

Municipal income from all sources rose from 14,973,133 rubles in 1901 to 39,805,022 in 1911, an increase of 166 percent. In the same period Moscow's population grew 39 percent, only one-fourth as much. Therefore the city had much more to spend per capita just before the war. After the change in the property tax, Moscow did even better in this regard. The expansion of revenues from city enterprises showed no signs of slowing down before the war; municipal income was improving in all areas, and that trend seemed likely to continue.

Nevertheless, local officials expressed much discontent with Moscow's financial position. Why did this feeling appear? Part of the answer lies in the very different ways that city and state came to look at local financial rights after about 1907.

This difference did not exist in the government's relatively liberal phase, which lasted for almost two years after the 1905 revolution. In March 1907, Prime Minister Stolypin suggested to the State Council that the solution to local financial difficulties involved "expanding the sphere of action of *zemstva* and towns." At the same time, a "thorough [*stroinyi*] reform of the tax structure" should take place. This would entail transferring "a certain portion of present state income" to towns and *zemstva*. After all, the "government is obligated to give them the opportunity to fulfill the obligations placed upon them."[88] The Council of Ministers also indicated its appreciation of local financial problems and their results. It reported in 1907 that "one of the negative characteristics of our financial policy" was the fact that taxation was "predominantly for the financial needs of the State." This meant that local governments were left without enough funds to meet local needs.[89]

The Moscow city government made similar points on several occasions. It had noted in 1904, "[the current] twenty-million-ruble budget is far from sufficient for the satisfaction of the various needs of city services and for the necessary development of their branches."[90] The fact that this statement was made before 1905 suggests that the Moscow duma did not develop its concern about people's needs solely as a response to that year's revolution. While the strikes and fighting of 1905 may well have pushed the city fathers to greater efforts to alleviate Moscow's problems, their subsequent programs were extensions of, not a radical departure from, much that had gone before.

In 1910, while debating its 1911 budget, the city duma unanimously agreed on the following statement:

> Under the conditions created by the active City Statute, city estimates of income and expenses cannot cover the most essential requirements of urban life; the efforts of the city government to correct and regulate the establishment of a budget will be to a significant degree without [satisfactory] results while the new sources of income for which the city has repeatedly petitioned are not opened, while the general state expenses with which the city is burdened, whose limits are still completely vague, are not removed, while petitions on the needs and requirements of the city are left unsatisfied, and finally, while the general rights of the city are not expanded through alteration of the City Statute.[91]

The municipality lamented its position and turned down, for lack of money, many requests from the population to extend its services and numerous ideas from its own officials.

While the Moscow city duma continued to emphasize the need for wider local rights, both Stolypin and his government became more conservative as time went on. In February 1910 he told the State Council, "*Zemstvo* and urban life does not go forward, in the main, not because of a lack of rights, but because of a lack of funds."[92] He had reversed his emphasis of 1907 and now gave no hint that there was any problem with where the power of administering or distributing money lay. Russia's poverty, not her governmental system, was to blame for severe local defects. Stolypin's comment was reminiscent of various government officials' suggestions in 1905 that workers were restless not because they lacked political rights but because they were not paid enough, an idea industrialists vehemently rejected. Once more, the government wished to shift the focus of concern away from its rights and policies to questions of someone else's money.

Stolypin probably changed his view for two reasons. First, he had become more confident about the future, at least in his public pronouncements. In August 1907 he remarked, "In Russia there is no revolution whatever."[93] By October 1909 he could say, "Give Russia twenty years of peace at home and abroad, and you will not recognize her."[94]

The second reason for his change of heart was probably his increasing reliance on conservatives in the State Duma, which was dominated by landowners after June 1907. Such men knew that tax reforms in the *zemstva* would only mean shifting the burden more onto their land. According to a work published in 1907, landowners' holdings were taxed by the *zemstva* at a rate forty times less than peasants paid.[95] The parties to the right of the Octobrists had no tax proposals,[96] and for good reason: there was only one realistic possibility for change, and that was putting more of the burden onto their shoulders. Even Octobrist landowners did not support broad tax reform.

In the countryside, an alert and educated person might possibly rationalize poverty, disease, and other defects with the thought that it was all traditional. Rural problems were much more spread out, just as the villages were, and the peasants took care of their own casualties much better than any urban population did.

A place like Moscow was in another category altogether. The city's problems were vast, concentrated, and growing. They were not traditional, and they were not absorbed by the populace. An epidemic in the countryside might quickly peter out for lack of human fuel. In the towns disease easily spread from person to person, including the poor and the rich. Unemployment could be hidden to a degree in the villages; in the cities, it quickly gave rise to crime. Urban dwellers were more often forced by circumstances to look their locales' problems in the face.[97]

The Moscow duma's complaints about finances stemmed from a situation in which the needs of the lower classes were obviously still far greater than the city's ability to provide services. As later chapters will show, it is evident from duma debates and publications that Moscow's government realized the extent of the problems in many areas, among them appalling conditions in housing, infant mortality, and higher education. The city had only begun to work on some of these questions by 1914.

According to a recent Soviet work one member of the Moscow duma wrote, in November 1912, "The consciousness of the masses is moving [ahead] incomparably faster than city income, and [this] presents the city with ever more complicated tasks."[98] Thus at least some municipal officials may have feared the ultimate political consequences of not finding more money for the improvement of urban life. The comment helps explain the ambitious city programs described later.

Liberals and government officials also found themselves in disagreement over local borrowing. Both groups were deeply concerned about this issue. In 1909 the Council of Ministers noted that the financial position of the empire's cities and *zemstva* was "extremely unsatisfactory" and that local governments were "deprived of the possibility, because of a lack of the necessary funds, of meeting the most essential needs of local well-being [*blagoustroistvo*]." To improve this situation it was necessary to create an organized system of credit as a "normal source [of funds]" for localities' special needs "and sometimes for their current expenses."[99] Such a system, in the form of a special state bank for loans to local governments, was created by 1912, to go into operation in 1913.[100] These loans could be up to one million rubles. The money was to be used for new projects or to retire loans made before the law was passed. The state agency would determine rates and terms.[101] However, there is no record that the new institution made substantial loans before the outbreak of the war.

In this case the state was willing and able to modernize, of course with the proviso that it still had to approve all loans and their uses by localities. The Council of Ministers recorded the opinion in 1911 that it "fully appreciated the importance of providing necessary [*nadlezhashchii*] credit to the *zemstva* and towns . . . but not without government participation."[102] By this the ministers meant state control. The council believed that the towns' money problems were just that: they stemmed from local poverty, not a lack of fiscal powers. Secondary cities like Kiev could not get favorable terms for bond issues despite state permission to make them.[103]

Yet it may have been the case that tax revenues, partly a function of restrictive laws, were so low to begin with in many towns that investors felt bonds issued there would be a bad risk. It is difficult to judge; but if Moscow could have raised more money under a different tax structure, it seems very likely that other towns could have, too. Lerkhe believed that that was possible. He argued that the "organs of local government in Russia will only be in a position to begin making large use of credit when the general question of the reform of their finances has been dealt with."[104]

Still another factor that produced rancor in Moscow regarding state fiscal policy was the general antipathy between the two sides that built up after about 1907. No matter how much the central government augmented its payments to Moscow, or how much more of local income it allowed the city to keep, it always retained control over finances. This continuous tutelage by the central authorities produced greater resentment as state-municipal relations deteriorated for other reasons. Local resentment was expressed about many matters, including the ones that were going fairly well, for instance education. The more the city of Moscow was able to accomplish for its own people, the less its leaders felt they needed state guidance, and thus the more it grated on them. These points will be developed in later chapters.

Such concerns also help explain why sometimes the duma could not or would not balance the city budget, which the law required it to do. The municipality, of course, did not publish information on its deficits, but various writers noted them at the time. One report claimed that the first city deficit, 872,000 rubles, occurred in 1905. This and further deficits in the two succeeding years were covered by drawing from reserve capital,[105] an illegal practice. Another report listed city deficits of 1 million rubles in 1905, 1.5 million in 1906, and 1.8 million in 1907.[106]

In a sense, the city government created its own budget problems. Had it been content to improve city services more slowly or to put less money into areas from which it received little or no revenues, it could have operated within the state's limitations. Instead, its fastest-growing expenditures by far were for profitless areas: education, welfare, public health, and "good structure" (*blagoustroistvo*),

the municipality's term for street paving, bridges, public buildings, and beautifi-
cation. In 1901 the city spent 6,455,233 rubles for these purposes; in 1912 it spent
14,928,657 rubles, an increase of 230 percent.[107] This rise was more than five
times the population growth in the same span. In other words, the Moscow duma
poured every kopeck it could find, including money from its reserve capital, into
programs intended to benefit the city's people, particularly the lower classes. In
March 1914 the Progressive Group of the Moscow duma, which then dominated
the council, introduced a broad program. Among its goals were "systematic measures to lower the prices of essential goods: meat, bread, and fuel."[108] The war
scuttled those plans. This is certainly not a bad record for the reputed defenders
of the propertied classes. Fear for their own position, that is, fear of revolution,
may have motivated the duma to some degree to spend so much on social programs. Yet it seems that the council also genuinely cared about the people and
conditions of the city.

There is no question that the Russian government after 1905 operated under the
burden of vast demands on its resources in both foreign and domestic affairs.
Russia was a very poor country, and the means to meet her needs were slim. Yet
the question remains of how well-equipped the conservative state was, in outlook
and institutions, to allocate these limited resources for the general good of the
nation. Was the state modern enough to cope with the financial requirements and
stresses of the times?

Most educated Russians, whether in the central bureaucracy or in liberal
groups, could agree that the financial situation of local governments was abysmal
and reforms were essential. The comments of A. I. Shingarev and G. G. Lerkhe
have already been noted, as well as the remarks on local finances made by the
Council of Ministers in 1907. Liberals and state officials could also agree that the
problem was of national significance, affecting all aspects of Russia's development and even threatening her status as a Great Power. "One of the most pressing
and urgent public needs in Russia is a reform in the finances of local self-government," Shingarev wrote in 1912. "Russia is culturally and economically behind
other countries, and cannot remain so without endangering her vitality as a state
and the normal progress of her public life."[109] Fear of another revolution is
implicit in his remarks.

Shingarev's words sound much like a memorandum the Ministry of Finance
attached to the state budget in 1911. It spoke of an "absolutely necessary measure—strengthening the means of local provincial and city institutions, whose
expenses are constantly rising, but whose sources of income are insufficient." This
was an "essential question, upon whose proper solution depends the further
development of the country's entire economic life."[110] Prime Minister Stolypin
and Finance Minister Kokovtsov both recognized in 1909 that local governments
faced severe financial problems and that reforms were necessary.[111]

Yet little was done in this sphere before 1917. Up to 1914 the central government achieved only the creation of new taxes on cigarette papers and tubes,
in addition to the treasury subsidies and the bank for local loans mentioned earlier. The most basic problems, the absorption of funds by the state and the limitations on local taxation, continued unaltered. Only under the pressure of the

war's financial needs, and only in order to satisfy those needs, was a national income tax adopted in 1916.[112]

The Russian political parties had very different views on tax reform after 1905. The Kadets and Octobrists insisted that taxation be shifted from indirect to direct forms, while the Nationalists and the Rightists had virtually nothing to say about the question.[113] In other words, they were more or less satisfied with the status quo, which protected the core of their membership, the landowners. Thus the state, in stacking its parliament to favor such groups, helped defeat its own interests. This was an important contradiction of the Old Regime: to win social support meant to block necessary reforms. In the process, urban liberals and many well-educated rural figures became intensely frustrated.

There is little evidence to support the contention that "members of society," other than rural conservatives, felt any willingness to accept the state's paternalistic guidance in financial or, for that matter, other areas.[114] Leading liberals became increasingly alienated from the regime as time went on. Above all, the limitations on national and local political life caused them to feel that way. Among Moscow's liberals, resentment of the state's determination to interfere in local affairs became stronger as the eve of the war approached.

The Russian state could not modernize without public support and participation,[115] partly because irrational and highly conservative forces became dominant over the few "modernizing" figures within it. For example, State Controller P. K. Shvanebakh and Minister of Agriculture B. A. Vasil'chikov opposed the income tax early in 1907 because they saw it as a "capitulation to leftist parties which would have shocking social and political consequences."[116] The war graphically revealed the failure of the state's attempt to improve Russia's general economic situation without broad national support; the government's favorite projects, the railroads and the army, were not prepared for the demands of modern combat. D. A. Filosofov, minister of trade and industry in 1907, had understood the situation: he argued that to win wide public acceptance for an income tax, it would be necessary to give local governments a stake in the results of the reform and a role in collecting the new revenues. Society had to be attracted to the project.[117] That is exactly what the government did not do, on this and many other issues, and that is a key reason why it ultimately collapsed.

Would it have been possible, given a different political complexion for the state, to find the resources necessary to solve Russia's manifold local problems? Shingarev argued in 1912 that, besides the additional funds that towns and *zemstva* would be able to borrow without state controls, tax reform would bring them substantially increased revenue. An income tax, if partially distributed to localities, would provide them with 120 to 140 million additional rubles per year.[118] Kokovtsov in 1907 thought that property tax reform alone could produce 50 to 55 million extra rubles for local governments in the first year, and that the figure would go up thereafter.[119] Stolypin certainly implied that more money could be found for localities in his remarks of 1907 to the State Council.

According to the Soviet economic historian A. I. Sidorov, taxes on capital, land, enterprises, and other unearned income produced only 8 percent of the state's revenue in 1913. All the rest came from indirect taxes, the liquor monopoly, state railroads, and customs receipts, also a form of indirect taxation.

"Nowhere did direct taxes play such an insignificant role in the budget as in Russia."[120] This picture could have been changed to the benefit of the towns. Certain other expenditures that had a political aspect might also have been altered, for instance subsidies to the Russian Orthodox Church; in 1914 the Church received over fifty-three million rubles in government funding.[121]

A few million rubles here or there could have greatly improved urban conditions, saved lives, and possibly started some areas on an upward cycle. But the conservative state did not make the changes necessary to improve urban budgets. In any event, it is important to note that neither liberals nor, in several cases, government officials thought that the basis of local governments' financial problems was Russian poverty pure and simple. Shingarev believed that the "*decentralization of public expenditure* and the improvement of the local budgets is the chief remedy for the situation which confronts us."[122] The Moscow city duma agreed. For its part the state did at least consider various ways to improve local finances, even if it missed some of the obvious, politically unacceptable ones. Though Russian backwardness may be held accountable for many of the localities' money problems, there is no question that a good portion of that backwardness stemmed from the political nature of the conservative state. Even given the country's poverty and low level of development, local finances could have been greatly improved under a more flexible system that put less emphasis on indirect taxes.

Though it seemed for a time after 1905 that the government would substantially broaden local fiscal powers, it soon reverted to its traditional desire for strong central control. The same desire dominated the regime's ideas for reforming the system of local government in general, a subject to which key state figures attached great importance in the early twentieth century.

V. K. Plehve, appointed minister of the interior in 1902, tried to move energetically to introduce reforms in local government. In 1903 he formed a commission on the issue in his ministry that announced, "History has established that the responsible director of the province should be the governor." He should therefore be given "the means of fulfilling" this charge.[123] Somehow, the broad existing laws were not enough.

Plehve's goal in aiming to strengthen still further the powers of the governors—and thus of the *gradonachal'niki* as well—was to remove all vestiges of collective responsibility, as opposed to concentrating power in the hands of one official, and to make the lines of responsibility clearer in local administration. As things stood, the provincial governors, who reported to the minister of interior, had difficulty controlling all the local employees of the other ministries, who were nominally both under the governors and under their respective ministers. Needless to say, a great deal of confusion resulted.

The one remedy to this problem that was never proposed by the tsarist regime before 1914 was to give substantially more responsibility to the local populace. On the contrary, a bill introduced in the State Duma in 1907 by the Ministry of the Interior would have given state officials still greater powers over local government. The bill proposed that the Council of Ministers have the right to dissolve a *zemstvo* or city duma and replace it for up to three years with appointed officials if the local body was unable to cope with a major calamity such as a flood, if its public services were inadequate, or if its finances were in prolonged disorder.[124] Most of Russia's municipal dumas could have been closed under this law, especially for problems in the second category.

Right up to 1917, the conservative state felt it knew best. The government's answer to problems of poor administration or arbitrariness at the local level was always more state control, more power for the police. A semiofficial newspaper, the *Police Messenger* (*Vestnik Politsii*), proclaimed in 1908, "The more cultured and enlightened a nation, the stronger its police, the broader police authority and prerogatives."[125] In December 1907 the Council of Ministers agreed on a similar thought, stating that under Stolypin's reform proposals for local government "the forthcoming widening of the competence of *zemstvo* and town institutions must carry with it the establishment of more active supervision of them."[126]

This attitude stood in direct contrast to the desire of Russian liberals for local government. In the platform they adopted in October 1905, the Kadets argued that "the jurisdiction of local self-government should extend over the entire area of local administration (including the security and ordinary police)."[127] Moscow's city government made its similar view clear on numerous occasions.

The following chapters will explore the disputes between the tsarist regime and the city of Moscow in more detail. But it should be stressed that these quarrels were not simply a product of tight central government supervision over a local government. The same or even tighter controls existed in Buenos Aires in the late nineteenth century. When the municipal council wanted to remove an old arcade from the city's central plaza in 1883, it had to get legislation through the national congress.[128] Yet in general, the central and local authorities worked together smoothly. This occurred for the simple reason that people from the same group, the "progressive elite" of the country, administered both the city and the nation.[129]

In another setting, nineteenth-century England, a high degree of centralization became the "origin of much positive municipal action." The towns were often determined to defend "municipal sovereignty and local control"; town reformers "were anxious to demonstrate by precept that municipalities had no need of central direction." Parliament often agreed and passed numerous "local acts" that gave wide powers to English towns.[130]

Reformers in Moscow after 1905 were every bit as eager as their nineteenth-century British peers to show that they could act on their own, without central control and tutelage. But the tsarist government was not Parliament, and it did not agree. The men who led Birmingham or Leeds could come to terms with the men who ran the state in London. They shared many views, especially the basic faith that the British parliamentary system was a just and proper form of government. In contrast, the men who ran Moscow had much less in common with Stolypin, Kokovtsov, and especially with Nicholas II, whose power remained the key to national administration. The two groups had difficulty communicating. A. I. Guchkov, head of the Octobrist party, was also a deputy to the Moscow city duma and brother of the city's mayor; their family was well established in business. In July 1906 Nicholas met with Guchkov for an hour, when there was a possibility that he might be asked to join the cabinet. The tsar became convinced that the Octobrist leader was "not a man of affairs, that is, of state administration."[131] In 1910 Guchkov was elected president of the State Duma; he ran for the office partly because it conferred the privilege of periodic audiences with the tsar.

But Nicholas disliked him and would not listen to him.[132] Even Guchkov's mild liberalism was too much for the tsar; it implied that the autocratic system of personal rule was inadequate for Russia's needs. Nicholas had come to conceive of 1905 as an aberration perpetrated by traitors, and he saw no reason to change the old ways. His view of Russia's future was so different from Guchkov's that the two men could not communicate meaningfully. Because of their political beliefs or activity other important Muscovites were barred by the central government from official positions or participation in politics in this period, among them Professors S. A. Muromtsev and A. A. Manuilov and Prince G. E. L'vov. Russia's urban liberal elite and her national, politically dominant elite, with its face set firmly toward the countryside and protecting its own authority, could not interact smoothly.

For the rest of his life Nicholas II abhorred and regretted the concessions he had been forced to make in 1905. He was determined to give away nothing more of the great power he had inherited from his father. From 1907 on, he hardened in his outlook on this point, and his government followed suit. Yet 1905 had only whetted the appetite of many Russians for a much broader role in directing their own local and national affairs.

3

Who the City Fathers Were: Social Composition and Politics of the Elected Officials

This negative attitude [toward service] pervades the whole structure of city self-government up to the present time.

I. I. Ditiatin, 1875[1]

The question of filling the post of Moscow City Mayor . . . is undoubtedly linked with extremely important questions of state order.

The Council of Ministers, 1913[2]

The Moscow duma was by and large a liberal body before World War I, interested in both wider civil rights and bettering conditions for the city's lower classes. Why should that have been so? As noted already, duma members had to own a substantial amount of property; in socioeconomic terms, they had little in common with the overwhelming majority of Moscow's residents. Were the duma deputies motivated largely by what C. Vann Woodward has called "the flattery of paternalistic impulses"?[3] Were they prompted to improve their city by fear of revolution? Why did a significant number of affluent men devote considerable time and energy to modernization and amelioration through the work of city government, when they had no responsibilities to the broad public, and when their counterparts in a city like Philadelphia paid little heed to pressing social issues?[4]

This chapter will begin to explore these and other questions by examining the social background and politics of the Moscow duma deputies. The issue of social origins is more complex than might seem at first glance, considering the franchise restrictions, which generally required ownership of substantial property in order to run for office. Men of various educational, social, and occupational backgrounds served in the duma between 1906 and 1914. To what degree, then, did Moscow's "bourgeoisie," as the large property owners are frequently called, dominate the city government? What was the nature of this bourgeoisie's influence? Did it follow the lines of "class interests" or not?

Moscow's elite was highly active and important in national politics, too, as several examples have already shown. In both national and local work, prominent Muscovites were very much concerned with the power of the state and its paramount role in determining the course and progress of modernization. What factors in the city's history before and after 1905 might have made its leading citizens cooperative toward the state, and what factors pushed them in the other direction? This chapter will begin to examine these questions and their significance for the development of both Moscow and Russia.

The City Statute of 1892 allowed the St. Petersburg and Moscow dumas 170 elected deputies each. In practice their total number often fell short of the maximum. This was possible because a candidate had to receive a majority of votes in his electoral assembly in order to win a seat. Besides the chosen representatives, the president of the local *uezd zemstvo* and a delegate from the clergy participated and had voting rights. The latter joined the duma only if the head of the diocese "found it useful to appoint one."[5]

Duma elections took place every four years. In the capitals, the eligible electors were all Russian subjects (and charitable, educational, or government institutions) who owned property within city limits assessed for municipal taxes at more than 3,000 rubles. For Odessa the limit was 1,500 rubles, for the more important *uezd* cities 1,000 rubles, and for the remaining cities 300 rubles. In Moscow commercial or industrial enterprises of certain state tax categories and steamship companies that paid over 500 rubles per year in the basic commercial tax also held the franchise.

Not all deputies personally met the large property requirements. Any male over the age of twenty-four could become an elector, and therefore a member of a city duma, by representing a business or institution that owned enough property to qualify for the franchise. After 1892, members of the intelligentsia sometimes entered the Moscow council in this way, as they often sat on the boards of educational or charitable institutions and held their proxies in the balloting. No precise figures are available on the number of such delegates, but surely many of the professionals in the duma fell into this category.

The law allowed women owning the requisite amount of property to vote only through a plenipotentiary, who had to be a close male relative. Propertied males under the age of twenty-four could also vote in the same manner.

Jews had no electoral rights under the statute: they were not permitted to participate in city electoral assemblies or in preelection assemblies of property owners. Nor could they hold posts in city government or any branch of it.[6]

The law specified electoral procedures, but these did not always guarantee an orderly vote, as the *uprava* reported to the duma in 1912.

> In two electoral assemblies in 1912 and in many in 1908 a dense crowd gathered by the balloting tables and screened the mayor from the boxes of uncounted votes and the tables at which the count was being made. In view of the great danger from the crowd in the hall . . . no one will be admitted to the hall until the count is complete.[7]

Under such circumstances, it is more than doubtful that all Moscow duma elections were fair and above board.

Nor could the elections be considered in any way representative of the population or even the wishes of the city's upper strata. The franchise under the 1892 City Statute was even less democratic than under the highly restrictive law of 1870. In 1889, during the last elections held in Moscow according to the earlier statute, there were 23,671 qualified electors, about 2.9 percent of the population.

The new franchise requirements cut this figure by almost 75 percent, so that in the 1893 balloting there were 6,260 electors, about 0.66 percent of the population. Only 1,376 electors actually voted, which meant that the duma in that year was chosen by 0.0014 percent of the city's people.[8] This pattern continued, so that by 1912 3,407 of 9,431 eligible voters took part,[9] about 0.2 percent of the population.

In late 1907 the Council of Ministers, apparently recognizing some inequity in the urban franchise, proposed the reduction of the property requirement by one-half and the extension of the franchise to those who paid a certain level of the state-levied tax on apartments, as had already been done for St. Petersburg apartment dwellers.[10] These changes would have expanded the Moscow electorate considerably but still limited it to a tiny group of property owners and prosperous renters. Such modest reform was the most extensive the government was willing even to consider before 1917; after 1907 the Council of Ministers did not return to the subject. No extension of the urban franchise whatsoever was adopted, and Russia's municipal affairs remained in the hands of a small elite until the revolution.

Though the Moscow duma members benefited from this situation in the sense that they were responsible only to men of similar background and not to the population at large, the deputies spoke against the narrow franchise. In June 1905 the council resolved that voting for any national parliament should be "universal and on a democratic basis."[11] Like other urban moderates, A. I. Guchkov believed that widening political participation would help achieve stability in Russia. Invited to a palace conference on the country's political future in December 1905, he said as much to the tsar and other notables.

> It seems to me that it is not at all proper to fear the popular masses. On the contrary, it is precisely the attraction of this mass into the political life of the country that will achieve its firmer and more serious pacification.[12]

Ironically, D. N. Shipov, co-founder with Guchkov of the Octobrist party, held virtually the opposite view. In 1905 he commented that political activity on the part of the masses would only "increase their dissatisfaction with their situation and arouse their selfish interests."[13] This was a classic conservative position.

Both Guchkov and Shipov were members of the Moscow city duma, although the latter served only a short time. But Guchkov was from an industrialist family, while Shipov was a noble, a large landowner, and a *zemstvo* activist. To be sure, personal factors and experiences affected each man's outlook, yet the two did personify the differences between the liberal-bourgeois and the conservative-landowner viewpoints. Certainly their opposing stances on suffrage fit into a broader pattern of urban-rural divisions.

Although Guchkov and the Octobrists in general did come to welcome the narrowing and weighting of the national franchise on the basis of property qualifications, a response that tallied with their general support of the government until about 1912, they still remained more liberal in this area than many gentry figures. And when the Octobrists disintegrated as a political party after 1912, it was Guchkov and the more urban wing of his followers who re-formed as the more progressive Left Octobrists. Mikhail Rodzianko, a large landowner, became head of the Zemstvo Octobrists, who were often rural gentry, and the right wing of the old Octobrist party moved into the gentry Nationalist party or into close cooperation with it.[14] In other words, to a fair degree the Octobrist party split along urban-rural lines after 1912, according to whether its members believed they could generally agree with state policy or not. The issue at stake was the country's peaceful development.

Within Moscow, in January 1914 the liberal daily newspaper *Russkie Vedomosti* editorialized, "Only reorganization of the electoral law, both local and national, can bring Russian political life out of its blind alley."[15] Although the context was very different, it is also worth noting that in early 1917, when all controls on its contents were removed, the same paper called repeatedly for the widening of the urban franchise;[16] *Russkie Vedomosti* was closely identified with the majority of Moscow duma deputies after 1912.

Before the revolution, the low voter turnouts in Moscow were probably largely due to the many limitations on the city government's competence. The restrictions encouraged the traditional apathy of urban citizens toward their local governments, which prior to 1870 had been thoroughly dominated by the state. After the passage of the Extraordinary Measures in 1881 and the new City Statute in 1892, many among the small electorate may have felt that this domination had been reinstated and that participation in municipal affairs would therefore be pointless.[17]

In any event, too little time had elapsed since 1870 to allow the development of a new attitude of participation and responsibility toward local government. Voter turnouts were often quite low for *zemstvo* elections, too, probably because of apathy engendered by the tradition of nonparticipation, restrictions in the 1864 law that had created rural self-government, the Extraordinary Measures, and the *zemstvo* counterreform of 1890.[18] Concentration of power in the hands of the state and the slow economic development of Russia had helped to retard the growth of public spirit; it was only in the 1860s that it became apparent on any scale, and then it was confined to a relatively small group in the cities and among the rural gentry. All of the Great Reforms encouraged the development of public spirit only in a very limited fashion. More thoroughgoing economic change and the spread of education would be required before many of the empire's inhabitants began to want a voice in local government. Recent scholarship on the period 1902–1905 in St. Petersburg and Moscow suggests, moreover, that even at that time workers and artisans in the capitals would have been satisfied with only minor improvements in their political situation, which did not include participation in city government.[19]

Among those who could vote after 1892, mostly wealthy men, another factor may have kept turnouts low. The city government did not have much power to regulate matters that directly affected the wealthy. It had a limited say in the amount of taxes the rich paid, for instance. It could set fares on tram lines, open public elementary schools and hospitals, and deal with a host of other urban issues. But wealthy people sent their children to private schools, rode in carriages or automobiles, and had private doctors. Even some of those who became duma delegates remained largely apathetic about such municipal services.

Yet from 1870 to 1917 there was always an active, decisive segment of the Moscow city council. An understanding of this group and of the duma as a whole depends to a large degree on an understanding of the delegates' backgrounds. As

TABLE 3-1.   300 Moscow Duma Delegates by
Occupation, 1906–1914

	Number	*Percent*
Business:	188	63
honored citizens	47	
kuptsy	43	
meshchane	7	
peasants	5	
iamshchik	1	
guildsmen	2	
artisans whose specific occupations are unknown	2	
Intelligentsia and professions:	78	26
Other:	34	11
nobles	11	
engineers	12	
reserve lieutenant	1	
agriculturalists (*agronomy*)	2	
individuals with ranks from the state's table of ranks	8	

Source: Author's card file, using over twenty-five primary sources.

Table 3-1 shows, the sources provide occupational or background data for 300 of 331 men, over 90 percent, mentioned as having served in the duma in this period.

Unfortunately, the many sources used for this study give far from complete information about the men who served in city government.[20] This was partly because of the way they identified themselves. Following contemporary usage, they tended to use the socially highest title or designation they had. This label was the *zvanie*; it could refer to official rank, conferred or inherited title, level of education, occupation, or more frequently *soslovie*. Thus a man who was a *kupets* (merchant) by *soslovie* might have gained a title in the table of ranks, the ranking of government and military positions according to importance implemented by Peter the Great, by working at some point in state service. The merchant would then use that title because it carried more prestige, even though for the rest of his life he might be a lumber dealer. Or a Moscow noble might be a prominent lawyer but would identify himself only as a noble. There are some instances in which members of the duma can be identified by *soslovie*, rank from the table of ranks, and occupation, but that is very rare. Usually only one of the three categories is available.

Both government and society in tsarist Russia had reason to use labels for people that were supposed to have social significance. The state's first objective was always control; in theory it was easier to control those who had been categorized. The *zvanie* gave officials an idea of where a person stood in society and therefore a notion of the degree of respect due to the individual. The upper strata cared about *zvaniia* for much the same reason: Russia was always extremely conscious of status, and human relations depended on it to a great extent. In the West this tendency also existed, of course, but industrialization and modernization had made such facile labels much less significant.

The same processes were having a similar effect in Russia before World War I. Perhaps the best example in Moscow is the category "honored citizen." People holding this title worked as lawyers, businesspeople, artists, publishers, and teachers. Some inherited the *zvanie* from their fathers and did no work at all. Altogether there were 120 honored citizens in the duma in this period, and several other delegates who had once held that rank but had advanced beyond it. Occupations are known for 64 of these 120. Only 4 of them worked in the free professions, while 55 were engaged in some aspect of business. In view of this overwhelming disproportion, Table 3-1, which describes the delegates by occupation, lists all the honored citizens whose occupations are not known in the business category.

Peasants, *meshchane* (a vague *soslovie* of townspeople, usually lower-middle or lower class), and *tsekhovye* (guildspeople) whose occupations are not known have also been grouped with business. The sources give no cases of delegates in these *sosloviia* who worked in the professions. If any from those estates had professional jobs, they would probably have announced the fact beside their names. For the same reason, the business category features one *iamshchik* (literally "postman"), an ancient tsarist *soslovie* that used to deliver the mail but was utterly devoid of significance by 1906.

Even when occupations are known for deputies, it is sometimes difficult or impossible to categorize them socially. Where should engineers be placed, for example? They might have been *intelligenty* or "third element" types, the surveyors, doctors, and other specialists who worked for the *zemstva* and were well known for their liberal tendencies. They might also have risen to high positions in business, in which case they would ostensibly have had the interests of that sector in mind. One engineer was listed as a firm owner, but the size of his operation was not given. The remaining engineers have been placed in the "other" column in Table 3-1 because of the various possibilities of their profession.

Something of the same problem exists for lawyers. Although professionals, they sometimes attained high positions in business. Four duma members were both lawyers and firm directors. All other delegates who were lawyers have been grouped with the professions in the table because at least their education provided a bond with this cohort. However, this decision is somewhat arbitrary.

There is also the problem of those who held high rank in the state's table of ranks. The occupations of thirty-nine men with ranks are known; for eight they are not. Some or all of the latter group were central government employees while they served in the duma; the Kadet newspaper *Rech'* reported in 1908 that the council had a group of "ten nobles and higher tsarist officials (*vysshie chinovniki*)."[21] It was fairly common at this time to find government officials in the St. Petersburg duma, and James Bater has argued that their presence is evidence of the local government's close ties to the state.[22] If similar bonds figured at all in Moscow, they did not bring the city government noticeably closer to the national one.

The nobles of the "other" category deserve some further discussion here. Two were large landowners and noted liberals: D. N. Shipov and Prince G. E. L'vov, head of the Provisional Government from February to July 1917. Another large landowner and noble was Count S. L. Tolstoy, son of the great writer, whose influence was purely local. Altogether, nobles played a small role in the city duma, yet certainly their influence was more liberal than conservative; Chapters 5–7 will show that such men, and for that matter the duma as a whole, promoted gradual social change and amelioration in Moscow.

Another gray area in Table 3-1 is the business category, though generally this refers to big business. There were some exceptions: two deputies owned grocery stores, one a skating rink, and one a tavern. Where business connections were noted, however, they were usually given as "firm director," "manufacturer," "industrialist," or similar designations, which imply a large scale of operations. The fact that most delegates owned at least three thousand rubles' worth of real property also suggests that they were usually not struggling small businessmen.

Leopold Haimson has written of Russia's "painful evolution" in this period from a "society of *sosloviia* to one of classes."[23] The major political figure of these years, Stolypin, recognized that this process was necessary. In February 1907 he told a close associate that the estate principle had lost all significance and had to be extirpated from local government.[24] Representatives of Russia's manufacturing class agreed. In November 1909 the first congress of the All-Russian Trade-Industrial Union resolved that every citizen should receive legal equality through the complete abolition of estate privileges.[25]

Sosloviia distinctions had already lost virtually any meaning in Russian urban life; electoral laws for local city elections considered only wealth, age, sex, and religion, but not estate. This situation reflected the realities of urban society, in which one could rise in status and make money on the basis of personal abilities much more easily than in the countryside. The essential fact of landowner-ship determined rural life above all, and most people there owned or did not own land by virtue of their birth. Urban society was at least more flexible and more characterized by opportunities for upward economic and social mobility; hence the presence of "peasants" in the Moscow duma. If Russia's population had been largely urban before World War I, or if the tsarist government had been more attuned to urban life and less oriented toward rural society, the old *soslovie* system might well have been abolished.

But it was precisely the government's concentration on rural life and politics after 1907 that bound the Old Regime to the *sosloviia*.[26] What appeared trivial at best in the cities—the *kuptsy* and *meshchane* organizations in Moscow had little more to do than look after their membership rolls and administer minor charity for destitute members—was very serious business in the countryside. There the original national electoral law of 1906, and the revised, much more skewed law of June 3, 1907, heavily favored the gentry.[27] The goal of the second law was to ensure gentry control of the State Duma: in the system of indirect elections the landowners (mostly nobles) chose 2,644 electors, while peasants chose 1,168 and industrial workers 114;[28] these electors then voted for deputies to the Duma. Thus about 20,000 fully enfranchised landowners controlled the parliament for a nation of 130 million people. The landed gentry had 47 to 49 percent of all seats in the Third and Fourth State Dumas and also had great influence over the

45–46 ecclesiastics in those assemblies.[29] In its final years the conservative state relied above all on the gentry and the clergy, and it could only do so by ensuring that the gentry had the automatic high status and privileges accorded them in the *soslovie* system. The "painful evolution" from that arrangement to a society of classes was long overdue, and it was necessary, in Stolypin's view, for local government. Yet where political weight really rested in the national scheme, in the countryside, there was no evolution away from the estate principle. On the contrary, that principle was enshrined in the electoral law of 1907, without which the government of the appointed officials, which still held most power, could not have achieved any kind of rapport with the State Duma. This situation left urban Russia to evolve on its own, away from the guiding ideas of state politics.

Moscow is an ideal case in point. The city duma deputies, though almost all wealthy men, came from widely varied backgrounds. Despite all the caveats given above about the limitations of the data, Table 3-1 gives a rough idea of the composition of the Moscow duma from 1906 to 1914. It reflects as well the dynamic jumble of types that Russian urban society had become.

The Moscow duma was indeed dominated by businessmen, as many contemporary and later authors have noted. However, these businessmen came from many different backgrounds. Some were well educated and some were not. Some were involved in manufacturing and some in trade, which might have produced different outlooks on business. Even within this group, such variations tended to produce a wide variety of interests and opinions on politics.

Among those in the professions, the range of backgrounds was still greater. And even when delegates had similar histories, their politics might differ widely. Indeed, the greatest political distance in the council was between Nikolai Astrov, a noble lawyer and liberal Kadet, and A. S. Shmakov, a noble lawyer, ardent monarchist, and vitriolic anti-Semite. Yet even Shmakov could exhibit a kind of social conscience. In early 1906 he urged the duma to consider the question of aid to the poor in regard to the high cost of food and fuel;[30] later the council did attempt to lower bread prices. Lawyers, engineers, and nobles appear in all three groups in Table 3-1. They cannot be put into convenient niches and neatly tied to certain political views.

One Soviet author has written, without specifying his sources, that of 146 members of the Moscow duma in 1913, 63 were capitalist industrialists, 32 were wholesale merchants, and 24 were large property owners.[31] All the materials used for the present study do not provide enough data to make such a statement, but it is conceivable that the writer is correct. Even so, it is simply not possible to conclude on this basis that the duma followed a certain line of policy.

Although available data on the composition of the Moscow council before 1906 are cruder than those of the preceding table, they nonetheless reveal some changes over time. In the Soviet work *Istoriia Moskvy* (History of Moscow), the duma in 1893 is described as in Table 3-2.[32]

The same work describes the council in 1896 (Table 3-3).[33] This information is somewhat problematic, because of both the roughness of its categories and the implication that no one from the professions served in the duma from 1893 to 1896. It is difficult to believe that eight professionals sprang into the council *ex machina* in 1896. The tables also show that the number of nobles decreased sharply after 1893. There is no apparent reason for that decline, and on this point

TABLE 3-2. The Moscow Duma According to Social
Status, 1893 (137 Members)

	Number	Percent
Peasants and *meshchane*	13	9.5
Merchants (*kuptsy*)	86	2.8
Nobles	38	27.7

the data also seem suspect, especially because of the number of nobles who served in the council between 1906 and 1914. Roberta Manning has suggested that the cities provided a "more congenial political climate" for gentry Kadets after 1906, and that they and gentry Octobrists, who "closely resembled the more modern and better educated of the new professional civil servants," often felt a "strong attraction" for the cities. After 1906–1907, some of these gentry figures moved from *zemstvo* into urban politics; one example is Prince G. E. L'vov of the Moscow duma.[34] This could explain the rise in the number of the council's nobles after 1908.

What appears beyond question in these descriptions is the factor that probably did not change dramatically before 1914, the percentage of businessmen in the duma. Their influence remained strong, though it was never monolithic.[35]

The Moscow council can also be compared in composition to the St. Petersburg duma in 1912. For all of the reasons given above, the information in Table 3-4 must also be treated with great caution. Even in this imprecise form, however, it reveals certain differences between the Petersburg council and its Moscow counterpart. The business community (merchants and honored citizens above) supplied a much smaller percentage of deputies in St. Petersburg than in Moscow, but the professional group in the capital was roughly the same size as the Moscow deputies in free professions. The noble category in Table 3-4 is somewhat hard to decipher, as it is not clear whether or not nobles were also included in the other categories. In any event, judging by the size of the group alone, they did not have major influence in the Petersburg duma.

The greatest difference between the two councils is in the categories of military officers and national government employees. No active officers served in the Moscow duma, and the number of state officials remains unclear, though it was

TABLE 3-3. The Moscow Duma According to Social
Status, 1896 (120 Members)

	Number	Percent
Peasants and *meshchane*	8	7.0
Merchants	81	67.5
Nobles	7	6.0
In professions	8	7.0
In a group of "bourgeois public [*obshchestvennye*] figures"	16	13.0

TABLE 3-4.   The St. Petersburg Duma Delegates by
Background, 1912 (160 Members)

	Number	Percent
Merchants and "honored citizens"	51	31.9
Nobles	10	6.3
Military officers	9	5.6
National government employees	26	16.3
Professionals	41	25.5
Others	23	14.4

Source: Bater, St. Petersburg, p. 359.

probably quite small. Almost 22 percent of the Petersburg deputies worked for the state, undoubtedly a much larger portion than in Moscow. This suggests that connections between the national and local governments were considerably stronger in the imperial capital.

Moscow's businessmen comprised a far larger group in the city's duma than did their counterparts in St. Petersburg. Pavel Buryshkin, who entered the duma in 1912, devotes a long section of his book *Moskva Kupecheskaia* (Merchant Moscow) to a discussion of the politics and influence in the council of leading business families. The Buryshkins were from the *kupechestvo*, the old merchant group mocked and applauded by Ostrovskii in various comedies. Once these merchants had been noted for their coarseness, for example the habit of blowing their noses into dinner napkins. But by 1906 many had achieved a high level of education and sophistication. According to Buryshkin, many merchants then left the business world for other pursuits. This was especially true in city politics.

> Those representatives of the *kupechestvo* who played a role in the city duma
> and influenced the course of affairs of the city administration usually belonged
> to those *kupechestvo* families, often to the dynasties [the leading families of
> merchant Moscow, in his opinion], that had already left the trade-industrial
> life and had turned toward either public affairs or the liberal professions.[36]

Sergei Bakhrushin, for example, later a noted Soviet historian and the winner of a Stalin prize, served in the duma at this time. He was from one of Buryshkin's "dynasties," but he taught at the Imperial University in Moscow as an assistant professor. He was an *intelligent* from the *kupechestvo* who had liberal views; that is, he cannot be neatly categorized. P. D. Botkin also came from a "dynasty." He was a director in his family's firm but had his own publishing house. He, too, did not fit into a precise sociopolitical niche. Mayor N. I. Guchkov, a leading Octobrist and a director of a company, was born into a *kupechestvo* family. He was also a lawyer. However, his whole career after 1906 was in public affairs; what interests did he then represent? The point is that Guchkov and others in the duma had a deep commitment to public service and to the city as a whole. There is little basis for the view that the class backgrounds of such men meant that they conducted municipal social policy solely or even largely as a defense of upper class interests. Like the Kennedys in America, these families often turned to civic pursuits as their raison d'être by the second or third generation after initial success in business.[37] Buryshkin and L. L. Katuar were industrialists and members of the duma's Progressive Group after 1908. But, as Buryshkin put it, "We were both more *intelligenty* than representatives of the class of exploiters."[38]

In one duma deputy, A. I. Guchkov, the zeal for service took the form not only of politicking in the Moscow city government and the State Duma and leading the Octobrist party, but also of pursuing trouble around the world. Leon Trotsky called him a "liberal with spurs,"[39] and certainly Guchkov loved to ride into a fight. His grandfather had been a serf, his father a Moscow merchant and a justice of the peace; his mother was "a graceful and clever French lady."[40] Guchkov first made a name for himself in Russian famine relief in 1891–1893. Next he fought on the side of the Boers against the English. He rode along the Great Wall of China and went to the Far East to serve with the Russian Red Cross, where he was taken prisoner by the Japanese. He travelled through Armenia in

A. I. Guchkov, the "liberal with spurs." Member of the Moscow city duma, head of the Octobrist party, head of the Central War Industries Committee in 1917, first minister of war in the Provisional Government.

1915, while the Turks were carrying out massacres. Perhaps he did represent "a new type in the Russian liberal movement," one characterized not by "philosophic idealism" but by "a quest for practical political and economic goals";[41] but he also displayed the bold confidence of the nouveau riche. It is no wonder that he was popular in Moscow and detested at Nicholas' court. As delegates to the Moscow city duma, A. I. and his brothers K. I. and N. I. Guchkov represented the kind of businessman whose deep concern for the future of his country eventually led him to a mild liberalism, a stance that was anathema to the conservative state after 1907.

Of course, not all Moscow merchants were liberal, but often the more conservative ones did not serve in the Moscow duma between 1906 and 1914. For example, G. A. Krestovnikov, a prominent industrialist who became head of the Moscow Stock Exchange in 1905, was not a member, though his brother N. A. Krestovnikov served in 1912. In any case, the old conservative merchants did not set the tone of city policy in this period.

Buryshkin categorized the families of the old merchantry according to their influence in Moscow. He listed five he believed were most important, as they played leading roles in both business and public affairs. Four of these had representatives in the duma in these years: the Bakhrushins, who gave millions to the city for hospitals and clinics; the Tret'iakovs, the same family that founded Moscow's well-known art museum; the Morozovs; and the Naidenovs.

A second group had earlier been in the same category as the above names, but by 1917 its members either had no outstanding figure left or had risen to the nobility. Of these, only the Alekseevs were represented in the council, by a professor.

Buryshkin distinguished several other merchant families that he felt were highly influential in Moscow, though not to the same extent as the above people. Among these were several clans who had men in the duma: the Mamontovs, who collected and sponsored art; the Botkins, publishers; the Guchkovs; one Riabushinskii, P. P., an industrialist, banker, newspaper publisher (*Utro Rossii*), and a leader of the national Progressive party; one Konovalov, A. I., also a leading member of the national Progressive party, who stayed in the Moscow duma less than a year before resigning in 1909; and the Krestovnikovs and Vishniakovs, important industrialist families.[42] Members of Moscow's old merchant clans had great influence in the duma, but they applied it according to a variety of interests and political outlooks. However, after 1905 their views were predominantly liberal.

Certain factors operating in Russia after about 1900 tended to make many businessmen less inclined to support the tsarist regime than previously.[43] First, they felt that the government, after a period of strong support beginning in the 1880s, had turned away from their interests in favor of powerful agrarian, antiindustrial elements within the bureaucracy and court circles.[44] Among the objectionable features of tsarist economic policy were tariffs that protected agriculture and state manufacturing enterprises, archaic laws regulating business organization and procedures, and restrictions on peasant mobility and development that retarded expansion of an internal Russian market.

By 1905, numerous businessmen in Moscow and elsewhere had recognized that the absence of safety valves for the venting of lower class grievances frequently caused disorders in the factories, which hurt economic life. The lack of a parliament also put commercial figures at a disadvantage in influencing state policy, as they did not have the connections to the throne that agrarian circles did. The problems caused for manufacturers by the "police socialism" or Zubatov experiments of 1901–1903, in which workers organized and were even supported in strikes by the police, helped produce a new mood of opposition to national policy among liberal Moscow businessmen. The repression of liberal *zemstvo* leaders carried out by the authorities in 1904 to dampen opposition succeeded merely in fueling it.[45] A final major factor in disillusioning businessmen about the regime was the utter failure of the war with Japan in 1904–1905.

The great bloodshed and unrest among workers in early 1905 dismayed industrialists, and their organizations began to protest loudly. Besides its objections to the *soslovie* system noted above, the All-Russian Trade-Industrial Union, a key group of business leaders, now criticized other features of tsarist policy. Existing law, it said, served as a "series of brakes" on economic development. The courts, consulate system, and credit facilities were all inadequate. Russian administration had a "police character," which did not follow "firm legal norms." Finally, the congress objected to "the constant interference [of the government] in the life and activity of the citizens, in particular in trade and industry."[46] Other groups of industrialists in Moscow and St. Petersburg issued similar statements.[47]

This volley of criticism was very close to comments made by the Moscow city duma in the same year, perhaps because so many businessmen served in it. In January 1905, just five days after Bloody Sunday, when troops in St. Petersburg had slaughtered hundreds of peaceful marchers carrying a petition to the tsar, the Moscow duma passed a resolution sympathetic to workers' rights. It began:

> The most important means for the support of internal peace, without which the life of the city cannot proceed normally, and trade and industry cannot develop, is the creation for the workers of legal pathways for the free, collective consideration of their needs and the transmission of them to enterprise owners and to the government.

The resolution went on to urge that workers be given the rights to strike, so long as violence was not involved, to hold meetings, and to form unions, with the "indispensable condition of the spread of this framework to all Russian citizens."[48] Until the October Manifesto, no Russian held such rights.

In the midst of the December fighting, the duma resolved as follows:

> The events that have taken place in recent days in Moscow have, unfortunately, a well-founded origin (*blagopriatnuiu pochvu*), . . . in the absence of a law regulating the freedoms introduced by the manifesto of October 17 and in the feeling of ill intentions [on the part of the state] and of lack of faith in the actions of the government, [a feeling] created in the population by the government's slowness in implementing its promises.

To rectify this situation, "liberal reforms" were necessary, "which alone can put the country on the path of peaceful development."[49] Despite the fact that the governor-general outlawed voluntary medical aid to the *druzhiny*, the people's guards and fighters opposing the troops, on December 12,[50] on the next day the duma voted unanimously to render all possible medical assistance to "everyone suffering in the current bloody events."[51]

Thus the Moscow duma in 1905 clearly marked out a political path quite different from that of the central government, which issued the October Manifesto only when forced to. City officials looked forward eagerly to a new political atmosphere in which they could speak out and work on local problems more freely; this milieu, they felt, would be more conducive to both economic development and political stability.

Dissatisfaction in Moscow with tsarist policies went well beyond the confines of the city duma. The general public evinced much sympathy for the *druzhiny*.[52] Further incidents in 1906 contributed to resentment of the government. On January 12, 1906 a Cossack patrol stopped a sledge carrying S. I. Chetverikov, a prominent industrialist, and his sister. For no apparent reason, a Cossack began to whip the two. Only the intercession of a policeman, who happened to recognize Chetverikov, saved the passengers from further harm. The Cossack officer in charge of the patrol told the industrialist that it had all been an "unpleasant misunderstanding." An account of the incident carried in the liberal newspaper *Russkie Vedomosti* ended with the comment, "Hasn't our entire life in recent times been one big 'unpleasant misunderstanding?'"[53] Two days later the same paper reported that a whole series of protests by various social groups had followed the affair.[54] Thus even at the beginning of the period often termed the "constitutional experiment," Moscow's elected government and a substantial segment of the public were deeply troubled by the regime's heavy-handedness and slowness in fulfilling its promises.

On the other hand, the December 1905 fighting had proved to be too much opposition for the city duma as a whole to tolerate. It had approved suppression of the uprising in mid-December, endorsing even the brutal methods of tsarist troops.[55] One member proclaimed that he was ready to shoot anyone participating in the fighting.[56] At a banquet celebrating the new year 1906, Mayor Guchkov clinked glasses with Admiral Dubasov and told him, "You must not doubt our support; each of us is ready to put all his understanding and all his strength into this cause [repression of the revolution]. Moreover, great significance has fallen to you as our leader in this cause."[57] Deeply frightened by the uprising, Guchkov had identified himself and the city government with the tsarist authorities. For most of the duma deputies, opposition to the regime was acceptable so long as it did not turn into violence. Naturally, the urban liberals shared conservatives' aversion to social revolution, and the two sides could toast repression together, though they would soon diverge on how to avoid another upheaval.

Yet many businessmen did not easily move into opposition to the regime, for other trends in the country's economic and political history and in their own backgrounds promoted strong loyalty. The Moscow *kupechestvo* was characterized in general by a conservative outlook, which stemmed from its success in traditional areas such as textiles, the lack of political opportunities throughout Russian history, and the dearth of outside stimulation that might have encouraged wider perspectives. The *kupechestvo* was also numerically weak and isolated from potential allies by social barriers and a certain snobbishness on the part of many political activists from the nobility and professions. All of these factors tended to make many Russian businessmen regard the government as their protector.[58] This helps explain why, despite their many economic and political grievances, most entrepreneurs became much more reconciled to the regime with the issuance of the October Manifesto, which granted fundamental civil liberties and promised a legislative parliament. Yet even this conditional support depended on sincere implementation of the Manifesto's provisions. In short, strong potentials for both a conservative and a liberal direction existed after 1905 among Moscow's elite. Time and state policy would determine which tendency would become paramount.

For its part the Moscow duma from 1905 to 1914 generally reflected the more liberal and oppositional strains among Russian businessmen and members of the *obshchestvo*. The unique position of Moscow's business elite in the country helped produce a group within it that maintained this political outlook. More independent of the state's economic power and freer of foreign influence than their counterparts in St. Petersburg, Moscow's business leaders were wealthier than most in Russia. They also had high social status in their city, as the nobility or the bureaucracy had long since ceased to dominate Moscow socially. Yet another factor that prompted some of the city's top businessmen to separate themselves from government policy was their origin or continued practice as Old Believers, a religious sect that had been severely persecuted by the state in Moscow and elsewhere as late as 1855.[59] And, as Buryshkin pointed out, the members of the *kupechestvo* who entered the Moscow duma usually had a higher level of education, culture, and public spirit than the members who did not serve. The general level of education among Moscow merchants increased greatly after about 1874.[60] These characteristics helped override the conservatism of the merchant milieu.

Petersburg's business leaders had different concerns and characteristics. The Soviet scholar I. F. Gindin noted, "Political-social leadership remained with the Moscow bourgeoisie because the Petersburg bourgeoisie developed later and was closer to tsarist politics."[61] Indeed, Petersburg's emphasis on heavy industry made it much more dependent on government orders than Moscow's "calico" or light industry. Petersburg industrialists like A. I. Putilov simply could not afford to take as independent a position as Moscow's leading businessmen did. One symbol of this difference is the fact that Putilov was welcomed in and consulted by the highest circles of the government while A. I. Guchkov was not.[62]

Moscow's intelligentsia had its own reasons to be liberal and to oppose the regime: the state hampered or made impossible its desires to organize, exchange information, travel abroad, teach without central direction, and publish. These factors, together with the feeling among many businessmen that workers had to have regular outlets for their grievances, led the Moscow duma to pass the liberal resolutions of 1905 detailed earlier. This spirit also appeared in the Octobrist party, which was very influential in Moscow, as shown by N. I. Guchkov's service as mayor from 1905 to 1912. When the party formed in November 1905, it called for the right of workers to assemble and strike.[63] These positions stood in stark contrast to those of the conservative state. Even after the pseudolegalization of unions in 1906 the government severely hampered their activities and even existence across Russia. (Chapter 5 will discuss this situation in Moscow.)

The large number of professionals and *intelligenty* in the Moscow duma probably also deepened its desire for reform, particularly of local defects. To enhance their own status and to stake their claim to a special role in government, professionals in the United States during the contemporaneous Progressive Era worked hard for urban improvements.[64] Professionals like sanitation engineers and statisticians had a natural interest in examining the problems that surrounded them and offering solutions. The tsarist government often opposed this kind of poking into Russia's problems and frequently rejected elections of doctors and other specialists to municipal *upravy*. This was particularly common in Moscow.[65]

In the period just after 1905 other cities' leaders appeared to share the state's view, but the picture was very different in Moscow. When tsarist police arrested numerous employees of the municipality's statistical department, the city secretary intervened on their behalf.[66] Moscow's civic leaders wanted to expose their city's problems and did so in various publications. The professional ethos and the liberal impulse complemented each other well.

To all these aspects of the background of the city fathers' liberalism we can add what Paul Miliukov called "the traditional Moscow spirit of opposition to the government."[67] Reaching back to the founding of St. Petersburg in the early eighteenth century, a cultural and political rivalry existed between the two Russian capitals; one can find echoes of it today. Moscow took pride in being the "first-throne capital"; to be crowned or carry out important ceremonial functions such as the tercentenary celebration of the Romanov dynasty in 1913, the tsars travelled to Moscow. For fun, but fun with a serious undertone, the royal family and elite Petersburg society dressed in old Muscovite costume. In the eyes of Moscow's people, their city was the heart of Russia; Petersburg was Western, almost an alien growth on the native soil. Moscow had risen to defeat the Mongols, and Moscow had suffered destruction at Napoleon's hands, while Petersburg remained untouched. All this pride fed the patriotism of people like the Guchkovs, P. P. Riabushinskii, and Prince L'vov, as well as their dislike of German influences at court, transmitted through ethnic Germans from the Baltic provinces and relatives of the emperors. The ancient distrust of the Germans, dating back through various wars to at least their invasion of 1242, deepened the Muscovites' sense of being the true Russians. Riabushinskii's newspaper *Utro Rossii* summed up these feelings in early 1912 while discussing an English delegation's visit. The editorial's title was "Welcome to Russia!" It began,

> On the way to Russia stands Petersburg. Our guests from England have been detained for several days in that entryway and only today come to us in Moscow, entering Russia.
> Welcome: to Moscow—to Russia![68]

Without question, this pride also promoted a desire among Moscow's civic leaders to make their city as fine as possible. To do that, they needed more freedom of action than the central government was willing to allow.

The opposition to tsarist policies by Moscow duma deputies, as well as their prominence in national politics, was further demonstrated in 1917. Of the ministers of the first Provisional Government, four had been members of the Moscow duma. They were the premier, Prince L'vov; A. A. Manuilov, the minister of education; A. I. Guchkov, the minister of war; and A. I. Konovalov, the minister of trade and industry. Surely there would have been one more, S. A. Muromstev, president of the First State Duma, had he not died in 1911. It might be added that, although he lived in St. Petersburg, Paul Miliukov, first foreign minister of the new government and its leading figure, was a graduate of Moscow Imperial University and had received his intellectual shaping there. M. V. Chelnokov, mayor of Moscow after the fall of 1914, was head of the important Union of Towns during the war. N. M. Kishkin, another Moscow duma deputy, apparently actually ran the union.[69] Guchkov also headed the important Central War Industries Committee during the war. Though all of these figures were to suffer complete political disaster in 1917, their early status and positions after the February collapse of the Old Regime reflect both their opposition to it and their importance as Russian liberals, in the days when that group believed it could determine the country's future.

Though he never joined the Provisional Government, P. P. Riabushinskii also played a prominent role in 1917. Along with another Moscow industrialist, S. N. Tret'iakov, Riabushinskii was one of the driving forces in the All-Russian Union of Trade and Manufacturing, which revived and assumed new importance in the changed political environment. In this role he became one of the leading spokesmen for Russia's industrialists. Unfortunately for himself and his peers, Riabushinskii's rhetoric greatly stirred class tensions, as when he spoke in Moscow in early August 1917 to a group of business leaders. To end economic and political chaos, he said, "We may have to employ the bony hand of hunger, and of national misery, to take these false friends of the people—the committees and the soviets—by the throat."[70] His words spread quickly across Russia, increasing the enmity between common people and the upper classes. In early 1918 the Bolshevik party newspaper *Pravda* singled out Riabushinskii as the prime representative of the evil, capitalist counterrevolutionary.[71] The self-confidence of Moscow's elite overreached itself in 1917 and helped lead to its own destruction; Riabushinskii's disdain for the needs of the common people and his suggestion that the upper classes might have to starve them into submission helped support the Bolsheviks' emphasis on class struggle as the essence of the revolution. Russia's poor could find reason to hate the Riabushinskiis and their peers and to support their arch-enemies.

Liberals were not the only national figures to emerge from the Moscow duma before and during 1917. A. S. Shmakov won a wide reputation as a leading anti-Semite. He authored several anti-Semitic tracts and in 1913 gained some notoriety when he offered his services as a "civil plaintiff to assist the prosecution" in the infamous Beilis case,[72] in which a Jew was charged with the ritual murder of a Christian child. Yet Shmakov stands out in the Moscow duma as a lone figure; no other delegate publicly repeated his anti-Semitism, a stance that was not uncommon among rural gentry.

Within the generally liberal framework of city politics before the war, Moscow duma delegates divided almost without exception into two groups, the progressists or Progressive Group (not to be confused with the national Progressive party) and the moderate-rights. Both acted as local parties: they adopted platforms and campaigned on them, held caucuses and conferences, tried to elect their own members as mayor, and published attacks on the other group's ideas and record.

Unfortunately, far less data are available on the delegates' political affiliations than on their social and occupational backgrounds. Therefore any analysis of correlation between social standing and political views must be highly cau-

TABLE 3-5.   Local Party Ties in the Moscow Duma, 1906–1914

	Right-moderates	Listed in Both	Progressists
In business	30	48 (includes 1 noble)	5
In professions	10 (2 nobles)	28 (5 nobles, 2 honored citizens)	4
Other	6 (1 noble)	3 (1 noble)	4

Source: Author's card file, compiled from over twenty-five primary sources.

tious. The sources provide party affiliations for 138 deputies. Table 3-5 shows the breakdown of these affiliations according to the categories of Table 3-1. Incomplete as they are, the data suggest several things. First, the nobles are found in five categories, indicating they were by no means a solid bloc in the duma. Indeed, in general the pattern of party affiliation seems quite random. None of the three occupational divisions tended to affiliate as a bloc; duma politics in these years were more complex than a simple expression of class interests.

Most accounts indicate that the council was fairly evenly split between the two groups from about 1908 to 1916. The newspaper *Russkie Vedomosti* reported after the 1908 election that sixty-six delegates were progressists, fifty-seven were right-moderates, and fifteen were on both lists.[73] The Kadet paper *Rech'* stated that sixty-six delegates were progressists, sixty-two were "Right-Octobrists," and ten were on both lists.[74]

The best indication of local party strength among the duma deputies after the 1912 election was the way they voted for mayor in early 1913. Prince G. E. L'vov, the progressist candidate, received eighty-two votes for and seventy against. N. I. Guchkov, the moderate-right choice, received seventy-seven for and seventy-five against.[75] The first figures more accurately reflect the parties' balance, as the duma was obliged by law to present two candidates to the government and thus had to vote positively for someone other than its first choice. L'vov's victory reflects the growing strength of the progressists in the duma, from a distinct minority before 1908 to rough parity with the moderate-rights between then and 1912 and finally to a small majority. This pattern reflects in turn a growing disillusionment with the regime among Moscow's elite. The 1913 mayoral vote essentially represented the victory of a Kadet over an Octobrist and had more to do with feelings about national politics than local events. In the previous year, Kadets won all four seats to the Fourth State Duma in Moscow's first and second curiae.[76] Even A. I. Guchkov lost his State Duma seat in Moscow. The Octobrists had become too closely identified with the national government and its failures, as perceived by Moscow's electorate. Buryshkin noted that by this time among the city duma deputies, "a majority of the industrialists were 'nonparty' or progressists. Almost all the *intelligenty* [were] Kadets."[77] In short, as will be shown in more detail below, by 1912 a spirit of opposition to the conservative state was very much on the increase among Moscow's elite.

This was true in other cities as well. In Riga and St. Petersburg, Octobrists lost their State Duma seats in the first curia to Kadets.[78] It is worth noting that, as far back as 1906, the Kadets "emerged as the major political party of virtually all Russia's cities and towns."[79] Kadet strength did decline thereafter for some years, as government policy became more conservative. But among the urban electorate, as well as inside the Moscow duma, that conservative trend had produced a reaction in the opposite direction by 1912.

National party differences spilled over into that body. Buryshkin recalled that the moderate-rights were "closely connected" to the Octobrists, and the progressists were likewise tied to the Kadets;[80] polemics between the two groups often concentrated on these connections. Before the 1908 elections, for instance, the Octobrist newspaper *Golos Moskvy* accused the progressists of being a screen for the Kadet party. The Kadets, the article sneered, wanted to reform the City Statute so that they could pull "workers and others" into municipal affairs. The party would then organize the city to put pressure on the government. Concerned only with their own goals, the Kadets had no real interest in improving the city.[81] There was a grain of truth in these words. Meeting in Moscow in April 1908, a conference of Kadet leaders had decided that it would not be appropriate for the party to campaign locally on a "broad municipal program." Rather, its members should use local slogans in order "to avoid sharp corners,"[82] which presumably meant confrontations with the government. But clearly Moscow Kadets did care deeply about their city.

Golos Moskvy also charged in 1908, "The ideal of the 'progressists' is the order and traditions of the terrible year 1905,"[83] a stock sarcastic Octobrist jab at the Kadets. Mayor Guchkov was also the editor of this paper, and as a leading Octobrist and moderate-right he had an interest in polemics with the other side, especially at election time.

After the balloting, however, the mayor had something different to say. In an interview with a paper more liberal than his own, *Rannee Utro*, Guchkov commented that both duma parties were interested in improving conditions on the outskirts of the city, in particular sewerage, water supply, street lighting, and pavement. Both were interested in reform of the City Statute, though he did not specify why. He went on to comment on the party programs.

> In my view, they are so close to each other, they contradict each other so little—if one does not consider unimportant details—that, it's true, each half of the Duma could sign with both hands [that is, endorse wholeheartedly] the program of the opposite group.[84]

In the liberal journal *Gorodskoe Delo*, a progressist deputy remarked about the opening of the new session in 1909, "The Progressive group was truly astonished, having heard from the mouth of the mayor almost the entire program with which it had campaigned before the voters during the elections." The main points of this program were decentralization of the city government and the improvement of finances through commercial management of municipal enterprises, especially the trams and gas works. These were the very enterprises, the author claimed, that the moderate-rights in their election speeches had wanted to give to concessionaires.[85]

After 1908 the trams again began to return revenue, and the question of turning them into concessions ceased to interest either group. The progressists never actively pushed for adoption of their scheme to decentralize city government by creating neighborhood or ward dumas, a favorite Kadet idea.

On many contemporary issues local party lines were abandoned, if they ever had any real significance. In December 1908, for example, twenty-nine delegates signed a statement to the duma calling for a protest resolution against the decision of the Moscow governor-general to ban certain published materials in the city and forbid their possession by any inhabitant. The list of prohibited items was to be expanded regularly, and it was the duty of every citizen to keep informed of all additions. The twenty-nine delegates protested the "almost complete impossibility of determining which materials were banned," which put the residents of the city in an extremely difficult position.[86] Among the signers of the statement were progressists and moderate-rights; it seems that irritation at the central administration's powers did not always depend on the label a delegate chose for himself. On this and various other issues the factors that united the duma were stronger than those that divided it. Almost all deputies shared a desire to see the end of the regime's tutelage and interference in personal and municipal affairs. They also shared a commitment to more open politics, broader political participation, basic civil liberties, and improvements in conditions and opportunities for the lower classes.

The contention that policy differences between the local parties were minor is further borne out by the tone of a publication the moderate-rights issued in 1912. Signing themselves the "group of nonparty and moderate electors," the authors assessed the duma's activities over the past three years with an eye to the upcoming elections. There was more praise than criticism of the session, despite the report's claim that the "Kadet group" had dominated it. The most severe objection in the whole document was to the so-called Progressive Group's attempt to ban all new construction in the city over three stories, ostensibly for health reasons. The moderates, "defending the interests of the average person," had defeated the measure because it would have driven housing prices up and was not important from a health standpoint.[87]

These criticisms seem contrived. If the moderates were able to defeat the progressists' measure, then the latter did not have a firm majority in the duma. And if this was the sorest point between the two groups, then there was really not much difference between them. This conclusion is borne out by a laconic comment in an *uprava* report on the years 1913–1916: "The composition of the duma delegates changed [more in favor of the progressists], but the general direction of city policy remained unchanged."[88]

Even at election time the differences between the two groups sometimes disappeared. A total of twelve deputies were listed in various sources as members of both factions, for instance. In the 1912 elections, according to one newspaper report, progressist and moderate-right electors made arrangements in some wards to support the same candidates.[89] The article does not say why; presumably this was done to ensure the defeat of the "property owners," a small group that wanted to cut property taxes. This faction rarely succeeded in electing deputies. Its defeats further suggest that the duma was not as dedicated to keeping property taxes down and defending property as some accounts indicate.[90]

While the moderate-rights and progressists may not have been far apart on most questions of local policy, there were differences in the tone, style, and general outlook of their politics. In this sense Guchkov's charge that the progressist group was only a screen for the Kadets had more than a grain of truth, though many local progressists joined the national Progressive party. In the corollary to the mayor's complaint, Nikolai Astrov wrote of the 1908 city election that the "Union of October 17 [the Octobrists], calling itself the moderate group, had as a platform general desires for reform of city affairs without any indication of how to do it." The Octobrists had claimed that the election had great national political significance and that on it depended the "further pacification of Russia." Astrov dismissed their platform as "impatience toward [their] opponents,"[91] by which he apparently meant that the moderates' differences with the progressists on local issues really stemmed from personal antagonisms.

The progressists did tend more strongly than the moderate-rights to oppose the national government when it thwarted the city's plans (as Chapter 4 will show). Yet the two factions often combined to try to avoid any state intervention' or, failing that, to skirt its vetoes. In most such cases differences between the parties disappeared. The duma's overall commitment to liberal goals and to establishing its independence vis-à-vis the state impelled it to unite at these moments.

To lay the groundwork for its policies and to obtain recommendations for their implementation, the duma created commissions for areas such as public health, education, technical problems, well-being (*blagoustroistvo*), and housing. It also set up temporary commissions to deal with ad hoc or special topics, such as Khitrov Market or ceremonies at the unveiling of a new statue to Gogol. Both types of commissions gathered information, interviewed experts, sometimes travelled within Russia and abroad, and made reports and recommendations to the whole duma. These reports were published each year, and the quality and thoroughness of their presentation, as well as the careful efforts to compare statistics and programs with those of foreign cities, are often quite impressive.

At the beginning of each four-year session, the duma elected an executive board, the *uprava*, which was headed by the mayor. Since their positions were fulltime and required special competence, *uprava* members almost invariably came from outside the duma. The board had responsibility for "direct administration of the affairs of the city government" according to law and the resolutions of the duma.[92] In Moscow the *uprava* was directly in charge of running city enterprises, keeping all books and statistics, and carrying out duma resolutions.

The *uprava* and duma were both headed by the mayor, chosen by the duma from among its delegates at the beginning of each term to serve for four years. As noted already, the duma had to select not one but two candidates for the mayoral position. The minister of internal affairs then ruled on these choices, either rejecting them or presenting them to the tsar. The monarch could choose one or reject both, in which case the government could appoint a mayor or direct the duma to start over. In 1909 all went smoothly and Nicholas II affirmed N. I. Guchkov as mayor of Moscow.

In contrast, the mayoral election of 1913 produced great difficulties with the state. Urban mayors had a sensitive and powerful role within city government: they controlled agendas and speakers in duma sessions. They were also largely responsible for liaison with the local tsarist administration and with the regime as a whole. The importance of the Moscow mayorship to the tsarist state was underscored in the law codes, which specifically allowed central government officials to impose "disciplinary fines" on the city's chief executive only with the emperor's approval;[93] that is, the mayor was monitored at the topmost level of the regime. Especially in Moscow, where the city council had been independent and recalcitrant and where rebellion had peaked, the national government wished to have a cooperative mayor.

The Moscow duma, however, did not oblige. It chose Prince L'vov, a prominent Kadet, and further displayed its stubbornness by refusing to submit a second candidate to the government. Acting mayor V. D. Brianskii went to St. Petersburg in early 1913 and talked with Minister of the Interior N. A. Maklakov, ironically the brother of the liberal Moscow lawyer V.A., who told him that if the duma did not choose a second person for presentation to the tsar it would not be permitted to hold more elections, and the government would appoint a mayor.[94] The duma then submitted Guchkov's name, but he indicated he would not serve if selected by the tsar.

According to the Soviet historian V. Ia. Laverychev, at this point Maklakov tried to persuade Guchkov and another leading Moscow Octobrist, A. N. Naidenov, to take the mayoral post by appointment from the tsar, as the law permitted. Naidenov, from one of the city's leading industrial families, was a Moscow duma delegate and a prominent member of the Moscow Stock Exchange Society. Thus he would have commanded respect from the duma; but neither he nor Guchkov could be persuaded to take the appointment.[95] Both men were moderate-rights, which made them reasonably acceptable to the state. In this case, even two members of the Moscow duma who ardently wished to cooperate with the government would not agree to become the city's mayor by imperial fiat. Although they were undoubtedly partly influenced in their decision by the desire to avoid offending their colleagues in Moscow, Guchkov and Naidenov surely believed that an important political principle was at stake. Why should the state have the right to override the choice of the Moscow duma, a body comprised of respectable men who had no thoughts of revolution?

For its part, the government did not want a Kadet as mayor of Moscow. As early as November 1906, in accordance with central government policy, the Moscow *gradonachal'nik* had ordered all city employees, whether elected or appointed, to leave the Kadet or "any other opposition party" or lose their jobs.[96] The mayoral issue must also be considered against the background of growing tensions in national politics. Beginning somewhat before Stolypin's death in 1911, but especially afterward, tsarist officialdom moved toward more reliance on administrative measures and away from cooperation with the State Duma. The "Third of June" system, which Stolypin had engineered in 1907 in the belief that the new electoral law would ensure such cooperation, had begun to break down as early as 1909 over bills on the naval general staff and religious freedom for Old Believers. The Octobrists supported both projects, but they were rejected by Nicholas II. In early 1911 Stolypin himself furthered the failure of his creation by persuading the tsar to approve a controversial bill to establish *zemstva* in the western provinces for the first time. The legislation was adopted under article 87 of the Fundamental Laws, the great loophole that enabled the central government to adopt laws whenever the State Duma was not in session.[97] Widely perceived as an assault on the parliamentary principle, this action angered many politicians, including some Octobrists who had previously strongly supported the government.

In view of the failure of much of his reform program to pass the Duma, Stolypin had begun an attempt to build a new political base by turning to the Nationalist Party, a group of deeply conservative men. The premier now abandoned some of his desires for reform, for example easing restrictions on religious freedom, but he counted on the Nationalists to support his agrarian proposals. In return he catered to the party's virulent Russian nationalism. In general, the Nationalists were wealthy landowners of the western provinces, acutely concerned about any threat to their preeminence from ethnic Poles or Ukrainians, who comprised the bulk of the population in the west.[98]

But by 1911, Stolypin had forfeited his credit with Nicholas, as a result of strong attacks on the premier from the Rightists, who hoped to wreck the Duma completely and return to unsullied autocracy, and supposed insults to the government in the Parliament. Stolypin's death thus did not cause the triumph of reaction in the government but merely enhanced its rise. In this context, a noted liberal and Kadet like Prince L'vov was unacceptable to the government as mayor of Moscow. It was not likely that those with influence at court could have established smooth relations with him.

The next step in the mayoral conflict came in April 1913, when the *gradonachal'nik* informed the Moscow duma that Minister of the Interior Maklakov had not seen fit to present either candidate, Guchkov or L'vov, to the tsar. Nicholas accepted his minister's decision, and the duma was directed to hold new elections.[99] It selected S. A. Chaplygin, a member of the duma's Progressive Group and a professor at Moscow Imperial University. He, too, was rejected. In the fall of 1913, L. L. Katuar, a progressist and banker, was elected, but his candidacy met the same response.

Maklakov then tried to have the tsar appoint B. V. Shtiurmer, a well-known reactionary who was later prime minister during the war. This idea was rejected by the Council of Ministers. According to Laverychev, the ministers did not want to provoke a conflict with the Moscow bourgeoisie.[100] V. N. Kokovtsov, who was prime minister at the time, reported that all the ministers except Maklakov opposed the choice of Shtiurmer. Kokovtsov argued to the Tsar that Shtiurmer's appointment would result in conflict with the Moscow city government. Nicholas then agreed not to appoint Shtiurmer.[101]

The Council of Ministers' records tell the story in a somewhat different way. (Appendix H provides a translation of its deliberations on the issue in November 1913.) According to the Council's own *Journal*, Shtiurmer requested that he be withdrawn from consideration after leaks to the press about his possible appointment resulted in a public outcry "against the very possibility of appointing anyone as Moscow's mayor who was not chosen as a candidate by the city duma." At the same time, the Council recommended that Katuar not be appointed; he was of foreign origin, was not Orthodox, and would be "only an obedient tool in the hands of the leftist elements in the city duma," who were now in control of it.

The Council of Ministers concluded that the present situation should be maintained: no permanent appointment should be made, and Brianskii should continue as acting mayor. This solution would avoid introducing "harmful bases of distrust, discord, and irritation" into relations between the national government and the municipality of Moscow.

Essentially, the Council had no suggestion about the basic problem except to wait and hope that somehow the situation in Moscow would improve from the government's point of view. "It is fully conceivable that, with the passage of a certain length of time, new elections for the Moscow City Mayor . . . can produce more suitable candidates."[102] Here, as in other situations, the government lacked a clear idea of how to proceed in regard to an urban dilemma.

Yet there was no reason to expect a progovernment shift in the Moscow duma's attitude, barring a fundamental change like the advent of war. The Council of Ministers certainly provided no indication that the Moscow duma would radically alter its attitude. And the evidence of recent events in the city pointed in the opposite direction: only Kadets had been elected to the State Duma in the top city curiae in 1912, the progressists had gained control of the city duma in the same year, and the latter body had stubbornly continued to elect mayoral candidates who were clearly unacceptable to the conservative state. The Moscow duma had come a very long way since its "typical display of fright and passivity before the tsarist bureaucracy" in another dispute in 1883.[103]

Only in September 1914, after the outbreak of war, did the duma choose a candidate acceptable to the government: M. V. Chelnokov, a Kadet, progressist, and *kupets*. The general feelings of renewed loyalty to the throne at the start of the war in the duma and elsewhere undoubtedly influenced the tsar to drop his objections to a Kadet. Even so, Chelnokov accepted the post over the objections of the Moscow Kadet committee, which changed its opinion only after the non-Kadet members of the Progressive Group threatened to resign in order to show their support for Chelnokov.[104] Even the heady patriotism of the war's first phase was not enough to override the antipathy built up between the city duma and the state before 1914; a significant part of the Moscow duma, most of its Kadets, was far from willing to bow to the state on local rights.

The duma reacted to this lengthy process along local party lines. After the first government rejection of mayoral candidates in April 1913, Nikolai Astrov, leader of the Progressive Group, said in a duma session, "The situation is painful. We must find a way out and not succumb to a feeling of grief and bitterness, so natural at the present time." Two moderate-right delegates immediately rose to contradict him. Both said that they did not share his grief. One, F. F. Voskresenskii, said that all was in order and according to law, where everything depended on imperial authority.[105] He thus echoed the sentiments of rural conservatives on tsarist law.

Feelings about mayoral problems therefore constituted one of the few issues on which city duma politics followed the lines of national party politics. At the same time, while the duma's conservatives may have been willing to support the central government's right to act as it did, most deputies resented the uncertainty and frustrations of the situation. The government had played its hand very forcefully on the mayoral issue, another instance of the way it fostered the alienation of the *obshchestvo* in Moscow and elsewhere.

Cases of state interference in municipal mayoral and *uprava* elections occurred regularly throughout the country. Between 1900 and 1914 the government rejected 217 mayoral choices and 318 *uprava* members.[106] Thus the regime tried in its crude, paternalistic fashion to ensure quiescent and cooperative municipalities. It may have achieved this shortsighted goal to some degree, but the legacy of such acts was bitter; they contributed to the erosion of support for the tsarist system before and during the war.

Businessmen dominated the Moscow duma from 1906 to 1914, though many professionals also served in it. However, these facts alone are not particularly helpful in analyzing the nature of municipal policy in this period. Both local parties included members from various socioeconomic backgrounds; there are no strong correlations between background and local political affiliation. Both groups worked to promote gradual social change and improvement in the city.

The existence of parties in the duma was usually not significant. Only minor squabbles occurred over local policy questions; following a trend begun in the 1870s, the council usually voted by large majorities to implement ameliorative programs. This pattern did not change in the period under investigation, despite the fact that control of the duma passed from the moderate-rights to the progressists.

On a few questions that involved larger political issues real differences between the two groups did emerge. The progressists adopted a more conciliatory tone than the moderate-rights toward striking municipal employees in 1913 and a sharper response to administrative vetoes (as subsequent chapters will show). However, in the same year two moderate-rights refused to accept appointments as mayor from the tsar; certainly they were not pliant supporters of the government.

In general, what the delegates had in common was more important than what divided them. The deputies believed in capitalism and in evolution toward a more open society, but that did not mean that they were dedicated first and foremost to defending their own property interests or that they were frightened by the prospect of revolution into more than temporary cooperation with the government. They might better be characterized as a body with a definite liberal slant that saw no alternative to working within the law, while bending it whenever possible.

In 1911 the liberal, Kadet-oriented journal *Gorodskoe Delo* published a comparison of Moscow's duma with St. Petersburg's.

> Moscow is significantly ahead of Petersburg in the composition of its leading city officials; its ruling majority with N. I. Guchkov at the head is still to a fair degree reactionary, opportunistic, and dependent on big capital [that is, on the wealthiest capitalists], but nevertheless the majority's cultural level is significantly higher than that of the Petersburg traders, flour dealers, tavern keepers, and financiers of the old duma camp. This [Moscow] majority is frequently prepared to listen to the demands of the progressists, whose chief is the leading delegate Astrov, to understand these demands, and to a great degree to meet them. On the other hand, the age-old neglect of the ancient Russian capital, especially its planning, geographical situation, and huge death rate—explained partly by the chaotic flood of people into Moscow, going there from our sick countryside to get well and to die—create for the city government great difficulties, particularly because Moscow's finances, like those of other cities, have been driven into a terrible corner.[107]

Several exaggerations and unfounded assertions appear in this appraisal, such as the charge that the moderate-rights were "dependent on big capital." As has been shown, that cannot be proven, while on the other hand many progress-ists also came from business backgrounds, including some from big business. Yet the statement accurately depicts the Moscow duma's liberalism, its differences from the Petersburg council, and its difficult financial position.

Gorodskoe Delo's appraisal of the St. Petersburg duma has recently been sup-ported by James Bater, who refers to its "absence of a 'civic spirit' and . . . preoc-cupation with minimizing the financial demands made on the citizenry." He goes on to say that "as a body, it was essentially conservative and for a long while remained the domain of the merchant and entrepreneurial elite."[108]

As in so many other respects, Moscow was the leader among Russian cities in regard to its duma. Progress came more rapidly and extensively there than in any other town.

The irony of the city's history before World War I is that the more the munic-ipal government achieved, the more it became hostile to the state. By 1913–1914 city and state had become locked in an apparently irreconcilable conflict over the mayorship. It is difficult to imagine anything that could have broken the impasse, short of the burst of patriotism produced by the declaration of war, without caus-ing much greater bitterness among Moscow's leading citizens. It was no accident that the Council of Ministers referred to the moderate liberals who dominated the Moscow duma by 1913 as "leftists." To the top officials of the state the term meant revolution and the destruction of all they held sacred. Close cooperation with "leftists" was out of the question.

To understand why this situation developed, it is necessary to examine first the nature and role of the tsarist administration in Moscow and then the inter-action between municipal and national officials as they both dealt with local prob-lems. The remaining chapters trace the checkered pattern of cooperation and antagonism between city and state that developed over measures to improve Moscow's life.

4

The Police at Work:
The Tsarist Administration in Moscow

Here, where the public is more hostile to the government than in any other country, absolutely everything must be done to avoid alienating the harmless and to show that we have parted company once and for all with the old police regime.

Stolypin to Bernard Pares, July 1906[1]

Properly organized police, dedicated to their duty, disciplined, and enjoying the confidence of the population, constitute one of the most important conditions for the firm guarantee of order and public safety in the state. Unfortunately, in a series of state requirements, the current arrangement of the police in Russia is far from corresponding to such serious significance.

The Council of Ministers, January 1912[2]

The Extraordinary Measures of 1881 and the City Statute of 1892, among other laws, gave extensive powers to Moscow's tsarist administration. Indeed, its sphere of competence was so broad that it allowed regulation of virtually all areas of city life. Yet upon the adoption of the first City Statute in 1870, the state had ostensibly ceased to run towns directly. In theory, tsarist officials operated on the premise that Moscow's affairs should be left to the elected city government, except when it acted against the "general well-being and needs of the state."

In practice, as with its approach to the Fundamental Laws and the State Duma after 1905, the regime could not keep its hands off its own creation, in this case the city government. The vague definition of the *gradonachal'nik*'s competence gave him the power to enforce state policy, make policy on his own, and block efforts of the municipality. The laws encouraged the administration to interfere in Moscow's affairs, which it often did on major and minor issues, increasingly so after 1911. The tsarist penchant for regulating all aspects of local life was growing stronger on the eve of the First World War.

Police functions, as traditionally defined in Russia, comprised the largest portion of the administration's activities, and policemen made up the largest portion of its employees. The story of the tsarist authorities in Moscow between 1906 and 1914 is therefore a case study of how local Russian police operated and of their relations with citizens, as well as a study of administrative history. In its structure and functions Moscow's force was similar to those of other large Russian cities, since the empire's police were organized on a national basis under the Ministry of Internal Affairs.

Throughout the imperial period, the regular Russian police (*ispolnitel'naia* or *naruzhnaia politsiia*) were supposed both to control and aid urban populations. To do so they exercised "police powers" in the original sense of the term as used in Europe. Besides maintaining law and order, they were to watch over morals, look after health and sanitation, and see that religion, most particularly Russian Orthodoxy, was respected. Tsarist police also traditionally supervised trade, transportation, and building construction.[3] In an official publication issued in 1896, the Ministry of Internal Affairs announced that to it was "allotted the very extensive task of caring for the universal welfare of the people, the peace, quiet, and good order of the whole Empire."[4] The police were the agency immediately concerned with carrying out this vast assignment.

Their role meant that the police were the government officials most often and most directly in contact with the people. For example, municipal police sergeants (*okolotochnye nadzirateli*, literally neighborhood supervisors) were expected to know all property owners, businesspeople, and tenants in their areas. The city police thus constituted the "most important link tying the [urban] citizens to the government."[5]

Besides these broad responsibilities, the Russian regular police had political functions. While the special political police, the *Okhrana*, were charged with infiltrating, reporting on, and stopping the revolutionary movement, the regular police carried out political repression on a day-to-day basis. The latter supervised publications, public meetings and organizations, and workers in their factories and gatherings.

In the period 1906–1914, the Moscow police occasionally attempted to improve conditions for the lower classes as well as to regulate their daily lives. As one would expect, the police concentrated on regulation, and undoubtedly their primary interest in ameliorative efforts was to reduce social tension; nevertheless, they were not indifferent to conditions in the city. Yet when they attempted to remedy local problems, they acted inconsistently and within the bounds of traditional tsarist paternalism. They were not equipped or inclined to be a modern force for progress.

The upheaval of 1905 led to relatively little change in police functions or practice in Moscow or elsewhere. When the liberal movement and the workers began to evolve in new directions, the administrative authorities responded with outmoded ideas. Because of the growing gap between tsarist notions and the demands of Moscow's people at various levels, police activity in the city contributed substantially to the growing friction between local and central authorities and to increasing resentment of national policy, especially after 1911–1912. In this sphere of city life, too, the tsarist regime demonstrated its inability or unwillingness to adopt measures that might have reduced social and political tensions.

Organization and Functions of the Moscow Police

On January 1, 1905 the central government designated Moscow a *gradonachal'stvo*, headed by a *gradonachal'nik* appointed directly by the tsar. Holders of the post were invariably army generals, now charged with the sensitive task of overseeing a rebellious and rapidly growing population. Moscow's new status as a *gradonachal'stvo* meant that state control of the city became more thorough, as the *gradonachal'nik* had only an area slightly larger than the municipal limits to oversee. In general, *gradonachal'niki* in all Russian cities placed under their control—Moscow, St. Petersburg, Odessa, Sevastopol, Kerch, Nikolaev, Rostov-na-Donu, Baku, and Yalta—had the same powers in their jurisdictions that governors had in their provinces.[6] Moscow's *gradonachal'nik* reported to the provincial governor-general, as did the governor of Moscow province. But the governor-general rarely intervened in the city's affairs, and the post was left vacant from 1908 to 1914.

In 1904 there were 2,335 policemen in Moscow. Evidently responding to the force's inability to handle the events of December 1905, the government boosted their number at the end of that month to 4,843. An additional mounted police guard of 150 was formed in April 1906.[7] These increases may well have been motivated in part by a desire to satisfy Moscow's propertied classes; in December 1905 a group of "Moscow factory owners" demanded increases in the number of police as well as higher pay and better working conditions for them.[8]

Moscow had more police per capita than other large European cities, including St. Petersburg, where there were 45 percent more people but only 18 percent more police. Table 4-1 compares police strength across Europe.[9] Before 1905, when Moscow's force was more than doubled, its ratio of people to police had been higher than those of several other European cities. It seems that order in Russia's ancient capital assumed even greater importance for the government after the scare it received in 1905. A new law of January 31, 1906 specified that there should be one policeman per four hundred residents in Russian towns and one per two thousand people in the countryside.[10] The government evidently believed that Moscow needed still more police attention than these ratios could provide.

The three thousand or so *gorodovye* (lower ranks) of the Moscow force took up posts on the streets, where they were supposed to stand within hearing distance of each other. In addition about thirteen were permanently stationed in factories. Nothing similar to American police beats existed in imperial Russia; these men generally waited for trouble to come to them. This idea of police organization has certain implications for their attitude toward crime and for the public's attitude toward them. First, they relied more on the public to report crime than did the

TABLE 4-1. Police in Selected European Cities before World War I, 1913–1914

City	Population	Number of Police	Residents per Policeman
Moscow	1,345,749 (1907)	4,843	278
Berlin	2,071,257	6,374	325
Paris	2,888,110	8,597	336
St. Petersberg	1,962,400	5,726	343
Vienna	2,031,498	4,596	442

forces of other countries, which meant that public sentiment toward law enforcement could affect the number and type of crimes reported in Russia more strongly than elsewhere. While any regular (nonpolitical) police organization relies on public support for effective operation, a stationary force is certainly more dependent on public approval than a mobile one. Soviet civil police (*militsiia*) have maintained Russia's prerevolutionary emphasis on social networks and communal responsibility. These concepts are firmly rooted in Russian history: in the medieval period and later *krugovaia poruka* (legal, collective responsibility) applied to certain *sosloviia* in regard to payment of taxes and commission of serious crimes; the peasants were obligated in this manner until 1903.

The early twentieth-century police were not so limited by their lack of circulation as one might at first suppose. Their effective range and penetration of the population's affairs were greatly extended through their official auxiliaries, the *dvorniki* (yard men or porters) employed in every apartment house and the night guards hired privately. Both groups were required to report crimes and even movements of persons to the police, to obey all police orders, and to arrest lawbreakers if possible. The number of *dvorniki* in the city was calculated at 17,214 in 1902, and in 1906 the newspaper *Russkoe Slovo* estimated the number of night guards at 2,000.[11] Through this network of auxiliaries, the police had informers and aides in almost all dwellings and important commercial sites.

Beyond these regular forces, the Moscow *Okhrana* detachment, whose commander reported to the *gradonachal'nik*, augmented the city police. The last prewar head of the *Okhrana* in Moscow recalled that in 1912 he employed about one hundred secret agents in the city.[12] However, as many as seven hundred agents may have been at work there.[13]

In the early stages of civil strife, the police chief could also call on the gendarme division stationed in the city; in such cases he assumed command of this group. If matters worsened he could call in regular troops, which remained under their normal leadership.

This complicated force, the Moscow police, with its great power and responsibilities in the city, was the latest stage in the long development of Russian institutions that supervised, investigated, and regulated the urban population. In this process the legal changes of 1881, 1892, and 1905 marked efforts toward progressively tighter control of municipal inhabitants and public life. Moscow's enforcers (and makers) of the law in the period 1906–1914 generally followed long-standing traditions of Russian police practice but had wider powers and greater latitude to interpret the law than their predecessors. The city's police usually, though not always, obeyed the laws. But it cannot be said that the German ideal of a state based firmly on precise laws, a *Rechtsstaat*, existed in Moscow. The statutes themselves were so broad that great arbitrariness was possible within their limits. Both the laws and their application continually worried liberals.

The Moscow *gradonachal'stvo* also had a wide range of non-law enforcement employees and departments, reflecting the breadth of its responsibilities. For instance, it had veterinary and technical departments, which overlapped with and supervised municipal agencies with the same functions. In each precinct headquarters there was a clinic open to the public, staffed in theory by doctors, *fel'dshery* (paramedics), and midwives. It was the police who operated the first aid and ambulance service in the city, called then and to this day the *skoraia meditsinskaia pomoshch'* (literally rapid medical assistance). In 1899 the current *oberpolitseimeister*, as the police chief was then called, D. F. Trepov, founded a receiving clinic for the mentally ill. (By 1910 the city supplied most of its funding, however.[14]) Trepov, an important arch-conservative close to the tsar after 1905, was acting in the traditional Russian spirit of solicitude for the needy. Traditionalism could sometimes foster modernization, as in this case, when the local government took over the operation of the facility on a permanent basis.

Another branch of the *gradonachal'stvo* was the Address Office, which carried out the long-established function of the Russian police of monitoring the population's movements and domiciles. Every citizen of the empire had to keep his or her residence registered with the police at all times.

The *gradonachal'nik* also headed the Moscow Office on Press Affairs, which had the power to "arrest" (seize) publications in the city and to fine editors and writers. Its decisions, however, were subject to legal review. This office ordered the seizure or prohibition of more than 150 editions of periodicals in the city from 1907–1912. In 1907 alone 14 newspapers were closed for various lengths of time.[15] The police also frequently imposed fines on periodicals, typically on the order of five hundred rubles or three months in jail for an editor.[16] This sum was not insignificant; it was more, for example, than a year's salary for most of Moscow's public school teachers.

The national government occasionally sent out lists of undesirable published materials to local administrations "for [the chief administrator's] information and corresponding directives on [his] part."[17] However, the *gradonachal'nik* or the Moscow press office could also act independently to seize publications they deemed harmful to state interests.

The city archives contain some records of cases in which the courts reversed decisions of this office. In several of these no explanation was given. In others the courts showed what seems to have been a readiness to thwart the tsarist administration on technical grounds. For example, in April 1911 the press office asked the district court to confirm its seizure of an issue of the Moscow newspaper *Gazeta-kopeika*. The issue had featured an article containing the line, "The present-day militant high officials of the Orthodox faith follow Christ only externally and with their tongues." The judge who took the case ruled that the phrase did not insult the clergy as a class, as the press office had charged, but referred only to the church administration. Therefore the office's suit was improper.[18]

In a similar instance, the press office seized *Utro Rossii* for November 17, 1912. The offending article concerned a possible speech that M. V. Rodzianko, president of the Fourth State Duma, could appropriately give to that body when it opened later that month. "Go home, fools," the article had Rodzianko say, implying that the parliament was a sham. The fictitious speech went on to describe the power of the Rightists in the Duma, saying that it had caused the chamber to become precisely what the Rightists wanted, a mere advisory body.

On December 21 the Moscow judicial chamber ruled that the issue should not be seized. It found that the supposed speech "contained no insolent thought whatsoever in regard to the Supreme Power," contrary to what the press office had claimed; nor had the office defined the words "caddish notes," which its protocol charged had characterized the article.[19]

In other cases the courts simply stated, without any elaboration, that they disagreed with the office's decisions. There is not sufficient evidence to determine a pattern of greater liberalism in the courts than in the administration,[20] or of antagonism on the part of the former toward the latter. There is only the suggestion in certain instances, such as the *Gazeta-kopeika* case mentioned above, that such attitudes may occasionally have motivated the judges. A similar difference between the court system and administration did appear elsewhere in Russia in this period,[21] and it was partly for this reason that the government transferred so many cases to military courts or decided them administratively, as the Extraordinary Measures and other laws made possible. One may speculate that the views of Russian "society," so often expressed by liberal lawyers, had some influence in the Moscow courts.

The *gradonachal'nik* could bypass the courts or even the Office on Press Affairs if he wished. It is this sort of capability that made him much more than a mere agent of state policy. For the most part, he chose when, how, and what type of action to take in regard to publications. At times this approach included a personal, persuasive touch. For example, in April 1907 the current *gradonachal'nik*, Major-General A. A. Reinbot, called the editors of *Russkie Vedomosti* and *Novosti Utra i Vechera* into his office. To the first man he complained about a recent article's statement that in an unnamed factory the management had docked workers' pay for time they spent talking to state factory inspectors. According to the newspaper, local police had sided with management. The *gradonachal'nik* explained to the editor that he could not take action against the paper because the factory was not named, but that he did not wish to see more such articles, as they could worsen relations between workers and management. He added that he would present newspaper reporters with a wide range of material on such questions so that they could check their stories.

Reinbot told the second editor that recently his paper had adopted an undesirable tone and had been inciting certain segments of the population against others. He had warned the editor once before about the same thing. When the man replied that politics would no longer be featured in his paper, Reinbot said that that was not his object. The paper could be full of political articles, but not of a strident tone that could inflame workers and youth. The *gradonachal'nik* noted that the only reason he did not ask the governor-general to close the paper was that its employees might sue him for loss of pay; of course, this was a specious reason, for the Extraordinary Measures ensured his right to close any paper he did not like. Reinbot then promised that if *Novosti Utra i Vechera* continued to publish articles written in the same offensive manner he would take action not against it but against the editor personally.[22]

The incident illustrates the flexibility of the law and of the *gradonachal'nik*'s position in Moscow. Reinbot often took a conciliatory and personal approach to publications and workers' problems, perhaps partly because his personality inclined him to do so, but probably also because he hoped to reduce the kind of tension that had led to the revolution of 1905. In adopting this stance he made his own policy in the city.

From the point of view of the city's inhabitants the flexibility of the tsarist administrators was often quite aggravating, for it made policy, acceptable behavior, and punishments unpredictable. The vagueness of the laws, which high officials had long felt was all to their advantage, contained a great potential for weakening the regime: citizens could not be sure of policy from one *gradonachal'nik* to the next or even one day to the next, and they objected to shifting rules. Russian liberals had to rely on law to secure their positions and goals, since personal connections with the authorities were weak. As we shall see, the personal and paternalistic approach to censorship no longer sufficed in Moscow, and the issue produced strong resentment by 1914.

It has been argued that after the abolition of prior censorship in October 1905 the Russian press had almost complete freedom of expression. Recent studies maintain that government attempts to seize issues once they had appeared were ineffectual, and fines levied on periodicals did not amount to a serious financial burden, even for the Bolshevik press. Russian newspapers in this period printed numerous statements highly critical of the state;[23] a large number of such expressions by Moscow's press are noted in the present study.

Very wide opportunities to express opinion certainly existed in Russia after 1905. However, the state retained means to coerce editors and publishers through the Extraordinary Measures and other laws, as just illustrated in Moscow. Such cases surely had the effect of intimidating some editors into silence. Official statistics on newspaper fines, of course, did not record this kind of pressure. Neither was the outright closing of a paper unheard of, though a periodical suppressed in this fashion was often able to reopen under another title.

Nevertheless, there was considerable freedom of expression in Moscow and elsewhere after 1905. Yet perhaps the most salient point about this development is that it was unfavorable for the conservative state. Its agents now engaged in a hit-or-miss kind of repression. Editors and writers were only occasionally fined or jailed; most of the time they got their points across. Thus the state became no more than a nuisance factor for the press.[24] This erratic behavior, which appeared in other areas of Russian life as well, was the worst thing the state could have done for itself. It raised expectations about what was permitted, then tried to crush them. It made the state appear querulous and ineffective, as though it was simply unable to do what it really wanted—to end the new freedoms completely. This approach again demonstrated the regime's lack of coherent policy for the more liberal life of the post-1905 period. It could not satisfy conservatives, who wanted more repression, and it deeply angered liberals.

Inconsistency also characterized the *gradonachal'nik*'s role as head of the Special Office on City Affairs, which had members from the city government but was dominated by tsarist administrators. There is no record of the Special Office voting against its chief in this period, which it had the legal right to do. But as much as several months occasionally elapsed between its meetings, which meant that in such periods it did not even formally review the legality of the *gradonachal'nik*'s vetoes. At other times, the Special Office suddenly became active after a period of quiescence, as in August 1913, when it met and vetoed six resolutions of the city duma, some of which had been passed six months before.[25] The municipal government could therefore never be certain that its measures would remain legal, even if they had been in effect for some time, or even if they repeated previous decisions that had not been invalidated. For example, the Special Office rejected rules on the construction of nightlodgings that had been in force for years when they reappeared in 1913 in a new duma resolution.[26]

Mundane questions also received the Special Office's attentions. In April

1914, for example, it vetoed a city duma resolution not to return money to a man who had complained of excessive taxation.[27] Therefore the office served at least occasionally as a court of appeal for citizens. This was a natural result of the fact that two sets of officials existed in the city; sometimes people protested against the administration to the municipality. Since most Muscovites could not vote in municipal elections, their only means of protest or of influencing policy was to appeal personally to the duma or administrative officials. This recourse, an integral part of traditional tsarist paternalism, was unpredictable and slow at best. Such appeals also meant that the city government did not have ultimate control over even trivial, day-to-day matters, and the Special Office's vetoes served as a reminder that the state did not consider municipal officials competent to manage even minor issues.

The Special Office played a central role in the imperial government's "new course" toward Moscow, as several city government figures termed the pattern of events, evident in the problems with mayoral elections discussed earlier. Starting some time after Stolypin's death in 1911, the Special Office began to veto more city duma resolutions than previously, and the tsarist administration began to reject more people chosen by the duma for posts in municipal government and the school system. After the mayoral election of early 1913, relations between the two sides deteriorated further. Nikolai Astrov later wrote that in that year the "new course" became a "systematic campaign against the Moscow city government." The administration "created a whole series of hindrances and difficulties for the conduct of city affairs" and vetoed duma resolutions on "large and small questions, touching public and private interests." Among these were decisions on starting pension funds, purchasing land, repairing run-down city buildings, and developing city enterprises.[28] In 1913 the *gradonachal'nik* protested and sent to the Special Office forty-five of the council's resolutions.[29] M. V. Chelnokov felt that Gradonachal'nik Adrianov had "carried out persecution of the city" in the period just before the war.[30]

The Moscow police also played an important role, mostly a political one, in the city's educational life. (Chapter 7 shows this in more detail.) As representatives of the conservative state, the police were especially careful to make sure that dangerous political tendencies did not develop in educational institutions. In 1907, for example, the *gradonachal'nik* informed the administration of Moscow Imperial University that the school would be closed immediately for even a single antigovernment lecture.[31]

During this period the Moscow duma often adopted circuitous tactics in its attempts to nullify the administration's vetoes. It resisted state interference as best it could, but under the circumstances its maneuvers and protests could not seriously challenge the regime's power in the city. The municipality had to operate with the knowledge that the *gradonachal'nik* could remove matters from its agenda, thus silencing it altogether on any question, or could even close the duma completely. The administration could bypass the duma and simply issue its own regulations and, as shown earlier, could introduce items into the city budget if the municipality refused to pay a state demand. Effective power lay with the tsarist authorities.

Nevertheless, the duma sometimes tried to resist, usually by stalling or not carrying out the administration's orders. In 1913 the *uprava* fired a city doctor;

he appealed to the Special Office on City Affairs, which ruled in his favor. The duma voted to stand by the *uprava* and not rehire the doctor. At the same time, the city protested the Special Office's decision to the Senate, informing the *gradonachal'nik* of its action. If the *gradonachal'nik* did not object further, the duma resolved, it would recall its complaint.[32] Despite the legal requirement to implement the Special Office's decision, the city hoped it could simply proceed as it wished. In this case the ploy worked. It seems that on minor issues the system of administrative control was not as thorough as it looked on paper.

The duma resisted the Special Office on other occasions as well. Its elected delegate to the office resigned in March 1911, after he reported to the duma that the *gradonachal'nik* had insulted him in a conversation. The chamber then voted not to elect another delegate until it received an explanation from the Special Office. The office vetoed this resolution. In September the whole cycle was repeated, and the duma again decided not to elect a delegate.[33] The whole affair illustrates the city government's helplessness and lack of alternatives when confronted by such administrative actions; withholding its delegate certainly did not help the duma.

In the years just before the war the role of the tsarist administration in Moscow continued to expand still further under other provisions of the Russian legal codes. As noted earlier, the police chief could make regulations with the force of law on well-being (*blagochinie*), order, and security. Though such regulations were not supposed to contradict existing statutes, they sometimes did. In early 1913 the *gradonachal'nik* announced that for public drunkenness, disturbing the peace or the public, breaking windows, throwing stones, or entering any private place without permission, he would issue fines of up to five hundred rubles or jail terms of up to three months.[34] These punishments preempted the regular criminal code. Other regulations issued by Moscow's chiefs of police ranged from prohibiting open air meetings and carrying weapons to specifying details of clothing permissible for hack drivers.

The penchant of *gradonachal'niki* and governors for issuing detailed regulations went very far, too far even for Stolypin's taste. In 1910 he sent a circular to these officials informing them that the Extraordinary Measures were intended only to protect state order and public security. Regulations issued under them were not to affect ordinary crimes or "frivolous matters" such as scalping tickets, playing billiards, playing harmonicas, or swimming too close to steamships.[35] Yet the vagueness of the statutes had clearly encouraged local tsarist administrators to regulate such minutiae, and in so doing they were merely following the guidelines of tradition and policy at the highest levels of government. The practices criticized by Stolypin harked back to the period before the mid-nineteenth century, when the police alone had responsibility for regulating and managing city life. Detailed supervision of local affairs also reflected long-standing state ideology, which saw local government merely as a minor branch of the state.[36]

The broadness of the statutes meant that Moscow's police were busier than in other large European cities. Large numbers of Muscovites were arrested each year, more per capita than in Paris or Berlin.[37] Roughly two-thirds of all arrests in Moscow between 1907 and 1910 were deemed "administrative," violations of regulations issued by tsarist administrators. A certain number of arrests in this category would undoubtedly have entailed simple fines or civil proceedings outside Russia. The large number of administrative arrests, reaching over forty-five thousand in 1910, more than the total number of arrests in these years among the larger populations of Paris or Berlin, underscores the extent to which the Extraordinary Measures regulated Moscow life.

A new *gradonachal'nik*, Major-General A. A. Adrianov, took office in early 1908. His presence may have raised the number of criminal arrests in the next two years. He was more conscientious and thorough than his predecessor, Reinbot, who lost his post because he seemed to regard Moscow as his own private farm: he extorted money from local groups and residents on a fabulous scale. Adrianov may have tried to compensate for Reinbot's faults by excessive zeal; under him the police newspaper reported many more arrests of hack drivers and other minor infractions of administrative rules.

The great majority of crimes in the city were minor. In 1910, for example, the Moscow *mirovye sud'i* (justices of the peace) sentenced 68,023 people,[38] while the Moscow district court, which handled more serious crimes, sentenced 1,728.[39] Most violations covered in the newspapers were minor, such as purse snatchings, small-scale swindles, disorders in taverns, and street robberies of coats, wallets, or even caps. These were the usual events with which police had to deal.

For a certain period after the upheaval of 1905, however, the police had much more serious trouble on their hands. Throughout 1906 and into 1907 assailants frequently abused, attacked, and sometimes killed policemen. Such attacks tapered off after November 1907 and did not occur again in large numbers. The Moscow press reported the following pattern of attacks on police by people other than those who were being arrested:[40]

1906	42	1911	10
1907	34	1912	1
1908	1	1913	2
1909	3	1914	0
1910	8		

(Undoubtedly some of the attacks on police were crimes committed with no particular political motive, for example a man taking revenge on a policeman for arresting his brother. Wherever the newspapers made such nonpolitical motives clear, attacks have not been counted.)

The assaults of 1906 seem to have been a new phenomenon. A check of several months of the city's papers of 1903, for example, revealed no attacks on police.[41] In May 1907 Reinbot complained to his superior, the Director of the Department of Police, about the "ever-increasing cases of armed robbery and political murder." The *gradonachal'nik* found the cause of this situation in the recent abolition of courts-martial for civilians;[42] that is, more repression was necessary. The police themselves reacted to the assaults with new policies. In August 1906 Reinbot instructed his men to be especially cautious, not to allow anyone to approach them, and at the first sign of attack to answer directly with arms. Police were to stand in pairs, six to eight paces apart. They were ordered to follow all speeding cabs and if possible to get their numbers and question their passengers.[43]

Toward the end of 1907 accounts of assaults on police began to disappear from the newspapers. Between that time and the start of the war, they appeared in significant numbers only in 1910 and 1911 but even then were far fewer than earlier. The small resurgence of attacks in those two years may have been related to the death of Leo Tolstoy, the disorders of November 1910 during his funeral in Moscow, and resulting tensions between the police and the citizenry. Tolstoy had been extremely popular as a writer and a thinker, and his excommunication by the officially-sponsored Orthodox church had been interpreted as an act of despotism. Hence his funeral became the occasion for a large political demonstration.

It is unlikely that the pattern of attacks can be explained by changes in newspaper policy, for the columns and editorial outlooks of the two papers studied were virtually unaltered in this period. Nor does it seem possible that increased police repression prevented many attacks after 1907, as the number of police was not raised in these years and the basic outlines of police activity were unchanged, judging by the *gradonachal'nik*'s orders of the day. When Adrianov became chief in 1908, he tightened supervision of the lower ranks but did not reorganize the police or introduce new methods. The extra caution police were ordered to take in 1906 may have reduced attacks somewhat, but they continued to occur frequently for more than a year after the order was issued.

The number of attacks in the years 1906 and 1907 strongly suggests that the social and political hostilities of 1905 lingered, though subdued, in the city. The ordinary policeman at his post was, as noted earlier, the lowest and most visible tsarist official, the one who most often enforced the authority of the state. When that authority declined, and when the police carried out overt political repression, as in December 1905, it was this most visible symbol that became the object of hostility.

Moscow was not unique in Russia in respect to attacks on state officials after 1905. The journal *Pravo* in August of 1906 ran lists of murders and attempts on the lives of officials so far that year that continued for four and a half pages. For the month of July 1907 alone, *Pravo* listed 54 Russian authorities killed and 47 wounded; 34 police were among these.[44] According to another report, in 1906 "terrorists" killed 1,126 government officials and wounded 1,506 others. In 1907 the toll was 3,000 killed and 3,046 wounded.[45] It is not clear if police were included in these figures.

The available accounts of attacks on Moscow police do not permit precise analysis of their motivation. Many of the attackers were not caught; in general, only the more unlucky or slower-footed ones were, which is not a scientific sample of all attackers. Most of the newspaper reports are very sketchy, and even when a suspect was apprehended they do not usually give a motive.

For similar reasons it is also difficult to analyze the attackers in social terms. Assailants were described in the press as "workers," "hooligans," "young people," or "peasants," though reports only rarely gave precise indications of their backgrounds or occupations. Yet it is highly unlikely that any but lower class people would have appeared in groups to attack police, as happened frequently. Articles sometimes specifically noted that assailants were well dressed, which suggests that they usually were not. The street fighters of 1905 were largely workers and other lower class people, and it is logical that this group would have supplied most of the attackers of 1906 and 1907. Unfortunately, virtually all the evidence available on the social composition of police assailants is indirect; but taken together it suggests that most Muscovites who continued to fight the representatives of state power in 1906 and 1907 were from the city's lower strata. The evidence further suggests that attacks in those years were largely politically motivated; that is, the word terrorism does apply, if it is understood to mean attacks on symbols or representatives of power stemming from a sense of injustice or oppression.

Assaults on police in those two years took various forms. On January 14, 1906 a *gorodovoi* followed a "suspicious woman" into a doorway, where several men described in the story as workers jumped him, beat him, and took his revolver.[46] During 1906 similar incidents involved twelve policemen, sometimes more than one at once. Robbery of policemen's weapons may or may not have been politically inspired, but in any case the number of such incidents indicates a serious diminution of police authority. And radical groups still coveted police weapons, for the idea of armed struggle with the government was far from dead.

Another type of attack on police, those committed by crowds, also suggests that widespread hostility toward the authorities continued in Moscow in 1906 and 1907. On June 1, 1906 a small crowd attacked a police convoy escorting a prisoner to a city jail; he escaped during the struggle.[47] The newspaper account does not indicate why the man was arrested, and the implication is that the crowd

"Muzhiks [peasants] absorbed in the Story-teller's narrative." Typical lower class housing. Note the policeman in the background.

did not know. Such incidents therefore suggest a general hostility toward the police and sympathy for anyone arrested. On June 15 and June 17 more attacks on police convoys occurred; in the first incident prisoners were being taken into custody for drunkenness, and the second involved a soldier running around with his saber unsheathed. Both reports stated that the attacking crowds formed away from the scene of arrest, which implies that their reaction sprang from general hostility toward the police rather than from personal knowledge or sympathy for the arrested parties. One article identifies the attackers as workers.[48]

Several incidents imply political motivation even more strongly. On August 8, 1906 three policemen on patrol met a crowd of one hundred young people singing the *Marseillaise*. The police asked them to stop and disperse, and they refused. Shouts of "beat the police" rang out, and the crowd began throwing stones. One policeman fired into the air, whereupon a man leaped on him and tried to take his rifle. Another *gorodovoi* shot and killed the assailant.[49] On July 4 a police captain was seriously wounded when he appeared at a workers' meeting.[50] To these incidents may be added an attack on the *gradonachal'nik*, who was the target of a bomb on October 30, 1906, and a similar attempt on the life of the governor-general in November 1907. In these incidents the police surely figured as symbols of tsarist authority.

Not all Muscovites were opposed to the police. The papers reported several cases in which citizens helped law officers pursue suspects. For instance, on July 29, 1906 a crowd joined police in a chase of five men who had tried to rob the apartment of an archpriest. A wild shootout on the street ended the pursuit; two policemen were killed and two more were badly wounded. Also killed was a *dvornik*, and a night guard was seriously wounded. The presence of these two illustrates their role as police auxiliaries.[51]

In the years just before the First World War there were some confrontations between workers or students and police, such as those at Tolstoy's funeral. But these incidents generally differed from earlier attacks. Most of the clashes after 1907 occurred after police took the initiative in attempting to break up demonstrations or otherwise to force the public to obey them. Thus violence between police and citizens after 1907 was largely a matter of direct popular reaction to police repression, unlike the generally unprovoked attacks of 1906 and 1907. The initiation of violence had shifted from the people to the police; Muscovites now used violence as a defensive, not an offensive tactic. The difference suggests that popular hostility to the police had subsided and that their authority had been reestablished to some degree. There are not enough provoked or unprovoked attacks in the later years to suggest a pattern of deep social or political disorder, even after tsarist troops massacred strikers at the Lena Goldfields in April 1912. One might have expected such attacks after that event, which evoked a wave of strikes and demonstrations across the country.[52] It may be that workers and other lower class people put their energies and anger into more organized activity after 1912 and that the new "revolutionary upswing" so often described for that period caused them to think more in terms of collective action. By the same reasoning, in 1906 and 1907 workers had recently suffered a major defeat, but their sense of anger and militancy remained high. This feeling probably contributed to assaults on police. The first head of the Moscow metalworkers' union later recalled this period.

The mood among metallists in March and April 1906 was such that it could not be confined in what seemed like a narrow organization, a trade union. The "rebellious spirit" of the metallists after the months of the revolutionary struggle they had just lived through and the December Uprising could not come to terms with the tedious and organic work that was required for the unity of the workers in a strongly organized labor union.[53]

One participant in the 1905 uprising in Moscow reported that armed detachments of workers drilled secretly in the city throughout 1906.[54] In short, the desire for some kind of immediate action or revenge may have been quite high, resulting in terrorism.

The decline of assaults on police in Moscow toward the end of 1907 was undoubtedly linked to the drop in unrest in Russia as a whole. The anger and frustration of 1905 had turned to demoralization by 1907,[55] and the combination of militancy and anger that had fed earlier attacks on police was gone. However, it is also likely that local efforts to deal with local conditions had something to do with the fact that police were not being shot or run over quite so often. One part of these efforts was increased discipline within police ranks under Adrianov. *Russkie Vedomosti* carried the following news item in April 1908:

> In view of repeated cases of insults to private citizens by police on duty, the Moscow *gradonachal'nik* in his order of the day to the district *pristavy* (captains) directed them to explain to police that for this they would be prosecuted and dismissed from their jobs.[56]

The police chief proceeded to carry out his threat. In October 1908 he demoted two policemen from active duty to the reserves. One had refused to pay a cabbie for a ride, had followed him into an apartment, and had started a fight there with the inhabitants. The second had refused a tavern keeper's request to enter his establishment and stop a quarrel between drunks, and had gotten into a squabble with the keeper. "Finding in these two cases evidence of complete misunderstanding of their duties by the police, the *gradonachal'nik* directed the *pristavy* to instruct police as often as possible in their obligations."[57]

In the same month the police chief fired two of his men for "creating disturbances and insulting women by their actions when off duty." Another policeman was jailed for seven days for "coarse treatment of a woman" and warned that he would be fired for any further misconduct.[58] Altogether fifteen policemen, including one sergeant, were disciplined in October 1908. Four had insulted women and at least four were drunk while on duty.[59] Drunkenness among police and their tendency to insult citizens seem to have been perennial problems in Moscow, for the *gradonachal'nik*'s orders of the day are full of instances of disciplinary action taken against *gorodovye* and officers for these habits.[60] By 1910 the police chief's patience had worn so thin that he was turning wayward policemen over to the civil courts for trial.

The publicity surrounding such cases must have reached a fair portion of the city's population, perhaps fostering some sense that police leaders were trying to act responsibly. It is also likely that disciplinary measures taken against police served to make them more careful in their approach to the public and thus had a positive effect on their public image, which police commanders realized was important to their work. In 1905 the current *gradonachal'nik* issued the following statement:

> True—our police service is not easy, but when there comes a time at which each inhabitant of the capital will see in the policeman a friend and not an enemy, for which much depends on the police themselves, then our task will be easier and more fruitful.[61]

After 1908 the frequency of disciplinary action within police ranks indicates that a good public image had assumed immediate importance for their commander. But while the police could work to improve personal behavior and methods, state policy and ideology put their practices into a mold that could not change. Paternalism could be improved but not abandoned.

In the same year the police had another compelling reason to reform themselves. Late in 1907 a scandal broke around the depredations of high police officials and of the *gradonachal'nik* himself, General Reinbot. An investigation conducted by Senator N. P. Garin in 1908 revealed that Reinbot had extorted large "contributions" from various private clubs and individuals in the city, had vastly exceeded his authority and circumvented that of the governor-general, had often worked only four hours a day, and had taken long hunting trips and vacations with his mistress. In his report Garin wrote of the "victorious return to Moscow of police bribes" under the "influence of his [Reinbot's] personal example."

The report also detailed cases in which the police chief had abused his right to exile people. For instance, he had banished a peasant from the city because he had eloped with a girl, and her parents had requested his removal. Reinbot had then accommodatingly charged the man with "political unreliability." On other occasions the chief had exiled innocent people for various offenses, through simple carelessness. Finally, he exiled "many people without giving any reason."[62] It took Senator Garin 154 pages to complete the recital of crimes committed by the *gradonachal'nik* and his staff. The vast powers of the Moscow police provided fertile ground for such abuses, as they did for arbitrariness and summary judgments. The scandal must have made the new police chief, General Adrianov, especially determined to run a clean force.

When Reinbot was finally tried in 1911 by a special court appointed by the Senate, he received a relatively light sentence. Besides the loss of all special, personal, and military rights, and a fine of 27,000 rubles, he was sentenced to one year in prison. But the tsar interceded, and Reinbot never served time. The reaction of *Russkie Vedomosti* to all this was the comment that the arbitrariness and illegality of Reinbot's activities were duplicated by many other government officials. Pointing to the arbitrariness of the whole system, the paper indicated that some officials were tried for such crimes, while others were not. "Here is the theory of [our] state system," wrote one editor.[63]

Reinbot continued to lead a charmed life and returned to serve the tsar another day. In 1914 he rejoined the army under the proudly Russian name Rezvoi.[64] Ironically, his more honest successor in Moscow, Adrianov, was also dismissed from his post. This was not for malfeasance; Adrianov had taken no action to halt anti-German pogroms in the city in May 1916.[65]

A more positive aspect of the relations between police and citizens in Moscow before the war can be seen in the administration's efforts to ameliorate certain municipal problems. For instance, the *gradonachal'nik* wrote to the mayor in May 1908 to ask what measures the city was taking in regard to homeless children. He emphasized his belief that care of such children was a direct obligation of the city government. Mayor Guchkov replied that the municipality was taking "such measures as were allowed by the budget." He indicated that the *uprava* was already working out a plan for homeless children.[66] (As shown later, it was not until 1914 that anything more was done for them.)

In October of the same year Adrianov queried the city about the possibility of establishing controlled prices for meat. He remarked, "The poorest part of the city's population either completely lacks the opportunity to use meat in its diet or is able to afford it only as a special luxury, every other day or once every few days." He concluded by saying that he

> did not find it possible, because of his responsibilities under the law, to permit any longer such an unconscionable exploitation by meat dealers of the population of the capital, which consists in large measure of the poor, working class, and because of the possibility of the appearance in Moscow of cholera, when reduction in the cost of food is essential.[67]

Nevertheless, Adrianov eventually accepted the city's conclusion that the high cost of meat was due to external factors and that price controls would only serve to reduce its supply in Moscow.

Gradonachal'niki at least received some publicity for concerns of this type, as they did for fines imposed on property owners for violations of administrative or city regulations on sanitation. Police levied fines regularly for poor sanitation; twenty owners were punished in April 1909, for example, with fines of up to one hundred rubles.[68] Lists of similar fines often appeared in the police newspaper.[69] Also on the positive side for the police, a substantial number of Muscovites obtained free medical care each year at the police clinics. In 1908, for instance, 56,781 people visited the clinics, while police medical personnel made 6,095 calls to private dwellings.[70] Of course, it was the city that paid for these medical services as part of the "obligatory expenditures" for the support of the *gradonachal'stvo*. In any event, the public readily took advantage of a free service organized by police and operated from their stations. Thus Muscovites had reason to approve some aspects of police work in their city.

Police and "Society"

The city's *obshchestvo* regularly encountered a variety of police practices that engendered their resentment. Vetoes of duma resolutions and seizures or fines of popular liberal newspapers such as *Russkoe Slovo* and *Russkie Vedomosti* occurred frequently. Every public lecture had to have prior authorization from the administration and could proceed only in the presence of a police officer. In 1906 Reinbot forbade a planned talk on "Tuberculosis and Its Social Causes"; in 1912 a policeman halted a lecture by Paul Miliukov on "Nationality" when the noted historian remarked that nationalism had become a "banner of the liberal movement [*obshchestvennoe dvizhenie*, literally public movement]," to cite two of many such incidents.[71]

Police work also changed with the times: in August of 1913 an official circular demanded

> the strictest attention to films dealing with the lives of workers, and under no conditions whatsoever can there be allowed the exhibition of films depicting difficult forms of labor, agitational activity, or those containing scenes that may arouse workers against their employers, films of strikes, of the lives of indentured peasants, etc.[72]

Leading members of Russia's elite, Muscovites among them, objected vehemently in the State Duma to aspects of police activity in Moscow. In 1908 Governor-General Gershel'man ordered that anyone holding publications barred from circulation by the authorities had to turn them in to the police or face stiff fines or imprisonment. The difficulty with this measure even for a loyal citizen was in knowing which publications were illegal, for they were so declared by the police after their appearance and often after some sales or distribution. A. I. Guchkov angrily exclaimed to the Duma, "This violation [of legality] carried out by the Moscow governor-general establishes a situation in Moscow in which the inhabitants are given over to the complete arbitrariness of the local administration."[73] His words evoked applause in the center and left.

V. A. Maklakov, a prominent Kadet lawyer from Moscow, took the same stance. The governor-general, he complained, "can close a newspaper, can and does arrest, and if he arrests few, that is probably because the jails are overcrowded." His order on publications makes it "evident that there is no limit to the fantasy and arbitrariness of the governor-general."[74] Maklakov also received applause from the left and center benches.

There were some who took the opposite position. The odious N. E. Markov number two (there were two N. E. Markovs in the Duma), a reactionary anti-Semite who enjoyed saying outrageous things in the chamber, approved Gershel'man's order. It would "bring nothing but good."[75] For many conservatives, close state supervision of publications was a virtue in and of itself, if it helped to maintain order. This was more important than any inconvenience or injustice arbitrariness might cause.

The Moscow city duma did not agree. With only two dissenting votes, it resolved to send a petition to the governor-general asking him to rescind his order.[76] Urban liberals would not concede that state needs dictated such far-reaching measures; they put more emphasis on civil liberties than on controlling society.

Members of Moscow's elite, including city duma members, had reason to wish for limitations on the powers of the police. In 1907 Reinbot had exiled the industrial magnate P. P. Riabushinskii temporarily from Moscow. In the same year he also tried to exile the lawyer N. K. Murav'ev, but the governor-general overturned this order.[77] Reinbot's extortions took their greatest toll from the upper classes, too. In short, Moscow's elite had many reasons to resent the administration. On the other hand, the police were the only force that protected the *obshchestvo*'s property on a day-to-day basis; hence the industrialists' call for more police in 1905. This protection was a valued service, but "society" was quite capable of organizing and running a regular police force without the aid of the central government.

There was another dark side to police activity in the city after 1905, one particularly offensive to liberals. In April 1909, Governor-General Gershel'man received a delegation from the Union of the Russian People. This was an organization of the Black Hundreds, the reactionary Russian groups infamous for their crudeness and violence against minorities, especially Jews. The group gave Gershel'man a certificate making him an honorary member,[78] as it had done for Nicholas II. E. K. Klimovich, head of the Moscow *Okhrana* from early 1906 to March 1907, told an investigatory commission of the Provisional Government that Gershel'man and Reinbot had taken the Black Hundreds under "special protection." However, according to Klimovich, Reinbot "soon noticeably cooled toward them." The former *Okhrana* head nevertheless continued to aid them on his own: he stated that while permits to bear arms were generally given out to Black Hundreds "according to the usual procedures," he personally made this process easier if he believed that the member in question was trustworthy.[79] Thus the police extended aid to an unofficial, violent, and disruptive segment of the populace. Tsarist officials themselves undermined law and order in favor of their political concerns.

Before the war, members of Moscow's elite voiced their irritation at various aspects of police activity. In 1913, a year in which the *gradonachal'nik* vetoed many city duma resolutions, an angry writer complained in *Russkie Vedomosti* about "lively interference" in the affairs of city government by the administration. He went on to say, "That which was legal and appropriate yesterday suddenly became illegal, harmful, and impermissible today." The article concluded, "The life of a great city cannot be reconciled with this unnecessary struggle."[80]

After the *gradonachal'nik* held up the city budget at the beginning of 1914, the Progressive Group of the duma met and declared, "Under such conditions and inclinations of the administrative authorities any kind of correct activity of the city government is made completely impossible."[81] Since the Progressive Group comprised a majority of the duma at that time, as demonstrated by their ability to elect their choices as mayoral candidates, the statement reveals deep dissatisfaction in the city council. Several months earlier, the progressives had reported that the vetoes of the Special Office "elicited protests from all sides" of the chamber.[82] This picture is certainly somewhat exaggerated; as noted before, moderate-rights rose in the duma in 1913 to defend the government's right to reject mayoral candidates.

One can only speculate about the eventual outcome of the growing tension of 1913 and early 1914 between the city government and the tsarist authorities, had the war not intervened. In any case, it is important to note that leading elements in Moscow felt increasing resentment toward the state just before the war. Support for the regime was steadily eroding among the urban-based, educated, middle and upper classes. The broad powers of the police and their frequent interference in daily life, much more evident in the cities than in the countryside, and much more problematic in its results, was an important cause of growing dissatisfaction. The Moscow newspaper *Utro Rossii*, financed by the industrialists P. P. Riabushinskii, A. I. Konovalov, and S. I. Chetverikov, of whom the first and second served in the city duma, complained bitterly about the police in May 1910. The Russian bourgeoisie "is not coming to terms [*miritsia*] with the all-penetrating police tutelage and aspires to the emancipation of the people,"[83] said the newspaper.

In early 1912 the Council of Ministers considered the current state of the Russian police. The cabinet cited the following defects: an absence of coordination between police forces, for example the gendarmes and the regular police; a lack of special police for certain tasks; problems in internal police organization; the small number of policemen in absolute terms and per capita; low pay and poor benefits; too heavy a workload; and the lack of a general police code.[84] In other words, the Council wanted more and better police, with better pay and working conditions. The top officials of the conservative state did not suggest that the powers of the police were too broad or that the laws afforded individual citizens little protection from arbitrary police conduct. Arbitrariness remained a guarantee for the tsarist government of flexibility and quick response in its relations with the public.

G. B. Sliuzberg, a Russian lawyer and emigre after 1917 who did not allow his hatred of the Bolsheviks to alter his judgment of the old regime, had this to say about the prerevolutionary police:

> The entire civil life of the average person took place, as it were, through the supervision (*kontrol'*) of the police authorities. For the average man, the ideal was to live without any kind of contact with the police. But for that, it would have been necessary to withdraw oneself from civil affairs (*oborot*).[85]

Sliuzberg may have exaggerated, but not by much. Neither *obshchestvo* nor *narod* had much reason to love the police by 1914; the "old police regime" that Stolypin wanted to abandon in 1906 had not changed significantly. He was probably sincere in his desire for police reform and greater adherence to a rule of law. But here too the prime minister's moderate progressivism did not fit tsarist tradition and the desires of conservative gentry. Police powers and activities continued in their old vein, and those who wanted to improve "the life of a great city" found this situation less and less tolerable.

During the "years of reaction" after 1907, as the Bolsheviks termed the period, lower class Muscovites had little to hope for from the police except occasional, usually minor benefits of paternalism. With the workers' movement in disarray and their mood often depressed, reacceptance of police control was unavoidable for a time. However, the experience of 1905 had seriously damaged the tsarist administration's prestige and authority, and strong latent tensions remained among Moscow's laboring classes. The next chapter examines the efforts of both state representatives and the city's *obshchestvo* to bring stability to the potentially volatile workers' world.

5

Responding to Labor Issues:
The Approaches of the State and
"Society" in Moscow

The *gorodovoi*'s whistle blows, but it can't be heard above the [revolutionary] song.
T. V. Sapronov about April 1912 in Moscow[1]

A catastrophe of state power. . . . Only the word murder can be applied.
P. P. Riabushinskii's newspaper Utro Rossii
about the Lena massacre[2]

The extensive and valuable literature on Russian labor unions, the revolutionary movement and workers, and capitalists between 1905 and 1914 has not included many local studies.[3] It seems both useful and necessary to explore the multifaceted interaction among the various groups and forces that operated on the local level, conditioning the ideas and policies of all the actors. Russian industrialists, for example, conducted business in a particular economic and cultural context, whose nature reflected state policies on education, freedom of the press, and foreign policy, as well as economic developments. The struggle between the city and the state in Moscow also had an impact on industrialists' concerns in general, including their thinking on labor questions. It therefore seems wrong to explain the relatively high degree of liberalism among the city's capitalists in regard to labor issues by "the straitened situation of Moscow industry, above all textiles, as a result of the limited internal market."[4] Although local industrialists expressed deep concern about that market, a number of other issues were more important in shaping their judgments on labor and politics. Moscow's capitalists also showed more ability to compromise with the labor movement than they have been credited with.[5]

A complex array of issues operated for labor leaders and spokesmen, too. Moscow, already evolving away from the conservative regime in other ways, presents a good milieu in which to examine the conflicts and forces at work in shaping approaches to the workers' movement at various social and political levels after 1905. One aspect of this story deserving of more attention than it has received to date is tsarist paternalism and its role in efforts to diminish labor tension. Nor has workers' affinity, or potential affinity, for liberal programs been explored. Discussions of radicalism among Russian workers remain incomplete without attention to roads not taken and why.

Moscow workers seem especially notable for their willingness to consider liberal solutions to their problems, not only in 1905 but also later. Whether workers are more naturally inclined to radical solutions, including some form of socialism, or to a compromise with capitalism, is certainly beyond the scope of this study and is a subject fit only for speculation in any case. Yet it is worth mentioning that even Lenin worried about Russian workers' susceptibility to the dread disease of "*tred iunionizm*," to use the term that crept into Russian in his pamphlet *What Is To Be Done?* of 1902.[6] In other words, the workers might be willing to make a rotten compromise with the capitalists that would preclude revolution.

Some evidence suggests that Moscow workers were more fundamentally interested in such a compromise than in radicalism throughout the period 1905–1914, and there are indications that this attitude continued into 1917. Had the municipality and the city's industrialists been left to their own devices, worker radicalism might not have developed very far in Moscow. In many cases state policy and practice became the foci of workers' complaints, and this worsened both workers' and leading industrialists' attitudes toward the regime. Policy toward the working class thus had become another source of serious antagonism between the city's liberals and the state by the eve of the war.

Finally, it is important to recognize that the tsarist authorities had a calculated policy toward labor between 1907 and 1914, one they believed was effective in achieving their goals—until it began to fall apart in 1912. This policy, rooted in tsarist tradition, was indicative of the state's general inability to respond effectively to urban developments.

As early as the 1880s, Moscow's liberals had devoted some attention to the plight of working people and had tried to help them organize. In the second half of that decade a waiter and one of the "liberalizing intelligentsia" tried and failed to form a mutual aid society for restaurant workers. However, in 1897 a waiter published a letter in the press describing his atrocious working conditions, and liberals again became interested. Two members of the city duma, Professor V. I. Ger'e and hotel owner S. A. Popov, were especially active in helping to win approval for a mutual aid society charter, which was granted in 1902. Such aid societies were not unions but groups intended to provide mutual support and funds for difficult occasions like funerals and injuries. Ger'e was concerned about reducing class antagonism, for he hoped that the waiters' organization would draw workers and employers together.[7]

The state's most important effort to reduce class tension and win workers' loyalty for the government was the Zubatov experiment in "police socialism," which originated in Moscow and had its heyday in 1902–1903. Sergei Zubatov, head of the Moscow *Okhrana*, believed almost fanatically in tsarism and realized that the regime had to act to counter radicals' influence among workers or run the risk of losing their support altogether. His notion of how to win workers back to loyalty was to develop various programs designed to meet their needs; tsarist police sponsored lectures, educational programs, and organizations in several cities. The term *police socialism*, though commonly applied to Zubatov's plans, is a complete misnomer, for his goal was to combat socialist influence through an extension of tsarist paternalism. At first Moscow workers expressed enthusiasm for several aspects of the program. They were particularly interested in talks on scientific and popular topics,[8] but they also liked the opportunity to meet, express their interests, and organize, if only in a limited fashion. In the early stages of Zubatov's activity, the police unions attracted many workers and "hurt the radicals' fortunes a great deal."[9] Despite this appeal to workers, perhaps only because no alternative existed, Zubatov's program failed rather quickly. Its collapse came because it opened new possibilities to workers that tsarism could not tolerate, angered industrialists and conservatives by appearing to pit workers against them with government help, and contributed to strikes. Workers soon learned that they could use even the limited Zubatov unions to conduct work stoppages.[10]

The experiment illustrated the difficulties for the administration in encouraging workers' organizations, given its determination to retain control over every aspect of their activities. After the experiment ended the Moscow police made few attempts to organize or direct the workers' movement, but they still faced the dilemma that had proven to be Zubatov's undoing: to give no aid or support to workers meant to let them drift toward radicalism, while to intervene on their behalf meant exciting them and angering the regime's staunchest supporters. Thus the police found themselves walking a tightrope between helping the workers too much and alienating them completely. The result, as in so many other respects, was vacillations in policy that appealed strongly to no one.

However, the failure of the *Zubatovshchina* (the Zubatov phenomenon) did not mean the end of all workers' hopes for peaceful evolution and improvement of their situation. Indeed, several resolutions adopted by their organizations in 1905 are highly reminiscent of liberals' goals of the same time. A proclamation issued in February by the Moscow committee of the Russian Social Democratic Workers' party, said to be Bolshevik already, emphasized that the working class should elect deputies to "popular representation" and should have the right to freedom of speech and personal inviolability, to strike, form unions, publish newspapers, and hold meetings.[11]

A commission of delegates from among city government employees meeting on October 12, 1905, five days before the issuance of the October Manifesto, placed great emphasis on civil liberties and called for the reorganization of city government on a democratic basis.[12] The Manifesto, despite its vagueness, went part way to meet the desires of such groups. It may be true that many workers were still suspicious of politics in the abstract,[13] but even that attitude could work into the hands of the liberals, who thought that only they were educated enough to direct political life.

The strike experience in 1905 also contained some elements that prompted worker support for liberals. The October general strike had the "support and active participation of the entire urban community" in Moscow and "represented the high-water mark of the liberal-socialist alliance and of interclass cooperation in 1905."[14] Even the Marxists shared this attitude for a while: on October 15 Social Democrats took part in a session of the Moscow duma to consider how to defend the city's working class and intelligentsia from attacks by Black Hundreds. The local Bolsheviks issued a report of the meeting that shows their clear sympathy for students and professors.[15] Unfortunately, the duma was not yet willing to express the independence necessary to draw on the "liberal-socialist alliance" and set up a defensive force in the face of certain government opposition.

Left to choose their own path the Russian liberals and the working class would surely have come to some modus vivendi, at least in Moscow, but probably in the whole empire. After all, that was the pattern elsewhere in western Europe and eventually in the United States. In Russia, as epitomized in Moscow, opposition to the central government increased cooperation among classes and led to greater sympathy for the workers, so that the process of making concessions to workers' desires moved along very quickly in 1905. It is not clear that the October Manifesto broke the liberal-worker consensus, as some accounts have argued for Russia in general,[16] by satisfying a large portion of the educated elite but leaving the essential desires of the lower classes untouched. Some members of those classes had already posited political reform as one of their most important wishes.

Meeting after the Manifesto appeared but before the December Uprising, representatives chosen by twenty-one textile factories, with a total of 21,000 workers, stressed the need for economic improvements but also urged changes in urban life.

> With the goals of satisfying the spiritual needs of the workers, the [projected] union strives for free education for children [and] unhampered arrangement of reading rooms, libraries, public lectures, concerts, plays, and the like.[17]

These desires, too, were completely acceptable to liberals, and in fact the Moscow city duma implemented or promoted all of these items in subsequent years.

The tsarist regime, however, now entered the picture with a particularly heavy hand, first by arresting leaders of newly formed unions, which had the effect of radicalizing them. This kind of activity, coupled with an incident on December 9 when troops fired on a peaceful crowd, led to the December Uprising.[18] In effect, workers backed into the fighting, provoked by the government, which probably wanted a confrontation.

This violence certainly marked a severe though temporary parting of the ways for city officials and the workers' movement. While the Moscow soviet of workers' deputies had endorsed and eventually directed the uprising, the city duma by and large approved its crushing (as noted in Chapter 4). Workers' spokesmen immediately picked up Mayor Guchkov's endorsement of repression and publicized it to their constituents in order to discredit the city's upper classes as a whole and to strengthen the sense of class struggle against the "propertied authorities," both local and central.[19] At this point the leadership of the municipality, despite its grave misgivings and criticisms of central government policy in 1905, was more afraid of the threat from below than of mistakes at the top. As we shall see, that attitude changed.

For its part the central government now recognized some need to placate workers. It therefore issued the law of March 4, 1906, detailing temporary rules on organizations of workers and others. The statute, adopted before the first meeting of the new State Duma in an attempt to head off discussion of this volatile issue and to keep popular representatives from having any say in the policy, created City Offices on the Affairs of Societies and Unions in numerous large Russian towns. The Moscow office was headed by the *gradonachal'nik*. It approved, rejected, or recommended changes in the charters of all societies and unions in the city. Rejection meant that an organization could not legally function. The office could also close any existing group that seemed to it to threaten "public safety and calm or to take a clearly immoral direction."[20] The membership of the office paralleled that of the Special Office on City Affairs (discussed in Chapter 2): the police chief and his appointees comprised the majority. The city mayor, the president of the provincial *zemstvo*, and one person elected from the city duma also served in both offices.

The new law on unions did not alter key aspects of the Moscow factory inspectorate, also headed by the *gradonachal'nik*. In this post, he was already responsible for enforcing industrial legislation and for alleviating conflicts between workers and management. He carried out these duties through a staff of factory inspectors and thirteen specially designated factory police. They were assigned to—

1. carry out the general duties of a policeman at his post;
2. observe the workers and the appearance among them of any ill-intentioned and trouble-making persons with the object of preventing any disorders, disturbances, and strikes.

Factory police were supposed to become familiar with the plant, management, and workers, especially the more important ones. They were to investigate any dissatisfaction among workers.[21]

The government was wise, from its point of view, to be concerned about organizations for the working class. In Moscow these often became the focus of undesirable political activity. For example, the legal Society for Popular [*Narodnykh*] Entertainment served as a recruiting ground for radicals, who distributed their literature and made new contacts at its outings.[22] According to the metalworkers' chief, his union's meetings "were a school for workers, where they were trained in public [*obshchestvennoi*] life and became acquainted with the conditions of the class struggle." This happened despite police attendance at the sessions.[23] Like attempts it made in other areas to grant limited freedoms, the regime's half-hearted toleration of some new organizations for the lower classes probably further damaged its political support.

The Moscow *gradonachal'nik*'s ability to treat organizations as he pleased was guaranteed by the new law on societies and unions, which paralleled the Extraordinary Measures and similar legislation in its vagueness and the sweeping powers it granted to local administrators. Labor spokesmen immediately grasped that essence but still called for activity under the terms of the statute. The Menshevik V. Ginevich put it this way in March 1906 to the Second Conference of trade unions, held in Moscow:

> It is essential to utilize the law, which nevertheless gives the opportunity for the existence of broad workers' organizations. But to utilize it, considering it only formally, the activity of the trade unions should remain such that it will facilitate the economic struggle of the workers against the capitalists. In that situation one task arises before the trade unions—to widen the limits of the law to full freedom of coalitions and strikes.[24]

At least one organization, the Moscow tailors' union, reacted to the new law in accordance with Ginevich's statement. Tailors' delegates meeting on March 16, 1906 resolved the following:

> Considering that the law of March 4 ... represents an attempt to befog the consciousness of the workers, that this law strives to divert the movement of

the workers from the struggle for emancipation and lure them onto the path of the petty and fruitless tasks of mutual aid, that it binds even the trade union struggle of the workers with strong means . . . nevertheless [we] will use even this law for the organization of the working class.[25]

While information on the number of trade unions that arose in Moscow during 1905–1906 is contradictory, there is no question that workers responded in large numbers to the new chance to organize. One early Soviet account mentions 46 Moscow unions with 48,000 members by the beginning of 1907, another Soviet work speaks of 120 unions in the city in 1906–1907, and a newspaper report of September 1907 notes 52 unions in existence during the previous two years.[26] A recent Western study counts over 100 unions in the city by December 1905 but only 63 by March 1906.[27] Even the metallists overcame their early mood and formed a viable union. One contemporary writer on the labor movement summed up the hopes of Moscow's workers: "The individual hiring agreement is being replaced by a collective one, and in place of the autocratic structure in the factories a constitutional regime is being established."[28] Nothing could have expressed the liberal outlook for labor more succinctly.

The acid test of how broadly this view would penetrate the workers' movement would be the implementation of the new law, so open to interpretation. The test would also be in the practice of the liberals—in how well they could appeal to the working class in one way or another. Both liberals and the tsarist regime had to dissociate themselves from the old "autocratic structure" at the workplace and in regard to workers' demands and organizations; the next few years would be the crucial period for these issues.

But tsarist officials in Moscow did not break completely with their old methods. They took the same general approach to the labor movement after 1906 as other areas of urban life: they proceeded with a mixture of carrot and stick, paternalism and confusion. Both Adrianov and Reinbot, especially the latter, continued the tsarist tradition of paternalism by personally intervening with unions and in strikes. Both tried to make workers feel that they should bring their grievances straight to the chief and that the police would take a direct interest in their affairs. For example, Reinbot visited the Giubner factory during a strike in June 1906. He spent about three hours listening to the workers' demands, after which he toured the living quarters provided for them by the factory. There he found violations of his regulations on overcrowding, which he ordered corrected. He also directed a factory inspector to transmit the workers' demands to a conference of manufacturers and to report the results to him.[29] The *gradonachal'nik* acted here as mediator, combining his roles as chief of police and head of the Moscow factory inspectorate.

In a similar incident one local newspaper reported that the board of the metalworkers' union was arrested in May 1907 after the union passed a resolution stating that individual strikes were harmful for the labor movement and that workers had to prepare for a general strike. At the Dobrova and Nabgol'ts factory, workers elected a delegation to protest to the *gradonachal'nik*, which he received. The group told him that the board members from their factory had not signed the resolution and that the factory workers had not supported it. Reinbot promised to release the arrested board members from Dobrova and Nabgol'ts if the workers would sign a letter saying they had not supported the resolution. He also asked the workers to avoid strikes and to come to him personally in case of any trouble with their employers.[30]

Personal attention by the *gradonachal'nik* sometimes succeeded in dampening labor trouble. In February 1907 the Gustav List factory went on strike. Besides "insignificant economic demands," workers were protesting the firing of a man and his subsequent arrest for "agitation." A delegation from the factory met with the police chief and told him the worker had conducted no agitation; that was done by outsiders. The *gradonachal'nik* agreed to release the man if work resumed at the factory. Both sides kept the bargain.[31]

At times the Moscow police chiefs of this era went so far as to encourage organization and economic strikes by workers, a tactic reminiscent of the Zubatov campaign. For instance, in August 1906 Reinbot reportedly forced factory owners to pay workers for time lost in recent strikes, despite the employers' protests.[32] In 1908 the *gradonachal'nik* even blocked efforts of print shop owners to lengthen hours and reduce pay.[33] Adrianov met in May 1909 with members of the board of the waiters' society, so named because the Office on Societies would not permit the word *union*. The waiters had sent a statement to the *gradonachal'nik* about ill treatment and poor working conditions in the city's restaurants. After a discussion of the general situation of Moscow's waiters, Adrianov promised to take all possible measures to improve their working conditions and to investigate violations of sanitary regulations, tax rules, and conditions for apprentices. The chief told the delegation that police measures alone were insufficient; solidarity among workers was also necessary. He had nothing against the organization of a general meeting for the consideration of the waiters' difficult situation and how to improve it.[34] In 1912 the *gradonachal'nik* rejected a request by tailor shop owners to arrest the leaders of a strike against them. Adrianov maintained that the stoppage was economic,[35] so he had no grounds for interference. Most of these efforts took place during an economic slump and at a time when the revolutionary movement as a whole had greatly declined; they undoubtedly had something to do with the relative quiescence of Moscow's workers until about 1911 or 1912, though they may well have angered employers. Clearly, Adrianov and Reinbot hoped to impress workers with their solicitude; they wanted to convey the notion that the tsar and his officials protected common people. At the same time, the police expected, and sometimes succeeded in preventing, labor trouble.

The readiness of some workers to accept the limitations of tsarist policy was apparent even after the bloodshed of 1905, as delegations came to the *gradonachal'niki* to voice their grievances and ask for support. This acceptance was surely due in part to the fact that, for the time being, opportunities to resist the regime had evaporated. On the other hand, workers' visits to the *gradonachal'niki* continued into the more radical period following the Lena Goldfields massacre of 1912, indicating some expectation on the laborers' part that the administration would respond positively to their desires. Workers came to the police chief as late as July 1913. Police had raided the offices of the Moscow metalworkers' union, usually considered one of the more militant workers' groups. Several days later a peaceful delegation from the union visited the *gradonachal'nik* and informed him that the arrested members had not been holding a meeting but had merely been reading, paying dues, or enrolling in the union.[36] Occasionally workers or artisans wrote to the *gradonachal'nik* to protest conditions in their workplaces or living quarters. The city archives contain several records of quick responses from the police, including a few cases in which owners were forced to improve food and housing.[37]

Thus there was probably some positive assessment of state paternalism among workers. Had it been possible to maintain police intervention on a broad and regular scale and to direct it frequently in favor of the workers, it might have been effective in stimulating labor support for the government. But regular intervention was impossible—a policeman could not be stationed beside every workbench, and the *gradonachal'nik* hardly had the time to monitor or intervene in every factory or workshop.

Together with paternalism regarding economic issues, the Moscow *gradonachal'niki* moved energetically to quash any activity by workers that hinted of politics or threatened the legal rights of employers. During one strike, in 1907, Reinbot told strikers from the Tryndin factory that they could continue their stoppage but could not commit any violence against their fellow workers who remained on the job, or they would be exiled from Moscow.[38] "Violence" in this context implied any attempts to prevent nonstrikers from working.

Reliance on the court system would have vitiated Reinbot's threat. His interest in this case was in keeping the factory open and in seeing that the strike was as short-lived as possible. Therefore he based his remarks on the Extraordinary Measures, which guaranteed that he could act immediately. Even the requirement of clearing all exiles with the Ministry of Internal Affairs was largely formal and usually done after the fact.

In several cases police intervention on the workers' behalf went hand in hand with repression of labor organizations; the Moscow administration tried to act as a substitute for workers' own groups, an attempt to ensure a politically safe direction for labor. Reinbot arranged a conference of bakery owners and workers during the strikes of July 1906 and at the same time arrested and exiled several workers.[39] In the summer of 1907 the chief closed the Union of Graphic Arts Workers, ostensibly because it had tried to start political strikes. Since the phrase *political strike* could apply to a broad range of work stoppages, often arbitrarily categorized,[40] the *gradonachal'niki* had great freedom of action in this regard. Shortly after this incident Reinbot received a delegation of Graphic Arts members but refused their request to reopen the union. He promised, however, to put pressure on employers to allow a general workers' meeting so that they could discuss conditions on the job and disagreements with management.[41] Paternalism and the heavy exercise of power proceeded simultaneously; workers cannot have been overly pleased.

In another account of this audience, the delegation reportedly told Reinbot that the union was necessary to regulate relations between them and their employers. The *gradonachal'nik* replied that he would take it on himself to monitor these relations and that the workers should not hesitate to come to him about any dispute.[42] Personal intervention by tsarist officials was supposed to ensure labor peace in Moscow. But this approach was not modern; it could not substitute for permanent institutions designed to handle problems as they arose. The Graphic Arts members and many businessmen, at least in 1905, recognized the utter necessity for such institutions, but the conservative state was unwilling to let control of events pass out of the hands of its appointed officials, especially where workers were concerned. Even with the best of wills, the government's policy could not have succeeded; besides its limitations of time and personnel, the police usually entered the picture only after problems had erupted into conflict.

By mid-1907, the time of Stolypin's coup d'etat, repression clearly predominated in the Moscow administration's approach to the labor movement. A newspaper account in September of that year claimed that of the fifty-two unions that had existed at one time or another in the past two years, twenty-one had closed voluntarily or had been closed by the police, while the rest had become "humble mutual aid organizations." The article observed,

> Complete indifference among workers to the future of their unions is notice-
> able, which is explained by the loss of faith in their correct operation and by
> the involuntary removal of leaders and other active members.[43]

In 1912, even after some revival, there were only about thirty unions in Moscow.[44]

Two years earlier, General Adrianov bragged to the Department of Police that his activities in removing union leaders and in disorganizing union ranks had "already weakened the strike movement to a significant degree." He pointed as well to the "absence of leadership, solidarity, firmness, and planning" among the unions as a result of his work.[45] Doubtless exaggerated to enhance his own position, Adrianov's statement nevertheless illustrates his conviction, shared by the regime in general, that repression of legal organizations was the most effective way to minimize labor trouble. At this quiet point in Moscow's labor history, Adrianov appeared to be right. His reports to the Department of Police on the mood of the city's workers regularly mention calmness and indifference to political goals, from August 1907 until late August 1910. Only then did the *gradona-chal'nik* note, "Among workers interest in the strike struggle is again awakening," adding that revolutionaries were taking account of the new spirit.[46] Such reports were probably accurate, judging by the low strike activity in Moscow and the fact that later police discussions of the popular mood were detailed and frank about dissent.

The administration's files recount deep, continuous interference in the labor movement by the Moscow police. This activity was often purely political. In April 1906, for example, Reinbot refused to legalize the ribbon makers' union because, in his view, its charter promoted "the education of workers and the development of their ability to participate in the so-called liberation struggle."[47] However, the Moscow police chief did not go as far as the Odessa *gradonachal'nik*, who threatened exile for workers who did not cooperate with "legally authorized" parties.[48] This meant only groups to the right of the Kadets.

Occasionally the police relied heavily on repression to halt strikes. For example, when most of Moscow's bakery workers struck in July 1906, police arrested and exiled an unspecified number from three shops. Ten more were jailed for various lengths of time.[49] Four leaders of a stoppage at the Kushnerev printers in the fall of 1907 were arrested and banished from Moscow. Officers interrogated other strikers at Kushnerev and even some employees who had stayed on the job.[50]

Reinbot also used arrests as a weapon against management, for instance during the bakery strike of 1906. He ordered inspections of living and working quarters in Moscow's bakeries while the walkout was under way; at least thirteen owners and managers were fined or jailed for violations of sanitary regulations and space norms issued by the governor-general in 1903.[51]

It is difficult to imagine that in such cases police actions pleased either workers or managers, for both sides were subjected to repression. Sometimes police interference made management's position vis-à-vis the workers especially awkward. For example, a report on an unnamed Moscow factory in 1907 related an incident in which workers had requested a meeting with the state factory inspector about a potential conflict with their bosses. The inspector talked to the men for three hours, and the problem was resolved; the system worked in this case. Yet at that point the police ordered the factory owner to withhold pay for the time of the meeting, evidently considering the session an illegal work stoppage, despite the fact he was satisfied with the results and wanted to pay his men. The police threatened him with a large fine if he did not obey the order; he had to comply, although he was afraid of angering his workers. Police interference had put the owner into a no-win situation.[52]

On at least two occasions during Adrianov's tenure, arrests of workers backfired and caused strikes. At the request of management at the Bromley factory, its workers elected a delegation in February 1911 to discuss a minor issue regarding lunch hours on preholiday workdays. Police arrested the delegation the day after the election, and this so angered the eight hundred other workers of the factory that they went out in protest.[53] The positive side of paternalism paled in comparison to such provocation.

Relations between tsarist administrators and workers in Moscow entered a new, sharper phase after the Lena massacre. T. V. Sapronov recalled the reaction of his fellow construction workers to the killings.[54]

> During the reading of news about the shooting, the whole tavern fell silent. A deathly silence began. The reading ended. A minute of silence.... It seemed that no one wanted to say a word, they were so crushed. But then suddenly the tavern burst into noise, curses resounded, oaths were hurled at the executioners, and the expressions: "Again shootings, again a bloodbath for the workers." ... Demonstrators are walking along the street and singing a revolutionary song. The confused *gorodovoi* half tries to stop the demonstrators, half tries to break them up, but it is as if they didn't notice him. They continue on their way, and even louder and more confidently resounds their fighting song. The *gorodovoi*'s whistle blows, but it can't be heard above the song.

For this group of workers and many others, the Lena massacre ended a period of quiescence and began one of renewed militancy.

The increasing labor unrest in various cities spurred the Council of Ministers to consider "measures for the struggle with workers' strikes" in August 1913. The Council regarded recent strikes as a state issue, since they often affected defense production, and as a political issue, since the basis for the strikes was often "insignificant"; this suggested to the Council the presence of "criminal influence on the working people from outside." The state's highest officials had forgotten nothing and learned nothing. They paid little attention to workers' obvious grievances of poor pay, housing, working conditions, and the lack of outlets for protest and resolution of issues.

The cabinet's answer to working class unrest was essentially increased repression, though some concessions might be made as well. Local tsarist administrators were to remand instigators of strikes to the courts. In "exceptional cases, for especially pressing reasons," officials should apply "measures of administrative action" to workers, under the terms of the Extraordinary Measures. Workers could even be removed from factories if need be. At the same time, officials could apply "one of the more effective means of preventing strikes" by taking a "more sympathetic attitude" to workers' economic demands.[55] As in 1905, the government tried to deflect workers' attention from politics by emphasizing economic concessions. And, again replicating 1905, this course of action angered many factory owners, who resented government interference in their businesses and thought the workers' grievances were largely political, not economic. (This resentment will be outlined below.)

The Moscow *gradonachal'nik* received the Council of Ministers' ideas on the workers' movement, which were to be transmitted to the "chiefs of all interested agencies." Of course, the Moscow police were already using the ministers' recommended techniques, but the cabinet was clearly exhorting local administrators to be less conciliatory toward strikes and worker unrest in the future. Faced with a mounting wave of labor stoppages after the Lena Goldfields massacre, the government was determined to prevent or at least control them.

The *gradonachal'nik* now applied the minister's suggestions. In September 1913 *Okhrana* agents arrested a number of municipal tram workers as they were preparing a statement to management on labor conditions and pay. Instead of forestalling unrest, the arrests stirred the workers to strike; other municipal workers also walked out, as did some from private factories.[56] Eventually, forty-five workers were exiled from Moscow for their part in the strikes,[57] which must have further spread hatred for the tsarist administration. According to an early Soviet work, the minister of internal affairs then ordered the *gradonachal'nik* to take "decisive measures" to end the walkout. Adrianov responded by directing the municipal *uprava* to fire the striking workers.[58]

At the height of the strike, a delegation told the *uprava*, "We state categorically that if there had been no arrests, there would have been no strike." The delegation vowed that work would not resume until the *gradonachal'nik* released the arrested men and guaranteed their immunity from prosecution.[59] This declaration put city officials in a very awkward position, for they could do no more than appeal to the police for the workers' release. Privately, municipal leaders must have resented the way the government's political agenda made their lives harder.

For a while the strikes produced a very threatening situation. Fighting took place between workers and police as crowds formed to stop some of the few trams that were still moving. Two estimates of the total on strike in late September are available—23,000 by the *Okhrana* and 55,000 by a workers' newspaper.[60] Police with drawn sabers met crowds of workers on the streets, according to one eyewitness. He described a meeting on Triumfal'naia Square that adopted a resolution criticizing the administration for "political violence and arbitrariness against the workers' press and workers' organizations." The document ended with the words, "Down with the tsarist government! Long live socialism!"[61] However, there was not enough momentum nationally or locally to replicate 1905, and the strikes soon ended.

Another report from 1913 describes an assault by police on a workers' barrack in Moscow. The police drove a group of workers from the street into the barrack, forced them to kneel, beat several unmercifully, broke dishes, and arrested thirty people.[62] Far from discovering a policy that could defuse labor unrest, the conservative state was doing much to create more opposition.

The Moscow administration now increasingly found itself involved in clashes over symbolic political issues. On the anniversary of Lena in 1913 and again in 1914 workers at one factory in the Sokol'niki district tried to stage a memorial march. Each time, the police knew about the demonstration in advance and surrounded the plant to prevent it.[63] The annual May Day protests featured similar confrontations and resulted in many arrests.

Simultaneously, the government tried to mollify workers by allowing somewhat more union activity and a labor press, including both Bolshevik and Menshevik newspapers.[64] But the overall impression of the state's approach to labor in Moscow must have been negative for the workers. The government's message to them was still summed up in a remark to the State Duma by Minister of the Interior A. A. Makarov after the Lena shooting. Labor unrest would be met with force: "It was ever thus, and thus it will ever be."[65]

It may be somewhat misleading to judge the workers' mood by those who were organized, for they tended to be more active and concerned in the first place. Yet it is significant that by 1913 Bolsheviks had triumphed over their less militant Menshevik rivals in all thirteen Moscow unions in which elections took place.[66] A majority of the city's workers also voted for Bolshevik candidates in the Fourth State Duma elections in late 1912. The deliberations of the Council of Ministers described above and a memorandum written for the tsar by the new minister of the interior, N. A. Maklakov, in October 1913 reveal deep concern at the highest levels of government about the mood of Moscow's workers.[67]

Despite all the vacillations in national policy on labor, in the period 1906–1914 more remained constant than changed in the Moscow administration's policies on unions and the workers' movement. Disruption of unions, personal involvement by the *gradonachal'niki*, some interest and intervention by police in problems of housing and working conditions, and a certain willingness to tolerate workers' activities and organizations designed to better their economic position were constant features of administrative practice in these years. Some workers responded positively to the latter efforts.

Moscow's proletariat, and the lower classes in general, had reason both to support and to resent the administration. The police were sometimes protectors of the people. Yet it must have been the repressive, political side of police activity that made the strongest impression on the city's workers, and possibly on the lower classes in general. Workers directly blamed the police for provoking strikes such as the Bromley incident and the tram walkout of 1913. Police harassed and closed unions, seized and prohibited publications for workers, and hampered the development of educational courses for them. If tsarist labor policy had appeared to work fairly effectively between 1907 and 1911, it could not continue to accomplish its goals when workers were inflamed by overt and highly publicized violence against them.

One of the worst aspects of this repression was, once again, its erratic and unpredictable nature. Workers' hopes were raised and then dashed, which angered them more than a straightforward policy of unmitigated repression would have. The state again appeared confused and ineffective.[68] However, before concluding that this picture amounts to pervasive radicalism among Moscow workers by 1914, it is necessary to examine other sides of the story.

"Society" and the Workers

While the central authorities appeared to move ever farther away from a comprehensive and satisfactory labor policy, Moscow's liberals were trying to fashion one on their own. In so doing they met opposition from the state, local conservatives, and the working class, and their own actions were filled with hesitancy and shifts in policy. But over time they found themselves increasingly opposed to central government practice.

Major N. I. Guchkov personally reflected some of the contrasting aspects of the municipality's approach to workers. He lauded their suppression in December 1905 but received a delegation from the unemployed in the next year and set up public works for them. The city government as a whole adopted a mixture of old and new methods in dealing with the constant problem of unemployment. At times the city even resorted to the traditional technique of sending the unemployed back to the countryside. By 1906, however, Moscow had its first public employment bureau.

The oldest approach to the question, dictated by national law, had begun in Moscow in 1836 as a means of dealing with begging. This was the workhouse, originally run by the police but transferred to the city in 1893.[69] At the same time the municipality had also taken over the Office for Investigation and Observation of Beggars. In theory, police were supposed to arrest all beggars in the city and bring them to this office, which decided what to do with them.

Of 6,914 arrested for begging in 1912, a typical year, a little less than half went to the city workhouse for various lengths of time. The tsarist administration exiled 3.3 percent from the city, presumably because the police believed these were dangerous to "public order and calm." A small percentage was charged with other crimes, while 55 percent were released with a warning not to repeat within six months. Almost certainly, this number was so large because there was not enough space or work at the city's workhouses. The percentage released with a warning was more or less average for this period.[70]

Beggars were numerous in Moscow. Despite the police responsibility to arrest them all, the tsarist authorities acknowledged the hopelessness of the assignment. In 1908 the *gradonachal'nik* reported that beggars "continue to fill the streets of the capital," and some areas were "especially overpopulated by beggars."[71]

Besides those arrested, the workhouse accepted men and women who came voluntarily on a space-available basis. The percentage of volunteers rose from 59.2 percent in 1900 to 78.5 percent in 1908.[72] Compared to the alternatives, the workhouse was an attractive place to those who were down and out. If they could not get in as volunteers, reported the *uprava* in 1906, many people took to begging in the hope they would be arrested and sent to the house.[73] By 1902 there were so many volunteers that the city divided its facilities into a workhouse (*Rabotnyi Dom*) for those sent by the City Office on Beggars and a House of the Love of Labor (*Dom Trudoliubiia*) for volunteers. On some days as many as five hundred people appeared before the latter, trying to get in.[74] A certain number also fled the *Rabotnyi Dom* every year, though guards accompanied work parties.

The *Rabotnyi Dom* and the *Dom Trudoliubiia* served 18,290 people in 1911, about 25 percent of them in the former and 75 percent in the latter. Men comprised about 75 percent of the *Rabotnyi Dom*'s clientele and about 94 percent of the *Dom Trudoliubiia*'s. From 1909 to 1911 only 36 percent of all who sought places were admitted.[75]

Once inside the *Rabotnyi Dom* inmates were sent out to work on projects for the city such as street paving or on jobs for private contractors. At the *Dom Trudoliubiia* inmates might either go out to work or stay in one of the house's own workshops. Among others, there were a brass shop, a carpentry shop, a shoemaker's, and a tailor's. For youths there were three training shops, a bootmaker's, a basket and furniture shop, and a bindery.

The municipality made money on these houses, 207,836 rubles in 1911 alone.[76] If the city had followed the same pattern in service for the unemployed as in other areas, eventually this money would have gone into better facilities. The amount paid to inmates was low because the duma did not wish to make the house too attractive, which could have reduced people's desire to leave and find work in the regular economy. This was a long-standing principle in the city government, as it was in many other countries.

Neither the inmates nor the employees of the houses were particularly healthy, according to several reports. One of these related in 1908 that in the previous year city doctors had examined over ten thousand people in the *Rabotnyi Dom* and found only a small number healthy. Even the staff of the house had basement apartments that were very damp. Their children suffered from respiratory diseases, anemia, and other health problems.[77] These quarters were in violation of the city duma's own housing regulations.

Despite the low pay and poor conditions, the houses attracted many peasants who came into Moscow. These immigrants often had relatively little to offer on the job market; many were illiterate or lacked marketable skills for an urban environment. Municipal services benefited those who lacked jobs, and other volunteers may have left work to enter the houses. That would not be surprising, considering the abysmal conditions and pay in many occupations.

The much larger percentage of men than of women in the two houses partly reflects a greater structural capacity to accept them. It also illustrates the fact that it was still predominantly men who came to the city to look for work, leaving their wives and families behind. Undoubtedly most of the men who ended up on the doorsteps of the houses were recent immigrants who were still trying to get established in the city.

In 1913 the population in the two main houses, a tiny one for women only, and several small branches sometimes reached 2,500. The city planned to consolidate some of the expansion by building one large house, with room for eight hundred men and fifty women, while keeping the main existing buildings. Construction was planned for 1914,[78] but there is no record that it began.

In 1906 the city government encountered a situation that pushed it to deal with unemployment in new ways. During the summer of that year unemployed Muscovites advanced novel, militant demands, organized on a large scale, and became violent on several occasions. In response, the city set up a number of new programs. After the strikes and fighting of 1905 the duma was uneasy when confronted by large groups of angry people, especially when they began to organize and present their demands in a coherent fashion. In a statement characteristic of the duma's mood, delegate N. P. Zimin told his colleagues, "I consider it impossible to put off the question [of works projects for the unemployed]; otherwise the need will grow and be expressed in undesirable events."[79]

The main group that faced the city government during the summer of 1906 was the Moscow Council of the Unemployed. According to one Soviet author the council was organized by Bolsheviks,[80] though contemporary accounts do not mention a party basis or origin. Whoever was responsible for the organization and militancy of the unemployed, these were their distinguishing features in 1906, not their numbers, which fluctuated by day and by season. No precise figures are available on the extent of unemployment in the city in that year; one estimate by the Council of the Unemployed in July was 6,000, but other guesses put the figure at 20,000, and even 300,000.[81]

The first indication that something was different about the unemployed in 1906 occurred unexpectedly on May 16, when a group of men from the council came to a city duma meeting. There they presented a statement demanding organization of public works, food, and housing for the unemployed. The delegation asserted,

> The unemployed belong to the class of the city population on which, directly or indirectly, city taxes fall. You—the duma—enjoy wide political rights thanks to the efforts of the workers [i.e., the October Manifesto was a result of workers' strikes].
>
> You can't refuse us work by citing a lack of money. You have a lot of it, but you spend it unproductively, often not for the use but for the harm of the population. Not more than a few days ago you assigned over 1,500 rubles for policemen's apartments and declared the question of apartments for police sergeants pressing. And this at a time when all the city's poor are suffering such terrible need.[82]

It should be remembered that the state required Moscow to pay for policemen's apartments as part of the "obligatory expenditures" and that for years the city had resisted paying for the sergeants' quarters. In any event, the importance of the statement lies in its militancy and its low estimation of the duma's efforts for the general population. The last point should probably be taken with some skepticism, since the group was trying to impress its point of view on the duma.

Mayor Guchkov read the delegation's statement aloud and then referred it to the *uprava* and to a committee already considering such matters. At this and subsequent points the audience shouted out its displeasure. Guchkov finally interrupted the meeting and reconvened it in a smaller room, where it concluded without further disruptions.[83]

The mayor was still willing to talk to members of the Council of the Unemployed; the next day he received a delegation from it. After two hours of discussion, according to one account, he promised to present the question of funds for the unemployed to the duma and to arrange a place for the organization to meet if the duma did not object.

On the same day, the report continues, Guchkov held another meeting with the duma committees concerned with the question, representatives of the Council of the Unemployed and members of the Moscow Imperial Technical Society, a private group chartered by the tsar that investigated social and technical problems. At the session the decision was made to open several free cafeterias for those out of work.[84]

The mayor's reception of the delegation and the meeting with the council's representatives contrasted sharply with the governor-general's treatment of another, similar group of unemployed. When they appeared on May 17 at the governor-general's office and asked to see him, he had them arrested.[85] The city was much more flexible, either from fear or concern for the welfare of the unemployed, than the tsarist authorities, whose primary responsibility was public order. There was also a difference between the attitudes of the governor-general and those of the Moscow *gradonachal'niki* in regard to delegations from the lower classes. The latter officials received delegations, even of striking workers, on several occasions in this period. The narrower jurisdiction of the *gradonachal'niki*, who oversaw only the city of Moscow and thus interacted more closely with its people, perhaps made these officials more inclined to be conciliatory than was the governor-general.

The Moscow duma proceeded to appropriate money and plan public works projects, but their scale and pace did not satisfy the Council of the Unemployed. Delegates from it returned to the duma on June 13 with another statement, which charged that the latter's committees "did and are doing everything [possible] to create obstacles to the satisfaction of our demands." The duma had assigned sixty thousand rubles to public works, but the visitors claimed, "The paltriness of this amount is a direct insult to the unemployed."

Council delegates also complained about the lack of subsidies to dining halls, the *uprava*'s refusal to pay the council's expenses from May 16 to 25, and its refusal to allow regional meetings of the unemployed (this matter depended on the police, not the city). The statement concluded with the phrase, "We see in the conduct of the *uprava* a clear desire to call us to a confrontation."[86] The council clung to its militant tactics, perhaps because they had been successful in getting a quick response from the duma.

After hearing the statement, several duma members asked how much of the money it had appropriated for the needs of the unemployed had been spent so far. When an *uprava* member replied that "some" was left, the duma voted to add twelve thousand rubles.

In general, the duma reacted mildly to the Council's statement. Several delegates expressed concern about the situation of the unemployed in the city, but only two objected to the tone of the statement.[87] The duma was still willing to cooperate with the group.

The promised public works began on June 26 at Kalitnikovskoe cemetery. Workers received eighty kopecks per day plus housing and food at barracks constructed on the spot by the city. By July 1, 783 people were employed there. After a dispute over pay was settled, the workers seemed satisfied until one was injured on the job. A police investigation determined that it was his own fault, but this decision caused his fellows to riot and destroy a lot of equipment. When police arrived, many workers fled from the barracks, carrying with them mattresses, sheets, and other items supplied by the city. As they went, some of them set the barracks on fire.[88]

This disaster, which occurred in early August, ended the largest project of 1906 to aid the unemployed. Yet the municipality continued to support public works; in September the duma voted an additional 35,000 rubles for that purpose. In the summer alone the city funded 33,152 workdays on six different projects, spending a total of 48,620 rubles on pay for the unemployed.[89]

The Moscow city government had attempted to defuse a volatile situation by compromise and quick action. As the unemployed demonstrated, their presence in the city held great potential for social disruption. The fighting of 1905 and the new, legal opportunities to organize had encouraged workers to band together in defense of their interests, and in so doing the unemployed brought a new challenge to the city duma. The response was remarkable, especially considering the municipality's tight financial situation. It somehow found at least 84,000 rubles for the unemployed and went to great lengths to create work for them. All this, however, was not enough to override the militancy of those out of work.

Most of the city's initiatives were more successful than the works project at Kalitnikovskoe cemetery. It should be noted that even there working conditions and pay, though poor according to those hired, were better than average in Moscow for such work. Private contractors generally paid casual laborers less than a ruble a day and did not provide food or shelter. Much more than conditions at the works projects, the factors of organization of the unemployed and the lingering anger of 1905 led them to protest and riot.

The city again organized public works in the summer of 1907, but on a much smaller scale. In August about four hundred men were at work in two places,[90] and apparently in this case no trouble occurred. The newspapers and city publications make no further mention of public works before the war.

The municipal government also began a more permanent approach to the problem of unemployment in 1906: an employment bureau. The question of such an office had first arisen in the duma in 1897. A special duma commission and then the *uprava* had studied the issue and in late 1899 the full duma had approved a plan for a bureau. However, the Moscow governor would not allow it to open until the Ministry of Internal Affairs had approved its charter. "Despite multiple reminders and petitions," it was not until May 1906 that the ministry gave its approval. The city opened the bureau at the end of July.[91] In 1907 two branches opened.

Anyone living in Moscow or its immediate environs, no matter how long, could use the bureau's services without charge. Each prospective employer paid thirty kopecks to fill out a questionnaire about the work offered. After reaching a peak in 1908, the number of citizens using the bureau dropped slightly, but the number of jobs offered and people placed in them rose steadily. This pattern can be explained by the bureaus' tendency to become more and more a hiring service

TABLE 5-1. Moscow's Public Employment Bureaus, 1908–1911[92]

	No. Applying	Jobs Offered	Placed
1908	27,052	6,196	4,468
1909	25,647	8,126	4,511
1910	22,340	11,460	7,808
1911	21,731	20,002	12,088

for *dvorniki* and, above all else, for female servants. One report of 1909 noted that 92 percent of all those sent out to work from the bureaus went to these jobs.[93]

In early 1914 the municipality opened a second, larger bureau. The data in the table might seem to imply that no demand existed for another such service, but the opposite was true. In its first six months of operation the new labor exchange registered 23,744 job seekers and found work for 21,622. Most of those placed were unskilled laborers, watchmen, cooks, carpenters, and agricultural workers.[94] Though available accounts of its organization are sketchy, it is probable that the new bureau concentrated on jobs other than servant positions, leaving that field to the old bureau and its branches. In any event, on the very eve of the war the city had successfully entered an area in which there was a high demand for service; the bureau was beginning to meet a long-standing need engendered by economic change.

The municipality tried another sort of specialization in this field in 1914, an employment office ostensibly for those seeking white-collar jobs—employees as opposed to workers. Starting operation in the spring of that year, this bureau registered 3,400 people in its first two months. There were 400 requests for employees and 173 applicants were placed. Sixty-five percent of all positions for employees were for women, mostly nursemaids and office workers.[95] In this case, the city's efforts to fill a more specialized role in placing trained employees were only marginally successful, perhaps partly because it did not adhere strictly to its designated task. The experiment was still in its infancy when the war broke out and so cannot be judged a failure; yet it is likely that the need for such services among white-collar workers was much less than among the unskilled.

At the same time the city was operating employment bureaus and organizing public works projects, it continued to follow a very traditional approach to unemployment, sending people back to their villages. In February 1906 the duma voted one thousand rubles for that purpose because the *Rabotnyi Dom* and the *Dom Trudoliubiia* were overcrowded.[96] The *uprava* assigned another thousand rubles in December 1906 to journeys home "for Christmas" for the unemployed,[97] undoubtedly with the hope that they would not return. Such appropriations continued in 1907 and 1908, according to one newspaper, when the city spent over eight thousand rubles on tickets to home villages.[98] These expenditures were entirely futile, as the flow of people coming to Moscow looking for work was many times larger than the number sent out.

Nor was the program always well received. In May 1906 when the Moscow Council of the Unemployed was presenting its militant demands to the city duma, the *uprava* announced that the jobless could receive free tickets to the countryside. The unemployed of the Prechistenskaia district responded with the following resolution:[99]

> We will not go to our villages, where people are dying of hunger, but will stay in the city, and if the city duma continues its previous policy in relation to us, then we will make our slogan "Down with the bourgeois duma and replace it with one elected by a general vote."

Thus the unemployed calculatedly threatened the city government with revolution, flexing the muscles that had been strong enough only six months earlier to bring Moscow's economic life to a halt and to organize workers for pitched battles with the regime's troops. In the case of this resolution and in general, protesters from the city's unemployed wanted programs that would enable them to stay in Moscow and become better integrated into their chosen environment.

Paying third class rail fare to the countryside was cheaper than setting up permanent or even ad hoc services in the city for those out of work, but the municipality must have realized that providing tickets home was only a stop-gap measure in the context of rapid population growth. After 1908 the sources do not mention such payments again.

Between 1906 and 1914 the city duma modernized its programs for the unemployed by creating public works projects and new institutions—the employment bureaus—which were better suited to changing social conditions than the old practice of sending those out of work to the countryside. The city government recognized the existence of a municipal problem in unemployment and responded flexibly; previously, responsibility for this question was considered to belong largely to the home villages, private groups, or the urban *soslovie* organizations.

However, an ambivalent approach to the issue continued in Moscow. An exchange between two city duma delegates in November 1905 illustrates this point. The elderly conservative P. M. Kalashnikov, a merchant by *soslovie* and a deputy since 1877, maintained that the problem of begging in the city was a police matter. He demanded the "removal of the element of beggars and itinerants, whom it is impossible to avoid." In response, I. A. Aleksandrov, a member of the craftsman *soslovie* who had entered the duma in 1897, asked,

> Where should the police put them? The *gradonachal'nik* says he would remove them in a day, but there is no place for them. The duma should build an institution. In this case the city is the means of aid to the beggars, the police are certainly not; the blame can't be shifted onto them.[100]

The city's ambivalent approach to the destitute remained in effect until 1914. In some respects the unemployed were still treated as criminals: they were forced to go to the city workhouses when arrested. Police sometimes sent them to the countryside, a tactic the city could not control. The municipality even indicated tacit agreement with this practice until 1908 by funding passage to the villages for people out of work. Thus the city modernized in this area slowly and tentatively.

The same can be said of the municipal government's approach to strikes. Yet over time a clear difference emerged between the city's attitudes toward the issue of labor protest and the state's; by 1912 key figures in Moscow's local government and its industrial elite were actively seeking to dissociate themselves from central policy and to appeal to workers on other bases, while offering certain compromises to the labor movement. In some ways, the situation appeared similar to 1905: protest among the city's lower classes and its *obshchestvo* was finding common ground. The state's clumsiness pushed at least some members of Moscow's upper and lower strata together.

In the first case of labor trouble faced by the municipal government after 1905, the tram strike of 1907, it seemed beset by contradictions and hesitancy. Work stopped on the trams in February over the firing of a worker; deeper issues of relations between management and workers were at stake. Three separate workshops put down their tools. A delegation of strikers then presented a list of demands to the city *uprava*, and these were rejected because of their "anonymity." One newspaper account claimed that the workers were afraid to put their names on any demands for fear the signers would be punished;[101] it is not clear whether they feared retaliation from the city or the state. At any rate, a climate that would have facilitated open discussion of problems certainly did not exist.

The *uprava* proceeded to declare that all strikers would be fired if they did not immediately return to the job.[102] Yet the city managers eventually backed down and agreed to rehire the fired workers.[103] Meanwhile work resumed, and the municipal duma assigned its Revision Commission to investigate the whole matter.

The commission returned findings that placed virtually the entire blame for the strike on the *uprava*. "Why didn't the *uprava* ask the workers to select a delegation properly?" asked the commission's reporter, N. M. Kishkin. The *uprava* obviously didn't consider the demands so "anonymous" as it had claimed, because it listed them. City administrators should not have reacted so negatively and should have agreed to one key demand, a mediation chamber, which the *uprava* had already started to set up the year before. Workers had been "deprived of opportunities to find timely satisfaction of their needs, which would have been satisfactorily resolved given proper organization of a mediation chamber."[104] In other words, the Revision Commission believed that a modern, permanent institution for settling disputes was required in city enterprises; that would be the best means of avoiding labor stoppages.

Kishkin went on to say that the *uprava* had called the strike "original," that is, a product of outside influence. But he did not see how that could be true, judging by the *uprava*'s own report. Kishkin called the strike a "moral" one, caused by poor relations between labor and management.[105]

The mayor and the duma as a whole rejected the commission's findings. One deputy called the strike immoral, pointing to the fact that the workers did not sign their demands. The strike was wrong because it hurt other citizens, for example forcing a mother with a sick child to walk. Another duma member objected to the stoppage on the grounds that the city had to hold down the economic demands of the workers or they would soon ask for ten or fifteen rubles a day. Still another deputy railed against strikes in general: they were "a chronic illness that must be cured."[106] The last assertion would have drawn hearty agreement from the staunchest rural conservative.

Mayor Guchkov told the duma that if it accepted the Revision Commission's findings, it would create "great difficulties" for the *uprava* "in carrying out the legal obligations placed upon it." He explained away the commission's report with a reference to the haste of its investigation and said that the *uprava* hoped the future work of the commission would provide material for "the correct solution" of ways to prevent strikes.[107] Guchkov had completely and condescendingly rejected the liberal viewpoint.

In early 1907, therefore, workers had little to choose from between the city and the state when it came to strikes or even the opportunity to express grievances. In fact, the *gradonachal'nik* might well have been more receptive to the tram workers' complaints than was the city *uprava*; on other occasions at roughly the same time, Reinbot was more conciliatory toward workers and even strikers. However, the conclusions reached by the duma's Revision Commission were more than a straw in the wind for the future. Kishkin was an important Kadet and local progressist, and the attitudes embodied in his report were bound to triumph within the duma as soon as his group became the majority. That happened in a definite fashion only in late 1912, so that in the fall of 1913 municipal officials acted very differently in an incident that was otherwise nearly a repeat of the 1907 situation.

Once again, the tram workers struck, this time because of *Okhrana* arrests. Higher municipal employees and officials now chose a conciliatory course. Engineers at city enterprises sought out workers to talk, but police would not let large groups form. Workers who did talk to engineers in small groups "refused to relay information to their fellows because they were afraid the police would view this as agitation and they would suffer for it."[108] Thus communications between the two sides were severely hampered by the presence and policies of the police; the engineers and municipal officials in general must have been quite angry.

In reaction to the strike the Moscow duma divided once more, just as in 1907. Its liberalization was far from complete: one group, the progressists, addressed the workers and asked them to return to work. The city government would review the situation of its employees and would "propose to determine a possible form of their organization." On the other side of the chamber the "non-party and moderate members" called on the *uprava* not to give in to any workers' demands.[109] At this point the *gradonachal'nik* "proposed" to acting mayor Brianskii that he tell workers staying off the job that they would be fired and their names given to the police for further action. Brianskii's response seems somewhat tepid; he merely turned over the police chief's note to the tram administration for execution.[110]

In contrast to the approach of the police, the city government was sympathetic to the workers' position, though not without contradictions. Probably as a result of the *gradonachal'nik*'s pressure, the *uprava* issued a call to strikers to return to work or they would be fired.[111] But that move was overshadowed a few days later when a delegation of strikers visited Brianskii, who promised to make every effort to help workers arrested by the police and to prevent more arrests. On the next day a group of workers reported back to him that full movement of the trams had resumed; the news of the first meeting had made a favorable impression on the strikers.[112] The conciliatory attitude of Brianskii and the city engineers had appealed to workers and helped defuse a potentially volatile situation. The whole affair was a demonstration of how effective the liberal approach could be, as well as a lesson to the workers that the city and the state were not necessarily two peas in a pod. They were not the "propertied authorities" acting together, as the local Bolsheviks had claimed in 1906.[113] The police had defended the government's political position in a particularly maladroit way, and its policies could now stand in sharp contrast to the municipality's.

Of course, not only the majority within the Moscow duma had changed, but also the entire mood of the city's *obshchestvo*, as shown by the elections to the Fourth State Duma. A new spirit—or, more precisely, one reminiscent of 1905— was evident after Lena within the industrial elite. When P. P. Riabushinskii's newspaper *Utro Rossii* referred to the shooting there as a "catastrophe of state policy" to which "only the word murder can be applied," that was merely one of many expressions of disapproval from Moscow's elite. The head of the Moscow *Okhrana* now reported a "radical mood" among the city's business leaders. During a meeting of manufacturers at Riabushinskii's home, the host and many others outlined their view that it was not only wrong to struggle against the workers' strikes in protest over Lena, but that industrialists should give them moral support. They were an "extremely desirable political factor at the present moment."[114] Now, instead of calling in support from the central government to deal with economic strikes, key industrialists suggested aid to political stoppages. The two approaches were irreconcilable.

Russkie Vedomosti, linked to the Kadets, maintained that the Lena events "were deeply upsetting for all of the Russian *obshchestvo*" and spoke of "their horror, which has struck people of the most varied parties."[115] Another *Okhrana* report, of April 1912, noted "general indignation and dissatisfaction reigning in [Moscow's] *obshchestvo*. . . . The mood in the *obshchestvo* is rising ever higher."[116] In its report for 1912 the Moscow Society of Mill and Factory Owners found that "in general [the year] proceeded against a background of an increasingly aggressive mood among factory and mill workers . . . the workers put into motion an entire arsenal of pressure on the industrialists."[117]

Utro Rossii spoke of "whole streams of blood and horrors at Lena." The owners of the goldfields were guilty of the bloodshed because "they turned workers into slaves and did not obey the laws." But many local tsarist administrators "actively and passively facilitated this blind and ruinous policy." The article pointed to England, where strikes had taken place across the whole country without leading to bloodshed. That was because the government did not "identify the interests of the state solely with the capitalist class" but stepped into the situation to guarantee profitable operation of the mines for the owners and "for the workers—to secure the minimal demands of labor." In contrast Russian policy did not "guard workers from the influence of political agitators, using massive unrest for their own ends."[118] The government itself was feeding radicalism, whereas a more liberal approach would defuse it. Riabushinskii and others were hinting that the way to stave off revolution in Russia was a fundamental change in government policy, if not in the nature of the regime.

For this wing of the local industrialists, the so-called young group,[119] broader issues of Russia's future were at stake in the state's attitude toward the labor movement. *Utro Rossii* had earlier denounced "the police structure, under whose yoke the spiritual growth and economic development of the state suffer equally,"[120] and continued its criticism in commenting on Lena.

No conditions for the evolution of Russia's economic forces are present at this moment. There can be no talk of the flowering of industry where the chief mover, the main working force—man—is deprived of any rights, where a mass of miners gathered for peaceful conversations about their affairs are not guaranteed that they will not suddenly be subjected to shooting, although nothing provoked it.[121]

Even allowing for Riabushinskii's semimystical obsession with the ideas that the bourgeoisie could guide Russia to a brilliant future and that industrialists and workers were all part of one class, the *narod*,[122] his newspaper's dismay over Lena reflects deep concern that the central government was leading the country to disaster and that a liberal policy toward the workers was the only viable alternative.

Russkie Vedomosti, free of Riabushinskii's messianism, promoted the same view on labor issues. Months before Lena, a writer for the paper had this to say in its annual review of the workers' movement:

It is hardly possible to dispute the idea that the development of our industry at present has already reached such a stage that relations between labor and capital should be structured on a legal basis and determined by mutual activity of the [two] sides. The police point of view, seeing elements of "troubled times" [*smuty*] in manifestations of trade union activity and collective action by the workers, should be abandoned.

This was the way to head off strikes and "upheavals"; a "conciliation apparatus" should be created, which could settle conflicts without work stoppage. The "old police measures" could not do that. This writer, too, pointed to western Europe, where, he said, "experience shows that the practice of peaceful negotiations removes labor conflicts." The least number of strikes occur where there are the strongest labor unions. Suppressing unions, on the other hand, not only does not obviate strikes but increases their "uncontrolled nature [*stikhiinost'*] and chaos, which harmfully affect the interests of both sides."[123] In 1913 the Moscow Society of Mill and Factory Owners dispatched two members to western Europe for a look at industrialists' experience with strikes.[124]

In early 1914 even the Octobrist newspaper in Moscow, *Golos Moskvy*, edited by N. I. Guchkov, took strong issue with central policy toward the labor movement. The stimulus to the paper's objection was a draft of a new law on unions and societies, to replace the "temporary rules" of 1906. Written by the Ministry of Internal Affairs, the bill would retain the right of local administrators to close an organization if it was deemed a "threat to public order and safety" and would continue the Offices on Society Affairs as a permanent institution. The bill further specified that fired or unemployed workers could not be members of unions and set relatively high age limits on voting for union boards. These provisions prompted *Golos Moskvy* to comment, "It is not necessary to be a seer in order to predict that realization of the law . . . in the projected form will be a magnificent tombstone on the eternal grave of public organizations."[125]

In general, Moscow industrialists had begun to change their minds about labor unions. After their endorsement of the workers' right to organize in 1905, the December Uprising had led to a mood in which the city's capitalists largely opposed unions and welcomed their suppression.[126] But, paralleling N. I. Guchkov's own evolution, in 1914 the Moscow Society of Mill and Factory Owners recognized the existence of unions and indicated willingness to negotiate with them, though this did not occur widely.[127] The liberalism was faulty and incomplete, but a clear trend had been established.

The city's industrial leaders were willing to compromise with the labor movement in other ways. Instead of celebrating May Day by arresting workers, Moscow factory owners decided in 1914 that May 1 should simply be declared a holiday. Once again, they cited western European experience, where the creation of a holiday had already weakened demonstrations. A memorandum of the Moscow Society of Mill and Factory Owners stated, "It is our deep conviction that suppression of May Day is an unnecessary and fruitless struggle." Industrialists "cannot and should not permit the development of antagonism between the working class and themselves."[128] To achieve that goal, further compromises with the labor movement would have been necessary. However, neither the central government nor the St. Petersburg Society of Mill and Factory Owners could accept the proposal to make May 1 a holiday.[129] Relations between the Moscow and Petersburg factory owners' societies had become so bad over such issues by September 1912 that the board of the Petersburg group forbade its members to give their Muscovite peers any information about strikes in the imperial capital.[130] The Petersburgers' closer dependence on the central government and its industrial orders, in contrast to the Muscovites' greater independence, helped make the former more conservative.

Riabushinskii and another prominent Moscow industrialist, A. V. Konovalov, were able to establish contact with leftists, including Bolsheviks, in early 1914. The businessmen promised cooperation and money in the struggle against the government.[131] Of course, this was largely an arrangement of convenience for both sides.

Radicalism increased among Moscow's workers, just as the industrialists had feared it would. But, as labor organizers and workers themselves said on several occasions, this was a result of state policy, which had cut off opportunity for moderate development. In October 1906 the Moscow Bolsheviks announced, "The government has closed the path of peaceful struggle to the proletariat for the benefit of the capitalists."[132] The Bolsheviks' Moscow Committee on Arranging the Work of Labor Unions resolved in June 1908, "Under existing political conditions legal direction of the economic struggle is impossible. . . . It is essential to form illegal fighting centers of the trade unions."[133] A member of the city's Cooks' Society remarked that the workers' organizations were "trying here and there to move to open struggle, but this way is practiced more and more rarely."[134] In 1910 the journal of the Cooks' Society had glowed about the new legal possibilities for organization and publication. They signified that "Russian life is moving forward, and nothing will stop its movement." The editors were confident of the "final victory of labor," which would come after the system of "administrative pressure" changed.[135] Yet by 1913 the mood of the cooks had shifted, and the editors of their new journal were forced by the rank and file members to sharpen its tone regarding the class struggle.[136] Much sentiment existed among Moscow workers for choosing the path of liberal evolution in the labor movement, but this choice was blocked by state practice.

Despite the claim of the local Bolsheviks that ending any "peaceful struggle" by organized labor was a state policy favoring the capitalists, many of the city's industrial leaders were coming to realize again by 1912, as they had in 1905, that it was not at all to their benefit to deny the workers any real legal means of struggle. Mounting labor militancy after Lena had compelled many important Moscow business leaders and other spokesmen of the elite to urge greater concessions and recognition for labor. Capitalists could also see certain cases in which a liberal program would have obviated strikes, for example the walkouts in print shops and related factories in September 1913 over the issue of government repression of the workers' press,[137] as well as the simultaneous tram strike. Important city figures had reached a parting of the ways with the state on how to deal with the working class.

Whatever the inclination of Moscow's workers to accept liberal solutions, it may have been enhanced by other kinds of support the city's *obshchestvo* offered them. The various municipal employment services aided thousands of Muscovites. One worker participant in the labor movement recalled that in 1906–1907, under the auspices of the oddly titled Moscow Museum of Support for Labor, free or inexpensive legal help was available for unions and their members. The museum sent lawyers to any union that needed them. It also had a medical staff of about fifty doctors, dentists, and midwives, though it is not clear whether these charged for their services. In addition, the organization passed out coupons to union members to pay for visits to other doctors, which cost only twenty-five kopecks.[138]

The many educational, recreational, and transportation opportunities the city government made available to lower class people in Moscow (to be discussed in subsequent chapters) may have engendered some feelings of support for the liberal position. There is no record that a worker ever stood up and said how much he liked the liberals or how glad he was that they were on the scene to lead him to a bright future. However, there are some indications that liberal ideas were attractive to labor. In 1909 M. M. Novikov, a professor at Moscow Imperial University and a member of the city duma, organized a Society for the Guardianship of School Children in the Butryskii district. With evident satisfaction Novikov later recalled how the group once staged a play and party for the children at Christmas: "Upon seeing this paradise for children, many of the parents' eyes filled with tears of tender emotion." More such societies followed, he claimed, until there was a whole network of them across Moscow.[139]

Ironically, the Bolshevik newspaper *Pravda* produced virtually the same assessment of other children's activities in the city, in this case promoted by another creation of the liberal intelligentsia. In January 1912 the Moscow Society for the Arrangement of Generally Accessible Entertainment threw a party for workers' children, and in March it hosted a "children's morning." *Pravda's* writer maintained, "It is not necessary, of course, to state with what pleasure the worker-listeners, their families and children went to these affairs. This was not just relaxation for them, it was a holiday." This society also sponsored lectures on the history of the national economy, syndicates and trusts, industrial crises, and other subjects. Although by 1912 the president and members of the board were workers, the Society had been founded by "liberal *burzhui*" and *intelligenty*.[140] In this case the workers welcomed an organization, tailored to their needs, which liberals had created.

Like Lenin, *Pravda* sometimes worried that liberal programs might attract the support of workers. An editorial of April 1912 implied this concern:

> Is it true that management and enlightened owners will take care of the needs of the working class, if only the working class will display its well-intentioned patience and feed on the warm hope that the heavenly kingdom will come by itself?
>
> No! "No pain, no gain," [*pod lezhachii kamen' voda ne techet*] says the proverb. "[If] the child doesn't cry, the mother doesn't understand," but the evil stepmother, we add, doesn't want to understand.[141]

Surely the editors would have felt no need to warn readers about the "evil step-mother," the "enlightened" or liberal spokesmen, if there had been no workers taken in by her soothing words.

Pravda's anxiety on this point was even more apparent in an article of early 1914 on courses for adults. Sponsored by liberal *intelligenty* to provide education that state programs did not, such courses had appeared in a number of Russian towns (they will be discussed in Chapter 7).

> The cultural-educational institutions of the society of popular universities have enjoyed a certain popularity among workers up to this time. Unfortunately, not everyone correctly evaluates the educational role of these institutions and the true character of the persons standing at the head of these organizations. Conscious workers understand the hypocrisy. However, there are not a few people who sincerely believe in the democratization of these institutions. Especially sinful in this regard are people who have not fully freed themselves from the influence of liberal bourgeois ideology and are therefore incapable of coming to grips with liberal phraseology.[142]

The Moscow city government had gone well beyond the privately-run Society of Popular Universities to create a municipal People's University and to sponsor other courses for adults (described hereafter). These institutions spread liberal bourgeois ideology even further among local workers, who attended them in some numbers.

Other articles in *Pravda* also imply that the Bolsheviks feared the influence of liberal programs, especially in Moscow. In January 1914 the paper warned its readers "not to count for a minute on the firmness or principledness of the liberals." Labor could rely only on its own organizing ability.[143]

Municipal initiatives sometimes put the radicals in an awkward position. After the city opened its new employment bureau in early 1914, *Pravda* described it as having "warm, comfortable quarters" with an "inexpensive buffet." The account remarked, "A series of extraordinary sessions of Moscow labor union boards took place, to consider the question of further tactics in the struggle for participation by union representatives in the administration" of the bureau.[144] The establishment of the labor office gave radicals the choice of approving a venture by their rivals for the favor of the working class or disdaining something of immediate value for it. This dilemma has been a classic problem for radical movements in the face of a strong liberal response; either way they choose, would-be revolutionaries run the risk of boosting support for the liberals. In Russia the state hampered the liberals' programs and played into the radicals' hands.

Of course, one of *Pravda*'s key purposes was to castigate liberals and educate workers about class antagonism, so the newspaper may have been setting up a straw man in speaking of workers' affinity for the views of their social superiors. But the Bolshevik message regarding Moscow seems too often sounded to be based on nothing more than a desire to raise consciousness; it seems more likely that *Pravda* had identified an important strain of thought among Moscow workers.

Moscow industrialists had many reasons to become more moderate toward the workers' movement by 1912–1914. The problem of trying to do business in the face of low internal demand was one factor that promoted their dissatisfaction with government policy, but this seems less important than other features of the Russian political and economic landscape. Above all, the increasing fear that another 1905 was brewing prompted the city's capitalists to offer liberal solutions to workers. It was clear that the tsarist policy of repression and paternalism was no longer adequate. Although many of the industrial elite's ideas remained on paper, even when they could have been applied by the men who developed them, it seemed only a matter of time before more were put into practice. This prospect is evident in such behavior as widespread refusal to fine workers for strikes after Lena,[145] despite the endorsement of such punishment by the Moscow Society of Mill and Factory Owners, and in the meetings between some industrialists and socialists in 1914.

It is not true that the city's capitalists were unprepared "even to recognize the legitimacy of the workers' economic struggle."[146] A significant portion of Moscow's industrialists had taken important steps toward living with that struggle and the means of waging it, unions. The city's employers did "associate themselves with the workers' demands for political freedom," and they tried to "capitalize on the mobilization of workers" for their own purposes. But in this trend much more was at stake for Moscow's business and municipal leaders than a struggle against "gentry dominance,"[147] though that was important. The city's liberals felt that the entire future of the country hung in the balance, and they were right. Because of the stakes involved, they were deeply agitated after 1912.

Liberals also increasingly expressed their belief that compromise on labor issues was part of a much larger package of reforms that were essential if the country was to develop its economy properly and avoid revolution. In late 1912 the Kadet party drafted a bill for the State Duma that made trade union rights a key part of broader legal reforms relating to freedom of expression and equality for women.[148] We have already seen how leading spokesmen for Moscow's industrial elite made the same kind of connection between workers' rights and the country's stability. State policy toward workers and their organizations became a focal point for liberal dissent and pushed business leaders to develop their alternative scenarios faster than occurred in other countries; we could compare, for example, the willingness of Moscow's business elite to recognize unions and meet workers' demands on the eve of the war with American industrialists' vehement opposition to organized labor, extending into the 1930s. The pressures of 1912–1914 prompted Moscow's liberals to pay keen attention to the experience of their peers abroad and their apparent success in taming the workers' movement; the whole Western liberal experience became more attractive, both politically and economically. Even the Moscow Octobrists revealed something of this sentiment, as *Golos Moskvy* showed in 1914.

As for the city's workers, they remained considerably less radical than their counterparts in St. Petersburg. Available estimates of the numbers involved in strikes and demonstrations in the capitals after Lena are consistently much higher for Petersburg than for Moscow. For example, in all of 1912's political and economic strikes, an estimated 400,000–500,000 turned out in Petersburg, compared to 120,000–125,000 in Moscow. The scale of the difference is similar for 1913 and July 1914, when street fighting broke out in Petersburg but Moscow remained calm. The compiler of these estimates writes, "Admittedly, this is a crude yardstick of the intensity of the unrest in Russia's two capitals. Nonetheless, it is revealing."[149]

Many factors helped produce these differences between Moscow and St. Petersburg. Among them were the greater activity of radicals in the imperial capital, the existence of a socialist newspaper there, and a higher concentration of skilled, often radical workers such as metallists. The closer connections of Moscow's peasant immigrants to their home villages, stemming from the fact that they usually traveled shorter distances to the city than Petersburg's newcomers did, may have retarded the growth of working class consciousness.

In trying to assess the overall mood of Moscow's workers by the eve of the war, one must conclude that the picture is highly mixed. On the one hand, Bolshevik influence was rising; on the other, the total number of strikers and demonstrators was far from overwhelming, especially compared to the numbers involved in St. Petersburg. The radicalism that did exist in Moscow was largely a product of state policy, not of local industrialists' practice, which was becoming more conciliatory toward workers. The Petersburg owners were less flexible and more inclined to rely on the state for protection, as a result of their closer connections to it. In the imperial capital both local and national practice added to workers' unrest; in Moscow one of those sources of discontent decreased in importance.

Some of the differences in workers' behavior between the two cities must have resulted from the different programs available to them outside the workplace. Lower-class attitudes depended on the degree of overall integration into city life. The next chapters explore other policies of the Moscow municipal government and the results for the city's people.

6

Municipal Services

Besides ferocious measures against libraries in general, rules that are one
hundred times more restrictive are promulgated *against* popular libraries! This is the scandalous policy of promoting popular *ignorance*, the
scandalous policy of gentry landowners, who desire to make the country
primitive [*odichanie strany*].

Lenin, January 1914[1]

Robert Johnson has recently written of the "closed world of the factory" in Moscow at the turn of the nineteenth century, in which workers were forced to live
according to strict rules drawn up by management. Owners discouraged workers
in many cases from leaving their quarters at night; this together with distance to
entertainment in the city and lack of time, money, and appropriate clothing kept
many factory hands from ever attending a cultural event. One survey taken at the
Tsindel' textile mill in Moscow in the 1890s revealed that only 35 percent of the
workers had been to a concert, theater, public lecture, museum, or circus.[2] Similar
conditions and lack of opportunity for recreation prevailed among groups such
as the laundresses, domestic servants, bakers, and artisanal apprentices described
earlier. In short, the majority of Moscow's residents did not often have access to
formal, organized entertainment. This helped keep their connections with and
integration in city life at a minimum.

Given the budgetary constraints of the period and the existence of more
urgent problems in the city, it is not surprising that the municipality devoted only
a small amount of attention or money to the development of public recreational
facilities or libraries. Yet some innovations and substantial expansion of opportunities for the public did occur in this area, and the city government displayed
a concern for raising the general level of culture among the lower classes. The
question of the city fathers' motivation in promoting cultural opportunities, that
is, to what extent programs were designed to promote stability by integrating the
population into city life and to what extent they were simply intended to benefit
people, will be explored in this chapter.

As described earlier, housing remained one of the worst problems of the city
in 1914. The local government was aware of its scale and made a start toward
solving it but was hampered by the lack of funds and by its own belief that public
housing or shelters should produce income. Modernization of attitudes among
municipal officials, in terms of recognizing their responsibility for this question,
also proceeded slowly and haltingly. The greatest progress in housing occurred in

the construction of city nightlodgings, never intended as a permanent solution to the crisis. City programs in this regard thus affected only a tiny portion of Moscow's people.

Recreation

For the right price, any kind of entertainment was available in Moscow. Sometimes the price was not particularly high; for a few kopecks poor people played a kind of roulette in which they bet that a top would land on certain squares marked on a board. In other games they tried to put their fingers into a ring moved rapidly about by a gambler or to guess which of three cards he shuffled was a face card.[3]

Some seats in theaters were inexpensive. In 1906 the lowest-priced admissions to the Bol'shoi were twenty-eight kopecks for ballet and thirty-two kopecks for opera. The Malyi Theater charged as little as thirty-six kopecks for drama, the Novyi ten kopecks for drama and ballet, and the Korsh only five kopecks for some presentations.[4] All but the poorest stratum of Moscow's population could have afforded such prices occasionally. Yet the lack of time and decent clothing and a dislike for the diversions of the *obshchestvo* kept many lower class people away.

The city became actively involved in presenting entertainment for the general population. Starting in 1892, the municipal government subsidized summer concerts in Sokol'niki Park on the northeast side of Moscow. In 1910, for example, the duma voted five thousand rubles for the program.[5] By 1913 concerts were also given each night from April 28 to September 1 in the center of town and at other locations one or more nights a week.[6]

Another program begun by the city government before the war was the People's House. Started in 1904, at first it produced mostly operas, with full choruses. Later it formed an acting company, composed mainly of amateurs. The city decided that the repertoire of the company would be chosen for "artistic quality and importance" and commented, "It would not be appropriate to evaluate too narrowly the esthetic taste and capacity for understanding of the visitors to the People's House." Admission to the programs cost from seven kopecks to one ruble ten kopecks,[7] ensuring that all but the poorest people could attend.

The People's House also had a library, tea room, and lecture hall. Apparently it was successful; the city planned in 1915 to open a whole network of such houses, twenty-four in all.[8] The difficulties of the war years forced cancellation of the project. After the revolution, however, they reappeared in a new guise, the socialist clubs. One Western scholar who has written about Moscow workers in 1917 noted that "there was not much difference between the activities of circles centered in Peoples' Houses before the revolution, and those of the new socialist clubs created afterwards."[9]

The city stated the essential goal of the People's House program quite frankly in its 1915 plan: sobriety. Alcohol remained the favorite method of escape for Moscow's poor before 1917. Cheap taverns catered to workers and others and provided important social opportunities along with drinks.[10]

Civic leaders in and outside of the municipal government developed a strong penchant for lower class sobriety. In one section of Moscow well-to-do residents formed a "guardianship for popular sobriety," which ran its own People's House.

Here entertainment was offered year round, at a charge of ten kopecks to one ruble sixty kopecks.[11]

If the lower classes were kept busy and entertained, so the theory went, they would probably not drink so much. Perhaps the approach was paternalistic, but it provided some sophisticated presentations. And sober people, too, could have benefited from the activities in the People's Houses. In any event, these Moscow houses did not have the same kind of political goal as the workers' clubs organized by the police before 1905. There was no attempt to persuade workers to be more docile or more faithful to the tsarist regime.

Moscow was not alone in its support of People's Houses before the war. St. Petersburg had perhaps the most advanced arrangement, a house that had its own observatory and theater and offered lectures, classes for adults, and exhibitions. Other houses were located or planned in six other towns.[12]

Public parks also drew increasing attention and money from the Moscow duma in this period. In 1911 the city was still far behind most of western Europe in respect to park space.[13] Around this time, however, Moscow began to enlarge its park system rapidly. It constructed at least five new squares in the years 1911–1913, all in formerly dusty areas. In 1911–1912 three large new parks were opened and many improvements were made to existing ones. The money allocated to the development of parks and greenery in the city also increased dramatically in the same span, from 123,000 rubles in 1907 to 260,000 rubles in 1912,[14] about 0.6 percent of the municipal budget. In addition, the *uprava* worked out a plan in 1912 to plant trees on all Moscow streets, a total of 39,000 by 1916. The scheme called for eight more squares and almost a million new shrubs and flowers.[15] Needless to say, the war ruined these plans.

The first municipal recreation for children also appeared in this period. Summer street games were held for the first time in 1912, twice a week for an hour and a half in twenty-four places around the city. At least several thousand children took part, and in the next year over 2,700 played daily.[16] After that came the war.

In 1912 the city government also organized excursions to the countryside for children; about seven thousand participated.[17] A year earlier the city opened its first playground, built by children under adult direction. The primary goal of this facility and of the street games and excursions was to improve children's health.[18] Though it never said so, the municipality may well have had a secondary goal of steering children away from criminal activity or heavy drinking (noted among

TABLE 6-1.   Square Sazhens of Parks and
Public Gardens per Capita, 1911, in Selected
Cities

Berlin	1.6	Paris	0.3
Vienna	1.1	Moscow	0.1[a]
London	1.22		

[a] Includes the Kremlin garden, then administered by the state.

them in Chapter 7). The duma may also have hoped that these measures would help integrate children into society by teaching them to cooperate with adult directors and by instilling in them the feeling that the city government cared about its people.

All of the programs just described largely benefited the poor. The rich had their dachas and other chances to escape the dust and noise of summer; most Muscovites had only city parks. The wealthy and some middle-class citizens could afford to send their children to summer camps, or colonies as they were called then, but the poor had to keep theirs in town. Undoubtedly some poor children returned with their parents to the home villages in summer, but lower class families with children in the city were more often permanently settled there and had fewer strong ties to the countryside than those with no children in Moscow.

Libraries

The public library system was another municipal service available to the whole population but at least potentially of particular value to poor people. The system had two goals: to satisfy the intelligentsia and to "adapt to the interests and desires of readers from the people [*narod*]." In 1916 the city government reported that its libraries were still far from achieving either aim. They "perform neither one nor the other assignment well. The intelligentsia is not satisfied, and the working population uses them little," continued the report.[19]

The document discussed several specific library problems. One was inadequate staff, which meant that readers often had to stand in line for an hour or two to get books, only to find that the ones they wanted had all been taken. This in turn caused readers to order ten to thirty books at once, so that they would not have to return and waste more time. As a result, books were tied up needlessly. And library employees were so harried they had no chance to relate to readers individually.

Another problem specifically concerned workers. In a survey taken among readers in 1915, one respondent stated that many workers avoided the libraries because they wanted to be with their peers and not in places where the intelligentsia went. The library staff feared this might be a widespread attitude.[20] Already by 1912, the municipality had recognized the special needs and poverty of most workers and had reduced, from one ruble to fifty kopecks, the deposit required from them to take books home. The only other group so honored was children.[21]

The 1916 report also noted that, although strapped for funds, the city was trying to improve conditions for the working class in libraries and to attract more of its members. Special evening hours had been arranged, the system was improving its selection of technical materials and belles-lettres, and it was increasing its publicity by putting up posters on streets and in factory offices, cooperatives, and union offices.[22] As late as 1912 only 10–15 percent of city library users were "artisans and workers."[23] Keenly aware of this problem and concerned with its solution, the city attempted to reach the working class and offer it opportunities for enrichment, without including a political bias.

In 1914 the *uprava* endorsed what it termed the "American philosophy" of libraries: getting a good book should always be as easy as getting a drink in a bar. This implied that the libraries should have little paperwork and low fees; they should be open every day, especially in the evenings; and they should not limit the time of loans too severely or threaten people with fines for overdue books. The *uprava* noted that Moscow's libraries were too poor in books, funds, and personnel to achieve these goals.[24] In this case, as in other areas of recreation, the city government certainly hoped to divert poor people from alcohol and to attract them to cultural pursuits. Ultimately, the lower classes might thus become less violent, more sober, more hard working, and better integrated into urban life.

Before the war Moscow also operated a central library, the Pushkin. Lectures on history, literature, science, and music, as well as concerts, were given in its auditorium. All facilities and programs were free. There were also three municipal libraries that lent books; these were free and open each day. Four other free libraries were open three days a week, two free reading rooms were open daily, and one library that charged five kopecks per visit was open two days.[25]

Besides these city facilities, a private group called The Society for Free Popular Libraries ran fourteen branches in Moscow before the war. This system had more success attracting workers than the city's did. In 1913 it reported that about 50 percent of its 11,718 users in the previous year were workers. It seems that these reading rooms were places where workers could find their peers, and that they did not hesitate to use them, although the portion of Moscow's workers visiting them was quite small.

Realizing the city library system was inadequate, the *uprava* in 1912 drew up an ambitious plan for improvement. One large library would be located in the center of the city, while 20 somewhat smaller regional libraries would be built in various locations around town; the bottom level of the system would consist of about 250 small branch facilities.[26] Implementation of the plan did not begin before the war.

It is typical of the city's activities and approaches to problems in these years that the plans it made for library improvement were on a large scale—as large, relative to the existing system, as the earlier plans for elementary schools (Chapter 7 covers this subject). And, as with the schools, there is no reason to believe that the city would not have carried out its project. Moscow's city government was engaged in an almost frenzied expansion of its services and programs after about 1910: new parks, a million more plants for them, new schools, courses, tram lines, and more. The further plans the city made were even more ambitious. To some extent the larger number of progressists in the municipal duma after 1908 might explain the new pace of improvement. But it is likely that expanding city income made duma members in general feel that the municipality could do more, while the sense that success was in sight for some of its programs, for example in achieving general accessibility to elementary education and reasonably good coverage of the city by tram lines, caused it to believe that the time had come for development in other areas. One ultimate goal of these programs was better integration of the lower classes in Moscow's life and thus avoidance of further social unrest.

Yet in its library program, as in so many other activities, the city government found that its approach ran counter to the beliefs of the state and its rural supporters. Thus, in Moscow's case the following charge by two Soviet authors is simply wrong:

> In the years of reaction [1907–1917], *zemstvo* and city officials, frightened by revolution, worked together with the tsarist autocracy against the democratic demands of the masses in the area of library affairs.[27]

If anything, Moscow's city fathers were stimulated by revolution into greater attempts to satisfy the masses, though efforts in this direction antedated 1905. Certainly municipal officials did not hold the same views as the central government on libraries and did not work with it to hamper library development.

Blocking the spread of libraries for the people and controlling the reading matter in them were state policies for many years. In 1884 the government decreed that only books on an official list would be permitted in public libraries and reading rooms.[28] After 1890 lists of acceptable books were issued by the Ministry of Education.

In 1907, before its period of relative liberalism closed, the government abolished such lists. Theoretically all libraries then had to pay attention only to the official censorship and avoid all books and other materials printed illegally. But the state still controlled libraries tightly; all of them had to have official permission to open. Judging from resolutions adopted at the First All-Russian Library Congress in 1911, police sometimes closed libraries without court orders, undoubtedly under the Extraordinary Measures. This congress also protested "administrative arbitrariness" toward library employees and demanded that new books be allowed in their facilities "exclusively according to the existing general statute on the press."[29] Thus the police were clearly finding ways around the changes of 1907. By administrative order, according to Soviet scholars, public libraries and those organized by private groups were closed in a whole series of towns and rural areas after 1907.[30] In this period the Viatka provincial *zemstvo* complained to the Senate that police had carried out a "massive removal" of books from village libraries. The Senate replied that *zemstva*, and by extension city governments, had no right to be concerned with social and political issues, and therefore public libraries should hold no books touching upon those areas.[31] Almost any book could be banned under such a broad and vague rule. The state was really saying that only it could determine which social and political viewpoints should be conveyed to the people.

In 1912 the state made its position even more explicit. Minister of Education L. A. Kasso ruled that popular libraries located in schools, the mass of such facilities, had to follow new rules. Now they would be completely under school jurisdiction, which meant that they could acquire only materials approved for public schools by the Ministry of Education. Books allowed under the 1907 rules could be purchased only with permission of the ministry's school inspectors. Under this edict books like Leo Tolstoy's *Resurrection, Uncle Tom's Cabin*, and works on cooperative organizations were removed from some libraries.[32] In certain provinces officials confiscated 40–60 percent of all books.[33] Though Lenin may have gone too far in saying that government policy aimed at creating popular ignorance—for (as Chapter 7 will show) education did spread in Moscow and elsewhere before the war—he was not so far wrong about the libraries. It appears that wherever it felt its actions would not be severely protested, the state did shut down popular libraries after 1907.

All this was approved and promoted by rural conservatives, as Lenin suggested. At the beginning of 1911 a congress of the United Nobility, an organization of the most conservative gentry, unanimously denounced popular libraries; they were "depraving the people" and spreading revolutionary literature. The congress also demanded the reintroduction of official lists of permitted books.[34] For the rural diehards, the way to avoid revolution was to keep new ideas away from the people.

Although there is no record that repressive actions occurred in Moscow's libraries before 1914, and the city's library system did continue to grow until that year, it is important to note that the municipality promoted a course essentially opposite to the position of the state and its conservative allies. The city wanted to attract workers and other lower class citizens to reading, and it never expressed concern about what they read. The urban, liberal approach to avoiding revolution was to open new facilities and opportunities. Only the municipality, not the state, was moving to meet a need that was evident to city officials.[35]

Perhaps the central government did not hamper Moscow's library expansion because it feared alienating the city's Octobrists; it was also simply politically safer to close isolated rural facilities than ones in a large city, where news spreads fast. The volatility of Moscow's workers in 1905 probably also served to stay the government's hand. In any event, state and city library policies stood in sharp contrast to each other.

Despite the intensified efforts of the Moscow municipal government before the war, public recreational and library facilities in the city remained very limited. Nonetheless, the duma had established a clear upward trend and commitment to their improvement. The municipality had become highly visible in this field and had involved many thousands of residents in its programs. A number of its ideas were enthusiastically received in Moscow, judging by attendance. Thus the city may have created a feeling among Muscovites that it was doing something positive for them, particularly in contrast to the inaction or repression of the state.

Housing

The Moscow duma long recognized the extent of housing problems in the city, from before the 1899 survey of apartments (discussed in Chapter 1) through a report it made in 1915, which noted that workers and other low income groups had "unbelievably bad living conditions in economic, sanitary, and hygienic respects."[36] In response to the housing crisis the city government concentrated its efforts on public flophouses, or "nightlodging houses," as they were called then.

The history of such houses in Russia dates from 1872, when police in the city of Viatka opened one in a precinct station. Odessa followed suit in 1875, and the first city overnight shelter was built in Saratov in 1876. That city had six houses by 1906 with a total capacity of 1,100 places, of which 443 were on the floor. In 1912 one writer described them as very dirty, uncomfortable, overcrowded, full of bedbugs, and primary sources of disease for the city.[37]

The Moscow government opened its first nightlodging in 1879, strictly for the purpose of reducing the spread of infectious disease. By lessening overcrowding among the poor, disinfecting their clothing, and providing baths and decent food, the municipality hoped to improve resistance to disease. Thus the origin of housing reform in Moscow was the same as in England earlier in the century, where the upper classes also realized that poor housing conditions bred diseases that killed regardless of social standing. Since better health was the object, Moscow's first nightlodging was free, at least in its early years. Its initial capacity was 510 people but by 1886 it held 1,305. A second house opened in 1903 with a capacity of 350; in 1906 it moved and expanded to hold 400–500.[38]

By 1912 there were six city nightlodgings with a combined capacity of 5,650. In the two previous years these had provided space for an average of 4,857 per night.[39] Despite this capacity, the city houses were often overcrowded and forced to turn people away. Khitrov Market and other private flophouses still took in more people than did the city, about 7,500 per night.[40] Moscow had made no progress toward eliminating these sources of disease and crime.

Compared to the privately-run facilities, the city lodgings were quite attractive. In 1906 at the opening of a new public shelter with 300 spaces, 400 people appeared on the first night. The city houses turned away 55,823 people in 1913.[41] Thus the municipality had entered an area in which there was a huge, unsatisfied demand; the duma was able to make only modest strides toward meeting it.

Conditions in the municipal lodgings varied widely. Most had no special health facilities, but some had receiving clinics with doctors on duty. One house even had a bath hall and washing machines, presumably operated by the staff, on each corridor. Some of the houses had cafeterias and tea rooms where a dinner of cabbage soup and porridge cost five kopecks. Occasionally private contributions enabled the city to give out free meals. Tea and a pound of bread were sold in the tea rooms for two kopecks; these low prices were subsidized by the city.

Contemporary photographs of the city houses show long rows of narrow wooden sleeping platforms, each separated from its neighbors by a partition perhaps a foot high. The lodgers spread blankets and pillows on the boards. The houses were cleaned thoroughly every day and disinfected; thus their main advantages over private flophouses were that they were much cleaner and less crowded, a result of the city policy of turning away excess applicants.

Women comprised about 15 percent of the city nightlodgings' population in 1913, while children made up less than 0.15 percent.[42] The municipal government allowed women in only three of the six houses, and in 1912 it had considered barring them from one of these because of their "specific" influence there. It seems that many of them were prostitutes, an indication that this profession was more widespread in Moscow than the number of legal, registered practitioners alone, 1,611 in 1910,[43] would suggest.

The municipality charged money for accommodations in its shelters. In 1911 the *uprava* stated that providing free quarters to able-bodied persons was undesirable from the "economic or moral point of view." While it might be advantageous from a health standpoint, it could also lead to the growth of begging and parasitism. The low cost, from three to five kopecks per night, "could hardly overburden even the poorest people."[44] In March of the same year the duma voted to raise the lodging fees by one to three kopecks according to the quality of the house, stipulating that they should be free during epidemics or especially cold weather.[45]

In general the city did not provide free services in its housing programs. It believed that users should be made to pay something, as a protection of general moral standards. Moscow's government was determined to avoid the appearance of being prepared to support anyone who was not disabled. The only exceptions to the policy of charging fees for city services were some recreational programs and elementary education. In these cases the municipality was trying to entice adults and children away from alcohol and crime as well as to promote their welfare.

Most of Moscow's nightlodging problem in this period was related to Khitrov Market. Here the city's attention focused not only on problems of health and overcrowding but also on moral issues. An official municipal publication commented on this aspect in 1913.

> Tens of thousands of workers pass yearly through Khitrov Market, becoming infected there physically and morally and carrying this infection with them. Many honorable workers fall into the ready snares of the exploiting part of Khitrov Market, becoming drunkards and parasites.[46]

Moscow's ruling elite thus continued to deplore the problem of drunkenness among the lower classes, but it recognized that this moral crisis had identifiable social roots.

The history of the municipality's efforts to rectify the situation in Khitrov Market is a miniature study of city-state relations. In 1898 the special commission on Khitrov of the Imperial Technical Society stated its conclusions.

> It is impossible to correct the Khitrov system while the basic evil—the leasing system—exists, transferring all responsibility for the harm it does from the property owners to the leaseholders, whom it is forbidden [by the state] to fine.[47]

That is, Khitrov was a vast warren of cot-closet apartments. One person, generally poor, rented an apartment and then sublet space in it to even poorer people, crowding in as many subtenants as possible, to make ends meet. Khitrov was simply the worst such area in Moscow. This system was largely beyond the legal reach of the city, as will be shown. Only the police could levy fines for overcrowding, and their coverage in the area was spotty.

In 1903 the Moscow governor-general again called the duma's attention to conditions in Khitrov. He informed the duma that improvement there should be one of its primary concerns and was its legal obligation. In this case the administration's interest in ameliorating a social problem was doubtless stimulated, at least in part, by the role Khitrov played in the spread of disease.

Chapter 2 has already told a portion of the story from this point on: how the duma petitioned the government in 1903 to allow it to establish strict rules on building and maintaining flophouses in the Market area, the repetition of the request in 1907, and finally the reply from the Ministry of Internal Affairs that the duma could issue such rules only after a general reorganization of city government and the City Statute.

In 1910 the city decided anyway that it did have some power to control the flophouses. The *uprava* reported that the city government could issue regulations on various subjects, including fire safety, sanitation if there were tea rooms or cafeterias in the houses, and sewers and outhouses. The basis for such rules was the city's right to take measures to prevent and control infectious disease. The duma thereupon resolved that all flophouses in Moscow should be clean, have separate sleeping quarters for males and females, at least one cubic *sazhen* of air per person, and a separate bed for each lodger. It also set minimum requirements for the size of beds or sleeping platforms.[48] Enforcement depended on the police, of course, and was not thorough.

The city tried again in 1912 to improve the situation in Khitrov by planning a nightlodging there with space for three thousand. This time the minister of internal affairs blocked the project, giving no reason.[49] His action obstructed the city's general plan for the Market area but did not halt it completely. The duma had also decided to build free baths and a cafeteria there with a capacity of one thousand, to offer some free clothing, and to construct an "apparatus for disinfecting clothes." One city publication reported that "toward the end of 1912 the larger part of these resolutions had already been realized and the rest were being put into effect."[50]

The city's problems with the state in regard to Khitrov were not yet over. In 1913 the duma appropriated 316,000 rubles to build a nightlodging with 1,488 spaces. The *gradonachal'nik* vetoed the project, giving no reason, and it was not begun before the war.[51]

In another part of town the city ran into much the same problem. It purchased land and a building in 1910 and appropriated money to convert the structure into a nightlodging, but the administration refused to permit the plan, saying the site was too close to the provincial jail. In 1912 the city tried to obtain permission to build a small shelter on the part of the land furthest from the jail and find another site in the area for a second house.[52] This did not happen before the war.

In this long saga of the city's struggle with private flophouses and their attendant evils, the duma was not completely blocked by the government at every turn, but the whole process was prolonged and made much more difficult by the state's interference. It is doubtful that the central government had any malicious purpose in its tactics. As noted in Chapter 2, the state saw the issue in terms of the "widening of the rights" allowed to cities. The regime was simply not willing to permit municipalities great latitude in dealing with local social problems. Particularly when faced with a somewhat rambunctious and vocal city government like Moscow's, dominated after 1912 by the detested Kadets and progressists, the state was not inclined to give up any of its prerogatives. The result was slower improvement than the city could have achieved under a more flexible national government.

The latter's interest in taking its own steps to rectify Russian housing conditions was strictly limited. The Soviet scholar Iu. I. Kir'ianov found that there were only two central government projects concerned with housing before the war. The first, formulated by the Ministry of Finance in 1902, directed its attention to the improvement of factory barracks and spoke of the "urgent need for the construction of housing for underprivileged groups in the urban population." The second project was a bill, apparently presented to the State Duma, on "sanitary safeguards for housing." Both ideas "remained on paper" on the eve of the war.[53]

Nonetheless, the tsarist administration in Moscow was not always strictly backward in regard to nightlodgings or housing in general. It also exercised its power on the side of amelioration. In 1903 the Moscow governor-general issued sanitary regulations for all housing in the city, including rules on cleanliness, space per person, and number of persons allowed in certain buildings. These seem to have been enforced only sporadically at best, judging by the many reports of continued overcrowding in the city, but from time to time the police did make inspections, levy fines, or close lodgings altogether (as shown in Chapter 4). In 1910 the *gradonachal'nik* went so far as to close parts of a Khitrov flophouse for overcrowding,[54] but this probably only forced the inhabitants into similar housing elsewhere.

A particular concern of the tsarist administration of Moscow during this period was housing conditions in factories and artisanal establishments. The Moscow Office on Factory Affairs, headed by the *gradonachal'nik*, issued rules in 1906 on the construction and maintenance of sleeping quarters for workers. The regulations included specifications for bedding, washrooms, and ventilation.[55]

The duma for its own part passed some rules governing living conditions for factory and artisanal workers, on the basis of its right to take measures for the prevention of disease. As of April 1879, factory owners were required to provide one cubic *sazhen* of space in quarters for workers. This was also true in workshops, where quarters were further supposed to be light, dry, well ventilated, and well kept. In neither case could quarters be underground or in places "recognizably harmful or impossible."[56]

The police occasionally made inspections to see that all sanitary rules were enforced. In 1906 the *gradonachal'nik* ordered his men to inspect all workshops where apprentices slept to check for violations of the governor-general's 1903 order on their maintenance.[57] This action occurred at a time when tension was again high among the city's workers and artisans. Besides attacks on police, strikes had recently begun in bakeries, printing establishments, and the tram lines. The inspection of workers' and apprentices' housing and new rules on the subject fit into the *gradonachal'nik*'s campaign to reduce working class anger. It may also be that the police believed workers should not have to live like animals.

After 1905 factory housing became a greater object of concern to at least one city duma member. N. A. Tiuliaev, descendant of a merchant family, spoke in the council in 1910 and 1911 on the need to provide municipal housing for workers. He noted that the "movement" of 1905 had given "the most frightful push" to closings of factory dormitories, which had forced workers into apartments. The factory workers were "dark [ignorant] people, in most cases immigrants, who don't know how to orient themselves [to city life], and therefore they get the worst arrangements."[58] Workers were the "most needy class,"[59] Tiuliaev told the duma once, and the city should construct housing for them. In effect, he was saying that the duma should be concerned with a serious, general lack of integration into urban life among Moscow's poor. One year after Tiuliaev's second remark, in 1911, the municipality did adopt an ambitious plan to build inexpensive apartments, discussed below. In an indirect sense, the revolution of 1905 pushed local officials to undertake housing reforms.

However, the city government chose not to try to regulate housing conditions on a broad scale in Moscow. In 1911 the city Commission on Housing Problems decided that strict rules on conditions in cot-closet apartments would only force many to close, pushing thousands of people onto the streets.[60] In view of the extremely tight housing market in the city, the commission was undoubtedly correct. The only effective solution to the problem was to build a great deal more housing, either privately or publicly. Beginning in the early twentieth century, the municipality began to attack the housing situation by using private contributions to build apartments and by assuming the management of existing charitable structures.

The largest of the funds available for this purpose had been left to the city in 1901 by a wealthy merchant, G. G. Solodovnikov. Largely because of the inertia of his executors, only one and a half million rubles, one-fifth of the bequest, had been spent by 1908.[61] Two buildings of "inexpensive" apartments, one for families and one for single people, were finally opened in January 1909. And, as one observer wrote, "The question arises of the extent to which these apartments can be called inexpensive." The city charged ten rubles per room per month, which the writer thought a fair price considering a "whole series of conveniences" available to the residents.[62]

The relatively high cost ensured that the occupants were not from the city's poorest strata. *Russkie Vedomosti* reported that in the first group of renters for the married housing were eighty-three teachers, forty-three shop clerks, thirty-one other clerks, thirty-one tailors, twenty-five white-collar employees, and five workers.[63] In 1912 one city source stated that the Solodovnikov houses were "built luxuriously" and that the approximately two thousand people occupying them were mostly clerks, office workers, and others from similar occupations. The same publication lamented that these buildings constituted a step in the right direction but were only a drop in the bucket of Moscow's housing needs.[64] The same point, as well as the popularity of the houses, is illustrated by the fact that in 1912 the waiting list for them contained five thousand names.[65]

After much pressure on Solodovnikov's executors, they agreed to allow the city to spend the remaining money, which had grown by then to about thirteen million rubles, on low-cost housing. In the years 1915–1916 the municipality purchased a "series of buildings" for that purpose.[66]

The city government adopted a large-scale general plan in 1911 to build inexpensive apartments with its own money. This project represented a revolution in the attitudes of local officials, for the new dwellings would be run on a nonprofit basis.[67] For the first time the municipality had moved away from its strict business ethic in regard to housing. The magnitude of the problem had forced modernization in outlook. Altogether, sixty apartment houses with a capacity of 39,000 people were to be constructed. In 1912, according to one city publication, the duma planned to build three houses on a trial basis but did not because of disagreements over selection of land. Another source states that in 1914 the duma decided to build cheap apartments and had a project prepared to construct one building. The advent of the war scuttled the idea.[68] The latter two accounts cite the old basic principle of municipal housing: it should pay for itself in terms of both construction and upkeep. Therefore these quarters, too, would not have been for the poorest Muscovites. This contradiction in the sources may indicate that debate and vacillation continued in the duma over housing policy, although such problems did not appear in the stenographic records of council sessions

before the outbreak of the war. Nevertheless, all these plans suggest a new willingness on the part of the municipality to attack the root of the housing problem
with permanent facilities. Modernization of attitudes within the city government
continued on its erratic but generally positive course.

In 1914 the city gave another indication that it would begin to construct subsidized housing, though only for municipal workers. A special conference on
housing for them took place in February of that year. The president and vice-
president of the duma's housing commission and the heads of all municipal enterprises attended. The conference suggested building housing for tram workers first:
barracks for the lowest paid, rooms with cots and common kitchens for the next
echelon, and two- or three-room apartments with separate kitchens for married
workers and their families.[69] This new interest among city officials in the housing
needs of their workers appeared only after the tram and gas works strike of 1913.

Transportation

The important issue in transportation policy in this era was service versus revenue. To what extent could the city government lower fares, expand hours, or
extend lines to areas that did not promise to return net income on investment?
This question was of critical importance to Moscow's poor, who often depended
on the trams to get from their dwellings on the outskirts to their jobs in or near
the center. The municipality's policy began to shift more toward service before
World War I, though the duma clung to the badly needed revenue from the trams
as the largest single part of city income. Many of the city government's modernization efforts depended on this source.

M. A. Shtromberg, who published a book on the Moscow trams in 1913,
believed the city duma thought first of profits and second of service to the public.
The council would not build lines into the less densely populated areas of the city
or to the suburbs, he claimed, because such routes brought in less money.[70] However, building lines that were heavily instead of lightly used was also the best use
of limited resources.

Another contemporary writer made a charge similar to Shtromberg's in 1912.
The city, he maintained, "only built lines to those regions [of the outskirts and
suburbs] within which there would be a steady and more or less significant flow
of passengers." The uprava and duma sometimes carried this principle to a "clear
contradiction of the interests of the city population." However, the same author
noted that the duma in 1912 decided to build a line to the village of Bogorodskoe
even though it did not promise to be especially profitable. The recently completed
line to the Sparrow Hills was also not likely to make much money; these routes
seemed "to signal a new era in policy."[71]

It appears that once the city had achieved a certain level of service in transportation, it felt it could afford to build into less heavily populated areas. The
principle of service was becoming distinct from and sometimes superior to the
goal of earning revenue. The map shows that as of 1912 tram lines had already
reached the edge of the city at many points around the compass and that new
lines were under construction to reach out in several other places. In the center
the lines were well developed in all directions, though the network was not nearly
as extensive and convenient as, for example, Manchester's.[72] Nevertheless, in its

View of Sukharev Tower, built 1689 by Peter the Great, demolished under the Soviet regime. The tram line had not yet been electrified. Again, note the policeman.

quest for revenue, the Moscow city government had not neglected the poorer areas and had at least begun to serve the entire region. As with every other aspect of municipal life in this period, the city government had to obtain the tsarist administration's approval for new tram lines.[73]

The history of Moscow's streetcar fares in this period also indicates that the primary objective of the system was not always to produce income. In 1901 the city bought one of the two existing horse-drawn tram lines from the Belgian Stock Society, which had constructed them in the late 1870s and operated them since. The municipality retained the two-class fare structure adopted by the concession-aires until 1907, when it changed to a one-class system. Tickets were one and a half kopecks per *versta* (1.06 kilometers), minimum fare five kopecks per zone. This schedule had been used for second class by the Belgian Society.[74]

In 1910 the city adopted a new fare calculation. Until that year the trams had begun operation at 7 A.M., too late for the many people who started work at that time. The duma then voted to move the beginning time to 6 A.M. and to set a

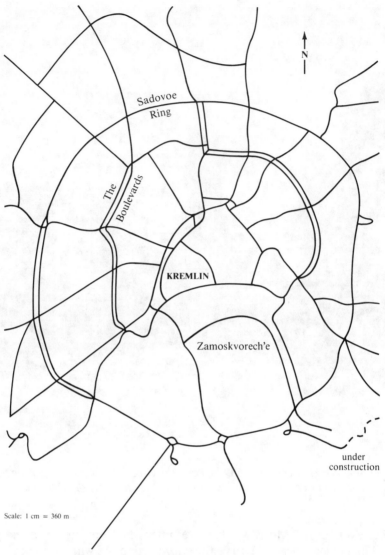

Moscow's tram lines, 1912

(*Source:* Moskovskaia gorodskaia uprava, *Sovremennoe khoziaistvo,* ed. Ippolit
Verner (*M.:* 1913], map following p. 416.)

lower fare of three kopecks per zone for the first hour, in view of the fact that
most users at that time were likely to be poor people.[75] This change followed a
pattern of lowering early morning and evening fares for workers all over western
Europe in the 1890s, an innovation pushed through by municipalities during
negotiations with private companies for tram concessions.[76] Surely Moscow's city
fathers were aware of this trend.

Almost two years after the experiment started, the *uprava* reported that riders
in the first hour were mostly working people: clerks, artisans, seasonal daily laborers, and so forth—"the least well-off class of the population, living for the most

part on the outskirts of the city." These people paid five or six kopecks to get to the center; ten would be too much for their tight budgets. The *uprava* concluded that "the lower fare is of substantial assistance to the poorer class of the population."[77]

On the other hand, one man who had worked as a seasonal construction laborer in Moscow on the eve of the war later recalled that even the post-1910 fares were too expensive for him and his coworkers. He had to travel through six zones, which cost him eighteen kopecks in the morning and thirty in the afternoon. Paid only one and a half rubles per day, he could hardly afford to spend one-third of his income on transportation.[78] It is impossible to determine how typical this situation, which contradicts the *uprava*'s findings, became in Moscow. Given the direction of public policy by 1914, perhaps even this laborer's costs would have decreased in the future. Long tram rides were often not very expensive: to get from Lubianka Square, almost in the heart of town, to Sokol'niki Park cost only ten kopecks at the regular fare in 1914.[79] This sum was still substantial for an unskilled worker, but at least the municipality was moving in the direction of reducing the cost.

In calculating its fares, any urban transportation system has to consider the possibility that it will actually earn less money if it raises fares, and vice versa. If fares climb too high, riders will seek alternate means of transportation. On the other hand, lowering fares may attract new riders. It is worth noting that a private tram company operating in Rouen, France made more money in the 1890s by adopting a special reduced morning fare for workers.[80]

With the lowered ticket prices between 6 and 7 A.M. the Moscow trams undoubtedly still made money during that hour. Income was quite large at all other times of the day, which suggests that all fares could have been lowered without causing an overall loss for the system. And the city would not have attracted nearly as many riders in the first hour as it did without a lower fare. Therefore it seems more than likely that the new policy increased the city's revenue; yet its motives in this instance had more to do with concern about serving people than had been the case previously.

In 1914 the *uprava* suggested that tram fares be raised one kopeck, but the finance commission of the duma refused. This would be, it said,

> a reapportionment of the shortcomings in the collection of the property tax to the predominately poor population for the use of a means of transportation that has become at the present time a vital necessity, which is why it is a monopoly of the city government.[81]

The changes in fare structures and priorities in construction of this period suggest that the duma had indeed begun to regard this statement as an underpinning of its transportation policy.

By 1912 the duma had come to believe that surface transportation alone would not be enough for the city. In March of that year it resolved that a subway was the best means of meeting the growing needs of Moscow and the suburbs. The city government was aware that the state was already considering the same question for Moscow, so it petitioned the Ministry of Finance, which had charge of the matter, not to grant a concession for construction of a subway system in the city without its approval.

The petition received no response, however, and in January 1913 the city learned that the ministry was about to begin considering proposals from several private groups for construction of a Moscow subway. The city government was not invited to participate because the ministry saw the question as pertaining to the central government alone under its exclusive right to build railroads. Moscow officials countered that a subway was much more similar to a tram system than to a railroad and that it clearly fell under the heading of local transportation, but this claim went unheeded.

Again the Moscow duma asked that it be allowed to rule on the proposals but was refused by the director of the department of railways of the ministry. At the last moment, however, the city was permitted to send representatives to the conference. After their strong protests at the meeting, the concessionaires whose plan was chosen agreed that they would not build without agreement from the duma. Negotiations between them and the city went on through the rest of 1913 and into 1914. As in so many other cases, the declaration of war put an end to the project.[82]

While the national government was proceeding on the issue without consulting the municipality, the latter was planning to build a subway on its own. In 1913 it published a pamphlet with detailed plans for an underground system, including stations, a fare structure, connections to tram lines, and a construction schedule. The scheme envisioned the opening in 1917 of three subway lines crossing in the center of town. As part of a master plan to improve transportation, the trams still operating with horse traction in the suburbs would be electrified by the same date.[83]

The city government seemed to be making great progress in transportation on the eve of the First World War. Programs were expanding and becoming more responsive to people's needs; track mileage and the number of passengers carried were growing faster than the population.

Welfare

Municipal welfare services received special attention and funding in this period. Here the central questions became who would provide and who would administer welfare services?

Russian state officials, beginning at least with Peter the Great, had recognized the importance for the empire of effective programs to deal with poverty. But, like many a more "modern" Western government, the tsarist autocracy never moved substantially beyond the position of viewing poor relief as largely a moral issue. As late as May 1914 the current minister of the interior, N. A. Maklakov, stressed the moral necessity to deal with poverty in traditional, religious tones. He indicated no willingness to meet the increasing demands for comprehensive welfare reform that came from *zemstva* and town councils.[84]

In a period when more and more peasants settled for longer periods in Moscow, were the old state and private agencies enough? Even before emancipation, the answer was clearly no, but the Moscow city government began to address the problem on a systematic basis only after 1890. Municipal welfare policies were modernized only tentatively and slowly before World War I; yet in this respect as well the city surpassed most Russian towns.

Substantial increases were made in welfare facilities: for instance, the city ran six almshouses in 1901 and twelve in 1911. Private groups also expanded their activities significantly in this period. These gains were remarkable considering that the city had not operated any permanent relief programs until 1879, when it had opened its first nightlodging. Before then there had been only temporary arrangements in time of war, famine, or other disasters. When these occurred the city had sold food, for example, at low prices. The municipality thus made vast progress in two decades.

The development of welfare programs depended heavily on private contributions. In 1912 a publication of the Group of Moderate and Nonparty Electors, that is, of the more conservative wing of city voters, complained that welfare development "has always depended not on the demand for one or another type of program, but on donations made to the city for this purpose."[85] The city government had been reluctant to use regular income in an area that in Russia and elsewhere had traditionally been administered by private groups with private funds.[86] For instance, the Old Believer community of the Preobrazhenskoe Cemetery ran the largest hospital in the Russian Empire, located in Moscow.

In this period, however, the duma began to change its welfare policy. Its expenditures on social services rose from 732,000 rubles in 1901 to 1,783,000 in 1911, an increase of two and a half times. In 1912 the municipality declared, "The right to assistance from the organs of social security is held by the poor person incapable of working, who needs social assistance, if he has no relatives or persons in general obligated to help him."[87] Moscow's government thus acknowledged a public, local responsibility for welfare, in place of the old reliance on the too-often uneven coverage of private organizations or the state. In this recognition of its duty in regard to welfare the city of Moscow was unique among Russian public institutions.[88]

Exactly why the change in policy occurred at this time is not entirely clear. It may well be that the steady growth of the city and its problems had produced such obvious need for change that the situation had to be handled in a more systematic way. In the 1890s the municipality had recognized the city's severe housing defects by conducting the survey of lower class dwellings mentioned earlier. As pointed out already, Moscow's elite could not ignore or rationalize poverty and misery in the way a landowner might. Moreover, there was a sort of safety net in the villages for the peasants: the communes normally did not allow a family to go under completely. Human support networks in the cities were scarce indeed.

The new attitude toward welfare paralleled the changed municipal views of about the same time on the importance of public services in education and transportation. In all three areas, the municipality was modernizing; it was starting to recognize the need for regular institutions in place of the old and uneven philanthropic services. The new welfare programs might also cushion the shocks of urban life for the poor and thus help ensure local stability.

But despite gains in several areas, the aid available to Muscovites in need or trouble was still inadequate in the years before the war. For example, one author commented in 1912 that regardless of the expansion of city and private homes for the aged, "there is a large demand for new ones. Many [applicants] are turned away each year for lack of space."[89] As in other areas, construction of these homes

had been undertaken on the basis of private donations. Three had been transferred to the city after years of operation by private groups. In 1912 the municipality planned to build one more home using regular revenue; its capacity was to
be 70 beds, bringing the total number of beds in such public institutions to
2,240.[90]

A similar situation prevailed in the city's homes for children. In 1906 a special duma commission on homeless children gave details.

> All existing children's homes in Moscow are overcrowded. For each vacancy
> there are dozens of candidates; children are often left helpless on the streets
> and are sent by the police to the city workhouse—all this is well known to
> anyone in Moscow interested in the problem.[91]

The public homes were essentially of two types, one that taught children trades
and one that sent them to regular city schools. There was also the City Rukavishnikovskii Corrective Home for Young Criminals. It conducted trade classes for
both boys and girls and had its own land in the countryside where children were
taught farming.

The Rukavishnikovskii Home occasionally had another function in Moscow. Parents or relatives of "morally spoiled" children, the special commission
on homeless children reported, sometimes "encourage them to commit small
crimes, for which the courts sentence them to the Rukavishnikovskii Home; thus
the parents get rid of them."[92]

In 1914 an *uprava* report, after reviewing programs for homeless and delin-
quent children in England, Scotland, and Italy, as well as in Moscow, proposed
several ideas. One was to build a new home with artisanal classes for fifty children. Another was to set up artificial families—small groups of children living
together with a supervisor. Last, the *uprava* wanted money to send homeless children back to their parents or birthplaces. The duma approved these programs,
which were planned to deal with two hundred children altogether at a yearly cost
of 51,135 rubles.[93] The war, of course, prevented implementation of the
proposals.

Besides the direct administration of welfare programs, the city organized,
subsidized, and supervised the "district guardianships," which were set up in each
police precinct. These bodies had their origin in a request from the Ministry of
the Interior in 1887 to the dumas of Moscow and St. Petersburg. The ministry
asked them to review their policies on poor relief, and specifically to decide
whether to continue subsidizing the old semipublic Committees on Begging or to
assume their functions altogether.[94] Petersburg typically chose the first option, but
in answer to a petition sent to the Council of Ministers in 1893, the Moscow
duma received the right to organize guardianships to "gather contributions, give
aid, and constantly observe those supported by charity." Another important purpose was to "struggle with professional begging, which was very widely developed." The guardianships, patterned after a German program, provided individual contact between their staffs and clients.[95] In 1899 the Ministry of Internal
Affairs issued model rules, based on Moscow's experience, for such institutions
in Russian towns.[96] In this case city and state stimulated each other toward modernization, though significant guardianship programs were instituted only in
Moscow.

Each of these bodies was directed by a council of five to ten volunteers from the community, mostly women, headed by a president appointed by the city duma. A case worker from the local guardianship visited each potential client to determine the degree of need and the type of aid to be given. The case was then taken to the council for a ruling. In urgent circumstances the case workers could immediately arrange temporary assistance. The original case worker stayed with the clients, visiting them regularly throughout the span of assistance. Following the lines of a directive of the Ministry of Internal Affairs issued to municipalities in 1894,[97] only those residents of Moscow who had lived in the city at least two years were eligible. The idea here was to prevent people from coming to Moscow expressly to take advantage of the city's welfare programs.[98] As late as 1906 it was customary for the police to investigate every case referred to the guardianships.[99]

These agencies cared for people temporarily or permanently. Case workers placed temporary clients in institutions or visited them at home, while arranging help with things like housing, fuel delivery, clothing, or subsidies. Permanent care was only for young children, the elderly, or disabled persons; they were given financial assistance or placed in institutions.

In 1911 Moscow's guardianships served 6,095 single people and 10,432 in families.[100] Among the single people aided, 77 percent could not work or had "low work capabilities (over 50 or under 15 years old)." These sought help for a variety of reasons, including senility, injury, "family misfortune," or because they were orphans or abandoned children. Among family members requesting aid, on the other hand, 70 percent could work. However, these often had no work or low pay, families too large to support on their incomes, or family problems. Senility or injury were also problems in this category. Almost three thousand clients in both groups were carried over from previous years, not an atypical number.[101]

Although the number of people aided by the guardianships had increased 50 percent from 1900 to 1911, the system showed many signs of stagnation. Expenditures lagged behind the growth of the client population and much further behind the growth of the city population.[102] Worse still was the decrease in the number of guardianship volunteers, which had occurred steadily almost from the program's inception. In 1895 there were 1,706 participants, while in 1910 there were 1,102. Of these, only 833 were case workers. The rest were council members and medical and legal volunteers.[103]

"The reasons for the failure of the guardianships to expand their work are many," wrote a reporter in 1912. A major problem, he believed, was that all affairs of a guardianship were directed by the president of the council. The lower-level volunteers, who did all the hard work, had no responsibility and no voice in administration.[104]

In 1908 another report criticized the guardianships more severely. Their work was "gray, humdrum, and not very noticeable." Among the city's educated strata and the workers who were touched by the guardianships' activities, there were "no illusions about them." In 1904 they gave no more than five rubles to about half of all those they helped; "This type of activity meant that no trace of the former interest in the guardianships remained among the *obshchestvo*." In other words, the ineffectiveness and paucity of the aid stifled the enthusiasm of the liberal volunteers.

Despite their German heritage, the guardianships represented the old concept of social services in Russia. They were largely run by volunteers on the basis of donations. They were paternalistic and concerned with the moral standards of their clients. They were small-scale and involved direct personal contact, a situation ideal for soothing the consciences of the *obshchestvo*. Criticism of their limited success in Moscow illustrates the changing public attitude toward welfare; it was becoming, slowly but surely, the concern of local government, not of groups or individuals from the upper classes. Moscow was gradually modernizing.

In this process the city was very far from meeting the welfare needs of its people. Part of this failure stemmed from the strains on its budget and the necessity to devote funds to other pressing aspects of city life; however, the problem was also one of attitudes. Members of the Moscow duma, for example the Bakhrushins, had long been among the most faithful and generous donors to charity in the city. They believed in the tradition of private welfare agencies. The old view that there was no "urban question" also lingered: if a peasant living in a city ran into difficulties, he should go home to the countryside. There the community to which he "really" belonged could take care of him. For many peasants that was indeed a possibility. For many others, Moscow was the only home they had. It is likely that a long span of time would have elapsed before the city government abandoned these attitudes entirely and assumed the greater share of responsibility for welfare programs.

Municipal services in Moscow showed great improvements and expansion from 1906 to 1914, though growth generally failed to keep pace with population increases. The city fathers' attitudes were modernizing, despite a good deal of hesitation. Expressly or indirectly, the municipality demonstrated deep concern for providing services that would appeal to the lower classes and which could help to integrate them into urban life. Motivated to some extent by the scare they had received in 1905, city officials worked hard and with some sensitivity to make Moscow's poorer people feel they had something worth preserving in the existing order, plus the prospect of better things to come. Residents touched or aided by municipal services quite probably felt that the local government played at least a partially positive role in their lives.

In its efforts to improve services the city government encountered state resistance at several points. For the most part this interference was not designed to block amelioration but to uphold the principle of central control. In this and other respects the state preferred to ignore pressing social problems or even to prevent their improvement in an attempt to maintain its ancient prerogatives; its contribution was often negative. The lower classes may have realized that the most active force on their behalf was the municipality, while the national government did little.

The attitude of the tsarist government toward Russia's severe urban problems, at least as expressed by Stolypin, was one of great concern. Yet his views also outlined the essence of tsarist policy toward the cities and all the difficulties it encompassed. "Think of the simple, poor working people," he told the State Duma in early 1911, "who live, or rather perish, in the most impossible circumstances." In a long speech he took his listeners on a tour of the most unhealthy places in Russia and then turned his full attention to St. Petersburg. He outlined the city's major problems in water supply and infectious diseases and then exclaimed, "I feel pain and shame when they point to my motherland as the source of the spread of all kinds of infections and illnesses." He wanted to be sure that in fifteen years Petersburg would have clean water and that "we will not perish in our own filth."

Stolypin's proposal for correcting this miserable situation was direct intervention by the central government. Probably sensing some skepticism in the Duma, he proclaimed that this was "not a question of the powers of local government. It is not a question of displacing the rights of local self-government, which perhaps, is mistaken, with the rights of the administration." Rather, he continued, the issue was "a question of faith in the government." Stolypin posed the matter this way: "How can *chinovniki* successfully do what city governments can't?" His answer was that the central government "has more technical means and a big circle of people in its service."[105]

The premier was asking once again that the public have faith in the tsarist government and recognize that central authorities were better able to handle local problems. Yet the government had consistently denied local officials the legal and financial competence necessary to make progress with local defects. It had also excluded the vast majority of urban residents from any role in solving their locales' difficulties. Though urban problems stemmed from many sources and were hardly exclusively the fault of the tsarist regime, it had not offered much in the way of opportunities or coherent policy for solving the mess in Russian cities. The government asked for faith but promised little in return and simply reasserted its ancient view of what Russia required: more central authority.

7

Education

A future historian, describing the events of current life, will halt with
amazement at this phenomenon [the idea of opening another Russian
university] and, probably, not being able to find any explanation, will
note it as a clear example of the inconsistency of the state authorities
peculiar to a revolutionary epoch.

Statement to the Council of Ministers by State Controller P. K. Shvanebakh
and Assistant Naval Minister Admiral I. F. Bostrem, April 1907[1]

Education was one of the most sensitive areas of Russian life in the last years of
the Old Regime. The government and most sectors of society recognized the terrible defects of the country's schools, which reached only a small portion of all
children. Almost everyone could agree without reservation that education had to
be greatly expanded if Russia was to maintain her Great Power status and
develop economically and culturally. At the same time, bitter debates occurred
between leading political figures and government officials on how improvements
in the schools should take place and what the nature of education should be.
These controversies really reflected the contenders' different views on the nature
of Russian society and its future development. In Moscow, struggles over educational policy reveal much about urban liberals' hopes and expectations for the
schools, feelings that stood in contrast to the regime's apprehensions about education in general. The very growth of education created political problems for the
tsarist state, a result best illustrated in a local study.

Some of the country's most important educational struggles and changes
occurred at the local level, not in the State Duma. At least, Moscow's story suggests that this was the case wherever local leaders tried regularly to implement
their ideas. The work and debates of the State Duma did not fundamentally alter
either Moscow's municipal educational policies or the tsarist administration's
approach to education in the city. A graphic illustration of this point is the fact
that the central government enacted major legislation on education not through
the Duma and the upper chamber of the parliament, the State Council, but
around them, under article 87 of the Fundamental Laws.[2] The State Council also
rejected school bills passed by the Duma on the grounds that they shifted control
too much from the government to localities;[3] the council thus facilitated the
regime's unilateral approach to the direction of education.

The existing literature about Russian education in this period commonly
focuses on events at the national level.[4] Most studies describe the clash over pol-

icy in terms of a prolonged struggle between the state and "society."[5] Several accounts argue that the *obshchestvo* wanted a "ladder system" of public instruction, a unitary and coordinated national school structure that would allow pupils to move from elementary institutions to secondary ones to the universities, if qualified. From the 1880s on, Russia had had a bifurcated secondary school network consisting of *gimnasii*, which specialized in classical languages and fed graduates into the universities, and *realschule*, which concentrated more on "practical" subjects and whose graduates could not enter the universities.[6] "Society" objected to this division, which seemed to promote elitism and hold back useful training, but the government was unwilling or unable to change its policy, despite the fact that from 1898 to 1916 the Ministry of Education drew up at least seven different plans for a ladder system.[7] Standard accounts of education in this period also depict a bitter debate between the two sides over control of schooling at the local level. In addition, the *obshchestvo* is said to have greatly resented the state's reduction of university autonomy, for example when troops broke up student meetings at Moscow Imperial University in 1911.

While many issues in education have been clarified by this concentration on national affairs, some important ones have not. Looking at the successes and defects of Moscow's public schools in this period, and contrasting local desires and policies to national ones, raises new questions and sheds some additional light on old ones.

First, who financed education, and where did the money come from? The state began to aid local governments in this sphere after 1908; what role did this assistance play in the expansion of education? Most important, what kind of education did the government want for Russia? What were its goals in the schools, and how did it relate its aims to politics and the country's future? How did liberals see these issues?

In considering prerevolutionary education in Russia, we have been beguiled to a degree by the writings of liberal emigres, chiefly Kadets. They have outlined the *obshchestvo* as a monolithic camp, opposed to the government as another monolithic camp.[8] Reality was far more complex; the regime found support to a degree from some liberals while encountering bitter opposition from others. The state's policies on education were not monolithic in this period, and changes over time revealed significant shifts within the regime on policy for Russia's development. Conservatives, for reasons dear to their own hearts and hearths, tended to support certain tendencies on education within the government. These patterns all appear in the story of Moscow's efforts to develop education and its relations with the state in that area.

Moscow's municipal government was proud of the level of learning its elementary school graduates achieved. In 1906 a subcommission of the *uprava* outlined their accomplishments.

> The children . . . have fairly broad mental development, interest in knowledge, and (in the majority of cases) a desire to continue studying. . . . The children have a sufficient grasp of elementary Russian grammar . . . in arithmetic those who finish the elementary school course can solve simple problems with abstract numbers and do mental calculations completely satisfactorily; . . . they have some elementary knowledge of history, geography, and natural science.

In many schools they learn to draw from nature—this work is extremely
satisfactory.[9]

O. V. Kaidanova, who taught for a time in the Moscow schools, also provided a
glowing account of their quality. They carried out "lively creative work" and
enabled their pupils to leave "fully literate and with general development corresponding to their age." Moreover, "the facilities of the schools were fully
satisfactory."[10]

The reality of Moscow's schools was far from this rosy picture, which was
probably heavily colored by civic pride. In attempting to expand and improve its
educational programs the city government encountered all of Moscow's inter-
locking social and economic problems (as outlined in Chapter 1). The dismal conditions of lower class life, existing in the schools as well, had a great impact there
on many children. In 1910 a writer reported on this in a national medical journal.

> Moscow city schools for the most part are crowded, gloomy, and dirty, so that
> not only do they not serve as a counterweight to the harmful influence on the
> children in them of their housing conditions, but they strengthen that influ-
> ence, adding to the harmful lack of clean air and light the deprivation of the
> freedom of movement, unnatural position of the body, nervous ailments, poor
> metabolism, nervousness, weakened muscle strength, suppression of spirits,
> and altogether an extreme weakness of the youthful organism in the struggle
> with many infections. Among these presently are scarlet fever and diphtheria,
> and chief among them, always active, tuberculosis.[11]

A few years later city doctors working in the schools noted that over 20 percent
of all pupils had poorly developed chest skeletal structures. These children were
prime candidates for tuberculosis. In addition, more than 20 percent of the boys
and girls in class had poor vision, 30 percent were anemic, and 20–25 percent
were undernourished. The doctors considered 48–51 percent of all the children
to be ill.[12]

Crowded housing and poor conditions in general may also have promoted
widespread drinking among school children. In 1912 one writer commented that
recent investigations in the West and in Russia showed that "the use of alcohol
among children of school age is much wider than one would think. We have to
consider that more than 60 percent of all school children are drinkers." There
were no such studies in Moscow, he continued, "but there is reason to think that
the picture [here] is even worse." He revealed that a teacher in one city elementary school had asked her children on the day after a big holiday what they had
done yesterday. Only two had not had any alcohol. Many had drunk until they
passed out. Some talked with great animation about their favorite kinds of
drinks.[13]

Sick, undernourished, possibly drunk or hung over: this is the picture of
Moscow's school children that emerges from contemporary descriptions. One
wonders how they could have learned anything. Before they could really learn, a
massive attack was required on the city's extensive health and housing problems.

Like the children, Moscow's adults were not in a position to draw all they
might have from the municipal educational programs available to them. A report
on adult education presented to the city duma in 1913 elaborated on the inter-

connected nature of the problems besetting public education and extended the discussion to the countryside as well.

> Every year Moscow attracts thousands of illiterate and semiliterate workers, who are at work at an age when school can do nothing for them. This dark mass of immigrants settles in Moscow and renders vain the efforts of the city administration to drive the gloom of ignorance from the walls of the city. Of course, in the present conditions of daily life it is impossible to dream of giving education to every illiterate adult in the population of Moscow. Moscow will be completely literate when there is no illiteracy in the surrounding countryside.

The author sadly concluded that "to correct the sins of several generations" in this area would take "many millions of rubles."[14]

In general, children and adults would not be in proper condition for classes until they were healthy and decently housed. Adult supervision and encouragement of children, essential to the success of any school system, would probably not improve until the elders' existence in the city was more secure. Parents had to be earning enough money to support their families without withdrawing their children from school and sending them to work. Thus a wide range of changes had to occur before the quality of public education in Moscow could improve substantially.

The city duma made at least one important effort in the schools to correct some of the defects of the children's home life. By 1913 the city was spending 199,000 rubles a year on school breakfasts for pupils "without means," an estimated 50 percent of all pupils.[15] To be "without means" in Moscow in 1913 was to be very poor indeed; the home life of such children did not prepare them to learn well.

The municipality assigned special priority to education for various reasons. Instructional programs for all ages and categories of the populace could serve to defuse social tension by opening the way to higher pay and better jobs or simply by providing an engaging leisure time activity. The lower strata could be alerted to the fact that the city government was doing something for them. These ends were particularly important in Moscow after the fighting of 1905, which may help explain the large amounts devoted to education by the municipality at a time when disease took a frighteningly large number of lives and many other problems demanded attention. For the purpose of creating a favorable impression among the public, it was also cheaper and easier for the city government to build schools and hire teachers than to construct the housing, sanitation system, and similar facilities necessary to correct the other problems of the day. And businessmen had recognized the economic importance of an educated population for some time.[16]

Solicitude for educating the lower classes had a long tradition among the city's leaders. As far back as 1863, the old Moscow general duma, operating under even narrower legal competence than the post-1892 institution, declared about popular education, "There is no public need that can be compared with this one. Any other necessity can be postponed for a time, in view of the unsatisfactory situation of city income; but this need cannot be put off."[17] Reflecting these sentiments, expansion of the municipal elementary school system took place steadily

TABLE 7-1.   Public Elementary Education in Moscow, 1870–1913

	1870	1880	1900	1905	1910	1913
Schools	5	40	150	215	288	324
Classes	12	119	501	753	1,170	1.850
Pupils	331	4,138	19,853	28,494	43,532	64,526
Money spent · (1,000 rubles)	10	165	795	1,504	2,100	4,086

after 1870, the year in which the first City Statute gave towns fairly broad powers to manage their own affairs.[18]

Moscow's relative success in drawing children into public school can be compared to St. Petersburg's. There 56,378 children were enrolled in elementary classes in 1914.[19] Since the imperial capital had more people than Moscow (1,907,708 compared to 1,617,700 in 1910, including suburbs), the latter city succeeded in providing education for a higher proportion of its children. A further comparison can be made with Philadelphia, another rapidly growing city with serious social problems, whose population of 1,549,008 people in 1910 was very close to that of Moscow. The former city enrolled 154,566 children in its elementary schools, almost 2.4 times as many as in Moscow.[20] Of course, Philadelphia did not operate under the constraints of tsarist law, had a wealthier population, and undoubtedly had more complete families than Moscow did. Nevertheless, the contrast underscores the relative difficulties of providing education in the Russian environment, even for a dedicated and progressive city government like Moscow's.

Few alternatives to public education existed for the city's poor by the early twentieth century. In 1905 there were eighty-one nonmunicipal elementary schools in operation with 7,300 pupils, of whom 700 were in private schools generally reserved for the wealthy and 3,700 were in factory or Sunday schools often attended largely by adult workers.[21] Later data are unavailable, but it is not likely that the number of nonmunicipal schools increased greatly before 1914. The public system expanded so rapidly that it probably drew pupils away from other institutions.

In 1909, a year after the State Duma adopted a plan to introduce compulsory education for the whole empire by 1922, the Moscow duma resolved to provide "generally accessible" primary schooling for the city. The municipal government also planned to build school rooms in the period 1913–1917 at a pace projected to be 18 percent greater than population growth.[22]

The cost of these developments was substantial. As Table 7-1 shows, between 1900 and 1913 the municipality increased expenditures on elementary education almost 5.14 times, from 795,000 rubles to 4,086,000 rubles. The proportion of the city budget devoted to primary schools also increased, from 5.9 percent in 1901 to 7.9 percent in 1912.[23] Under the terms of laws in 1908, 1909, and 1913 on state aid for primary education, Moscow began to receive government subsidies for this level. In 1910 the assistance amounted to 192,456 rubles; it jumped to

411,840 rubles in 1911 and increased to 466,830 in 1913.[24] These payments stemmed from the central government's recognition after 1905 that the "educational problem" was "very urgent" and "very difficult," as Stolypin told the British ambassador, Sir Arthur Nicolson, in 1908. Stolypin also avowed that it was "ridiculous" that the government spent only 8 million pounds (80 million rubles) annually on education from total revenue of about 250 million pounds (2.5 billion rubles).[25]

The budget of the Ministry of Education more than tripled from 1906 to 1913, rising from 44 million rubles to 143.1 million.[26] As a percentage of state expenditures, the increase was from 1.7 to 4.2.[27] Other ministries, for example the Ministry of Finance, also maintained educational institutions. Without specifying an exact date, a Soviet historian has estimated that education absorbed 5 percent of total state expenditures in this period. This proportion was "several times less" than in countries like Great Britain or Belgium.[28] While substantial, the increases after 1905 only began to solve a problem that left perhaps 55 to 60 percent of the empire's people illiterate in 1917.

State funds provided 11 percent of Moscow's budget for elementary schools and 9 percent of all municipal allocations for education by 1913. Far from opposing the spread of elementary schooling, the state was willing to help localities, and its aid proved quite important in Moscow. After 1910 the treasury subsidies of 1,512,996 rubles constituted the bulk of the city's increased spending on education, which totaled 1,986,000 rubles. This allowed the municipality to devote more money to other pressing problems: total city expenditures increased by almost 7.7 million rubles from 1910 to 1912. Of course, local revenues continued to provide 91 percent of all funding for public education in Moscow.

In terms of expanding education, cooperation between the government and the municipality was very good. After the city petitioned the Ministry of Education in October 1908 asking for state aid for elementary schools, the two bodies worked out a mutually satisfactory plan, and money quickly began to flow from the treasury to Moscow. The ministry's official journal praised the city's "huge results" in 1914 and indicated approval of its decision to set its own target of thirty-six pupils per class instead of the official figure of fifty.[29]

Yet because of its inability to generate more revenue, partly a function of remaining tsarist restrictions, the municipality still had much to do to upgrade the quality of education in its schools. For example, classes seem to have been too large for effective teaching. In 1913 they averaged forty-eight pupils in grade one, forty in two, twenty-five in three, and thirty-three in four. Many schools had larger classes, especially in grade one, where often there were fifty-five to sixty or more children.[30] Despite Kaidanova's appraisal, facilities were often poor; a report published in 1910 indicated that 38 percent of all city schools possessed insufficient ventilation, 78 percent lacked sufficient space for recreation, 44.5 percent were plagued by foul odors from gas formed in water closets, and 32 percent had insufficient light.[31] In 1912, 1,000 of the 1,364 elementary classrooms were in private buildings rented by the city. Forty-six percent of these, or almost half of all classrooms, were considered too small.[32]

Poor teacher morale, related to low salaries, may also have hurt the quality of education. In 1911 more than 40 percent of all teachers made only 460 rubles a year plus 240 for housing.[33] At this level they earned more than the average

Moscow factory worker, who received 325.2 rubles per year in 1913, but less than many elite members of the working class, for example the print workers discussed in Chapter 1. Teachers' salaries must have resulted in a certain degree of demoralization among city teachers and in the migration of the more energetic and qualified ones to private schools or out of education altogether—this pattern has been documented for the Moscow educational district and other areas at this time.[34] Of course, similar conditions and results are found today in a number of American school districts.

The Russian national government was concerned about teachers' low pay after 1905 for its own reasons. In August 1906 the Council of Ministers found that poor pay contributed to a situation in which many of the "unfortunate toilers of the people's school" are "pulled . . . onto the path of concealed or even open enmity toward the existing state and social structure." It was not "ideas, but feelings" that were "dangerous" in the schools. Apparently the ministers meant by this that teachers were susceptible to revolutionary ideas because of low morale, a result largely of poor pay. The state had "not devoted enough attention to this sphere, the sad results of which in the recent past are evident to all."[35] Yet, obviously, low pay had played only one part in producing dissent among teachers in 1905;[36] the ministers were really hinting at general distrust of the school teachers' political inclinations and influence, a state attitude that had a profound effect on teaching in Moscow and elsewhere.

Beyond the problems within the city's elementary schools were the thousands of children who stayed out of class altogether either by their own choice or their parents'. In 1912 there were 171,532 children between the ages of eight and fourteen in Moscow;[37] we may assume that five-sevenths, or some 122,522, of them were of officially designated school age, eight to twelve. Yet in the city's elementary classes there were only 64,526 pupils. Given the dearth of alternatives to public programs, possibly almost half of Moscow's school-age children received no classroom education at all, though the evidence does not allow precise calculations. The city's own estimate was simply "more than 10 percent."[38] In any event, municipal officials lamented a situation in which "there was no law requiring education" for children.[39]

Moscow's duma did everything it could in these years to ensure that primary schools were accessible to all youngsters, first by rapidly expanding the number of classrooms and second by making the schools free. Starting in the 1910–1911 school year, the city dropped the previous three-ruble fee for elementary education. The result was an annual decrease in municipal income of 150,000 rubles or more, at a time when such a sum was precious to the city coffers. The change was probably made possible by the new state subsidies. Abolition of the fee, of course, was most important to the poorest people of the city. At the same time, the duma approved another costly innovation in this area, the addition of a fourth year to the elementary program. This improvement implies that the city hoped both to teach children more and to prepare a larger number for secondary school. Because of these modifications and the treasury subsidies, expenditures on primary schools almost doubled from 1910 to 1913, as shown in Table 7-1, while the number of pupils rose only 1.48 times.

Preoccupied as it was with elementary education, the city gave far less attention and funding to secondary schools. The duma was aware of grave problems in this area but felt it could not spare the resources necessary for large-scale improvement. For many years the council also felt it *should not* operate middle schools. In 1905 its financial commission reported that it

> recognized long ago the lack of middle educational institutions of a general type. . . . But without the slightest hesitation, and unanimously, we have come to the conclusion that neither principles nor private considerations should be the basis for the city's taking part in the construction and maintenance of middle schools.[40]

Nevertheless, in the next year the Moscow *uprava*, elected by the duma, indicated a sharp change in municipal outlook by stating that general education beyond elementary school was "unconditionally essential for every person in our times."[41] The Revolution of 1905 must have prompted this reversal; it would be difficult to explain otherwise.

After almost fifteen hundred children were turned away from city secondary and trade schools in 1908, the School Department of the *uprava* stressed the imperative need to develop these institutions as fast as possible.[42] The duma itself resolved in 1910 that it was necessary to introduce "generally available" professional-trade education in the city.[43] Whether due to fear of revolution or simply a logical step after so much had been achieved at the primary level, the municipality made a beginning at this time toward developing a middle school system capable of greatly widening the lower classes' opportunities to train for better jobs.

One indication that the Moscow duma was thinking concretely about expanding secondary school programs was a questionnaire it distributed to parents of elementary school pupils in 1910. The duma wanted to know what sort of further education parents desired for their children. City officials received 35,000 responses, revealing a tremendous interest in the topic among Moscow's parents. Of the respondents, 92 percent wanted further schooling for boys and 90 percent for girls. Many parents specified that they wanted their children to continue in school only if classes were free of charge or if costs were less than twenty rubles a year.[44]

One striking point in the responses was the strong emphasis parents placed on general education for their children. Surely a large number of lower class parents returned the questionnaire; it appears that they felt their children could benefit by general education because that might facilitate their social mobility. Otherwise, the parents' stress would have been on acquiring skills. But instead of hoping that their offspring could become, for example, higher-paid workers, parents displayed more ambition. This in turn suggests that an important group of adults felt reasonably well integrated into Moscow life and had a positive outlook on the future. The evidence for this conclusion is slim, but it is reinforced by the desire that developed among workers in this period to obtain more general education and by the great response to the secondary and higher courses available to adults in Moscow (discussed later).

In the 1910 parental survey and in other cases, the privileged Moscow duma, comprised of representatives of Russia's urban elite, made a sizable effort to communicate across the gap between itself and the common people and to learn what the latter wanted. This is undoubtedly one of the rare instances in the history of

Russian local government before the Revolution when public opinion was solicited on such a large scale. The Moscow duma was not in any way responsible to the general public, but occasionally it acted as though it cared about what the city's people wanted.

However, the municipality's response to the survey was hardly on the scale desired by the 35,000 concerned parents. In 1912 the duma voted to set up sixteen classes in five new "independent higher four-class schools."[45] At the same time, the council decided to end supplementary classes in regular elementary schools, which had served until then as the most common form of secondary education offered by the city.

By 1907 the municipal government also operated five "urban schools of 1872." As conceived by the state these schools were originally designed to offer a six-year course of primary education for boys, which normally began at age seven. Toward the end of the nineteenth century the function of these institutions began to change. Local educational systems were permitted to drop the first two years of courses, which gave the urban schools much more of a middle than an elementary character, as pupils with good records could enter either state *gymnasii* or *realschule* after four years.[46] Girls were permitted to enroll. The Council of Ministers acknowledged these changes in 1908 without expressing any objection to them;[47] the state was certainly willing to be flexible where it perceived no threat to its prerogatives. Yet by 1913 only two more such schools had been added in Moscow, probably because of financial constraints. Tuition was set at twenty rubles per year.

Besides the general secondary institutions the city also ran a few trade schools for boys and girls. Altogether in 1912 there were only 4,048 pupils in municipal trade and academic secondary schools. These facilities could accommodate only 10–15 percent of the elementary school graduates each year;[48] the solution of this problem awaited more funding and the efforts of another generation.

Moscow's city government devoted less attention in this period to secondary schools than to adult education at various levels, a pattern that suggests a concern for adults' political stability and integration into urban life. The demand for middle and higher level courses among Moscow's lower class adults was great. A study conducted in 1896 by the city guardianships of the poor discovered that 93 percent of illiterate respondents and 56.8 percent of literate ones said they wanted to study.[49] Attempts to satisfy this demand were left to local and private organizations; the state made no effort to expand adult education. Any loyalty or gratitude engendered by the courses thus went to the sponsoring groups, not the regime.

The municipality ran evening and Sunday courses for workers and subsidized private organizations engaged in such teaching. One of these private groups, the Prechistenskie courses for workers, which opened in 1897 for men only, found as early as 1902 that there was a need for instruction beyond the elementary level. In that year a second course was added and women were admitted. In 1904–1905 a third course, and a fourth, preparatory course geared toward the examinations for *uezd* teachers and domestic tutors, became part of the program. The preparatory course also had the ambitious goal of readying students to enter universities.[50]

In 1912 the Prechistenskie higher (actually generally middle level) courses filled all 1,700 spaces on the first day of registration. The Miusskie Sunday and evening higher (also middle) classes for workers opened in 1907; by 1912 they had 514 students and had to turn away 76 more for lack of funds. The "most serious task" of these courses was to prepare pupils for entrance to the City People's University (discussed hereafter), "a goal unattainable for the masses of people without middle school education."[51] Each year the city contributed three thousand rubles to the support of the Prechistenskie group and fifteen hundred rubles for the Miusskie classes,[52] about 0.12 percent of the municipal educational budget in 1911.

Such courses apparently drew mainly from the upper strata of the lower classes; in 1910–1911 the Prechistenskie pupils were 35 percent factory workers, 12 percent print workers, 8 percent clerks and trade workers, 16 percent office workers, 17 percent artisans, and 7 percent white-collar employees.[53] This distribution reflects the greater leisure time and ambition that characterized the better-off workers. Nonetheless, such courses represented an important opportunity for enrichment, and possibly for social advancement, for the lower classes.

In addition to supporting these "popular" (nongovernmental) courses, the municipality ambitiously entered the field of higher education in this period in a more formal manner. Funded by a donation from retired general A. L. Shaniavskii, which was supplemented by public gifts and subsidies from the city government, a new institution opened its doors in the fall of 1908. Its full title was the A. L. Shaniavskii Moscow City People's [*Narodnyi*] University.

The university had three basic sections: "scientific-popular," academic, and practical. All were conducted in the evening. In the first section were an elementary and a basic cycle, designed to be successive stages in preparation for the academic section. These were generally middle school courses. A normal plan of study in this branch was considered to be two hours an evening five times a week for four years. Thus anyone with only an elementary education could prepare for the top level university courses, although the task was long and demanding. The school actively promoted upward social mobility and the spread of general, higher education among people who otherwise would never have had such opportunities.

The university's academic section offered a wide range of courses in history, law, languages, literature, and science. It did not include some subjects taught at state (imperial) universities, such as Roman law, ancient languages, and comparative linguistics; otherwise Shaniavskii's range of courses rivalled that of the imperial campuses. After the university opened its own building in October 1912 it had chemistry, physics, and several other types of laboratories. It maintained a library of more than 36,000 books, most of them donated.

The practical cycles varied from year to year. Among the most popular were library science, pedagogical science, administration of cooperatives, and local government. A. A. Kizevetter, an assistant professor at Moscow Imperial University and later a noted historian, also taught at Shaniavskii. He remembered that visitors from the provinces often came to the practical courses with a special goal. They observed the other listeners (so termed to distinguish them from imperial university students) for those who seemed to be most capable and then offered them jobs in "some provincial backwater." The directors of the university had to take special measures against such "capturers of people."[54] At least to some provincial officials, Shaniavskii's courses were effective; besides finding employees there, they sometimes sent staffers to attend practical cycles.

The university quickly attracted listeners, suggesting that a great desire existed in Moscow for an institution of higher education that was more accessible than the imperial university. By the start of Shaniavskii's second year, 1,106 people were attending classes; four years later, in 1913–1914, there were 5,372.[55] This high attendance occurred despite the fact that fees were charged, ranging from six rubles a semester in the scientific-popular courses to twenty-five for the natural history cycle of the academic section. This difference probably reflects an understanding that the scientific-popular courses would appeal more to those who needed them for "practical" reasons, generally less well-off individuals. Listeners could also pay for individual courses or, in the practical section, for individual lectures. The university was somewhat hard pressed for funds and could not afford to discount or dispense with fees very often. However, the Society for Strengthening the Funds of Shaniavskii University, a voluntary group of sympathizers, gave a "significant number" of scholarships in 1911.[56]

Kizevetter left a description of Shaniavskii students.

> What a variegated picture, what a mixture of ages, types, clothing. I saw there sitting next to each other an officer of the general staff and a conductor of a city tram, a university assistant professor and a shop clerk, a noblewoman with a feather boa around her neck and a monk in his everyday cassock.

He also noted that people of various parties, from Social Democrats to Octobrists, worked together in the university in an atmosphere of general harmony.[57] This picture could have developed only in Russia's cities, very probably only in Moscow.

Several surveys taken among its listeners by the University show that most of them were young: 62 percent in 1909–1910 and almost 64 percent in 1910–1911 were under age thirty. Young people more often had the energy and ambition required to follow a program that tied up as many as five evenings a week. Their preponderance also seems to indicate that the courses really were used as a means of social mobility, for young listeners were more likely than older ones to be able to improve their careers. Thus the city succeeded in providing a service for young people that promised their better integration into urban life.

The results of the 1909 survey also support the contention that social mobility was a goal for many who attended Shaniavskii: of 559 respondents, 466 were workers or employees. The rest were unemployed or from the professions, usually teachers. Lower class Muscovites were taking advantage of a chance for low-cost higher education, despite the fact that the school conferred no diplomas. On the other hand, the majority of listeners were also already fairly well educated before they started at Shaniavskii: 63.6 percent in 1910 and 64 percent in 1911 had at least finished middle school.[58] Therefore most who attended the university were not from the lowest strata of the population, who could not often have afforded the tuition in any case. Yet the academic and practical cycles provided probably the only chance almost all the listeners would ever have, prior to the downfall of tsarism, to obtain higher education. The typical route to the imperial universities, through the state *gymnasii*, was closed to all but a very few children of the middle and lower classes. Muscovites who had reached a middle level of education could hope to advance further in life by attending Shaniavskii University, and the approximately 34 percent of listeners in 1910 and 1911 who had not finished middle school stood to gain even more. The courses constituted an unprecedented opportunity for the residents of Moscow and numerous outsiders as well.

The university received steady support from the Moscow duma: yearly subsidies of 12,000 rubles, about 0.3 percent of the city's educational budget in 1911, and a gift of the land for its buildings. This type of support from the city government for higher education was a strong factor in the success of such programs in Moscow. The experience of Shaniavskii and the subsidies given to organizations like the Prechistenskie courses illustrate the privileged duma's interest in promoting the development of education at various levels. For its part, the state had neither the ability nor the inclination to meet the popular demand in Moscow for higher education.

Workers in particular responded positively to Shaniavskii University's courses. In a survey conducted in 1910, three worker listeners reported the following: "All the lectures [I] heard produced an impression on me"; "I am now beginning to think about the structure of our life"; and "The lectures—are our true teacher."[59] Such thoughts and impressions were unwelcome to state officials after 1907, as will be shown.

The university's success occurred amidst a burgeoning movement in popular higher education across Russia. The Society of Popular Universities, which had organized systematic lectures in thirty-six cities by 1910, attracted a total of 210,560 listeners to its sessions in that year.[60] Women's Higher Courses in 1914 had an attendance of about 25,000 in ten cities.[61] None of these classes had state support; in fact, the central government became quite suspicious of them as time went on.

In all of its educational programs the Moscow city government worked steadily before World War I to expand and improve public facilities at various levels.[62] In these efforts it had the active support of other members of the city's *obshchestvo*, those who served as "trustees" of the elementary schools. These figures were elected by the duma "from circles of society close to the city government." Although there were no requirements or rules for their conduct, they played a major role in hiring teachers.[63] According to another contemporary report, the elected trustees had "huge importance" in the schools: they were "the closest directors" and "handled all funds."[64] "Society" was both concerned and involved in education for the lower classes in Moscow.

What were the municipality's goals and concerns in promoting the development of education? How did those goals and concerns differ from those of the state? In this difference lay the source of conflict over education between the two levels of government.

Table 7-1 shows that the municipality's attention to education for the lower classes was not originally prompted by fear of revolution, as expansion of the elementary school system began in 1870 and proceeded at a steady pace until 1913. However, the city's new attention and funding for postelementary education after 1905 certainly had much to do with that year's upheaval. In General

Shaniavskii's proposal to create a municipal university, made only three months before the December fighting, he suggested to the duma that education in the city might play a role in building civil peace.

> In the present difficult days of our public life, one of the quickest means to its renewal and cure must be the wide expansion of education and the attraction of the people's sympathy to study [*nauka*] and knowledge.[65]

The general's statement implied a view of education in which it could serve to "cure" social unrest by integrating the lower classes into urban life, by attracting them to serious pursuits, by making them aware that opportunities for study and possible job advancement were available to them, and by showing them that the *obshchestvo* cared about them and was willing to work and spend money for their benefit. The Moscow duma accepted Shaniavskii's ideas when it approved his proposal.

In general, however, discussions within the city government after 1905 were remarkably free of open debate and even of deliberations on the nature and purpose of education. For example, there was little talk in 1910 when the duma voted on a subsidy for the Prechistenskie courses. One deputy, the merchant A. V. Buryshkin, remarked,

> The Prechistenskie courses are ... of great value [*pol'za*] in the sense of providing an opportunity to the workers and the poorest population.... If the duma finds it possible to give it [the courses] a subsidy, that would be a good thing.

Without further discussion the duma approved the subsidy.[66] Buryshkin's words suggest that he, like General Shaniavskii, believed that adult education could steer workers onto more productive and thus more politically stable paths.

Several factors at work in this period probably kept the city government from considering the nature and purposes of education more deeply. First, as shown above, the municipal authorities had recognized the general importance of education for the public more than forty years earlier. The pattern of attention to this area was very well established, and the city duma deputies may not have felt any need to discuss a long-standing tradition, despite their new devotion after 1905 to higher levels of training. Second, the job of setting educational priorities and philosophy belonged to the national government by law and force of habit, from at least the time of Peter the Great forward. Thus, while important debates took place in these years in the State Duma over the nature of education in the country, there would have been little point in such discussions in a forum like the Moscow city duma. In any case, the stenographic records of the duma and its other publications reveal no such deliberations. One must turn instead to the sessions of the State Duma. Here the central government outlined its ideas on the purpose of education and "society" responded; this provides a basis for discussing ideas on education within the city of Moscow as well.

In examining what happened in the State Duma in regard to education, it is important to note first that the government hoped to cooperate with "society." Premier P. A. Stolypin stated this in an address to the Second Duma in March 1907.

The Ministry of Education regards as its most immediate task the establishment, by the combined efforts of the government and society, of a system of primary education that shall be first accessible and in time compulsory for the entire population of the empire.[67]

This attitude carried over to the Third and Fourth State Dumas.[68] Cooperation, of course, depended on obtaining a fair degree of agreement between "society" and state on educational policy. Indeed, portions of "society" as represented in the Third Duma often did agree with the government in this sphere.

Besides the emphasis on spreading education mentioned by Stolypin and later repeated many times by various officials, the government believed that "schools must be the cement of the state, as in the West . . . the direction of education must agree with the state outlook."[69] This is a natural position for any government, but public acceptance of it depends on how relevant it seems to contemporary conditions.

Minister of Education N. N. Shvarts added another point to the government's approach to schooling in a statement to the Third Duma in 1908, during a debate on the budget for his ministry. In his view, education should "curb" the ancient "wild instincts" of man. This notion also prompted his arrogant response to criticisms of the government's school policy from State Duma deputies: they should give up their "childish playfulness" because "God sent us the Russian school."[70] His remark drew laughter and shouts of disapproval from the left side of the chamber. To Shvarts, the purpose of education was not so much to broaden children's minds as to discipline them in a politically safe direction.

A leading Kadet deputy, F. I. Rodichev, replied that everything on earth is given by God; the existing Ministry of Education and Minister Shvarts are given by God, "as from God cholera is received, as from God Russia was sent Tsushima and Mukden [devastating defeats in the 1904–1905 war with Japan]." At this the left benches began to applaud. Rodichev further suggested that the Russian school might have been sent by God as punishment.[71]

Shvarts' successor, L. A. Kasso, who took office in September 1910, outlined another fundamental principle of Russian public education later that year in a speech to the State Duma. He emphasized that church and secular schools should work "side by side on the same tasks and develop in their pupils equal love for the motherland and toward the people." Voices shouted "Bravo!" from the right.[72]

It was no accident that Kasso assigned the same purpose to church and secular schools, for at that time the government was turning more toward the Nationalist party as a source of support in the Duma. The Nationalists were generally ethnic Russian landowners based in the western provinces.[73] That area had a substantial population of Polish Catholics and Ukrainian Uniates, a faith that follows Orthodox rites but is subordinate to the pope. The Nationalists stood to lose social, religious, and political dominance if the majority ever came to rule in the western provinces. Kasso had the same background as many Nationalists; he was a "Bessarabian landowner of furious temperament."[74]

In its program on education, the Nationalist party stressed Russian patriotism and religion. "At the base of education must be placed the unshakable foundations of religion, love for the tsar and the motherland, the development and the strengthening of feelings of duty and legality."[75] These words were taken one step further in 1910 by the priest N. E. Genetskii, a Nationalist deputy who also came from the western province of Bessarabia. He informed the Duma, "To a significant degree" the "excesses of 1905 can be explained . . . by the decline of religious feeling, which especially the Left and the non-Russian [inorodcheskaia] part of our society facilitated." His words drew applause and shouts of approval from the right benches.[76]

In effect, the Nationalists and many Rightists had a prescription for social and political stability through education. This was an important aspect of the party's cooperation with the government. The Nationalists had formulated a brand of conservatism based on their desire to maintain their socioeconomic position in the face of the peasants' land hunger and the claims of non-Russian ethnic groups in the empire's borderlands. The emphasis on Russian Orthodoxy was a central component of the Nationalists' view of proper, conservative education, because the Church taught obedience and acceptance of one's fate on earth. Defending Orthodoxy's spiritual position was also a key part of their attempt to preserve Russian dominance over other nationalities whose religion was different.

In contrast, the Octobrists' leading speaker on the schools, V. K. fon Anrep, had serious reservations about the Church's contribution to education. He told the Duma, "My party believes that the clergy can do useful work in public education; but at the same time, many Church schools that are presently in existence cannot satisfy us."[77] However, like the Nationalists, the Octobrists generally believed that patriotism should be a foundation of education. Speaking for his party in 1908, fon Anrep endorsed the idea of developing the "Russian national school," intended to instill national pride and loyalty to the tsar in its pupils.[78] The "Russian national school" was also to have the specific assignment of Russifying other nationalities. In this regard, many moderate liberals felt great sympathy for the government's position, which after 1907 was to promote education in a "Russian state-patriotic spirit."[79]

Since there were relatively few non-Russians in Moscow, and there was little question of their threatening the position of the Russian population, this "national school" debate had virtually no meaning there. Nor did the desires of the urban lower classes have the same ruinous potential for their social superiors as the peasants' dreams of gaining all the land did for the rural gentry. Social progress in the cities implied not so much the massive expropriation of upper class property as simply more provision for upward social mobility. But such mobility was not compatible with tsarist ideology; it is indicative that the regime's staunchest supporters, the United Nobility, who were opponents of peasant upward mobility, fully endorsed Official Nationality in 1906.[80] The regime had made a number of attempts in the nineteenth century to limit access to higher education to gentry males, but these efforts ultimately proved unsuccessful.[81] This attitude on the government's part explains the failure to adopt a ladder system of education, which of course would have facilitated upward mobility.

The conservative state, concerned in its own way with national questions and social stability, heavily stressed religion in the laws of 1864 and 1874 on primary schools. These statutes, which remained in force until 1917, both began with this phrase: "The people's elementary schools have as their goal establishing in the people [*narod*] religious and moral understanding and the spread of useful fundamental knowledge."[82] The priorities in this statement were clear and political: first order and loyalty to the state, then knowledge. This reflected the government's long-standing and overriding concern for education at all levels—that it produce loyal citizens.[83]

The highly influential Konstantin P. Pobedonostsev, lay head of the Russian Orthodox Church and a member of the Council of Ministers from 1880 to 1905, certainly expressed such views. "However powerful the state may be," he said, "its power is based alone upon identity of religious profession with the people." Education had to be founded on religion. "On the Church lies the duty of teaching and direction." He maintained that "in the popular mind the function of a school is to teach the elements of reading, writing, and arithmetic, and in union with these, the duty of knowing, loving, and fearing God, of loving our native land, and of honoring our parents. These are the elements of knowledge." A purely negative example was France, which "in the last stage of political disintegration [1896], has organized its national schools without God." As noted earlier Pobedonostsev also insisted that each Russian should remain "in that place, in that area, in that corner where fate has placed him.[84] Ivan Delianov, minister of education from 1882 to 1898, took his main ideas from Pobedonostsev.[85] The latter was the ideal spokesman for a conservative state that relied on the Russian rural gentry: the Nationalists' stance on schools merely reiterated his points.

The curriculum outlined by the state for elementary schools also retained this focus, which was articulated in the law of 1874.

> Subjects of the educational course of the people's elementary schools are (a) the Law of God (short catechism and church history); (b) reading from the civil and church press; (c) writing; (d) the first four arithmetic functions; and (e) church singing where its teaching is possible.

Of five subject areas listed in the law, three were entirely or partly religious. In 1897 the Ministry of Education reaffirmed this emphasis in a model program for elementary schools. Of twenty-four classroom hours per week, nine were to be devoted to religious subjects. A Soviet author notes that "as a rule, schools added church singing three hours a week." This meant that about 45 percent of class time was assigned to religious instruction.[86] This refers, of course, to the secular state schools; the parish Church schools devoted even more time to religious studies. As shown hereafter, at least in the case of Moscow the rules for secular schools were not hard and fast. Nevertheless, they reflected the concerns of the regime about education and served as guidelines for the apparatus assigned to enforce the law at the local level.

The political content of Orthodox religious education, whether in the public or Church schools, was high. All pupils had to memorize the Orthodox catechism, which included the following exchange:

> *Question:* What does religion teach us as to our duties to the Tsar?
> *Answer:* Worship, fidelity, the payment of taxes, service, love, and prayer—
> the whole being comprised in the words, worship and fidelity.[87]

It is easy to see why liberals who objected to many state policies and to Nicholas' penchant for personal rule might have disliked such lines in the public schools. But these were golden words to rural conservatives.

Even with this reinforcement for their point of view, some conservatives expressed strong reservations about the spread of education. Echoing and expanding on the Council of Ministers' suspicions toward school teachers, conservatives objected to the introduction of general education "until a fully reliable cadre of teachers has been created."[88] In 1908 the Fourth Congress of the United Nobility pointed to "the school, the press, and the jury court" as "hotbeds of mutiny."[89] Conservatives generally favored caution toward and strict state control of these institutions.

The Russian government's goals for education before the First World War, at least for the lower levels, can be summarized as follows: the schools were to produce reliable, religious citizens who loved their country and their tsar. Pupils were supposed to acquire some basic knowledge of reading and arithmetic as well as religion. This view of education omits a great deal. There is virtually no indication in official Russian government statements that learning should stimulate children, let alone adults, or that it should broaden their horizons in any way. Certainly neither the Octobrists nor the Nationalists offered such a viewpoint. It was left to the Kadet leader Paul Miliukov, speaking for his party in the State Duma in 1908, to formulate a different conception of education.

> The Russian school should educate the growing Russian generation on the bases that have been created by the fundamental change [perevorot] in our government, [the school] should instill in the coming generation the idea of truth, the idea of legality.[90]

Yet even Miliukov, with his more liberal perspective on education, seemed less concerned with benefits for the pupils than with politics in the classroom. The notion of educating the mind to its fullest potential received scant attention at the national level in Russia after 1905, when many leading figures in and outside the government saw education and politics as intimately related.

Perhaps even more important than the differences over elementary schooling between the state and some segments of society was a quarrel over access to education at secondary and higher levels. Following a long tradition, the government was ambivalent and divided on this issue. In 1902 Stolypin welcomed the prospect of universal education in Russia. He compared the calm and loyalty of Germans to the anarchy of Italians and traced the difference to Italy's low level of education.[91] When he became premier he vigorously promoted the expansion of Russian schools, apparently without distinguishing upper from lower levels in social or political terms.

On the other hand, one of Stolypin's ministers of education, Shvarts, displayed considerable ambivalence about higher education. He told the Third State Duma in 1908, "It is my conviction that the path to higher knowledge should be opened to all, but it cannot be required to be presented to all." Shvarts avoided the crude references of earlier officials to "cooks' children" and the like who should not be educated beyond the station they were born to occupy in society, but his use of phrases such as education according to the "suitability of each to learning" had the ring of an old idea slightly updated.[92] And if Stolypin was not afraid of universal education, Shvarts was, at least for adults. In June 1908, during a debate in the State Duma over the charter for Shaniavskii University, he remarked that popular courses for adults "very often not only had nothing in common with a scholarly conception, but also with a healthy one."[93] He meant that this sort of education could serve to engender dangerous political views among the students. The Union of the Russian People, so dear to Nicholas II's heart, drew up a platform for the State Duma in July 1907 that called for "healthy" public schools guided by "rightists," the state, and the Church.[94] The statement of Ministers Shvanebakh and Bostrem quoted in the epigraph to this chapter also identified the universities as "supportive points of the revolutionary movement."[95] The rest of the ministers agreed that the situation in the universities was "abnormal" but argued that it was still more important to open another university because of Russia's great practical need for higher education.[96]

Thus the government appeared caught in the old dilemma outlined in a well-known dictum attributed to Count Sergei Witte, a key statesman and adviser to the tsars until 1906: "Education foments social revolution, but popular ignorance loses wars."[97] Would not education, especially higher education, undermine the very bases of the state? Once it gained some notion of the way things were done elsewhere, why should the *narod*, or anyone for that matter, continue to accept the notion that the tsar had some inalienable right to dismiss the State Duma, pass laws around it, and prevent the discussion of much of the country's budget? The long-standing ideological basis of the regime, Official Nationality, could well crumble in the minds of the people if they gained some perspective on Russian life.

If government officials of Shvarts' persuasion had ever doubted that education presented a threat to such notions, they had only to listen to State Duma deputy T. O. Belousov, a Social Democrat and former school teacher from Irkutsk. He told the Duma in 1908, "Science, education, and the school are undermining the principles on which our administration is based and are creating in the lower strata of the population a critical attitude toward [present] reality."[98] Left and right could agree on this issue, and from its point of view, the government indeed had reason to be worried.

The state's attempts to find a way out of the dilemma outlined by Witte reflected both its seriousness and the ambivalence within the government. Public groups created new educational institutions and programs with government permission only to find that the central apparatus then stepped in to hedge them about with restrictions and to insist on close central supervision.

In the case of Shaniavskii University, the state's approach was still more erratic. The original plan for the school, as developed by General Shaniavskii and approved by the Moscow city duma, stipulated that the university would not require any sort of prior education or grant any diplomas of its own. Courses would be conducted in various languages. Anyone over the age of sixteen would be admitted to classes; "this would open wide the doors of the university to all who were thirsting for knowledge."[99] The intention, therefore, was to meet a need the state would not meet.

Having accepted the general's ideas and donation, the Moscow duma resolved in May 1906 to plan courses, hire teachers, and open the university. The duma considered the school a public, municipal, higher educational institution, something apparently unforeseen by tsarist law. However unrealistically, the city hoped to avoid government interference in the project.

But that was not to be. The Moscow *gradonachal'nik* intervened and forced the city duma to work out a statute for the new school, which then went to the Ministry of Education for approval. The current minister, P. M. Kaufman, had no objections to the plan and passed it on to the State Duma as a bill in November 1907. But by this time the government was becoming more confident and conservative. It had surmounted the revolutionary crisis and dismissed the unruly First and Second State Dumas without serious effects. In a change that reflected this growing conservatism, Shvarts replaced the more liberal Kaufman as Minister of Education.

This move signalled the return of traditional tsarist suspicion toward the spread of higher education. Kaufman had come under attack in March 1907 by thirty-five Rightists in the State Council, who demanded to know why his ministry had allowed student meetings at the imperial universities in Moscow and St. Petersburg. For the moment the criticism was overridden in the council by the centrist faction.[100] But by December Nicholas II and Stolypin agreed that Kaufman had to go. For Stolypin, the issue was grave: he needed someone "to conduct the education of the youth with a firm and capable hand." He wrote to Nicholas,

> To drag out the matter is impermissible: once the weakness of the current Ministry of Education becomes indubitable, any delay would be a mistake, which would throw the shadow of a kind of imprecision and ambivalence on the general policy of the government.[101]

Restriction of the universities' autonomy was thus of crucial significance to Stolypin at this point, as it was to many conservatives.

Nicholas agreed with Stolypin and fully supported him. The tsar responded, "It seems to me that their simultaneous firing [of Kaufman and his assistant minister] will demonstrate to all Russia that I have not approved of the policy of the Ministry of Education."[102] The government was drawing the line on students' freedom of expression in the universities, and in the new atmosphere Shvarts moved quickly to rescind the bill on Shaniavskii University's charter and insist that central control over the institution be strengthened. He demanded that the school's charter require government approval of all members of the board of trustees, teachers, and courses. Moreover, he prohibited teaching in any language but Russian;[103] nothing would be allowed to detract from the ideal of the "Russian national school."

A number of liberal State Duma deputies were furious at Shvarts when he appeared before them to defend his actions in June 1908. The vacillation of the government on the project and the way it had been snatched from the Duma at the last moment undoubtedly contributed to their anger. Several commented with scorn on the length of time it had taken the bill to reach the Duma, more than two years after the Moscow city government had approved the project. Speaking for his party, the Octobrist P. V. Kamenskii accused Shvarts of tightening state controls over the university strictly for police goals. V. A. Maklakov, the Kadet deputy from Moscow, thundered that "here the only demand, the only request, the only hope presented to the government, that it would not interfere—in this hope society was deceived." The Social Democrat Belousov sarcastically noted that the minister's speech pointed to the "most decisive cessation of any sort of contact of the people with science and knowledge, those sources of revolution, strikes, and work stoppages."[104]

Nevertheless, the State Duma approved the government's bill, agreeing with its Educational Commission that it was better to have the university in a limited form than not to have it at all. The government's actions had evoked a bitter response from the parliament elected under laws the state had carefully tailored to ensure its own support.

The difficult birth of Shaniavskii University illustrates the problems faced by the Moscow city government in trying to make educational improvements or innovations it felt would meet local needs. The state was especially determined to monitor all aspects of higher education, which in this instance led to frustration and anger among liberal elements of "society." Shaniavskii University's trustees went to the trouble of publishing a pamphlet on the whole affair in which the noble aims of General Shaniavskii and the "police" goals of Shvarts are clearly meant to stand in sharp contrast to each other.[105] The publication was thus a sign of anger on the part of the trustees, who were chosen by the city duma from Moscow's *obshchestvo*.

Government supervision of the university continued after its opening. Several persons elected to the board of trustees were rejected by the Ministry of Education's district trustee, as were two presidents of the board. Police officers attended all lectures and sometimes intervened. In 1908, for example, an assistant professor from Moscow Imperial University was speaking at Shaniavskii University about the separation of powers in constitutional countries. When he began to discuss Russia, the police officer in attendance ended the talk. The audience reacted with much noise and whistling.[106]

In at least one respect, the government seemed ambivalent about what happened at the university. The authorities allowed the prominent Kadets A. A. Manuilov and S. A. Muromtsev to teach there despite their ouster from other posts for political reasons. Manuilov had been fired from his position as rector of Moscow Imperial University in 1911 after he allowed students to hold meetings on campus without police permission. Muromtsev, president of the First State Duma, had been barred from all political activity, including his seat in the Moscow city duma, after signing the Vyborg Manifesto of 1906; this document had called for passive national resistance to the closing of the First State Duma. The same confused approach applied in 1911 to more than one hundred professors and assistant professors who resigned from Moscow Imperial University and moved to Shaniavskii. They left in protest against the firing of Manuilov and the dispatch of troops onto the campus by Shvarts' successor as minister of education, Kasso, who was determined to end the student meetings.[107] The state again demonstrated its inconsistency when it allowed the protesting professors to move to an institution it clearly regarded as politically dangerous.

Government attempts to control education in Moscow extended well beyond its concern for Shaniavskii University. Under the vague national laws on public schools, the state had wide powers of intervention and control at the local level. For example, the 1892 City Statute charged municipalities with "care [*popechenie*] for development of the means of popular education," and "participation" in its administration, but did not specify the extent of municipal responsibility in this sphere.[108] Even the Council of Ministers complained about the imprecision of the law, though from the standpoint that the government's authority was not carefully defined.[109] This idea is ironic in light of the fact that it was

*A. A. Manuilov, member of the Moscow city duma and the State
Council, rector and professor at Moscow Imperial University until fired
by the government in 1911. First minister of education in the
Provisional Government, 1917.*

precisely the vagueness of this law, as with other legislation, that allowed government control to be so broad.

The Ministry of Education maintained an extensive apparatus to ensure that
its wishes were carried out in the country's schools.[110] The ministry's school
inspectors, who formed the first line of control, had great power over the institutions they supervised. They could fire any teacher they or the police deemed
unreliable; they could also delay implementation of any resolution of a provincial, *uezd*, or city school council, or of the city duma in Moscow's case, until it

had been reviewed by the "trustee" (*popechitel'*) of the educational district, the inspectors' immediate supervisor. This was double protection for the state, since the school councils were dominated anyway by state officials.

The Moscow school inspector played an active role in municipal education. For example, he informed the *uprava* in 1912 that city teachers were using books in class that had been banned by the Ministry of Education. He gave five examples of books that had come from city warehouses, which made teachers think they were all right to use. The inspector requested the *uprava* to tell the warehouse administration to keep itself informed of banned books.[111] It appears that in this case the city had hardly been eager to follow central direction on classroom materials.

At the next level in the Ministry of Education, the trustee had something of the same power over educational matters that the *gradonachal'nik* had over civil affairs. He could veto city duma resolutions on education or make additions or subtractions from curricula. He passed judgment on courses, teachers, and special programs. Above him, the *gradonachal'nik* had to approve instructions or rules for the operation of educational institutions, and the minister of education had the final say on all matters concerning schools. By the laws of 1864 and 1874 on elementary instruction, the state authorities could even close schools in case of "disorders" or their "taking a harmful direction." The vagueness of the laws assured the state's right to act without restraint.

During his tenure as minister of education, Shvarts directed his bureaucracy to report on the "political physiognomy" of all teachers and school personnel. He required the directors of school councils to study the performance of each teacher both politically and in terms of quality.[112] In this case he was simply using the apparatus for one of its intended purposes.

Occasionally the municipality of Moscow ran afoul of this supervisory framework; here too, great problems arose because of the ambiguity of the laws and the regime's unpredictability in interpreting them. One example of this kind of clash between the municipal and central authorities involved the elementary school curriculum adopted by the city duma in 1910, which began to diverge significantly from the Ministry of Education's "model program" of 1897. The city decided to apportion weekly classroom time in the following manner: only two hours of religious instruction; ten to sixteen hours of Russian language, combined with history, geography, or natural science, depending on the grade; four or five hours of arithmetic; and one or two hours of singing, usually religious in nature.[113] Hence the municipality's primary curriculum corresponded much more to the views of the Octobrists or even of Paul Miliukov than to the sentiments of Shvarts, Kasso, or the Nationalists.

Apparently no tsarist official objected to these changes until 1913. At that time, however, Kasso decided to review the courses personally. He eventually ordered the city to increase the hours assigned to penmanship. The president of the Ministry of Education's Academic Committee stated that the "task of the city school mainly consists of instruction in neat penmanship (most desirably calligraphy)." The city also had to cut the number of class hours devoted to drawing, manual arts, and singing. Kasso further believed that the first year of religious instruction was "too broad" and that pupils would not learn their prayers prop-

erly. Geography and history he also deemed "too broad," and Russian and arithmetic needed to be "strengthened,"[114] though in what sense the report does not
say.

While it might be argued that Kasso had the population's needs firmly in
mind when he spoke of improving the last two subjects, the same cannot be said
of his emphasis on religion or penmanship. In general, his approach to learning
was outmoded or designed to limit the perspectives pupils gained on their society
through such courses as history and geography. Last, it is difficult to believe that
he was in a better position than the businessmen of the Moscow duma to judge
how much time should be devoted to manual arts. As already noted, these delegates were almost certainly aware of the importance of such training for the city's
economy.

The national government interfered in Moscow's school system in other
important ways. It forbade, for example, all Russian cities and zemstva to give
translation tests from one foreign language to another in secondary schools. Stolypin, in his capacity as minister of the interior, informed governors and gradonachal'niki in 1908 that such tests were not within the legal competence of city and
zemstvo governments. His circular went on to reveal the real reason for the ban:
the tests were often "accompanied by criticism of the actions of governmental
agencies," presumably of national educational policy, in newspapers. Such articles "could only upset the minds of pupils in vain." Stolypin further instructed
governors and gradonachal'niki to tell local governments that they could not give
such tests and to remind them not to communicate with each other on "general
state questions," as they had been doing on this issue.[115] The prohibition of the
question's discussion among local governments is typical of the great difficulties
they faced under tsarism in simply trying to exchange information.

Yet there was a certain degree of flexibility in the tsarist educational bureaucracy. The municipality complained that the "greatest drawback" of the urban
schools of 1872 was the "limitation of the city government's rights" in regard to
them. In effect, the city had no rights at all. But in practice, Moscow's officials
had worked out an agreement with the district educational trustee under which
teachers would be appointed with the city's agreement, the uprava could introduce new courses with the trustee's approval after the fact, and the city's "honorary observer" as provided for by law took over economic management of the
schools.[116] The state's educational bureaucracy did permit local initiative, up to
the point at which a basic conflict developed over the nature of instruction.

The central apparatus also regularly entered into the process of adult education in Moscow. By 1912 attendance in the city's elementary courses for workers
was declining. There were few pupils who wanted instruction at that level, which
reflects a general trend toward increasing sophistication in the educational goals
of the lower classes: they now centered their desires more than ever before on
secondary programs. The city duma responded by drawing up a new, advanced
curriculum.[117] In July the improved program was ready, and the city submitted it
to the trustee of the educational district. Without waiting for a reply, the municipality opened several evening and Sunday classes on the new basis in October
1913. Here too it hoped to circumvent the state. The courses were arranged in an
eight-year sequence, with a special section intended to prepare students to
become city elementary school teachers. Such an ambitious schedule for sophis-

ticated adult education again illustrates the city's sensitivity to lower class needs and its willingness to work to meet them.

However, an old story was repeated here: the district trustee intervened and informed the city that the plan was unacceptable because the program was "extremely indefinite."[118] The municipality drew up new plans and submitted them to the trustee, but by the start of the 1914–1915 academic year he had not responded. With the outbreak of war, the plans were abandoned.

Other organizations conducting courses for workers had similar experiences. In 1912 the Prechistenskie group found itself in some difficulty because a series of people chosen as presidents of its commission on technical education had been rejected by the minister of education. The district school trustee had also rejected many teachers.[119] The Moscow Society of Popular Universities (a private group, not to be confused with Shaniavskii University) was ordered in this period to end lectures to workers in the auditorium of the Kursk railroad workshops. The gendarmes considered it impossible to allow the lectures without an officer in attendance, and none could be spared for the purpose.[120]

In such cases the state demonstrated its willingness to block the development of education for the sake of control over what was taught. The government was particularly determined to supervise anything done for or by workers. State control of adult education in Moscow operated continuously.

Outside the city, the government in 1908 closed popular higher courses or forbade their opening in at least eight places.[121] This represented a sharp change in practice from the period 1906–early 1907, when the government allowed such courses to begin or to be organized in several towns.[122] At the upper levels of the state, the previous fear and the spirit of conciliation it had produced gave way by 1908 to old habits, including opposition to the spread of adult secondary or higher education.

Moscow's city government worked energetically between 1906 and 1914 to meet the educational desires of the lower classes. The people of the city demonstrated very clearly that they wanted more access to education at all levels for themselves and their children, and as time went on they indicated an increasing need and desire for more sophisticated kinds of instruction. Municipal officials welcomed this trend and set up or helped fund programs to meet it. On occasion, leading figures in the city suggested that these efforts could be very useful in terms of further integrating the lower strata of the population into urban life, which in turn could produce greater social and political stability and cohesion. This goal was especially important after the scare of 1905.

On the other hand, many national government officials and their allies in the Third and Fourth State Dumas and the State Council strongly opposed any effort to move local curricula and programs away from the old emphasis on religion and toward more sophisticated training for adults. To a substantial degree, this dispute can be characterized as a split between the country's urban liberals, who saw the grave danger of allowing social problems to fester in their localities, and the rural, ethnic Russian gentry, who continued to stress religion and loyalty to the tsar in education. This approach was supposed to promote conservatism in the lower classes.

Differences in educational philosophy were at the heart of the quarrel between the state and some members of "society" over central control of the schools. Those who did not heavily stress religion, for example the Octobrists, became increasingly opposed to state control of education. An Octobrist deputy to the Third State Duma from the city of Samara, M. D. Chelyshov, told his colleagues in 1908, "All of us, gentlemen, accuse the *chinovniki* [of responsibility for the grave defects in the schools], saying that the bureaucracy is guilty of everything."[123] M. Ia. Kapustin, also an Octobrist, reported to the Third Duma in the same year on the deliberations of the budget commission regarding appropriations for the Ministry of Education. He pointed to "fundamentally dark sides" in the ministry, above all the "system of most strict centralization." "Confined in bureaucratic limits," he continued, school affairs "never go well."[124] G. Kh. Enikeev, a member of the Mussulman party, Islamic deputies who promoted their minorities' interests and naturally resented Russification, identified the "most important reason" for the sad results in education as "the activity of the Ministry of Education, its school policy." Its actions were based on "the violent realization of the old Russian bureaucracy's policy." This had "driven popular education into a horrible situation."[125] We have already seen the objections to government interference in education by the Kadet V. A. Maklakov.

On the other hand, a Rightist deputy and priest from Khar'kov, A. M. Stanislavskii, who valued religion in the schools most of all and thus felt comfortable with central supervision, insisted at the same time on the "necessity to strengthen [state] inspection of the schools."[126] The government could therefore feel that its educational values met the wishes of the political groups it tried to rely on after 1908–1909, the moderate Rightists and the Nationalists.

Conservative Russians had substantial reason to fear the results of broader and more sophisticated education for the general populace. For instance, one worker who attended the Prechistenskie courses in Moscow later recalled how a lecturer on geography "excited us with her stories of the lives and daily customs of workers in other countries."[127] The same man also recalled, "The more we penetrated into the kingdom of light, to which the [Prechistenskie] courses half opened the door, the more a feeling of protest rose up in us against all the hindrances and obstacles in our path."[128] The quotations noted earlier from the Shaniavskii University survey of 1910 also suggest the same reaction to education on the part of workers. Such feelings and perspectives on Russian existence were dangerous to a regime whose authority depended, even after 1905, on unquestioning acceptance of the tsar's right to dominate politics. Moreover, courses like the Prechistenskie program tended to attract the most politically conscious workers and other members of the lower classes, who then used this opportunity to recruit people for the Social Democrats.[129] In this instance, general education for adults in the form of "popular" courses bore out the worst fears of the conservatives.

Concerned about such trends, the state tried to make sure that the content of education at all levels was politically safe. Hesitating to prohibit popular courses altogether in the face of opposition from important segments of society, the central government allowed such programs to open and flourish in some places while attempting to regulate them strictly. This approach fell between two stools; it irritated many leading Russians and made state interference blatant to all concerned, yet it did nothing to halt the kinds of political recruitment or consciousness-raising just described. The state's erratic application of its principles further exacerbated these problems. Education expanded rapidly in the last peacetime years of the Old Regime; however, far from being a positive development for the future of the state, this growth served to engender anger and frustration among many citizens.

These sentiments were clearly visible among a number of Moscow's leading figures. They appeared, for example, in the mass resignation of faculty from Moscow Imperial University in 1911, the publication of the pamphlet on the birth of Shaniavskii University, and V. A. Maklakov's complaint to the Third State Duma about government control of that school. In 1914 P. P. Riabushinskii reported to a congress of representatives of trade and industry that he and his brothers had founded a trade school. They had then succeeded it getting it transferred from the jurisdiction of the Ministry of Education to that of the Ministry of Trade and Industry. The brothers, Riabushinskii said, had fled from the first ministry "as from a plague."[130] The state's formal educational apparatus and its outlook were thus deeply unattractive to a man who styled himself a liberal and who was the dominant personality of the national Progressist party.

A particularly sharp protest against state interference in education appeared in Moscow in 1911, after the massive resignations at Moscow Imperial University. The objection, courageously signed by sixty-six prominent business figures, was published in *Russkie Vedomosti*.

> There are moments in the life of the *obshchestvo* when its silence can be taken as a sign of sympathy. Yielding to material force does not cover people with shame. Some defeats are more honorable than victory. But to refuse any kind of defense of this affair in respect to right and truth, that is undoubtedly a symptom of defeat and the collapse of spiritual strength in the *obshchestvo*. . . . We . . . would not consider it correct to be silently present at the disintegration of the higher school.
>
> . . . is it really possible to make the higher school itself an object of punishment [for the excesses of some students]? No, in the great cause of popular construction, anger is a poor counselor, and measures of material force alone will not resolve the conflicts that are so deeply affecting the spiritual forces of the Russian people.
>
> The *obshchestvo* would render a poor service to the government and the country if at a moment of spiritual collapse it gave the government grounds to think that it had the moral support of the country.[131]

Among the sixty-six signers were a number of prominent members of the Moscow duma. Although the conservative president of the Moscow Stock Exchange Committee, G. A. Krestovnikov, issued a rejoinder, the statement did represent deep *obshchestvo* anger and resentment toward the state because of its actions in higher education. The signers were clearly convinced, moreover, that the government was losing "the moral support of the country" as a result of its behavior. All this might well lead to new unrest, as the document implied: "The revolutionary wave among our student youth has undoubtedly yielded in recent years to the pursuit of learning." Thus the state's actions might well upset progress toward stability.

Once again an important group of urban liberals found themselves bitterly opposed to state policies. Such conflicts over education fed the general spirit of resentment and opposition in the Moscow duma in 1912.

Patrick Alston has argued that by 1914, "Despite its reluctance to accept political constitutionalism, the state appeared ready to extend guarded recognition to society as co-partner in the campaign for national enlightenment."[132] But his evidence for this conclusion is slim: it rests on the fact that, in contrast to 1901 when it barred such a gathering, the government allowed an All-Russian Congress for People's Education to be held at the end of 1913. Yet this same meeting formulated a series of goals the central government had been moving away from in recent years: freedom of instruction, private initiative, and decentralization.[133]

Certainly even many Octobrists did not feel like "co-partners." In 1909 Kapustin broadened his criticism of the government's educational policies. He castigated the laws on education as "most severe" and "draconian."

> If the state administration seeks support not in the educated circles, if the upper intelligentsia stands aside from the Sovereign's cause, if [it] regards [the government] not with trust, [but] with suspicion, if [it] goes out, so to speak, into the opposition, no matter what happens, then the cause [of education] will not go well.[134]

To this important Octobrist, educational issues might be the catalyst for a very serious political division between the government and society.

By 1914 the "draconian laws" had not changed significantly in regard to the government's role in education, and opposition from the intelligentsia was indeed growing. In early 1909 Shvarts told the Council of Ministers that a proposed new law on elementary schools "did not introduce any kind of essential changes in the area of school instruction but only strengthened those norms that the school has already attained in its development."[135] Among those norms were strict state control and tutelage of the schools.

Moscow's city government, firmly in the liberal camp, frequently resisted or avoided state control over education. Supported by many conservatives, the national authorities opposed this trend. The stakes in this struggle were high, for each group thought that it recognized a key to social and political stability in a certain kind of education. Neither Moscow's elite nor its lower classes could derive much satisfaction from the state's educational policies, and the result was further deterioration of support for the regime.

Conclusion

The Russians' bodies were freed in 1861. Now the time has come for the
emancipation of their souls from the guardianship of the bureaucracy.
From a "memorandum compiled by a group of the biggest factory and
mill owners of Moscow and the Moscow region, 1905."[1]

Neither Moscow's elite nor various key figures in the national government were
indifferent to Russia's urban problems after 1905. The Moscow municipal duma
consistently worked hard and voted money, even when it hurt the pocketbooks
of the upper classes, to improve conditions in the city. In case after case Moscow's
leaders demonstrated their support for the vast efforts required to begin correcting
local problems; the result was a wide array of programs beneficial to the city's
poor.

Many of the services and plans developed extensively after 1905 had their
origins in the 1890s; for instance, welfare reform, new attention to the desires of
the poor for education, and a survey of the housing situation all appeared in that
decade. By then, several factors that tended to promote reform had begun to coa-
lesce in the city duma. First, the famine of 1891 shook educated society out of
the torpor that had fallen upon it since the assassination of Alexander II ten years
earlier. Second, Russia's urban problems had certainly already reached alarming
proportions, and it was clear that the central government had little to offer in the
way of solutions. While the rural elite could more easily ignore local poverty, poor
health, and other lower class problems, town dwellers could not avoid daily contact with them. The urban elite had more reason than the rural gentry to seek
solutions to local defects.

A third factor that prompted reform in Moscow was the relatively high level
of education attained by many of its leaders toward the turn of the century. Landowners who possessed higher education were also more inclined to advocate
ameliorative programs than their more ignorant peers. A growing consciousness
of Russia's backwardness vis-à-vis the West, which had certainly not characterized the old *kupechestvo*, came with the new level of education in Moscow. This
awareness was enhanced by the numerous professionals in the city duma, especially after 1892. The humiliation of the war with Japan in 1904–1905 drove
home the feeling that Russia had to make vast efforts to catch up with the
advanced countries.

The Old Believer background of many civic leaders in Moscow, which gave
them a keen awareness of past state injustice, may have prompted a greater sense

of duty to the local population. At the same time, a fair number of city duma deputies were still classified as peasants by *soslovie*, so that they may have felt closer to the immigrating peasants than one would normally expect for urban elites; P. P. Riabushinskii argued that the two groups were part of the same class.

In considering why a high level of solicitude emerged in Moscow but not in cities like Kiev, Philadelphia, or Buenos Aires, which were experiencing similar problems at the same time, the ethnic mix of each locale is important. Unlike the towns just listed, Moscow's people were overwhelmingly of one ethnic group. The leaders of Kiev wasted time, energy, and concern over issues of nationality and language and paid less attention to the local poor because they were often of a different ethnic group. Philadelphia's city fathers could always comfort themselves with the prevailing "racial" stereotypes of the day, which argued that immigrants from "inferior" countries were poor because of their "blood." Moscow's leaders had no such rationale to fall back on. It was Russia's own backwardness that they saw every day.

These characteristics of Moscow's life help to explain why the city government made many ameliorative efforts for the local populace before the threat of revolution became so perfectly tangible in the December Uprising. However, the severe upheavals of 1905, which culminated in grotesque bloodshed on the very doorstep of the city duma, naturally prompted local officials to bolster their reform plans. On many occasions after that year Moscow's leaders spoke of impending unrest if some specific improvement was not adopted. A heightened concern for integrating the city's poor into urban life and for improving their lot was expressed in measures to achieve better library facilities, housing, and education, to cite just a few areas. After 1905 Moscow's locally elected government seemed to sense that it was engaged in a race against time and immigration to win the loyalty of the lower classes.

Leading figures in the central government like Stolypin and Kokovtsov also recognized the depth of urban troubles and the necessity to correct them if Russia was to improve its economic and social life and to maintain its status as a Great Power. Yet little improvement in municipal services occurred by the eve of the war, even in the most developed parts of the country. A survey of town governments taken in 1911 revealed the appalling figures shown in Table C-1.[2]

No discussion of the quality or extent of these services was published with these data; judging from the difficulties involved in extending trams, water supply, and sewerage in Moscow and St. Petersburg, coverage of these networks was

TABLE C-1.   Municipal Services in Russian Cities, 1911

Area	No. of Cities	Have City Water	City Sewerage	Fire Depts.	City Trams
European Russia	762	149	27	742	42
Vistula region	121	9	5	118	7
Caucasus	103	27	6	86	5
Siberia	50	2	—	49	—
Asiatic Russia	46	5	—	37	1

probably much worse in smaller cities. Of course, the most striking feature of the table is how many Russian municipalities were not even attempting to meet the needs of their inhabitants in the years just before the First World War. This picture was growing steadily worse, because virtually all the towns also had to cope with rapid population growth. Why wasn't more done to alleviate urban conditions?

In some cases, the answer does lie in the apathy of the local elite, as Western and Soviet authors have suggested. But this tendency was originally fostered by a low level of education and, especially, by the traditional lack of opportunity for local residents to influence their own affairs. These characteristics of Russian urban life had their roots in state practice reaching back for centuries. The central government also kept the towns on a tight financial rein for far too long, and although this picture was changing around 1912, by then much damage had already been done. In addition, the state's political concerns still precluded any move to resolve the basic tax inequities of the country, which were built into the system of indirect taxation. Thus even the treasury subsidies and other positive changes in the cities' finances on the eve of the war would not have been enough to make more than an initial contribution to solving urban problems.

Finally, the centrally administered police still had vast powers on the local level after 1905; this situation also discouraged local initiative. In this regard, more remained the same than changed in Russia during the "constitutional experiment." Where power was actually exercised, old practices continued. The extremely vague statutes still gave the police the ability to act virtually as they pleased in enforcing the will of the regime. While urban liberals chafed under this yoke, rural conservatives found it to their liking; the laws and the powers of the police, they felt, were the best protection against revolution in their milieu. State officials were comfortable with landowner support, especially after 1907, because it dovetailed with tsarist tradition.

In sum, there were many reasons for the dire situation of Russian cities by 1914, but among them the actions and attitudes of the Old Regime played a very prominent role. Simply leaving the towns alone would have been more beneficial than the approach taken by the state, but that would have contradicted tradition and the central government's fears about the growth and nature of cities, which dated back to the 1840s.[3]

Judging by his own words, the man on whom so many upper class Russians pinned their hopes for the future, Stolypin, wished to change much of this picture. We can sum up his desires for urban reform along the following lines: he decried the low level of education in Russia, advocated its expansion and improvement, and called for better public health measures. Into 1907, he spoke in favor of decentralizing financial prerogatives, and his statements regarding police reform also implied some lessening of the state's authority at the local level. He denounced the old police system and advocated the rule of law. In fact, it is ironic that no one stated the liberal position on law better in this period than Stolypin. In March 1907 he spoke on this issue to the largely conservative men of the State Council.

> Our fatherland must be transformed into a state of laws, since until written
> law determines the obligations and limits the rights of individual Russian sub-

jects, these laws and obligations will remain dependent upon the interpretation and will of individuals, that is, they will not be firmly established.

Legal norms must also rest upon exact, clearly stated law because otherwise life will constantly give rise to confrontations between the new bases of public and state life [obshchestvennosti i gosudarstvennosti], which have received the approval of the Monarch, and the old arrangements and laws, which are in contradiction with them; [the latter arrangements and laws] do not correspond to the new demands of the legislator, nor to a productive understanding of the new bases on the part of private and official persons.[4]

The Moscow liberals could have endorsed these ideas without reservation.

After 1905 a number of influential Russians expected to be able to work with Stolypin on a reform program that addressed these and other issues; this hope was the raison d'être of the Octobrist party. But as time when on he found that this approach appealed neither to his tsar nor to conservative landowners. They liked the great scope of police activity, central control of education, and the status quo regarding taxation. In several key cases Stolypin found his reform plans blocked by the institution he most counted on for aid, the State Duma. If the Duma failed to act conservatively, the State Council stood ready to perform this role. The price for the regime's remaining social support among the nobles was the derailment of social change. After the "coup d'état" of 1907, which changed the national electoral law to insure gentry domination of the State Duma, there was little prospect that the reforms appropriate and necessary for Russian urban life would be adopted. The Russian gentry as a whole did not want such change. Even Stolypin's mild reforms for the cities ultimately failed, as did his plans overall. In retrospect this outcome seems inevitable, for he had tried to square the tsarist circle: his ideas were an assault on the regime's ideological bases.

The fundamental source of the dispute between liberals and the state lay precisely in the sphere of ideology. Many of the arguments between leading Muscovites and central officials can be traced to their very different conceptions of what Russia should be. The state's ideology, perhaps reasonably well suited for a medieval, agrarian society, was by no means appropriate for a country undergoing rapid urbanization in the twentieth century. Ideology was also an important part of the reason for the government's greater attention to reform for the peasantry than for townspeople.

The tsars had long identified with the landed gentry and even pronounced themselves members of that group. During the Pugachev peasant and Cossack rebellion of 1773–1774, Catherine the Great declared that she was a "proprietress of Kazan'." The integrity, well-being, and security of the gentry "are indivisible with our own and our empire's security and well-being," she continued. The nobles of Kazan' responded that the gentry are the "veritable shield" of the country, "the supports of the tsarist throne."[5] Nicholas II followed Catherine's lead. For the census of 1897 he called himself a landowner and "the landlord of the Russian soil."[6]

Another aspect of tsarist ideology that affected its approach to the towns was the estate principle. Although soslovie privileges seemed insignificant in most respects by the turn of the century, the importance of the estate system was still immense. It continued to ensure gentry control of the top levels of government, the *zemstva*, the State Duma, and the State Council—the whole of the country's policy-making structure except the city dumas.

That the town councils were chosen according to a different principle was no accident. Wherever it could the conservative state relied on the gentry, increasingly so after 1905; but there were simply not enough nobles in the cities to do the job. Trying to depend on the propertied elements in the towns, the next best choice from the government's point of view, was hardly satisfactory; in the case of Moscow, this stratum turned steadily against the regime toward the eve of the war.

Tsarist ideology also hampered the development of something else dear to urban dwellers, the rule of law. Again, Stolypin's ideas on law, which were never even put into concrete proposals, were bound to fail. The rule of law would have afforded the business elite the personal protection and chances to speak out it craved, while offering workers some legal and regulated ways in which to express their grievances. But it was the old, vague laws and norms, which ultimately had more support from the gentry, the emperor, and the state, that remained dominant in Russia.

Conservative nobles often approved the old ways and said so in the State Duma. Tradition ensured their status, and when the state intervened in the countryside it was to protect their lives and property by oppressing the peasants. Among the provincial gentry after 1905 a "law and order tendency," which meant above all control of the peasants, produced wide rejection of civil liberties.[7]

The last area where tsarist ideology hampered a modus vivendi with modern urban life concerned elected local government. Over the centuries the Russian state made only hesitant and limited attempts to promote self-government in the towns. Even the promising municipal reform of 1870, already greatly weakened in 1881, remained in effect for only twenty-two years before the state strongly reasserted its control over city government.

This counterreform of 1892 was also firmly based in tsarist ideology and was heavily promoted by Pobedonostsev. He had decided that the essential principles of both the *zemstva* and the municipal dumas, their elective and legislative characteristics, were "immoral." In order to preserve Russia, these institutions had to be eliminated.[8]

Count Sergei Witte, who was even more prominent than Pobedonostsev as a statesman and adviser to the tsars in the 1890s and early twentieth century, also found that tsarism and elective local governments were completely incompatible. He recognized that reliance on an unlimited bureaucracy was a fundamental state principle. Yet "in their relationship to the supreme power," he wrote in 1899, "organs of self-government are essentially different from bureaucratic organs." That is, by definition self-governing structures were not completely creatures of the state. They were partly responsible to a local electorate, which contradicted the principle fulfilled by the bureaucracy: all levels of government were responsible to the tsar. Self-government limited, however narrowly, the ability of the autocratic state to maintain control everywhere.

Witte further criticized the concept of elected local governments by linking it with one of the words most detested by the tsars and their conservative advisers—*constitution.*

A constitution, as self-government at the top, and *zemstvo* self-government as
a system of local administration, are based on one and the same principle, of
popular rule. That is, [they are both based] on society's participation in state
governance (the first—at the top, the second, locally); therefore, my memorandum shows that the system of administration at the top is closely linked to the
system of local administration. The organization of these systems on different
bases produces an inarguable contradiction, [and this] will hamper the correct
action of the administrative machinery and sooner or later will lead to a
reform of one [system] on the bases of the other.[9]

Thus, like Pobedonostsev, Witte believed that elected local self-government had
to be abolished if the tsarist system was to survive. Virtually the same point was
made by a writer in the liberal newspaper *Russkie Vedomosti* in early 1914.[10]

All of these ideological differences between city and state help explain why
Moscow's leaders, like so many liberals, opposed the centralization of power in
Russia. The exercise of that power hindered the modernization liberals felt was
essential. On the eve of the war, the country's crisis was as much ideological as
social or political, and ideology conditioned social and political tensions.

By 1911 Stolypin could find a majority in the Duma only on so-called
"national issues" like the reduction of Finland's autonomy. Moving in this direction and away from social reform, he relied more and more on the gentry of the
Nationalist party. Although he also found support among the Octobrists, many
of them realized that this tack was of little value for Russia's urban situation.
After 1907, when the prime minister did offer suggestions for the towns, they
always included provisos for increased central tutelage of local governments. Following Stolypin's death in 1911 tsarist officials paid even less attention to reform,
and their interference in urban life and government grew. Moscow's liberals
found this situation less and less tolerable as time went on.

In assessing the Old Regime's record toward the towns by 1914 it is evident
that some initiatives and efforts for improvement did come from the center. The
better funding for city governments, the subway plan for Moscow, and the suggestions for welfare reform are only a few examples of this pattern. Especially
when directed by Stolypin, the central government displayed regular concern
about urban conditions. Nevertheless, tension between town authorities and central officials, not just in Moscow but in many places, continued to grow. There
were several reasons for this widening antipathy. First, urban difficulties, fed by
population increases, outdistanced the limited innovations possible under the
given legal and financial restrictions. Second, Russian liberals came to believe
that the central government was paving the way for another revolution; it had not
made necessary reforms or shown sufficient concern for the needs of the lower
classes.

Nowhere were these sentiments of opposition and impending disaster
stronger than in Moscow. After the sentencing of former *Gradonachal'nik* Reinbot in 1911, *Russkie Vedomosti* announced that such punishments for crimes by
officials were extremely infrequent and erratic. This was no surprise, for "the
obshchestvo well knows that we live in a country where considerations of public
interests are not of primary importance."[11] M. M. Novikov, a liberal member of
the Moscow duma, noted in his memoirs that "in the corridors of the city duma

... antigovernmental tendencies [had] clearly emerged" by 1908, growing stronger in the elections of 1912 and 1916.[12] The difficulties the municipality encountered with tsarist officials over educational programs and mayoral elections after 1912 brought forth similar feelings.

Leading Muscovites made numerous gloomy predictions about Russia's future on the eve of the war. Arch-conservatives like the former revolutionary Lev Tikhomirov, editor of *Moskovskie Vedomosti*, felt the ground slipping away beneath them. In his diary for December 1910 he noted that subscriptions to his paper were steadily falling. "No information (permitted by me) attracts readers, so long as I maintain a monarchist, Orthodox, and decent tone." In July 1911 Tikhomirov predicted, "In about ten years, not a trace of old Russia will remain. Finis Russiae." On September 5, after the news of Stolypin's death, Tikhomirov entered the opinion that "before Russia a kind of black darkness of unknown and, probably, cruel misfortunes is opening. Probably no one will be able to cope with the situation."[13]

Tikhomirov blamed this prospect on the regime's supposed divergence from its true principles, especially Orthodoxy and nationalism. But he was admitting that those foundations no longer attracted many people. More liberal Muscovites, approaching the question of Russia's future from a much different viewpoint and set of experiences, nonetheless reached similar conclusions about the chances of another upheaval. A. I. Guchkov addressed the problem at a meeting of Octobrist party members in 1913.

> What is to be the issue of the grave crisis through which we are now passing? What does the encroachment of reaction bring with it? Whither is the government policy, or rather lack of policy, carrying us? Towards an inevitable and grave catastrophe!
> ... the attempt to effect a peaceful, painless transition from the old condemned system to a new order has failed.[14]

V. A. Maklakov had issued a similarly dire warning to the State Duma six years earlier.

> Reform cannot [*nel'zia*] be postponed; whoever does not put it into effect now will be guilty before history, if he by this [failure] calls forth, to our misfortune and woe, another paroxysm similar to the revolution [of 1905].[15]

By early 1914, the Moscow industrialists P. P. Riabushinskii and A. I. Konovalov were so convinced of the regime's inability to change that they met with members of leftist parties, including the Bolsheviks, and offered them cooperation and money.

Much of this mood of criticism and pessimism stemmed from state interference in local governance. Guchkov proudly described Moscow's defiance of the central government to the Congress of Municipal Representatives held in Kiev in 1913.

> In Moscow we do not permit such a limitation of freedom as has hung over us in Kiev. In Moscow we do not stand for interference by the police in considering issues of municipal government. In Moscow we are preparing a basic reform of the city statute.[16]

Of course, the powers of the tsarist administration meant that these words were much more indicative of an attitude than of practice. But as such they were deeply significant, not only for Moscow but for all urban Russia.

Guchkov also denounced "those general conditions that prevent, among other things, the advancement of our municipal affairs." This situation was rooted in "the attitude of the government to the organs and to the very idea of local government." Police closed the congress after his remark that delay in reforms and deviations from the October Manifesto "threaten the country with grave convulsions and ruinous consequences." Guchkov, like the Moscow duma, had traveled a long political distance from the period between December 1905 and 1907, when he and his brother had identified themselves with key tsarist officials and policies. As the police were ending the meeting the assembled municipal activists gave Guchkov a resounding ovation.[17] A "militant mood reigned" at the conference, according to a Moscow duma deputy who took part.[18] Another reported that the meeting adopted a resolution that repeated Guchkov's general remarks almost word for word.[19] In all likelihood a similar session of *zemstvo* delegates in the same period would have tried to make sure that a speaker with his outlook did not appear on the rostrum in the first place; failing that, it would have greeted similar remarks with strong hostility.

The urban elite's mood was different, and Moscow's liberals had found widespread sympathy and support by the eve of the war. Several factors demonstrated this trend: the Kiev congress; the growing strength of the Kadet party in urban curiae by 1912; the fragmentation of the Octobrists, finalized by Guchkov's speeches and activities, over the issue of the party's attitude toward government policy; the fact that the national Progressive party centered in Moscow; the prominent positions held by Muscovites in the Union of Towns, the Union of Zemstvos, and the War Industries Committees during the war; and finally their virtual domination of the first Provisional Government. Moscow's leaders set the tone of liberal activity for the whole country by 1912–1914.

At least two members of the city duma sensed and commented on the depth of the differences in outlook that separated them from the main tendencies of the regime. In 1910 P. P. Riabushinskii wrote that five years earlier the bourgeoisie had helped "the people of the old regime put down revolution. But now reaction, just as crude as anarchy, begins in its turn to evoke resistance from the bourgeoisie." The unheard-of was happening: "the *arshinnik* [petty merchant], always so submissive, so silent" is suddenly mixing into politics "fully consciously." He meant that at last the bourgeoisie was attempting to claim its rightful political role, in opposition to the regime. Perhaps this will come to nothing, he wrote, but the "idea of the bourgeoisie, the idea of cultural freedom—this idea will not perish."[20]

Pavel Buryshkin seconded Riabushinskii's opinion. He noted that after 1905 the Society of Mill and Factory Owners of the Moscow region worked to defend "the interests of industry and commerce on the one hand against the government, on the other against the workers." Before the war with Japan, "no one [among the Moscow commercial class] thought of considering questions that were connected one way or another with politics." This was because the people of that group already knew "what was necessary for the development of the productive forces of the country and the growth of the Russian economy," and that was "to change the general conditions of Russian life—both political and social."[21] Thus two members of the Moscow city duma expressed their conviction that fundamental liberalization had to take place before Russia could hope to realize her full economic potential; Moscow's liberal press did the same in 1912. Especially in Riabushinskii's remarks, there is the implication that the bourgeoisie had the correct vision to achieve that development. As far as possible, the Moscow city government worked to implement this vision between 1906 and 1914.

In making that attempt the municipality frequently found itself in conflict with central authorities. The same clash occurred in other towns as well. Bernard Pares, who had extensive contacts among the Russian *obshchestvo* and spent considerable time in the country before the war, remarked, "It is impossible to count up all the disputes between a Town Council and the Government, or the cases in which the Government has treated the Town Council with negligence or even contempt."[22] Nor were Moscow's difficulties in choosing its own mayor unique. As Chapter 3 noted, between 1900 and 1914 the state rejected 217 mayoral choices and 318 *uprava* members in Russian towns. On the other hand, such problems have not been reported for the *zemstva*.[23]

That so much was accomplished anyway in Moscow was both a tribute to the perseverance and resourcefulness of the city leaders and a reflection of the regime's logical and policy weaknesses in regard to the towns. The central government was not so much against innovation in urban life as it was for change on its own terms, under its control. Its halting, stumbling, erratic approach to new programs in Moscow stemmed from its basic inability to accept the nature of city existence. The government had few ideas of its own for the towns; when confronted with an energetic municipality like Moscow's, it allowed many things to go forward, hampering them just enough to cause local resentment. Without the government's restraints and interference, much more would have been achieved in the city before the war.

Nonetheless, it is possible that municipal programs did succeed to a degree in making the lower classes feel that they had a real place in the city's life. From 1912 to 1914, as the workers' movement gained vast new energy in the wake of the Lena Goldfields massacre, Moscow's working class remained much quieter than Petersburg's.

There are few indications of appreciation for municipal efforts or programs among Moscow's lower classes. But many of the thousands who attended city-sponsored courses, used city libraries, slept in municipal flophouses, or sent their children to free schools, must have reacted positively to these opportunities. Evidence on the degree to which Moscow's people came to support their liberal leadership is only fragmentary. Still, it seems important that radical spokesmen regularly worried about a liberal mood among the city's workers, and that strikers responded positively to municipal efforts in 1913. Why shouldn't that attitude have deepened as the city did more for people and the conservative state appeared as its foil, as happened so frequently after 1912? In short, one may offer the conclusion, however tentatively, that the bulk of the city population was becoming more open to liberal solutions as time went on. Moscow's experience in 1917 (discussed in the epilogue) provides further indications that support this finding.

The Soviet scholar L. M. Ivanov, writing about the "ideological influence on the proletariat of tsarism and the bourgeoisie," was also impressed by the scope and success of the bourgeoisie's efforts to attract workers before the war. "Government and liberal-bourgeois" programs "drew in, especially in the cities, not a few workers." The Moscow Society for Popular Sobriety "attracted a significant number of workers." Ivanov also concluded, "The liberal bourgeoisie in large measure attracted literate and developed workers," a surprising finding for a Soviet writer, as such workers are typically considered to be the backbone of Bolshevik support. However, he added, "severe social contrasts, the sharpness of class contradictions acted in the opposite direction to government and liberal propaganda."[24] In light of his lengthy discussion of liberal programs and his more specific conclusions on their effectiveness, the last phrase seems largely a pro forma nod in the direction of the orthodox Soviet view.

Yet for all the efforts and improvements that occurred in Moscow by 1914, most residents still had inadequate housing, lacked protection from disease and epidemics, and were desperately poor and exploited. There was much tinder in the city for revolution, a fact that local officials recognized and that added to their growing worry about the future. The liberal approach might have worked in Russia, as it did elsewhere, in the sense of forestalling revolution. But the state's ideology and policies prevented its implementation soon enough or on a broad enough scale.

Russian liberals came to see that the promises of October 1905 would not be fulfilled, and they came to distrust the regime's political and social policies more and more. Thus even when conditions improved in certain respects, as they did in Moscow from 1906 to 1914, and the regime allowed local leaders some opportunity to act on their own, the result was only to underscore how different the regime's view of Russia was from the liberals'. The latter came to see the central government as little more than a nuisance blocking the way to real amelioration, which is hardly a view conducive to substantial support. Every halfway measure granted by the government or allowed to go forward without its approval only pointed up how much more might have been accomplished without central interference, or if the political bases of the country were different.

After Stolypin's death, the government moved further away from constitutional rule. Reliance on the police increased, ministers no longer submitted important bills to the State Duma, and Nicholas II considered trying to reduce the legislature to a consultative body, "which is in accordance with the Russian tradition,"[25] as he put it. The regime also gave no indication that it would change its attitudes toward the rights and competence of local self-government after 1905. There is a clear continuity and tendency toward greater central control, from the Extraordinary Measures of 1881 to the *zemstvo* and municipal counter-reforms of the 1890s to the regime's proposals on local government of the period 1907–1912. Moscow's leaders felt this trend more strongly in the two years prior to the war's outbreak than ever before, and they reacted to it with anger and resentment.

A number of Soviet scholars, following Lenin, have argued that the liberals veered back and forth between support of the government and opposition to it in the years 1906–1914. On the one hand, this view argues, the liberals had many economic ties to the state, were afraid of revolution, and saw the preservation of the regime as their best guarantee that it would not take place. On the other, they detested many features of the political situation.[26] Lenin asserted that the Russian bourgeoisie "became liberal-monarchist and antidemocratic, antipeople [*protivonarodnoi*]. . . . it feared democracy more than reaction."[27] However, the opposite is more correct: what occurred by 1914 was a general decline of support for the regime among leading urban liberals, precisely because it was apparent that the government's policies were likely to foster, not prevent, another revolution.[28]

Even less convincing is the idea recently advanced by an American scholar that a "revolution in consciousness" was occurring before the war among industrialists, professionals, and the middle class. This trend, the argument states, moved such people into a kind of loyal opposition to the regime, akin to the British system's party out of power.[29] If this happened for some educated Russians, many others felt that the Old Regime simply had to go. In Moscow, a major venue of industrial, middle class, and intelligentsia thinking, important spokesmen emphasized over and over their active opposition to the central authorities by 1914, and the Council of Ministers and the Tsar returned the compliment by referring to the city duma's majority as "leftists." The dominant political consciousness in the city's elite on the eve of the war, evident as well at the Kiev city conference, was hostility to the regime.[30]

In the realm of complete implausibility is the opinion that "before 1917 the Russian liberals had squandered their opportunity not through upholding the claims of political liberty but through demanding in so backward and regimented a country and so vast an empire too much liberty too soon."[31] What "too much liberty too soon" might mean must remain a mystery. But surely more liberty, not less, would have helped produce stability; more attention to urban problems was absolutely essential. This was the liberal program.

Moscow's leaders did what they could from 1906 to 1914 to avoid another revolution. The scale of the problems they faced was great, and their efforts were insufficient. The state also tried very hard to prevent another upheaval, yet its tactics could not satisfy the urban populace, which demonstrated its ability to decide the fate of the country in 1917. Even when the regime tried to placate town dwellers, it was trapped in the major contradictions recognized by Pobedonostsev, Witte, and Stolypin. When the government moved to correct the country's severe problems, or even to allow their solution by others, it undermined its own social and political foundations. The state moved in one direction, Moscow in the other, and their divergence epitomized the kinds of cleavages in the body politic that led to revolution three years later. Even abstracting the immense effects of the war from this picture, it is difficult to imagine Russia's peaceful transition to a stable future.

Epilogue: War, Revolution, and Beyond

The outbreak of World War I and the new demands the conflict placed on Moscow's resources meant the end of numerous municipal plans. To name just a few of the cancelled projects, fifty-one new schools and eight other educational buildings were not constructed, the subway did not become a reality, the branch library system did not open, and inexpensive or free housing for the lower classes was not built.[1] By 1916 the city was spending five hundred thousand rubles a month on the care of refugees alone. Following a tradition established in the 1812 war against the French and continued in the Crimean conflict, the Russo-Turkish war of the 1870s, and the Russo-Japanese war, the Moscow duma also made various financial contributions to the effort against the Germans, usually in the form of payments to Belgium, Serbia, and other areas affected by the fighting. This funding amounted to additional hundreds of thousands of rubles.[2]

The beginning of the war also brought the temporary end of all differences between the municipality of Moscow and the state. The city duma unanimously voted to send a telegram to the tsar that included the following passage:

> The Moscow city government . . . places at the feet of your majesty an expression of its age-old love and devotion and full readiness for unity with its sovereign. With all its strength [the city government] will embark on the defense of the dignity of the fatherland and of the independence of our brother peoples. God bless the good impulses of your heart, Sovereign.

The stenographic record of the session notes "applause" at this point.[3] Reflecting the mood of the *obshchestvo* but not necessarily of the lower classes regarding the war, the city duma's words suggest a fervent hope that the conflict would somehow resolve the strong tensions and divisions that had developed between it and the central government.

However, the sentiment of unquestioning loyalty to the state could not survive the terrible defeats of 1915 and the government's determination to exclude "society" from any major role in the war effort. Soon Prince G. E. L'vov, earlier denied his chance to become mayor of Moscow, was trying to use his position as head of the Union of Towns, formed in 1914 to aid the war effort, to gain political leverage for the Russian liberals.[4] Other leading Muscovites were pursuing the same course in the War Industries Committees.[5] The conflict between state and liberal society thus flared up again very quickly during the war, in contrast to the relative political tranquility that obtained in other belligerent countries. This tension in Russia greatly hampered efforts to organize the economy for war and contributed to defeat and revolution.

As the military and economic situation deteriorated through 1915 and 1916, and charges of treason were levelled against Tsarina Alexandra and the court, Moscow's electorate turned against the dynasty and its chosen officials more strongly than ever before. City duma elections held in 1916 led to the "absolute victory" of the progressists, and the government refused to confirm the voting; the duma had to continue with its old complement.[6]

By New Year's Eve of 1917, relations between the tsarist administration and Moscow's elite had reached a dead end. On that day the last *gradonachal'nik* of the city, General V. N. Shebeko, gave a reception to celebrate "the unity of [state] authority and society." Only a small group appeared, and it included no one from the city's important circles.[7]

Although there is no record that members of the city government took an active role in the events that finally brought down the tsarist state, a story centered in Petrograd, the entry noted in Chapter 3 of present and former Moscow duma deputies in the Provisional Government certainly demonstrated a high level of enthusiasm for the Old Regime's collapse. This feeling was expressed sharply in April 1917 by A. I. Konovalov, who had briefly served in the city duma, when he spoke of the "economic and political fetters . . . of the hateful old order."[8] N. I. Astrov, who now became mayor of the city, waxed even more bitter about his former sovereign.

> The senselessness, the Byzantine quality, the lack of will, the vindictiveness, the fear, the lack of understanding and hatred toward the people [*narod*] of Nicholas II—these are the distinct lines of [his] personality.[9]

So much for the good impulses of the tsar's heart.

The chaotic March days in Petrograd, where the Soviet of Workers Deputies was already moving into the realm of policy-making and thus encroaching on a right the Provisional Government considered its alone, passed without much sign of such "dual power" in Moscow. There the Committee of Public (*obshchestvennykh*) Organizations, formed by the educated elite of the city, was able to see that local authority remained in the hands of the Moscow duma, though the latter body now seated the new members rightfully elected in 1916 and chose Astrov as mayor. The committee adopted its position in defiance of a resolution passed by the Moscow Soviet's Executive Committee, which stated that a new city duma should be elected by general, equal, and secret ballot. In the words of one Soviet scholar,

> the bourgeoisie, not meeting resistance from the masses and their political parties, relatively easily organized itself and created in Moscow its organ of authority in the form of the Committee of Public Organizations, having seized the key positions of the city administration.[10]

The same writer also speaks of the "unconsciously trusting attitude of the petty bourgeois masses toward the capitalists," which he attempts to explain by reference to "support [for the bourgeoisie] from some part of the petty bourgeois masses and the bureaucracy." This in turn developed out of these groups' "economic power and organizing ability [*organizovannost'*]."[11] Perhaps, but most of the city's people were not petty bourgeois. The easy initial victory of the Committee of Public Organizations and the "trusting attitude" of the masses toward the city's elite, which were certainly not evident in Petrograd in the same period, might well have had part of their origin in the ameliorative programs of the municipal duma before 1914. In general, the liberal revolution of February 1917 seems to have been well received at first by Moscow's lower classes. In March "a more radical revolution seemed extremely remote," and there was "no sense of urgency" about the future.[12]

From February 1917 until the October Revolution, there also seems to have been relatively little talk in Moscow about urban problems. The Bolsheviks, who might have been expected to seize every opportunity for agitation, deliberately steered clear of "minor community affairs" in favor of "the most important political issues," like the war.[13] Again, one wonders if this was because Moscow's *obshchestvo* had already made a start toward solving many urban problems.

Nonetheless, the feelings of March that had allowed the elite of Moscow to retain local power had faded substantially by June. Democratic elections for a new city duma held in that month returned a 70 percent majority for the Socialist Revolutionary (SR) party, the agrarian socialist group that catered above all to the Russian peasantry. The Kadets received 17 percent of the vote, leaving only 13 percent for the Bolsheviks and Mensheviks together.[14] In all likelihood the SRs won so strikingly because they were the best-known party among the peasants, who still comprised the overwhelming majority of Moscow's residents by *soslovie* and who had migrated to the city in vast numbers. The SRs had also acquired political capital from their "fine traditions of the past long struggle with tsarism," according to one witness of the elections.[15] At this time the SR leadership was dedicated to maintaining the bourgeois revolution and did not want to see the introduction of socialism. Therefore the vote can also be read to some extent as an endorsement of the politics of moderation and acquiescence in a coalition with the liberals, one that would follow their program.

Yet by September 1917, for reasons that have been excellently covered in recent literature, the Bolsheviks had gained much political ground in Moscow.[16] Among the factors that helped produce this change were the inability of the Provisional Government to solve the growing economic problems, its increasing identification with the upper classes and their political parties, its failure to sanction efforts by the lower classes to control the land and factory life, and above all the deepening unpopularity of the war. In short, it appears to have been the specific context of 1917, especially the war and the pressures it exerted throughout the economy and society, that produced the growth of radicalism. Elections for district *dumy* held in Moscow on September 24 returned majorities for the Bolsheviks in eleven of seventeen areas and gave them 350 of the total of 710 seats. The Kadets won 184 seats and the SRs 104, still a sizable moderate vote.[17] The Moscow Soviet also began to pass Bolshevik resolutions in September; the situation in Petrograd and several other cities was analogous. Thus Lenin had reason to believe that his party could take and hold power in Russia's two largest cities and many other areas as well. His estimate proved correct, though the initial victory in Moscow came only at the cost of considerable casualties among both Red and anti-Red forces.[18] This fighting, which stands in contrast to the relatively peaceful seizure of power in Petrograd, may also indicate that the local bourgeoisie had found more support and had a stronger position in Moscow because of its prewar record on programs for the lower classes. The fact that the tide of the October fighting turned in favor of the Bolsheviks only when Red Guards from factories in the countryside poured into the city also seems significant; until that point a standoff had existed between Moscow's Red and counterrevolutionary forces.[19] Though the evidence of 1917 in Moscow is certainly indirect and quite tentative, it lends itself to the interpretation that the local bourgeoisie had by no means completely alienated the city's lower classes.

The new authorities in Moscow inherited a great deal that had been produced by the efforts of the old municipality. Schools, hospitals, parks, and the like passed into the hands of the Soviet regime and served as the nucleus for later expansion. In the case of higher education, the new government even borrowed a model for several years in the form of Shaniavskii University's statute. Such debts to the old city duma have never been properly acknowledged in Soviet works.

This ingratitude is certainly partly a political judgment, but it probably also stems from the fact that so much remained to be done. Urban problems had worsened from 1914 to 1917, and Soviet authorities had little time to look back.[20] It took years to remedy the underlying causes of poor public health in the city, and housing remained in terribly short supply into the 1960s; there has been considerable improvement since, but the goal of a separate, decent apartment for every family is still not in sight. Not even the Soviet government has been able to control the flood of people migrating to Moscow or the hordes of peasants from the surrounding regions who descend upon the city daily in search of food and goods. However, in working to raise the quality of urban services, Soviet municipal officials have not been faced with a major problem of the tsarist era, for they have shared general political and social goals with the USSR's ruling circles. From Nikolai Bukharin in 1917 to Boris Eltsin in the 1980s, Moscow's communist leaders have often been part of that select group. Even when the city's top officials were ousted or executed by other Soviet leaders, that occurred as a result of political in-fighting or disputes on how to reach the common goals. This is one of the fundamental differences between the history of Moscow before and after October 1917: the old ideological antagonism between city and state in the late tsarist period, with all its profound implications and impediments to change, disappeared as the Bolsheviks came to power.

Appendix A

Comparative Infant Mortality and Death Rates

Infant Mortality to the Age of One Year per 10,000 Infants,
1909

Moscow	3,160	Munich	1,920
St. Petersburg	2,420	Odessa	1,760
Bucharest	2,120	Vienna	1,730
Madrid	2,100	Cologne	1,730

Source: Shtromberg, *Gorodskie zheleznye dorogi*, p. 26.

The year was not atypical; Moscow also led almost the same group of cities in this regard in 1911, for example. Moscow's claim to the title of deadliest European city is supported by these data:

Death Rate in European Cities per 10,000 Population,
1881–1910

City	1881–85	1906–10	1910	Percent Decrease
Berlin	26.5	15.5	14.7	41.5
Vienna	28.2	17.0	15.8	39.7
London	20.9	14.0	12.7	33.0
Paris	24.4	17.5	16.7	28.3
Oslo	19.9	13.0	11.9	24.7
St. Petersburg	32.8	25.5	24.1	22.3
Moscow	33.3	27.6	26.9	17.1

Source: Alaverdian, *Zhilishchnyi vopros*, p. 69.

Appendix B

Moscow's Population by Estate

Moscow's Population by Soslovie, 1871–1902, in 1,000s

Estate	1871	1882	1902	Percent of Population		
				1871	1882	1902
Nobles	48.2	55.8	59.6	8.0	7.4	5.0
Clergy	11.2	13.1	10.6	1.9	1.7	0.9
Honored citizens	7.1	9.2	40.7	1.2	1.2	3.5
Merchants (*kuptsy*)	29.2	22.9	18.5	4.8	3.0	1.6
Meshchane, guildsmen	153.9	181.2	227.6	25.6	24.1	19.4
Peasants	260.4	370.7	789.6	43.2	49.6	67.2
Lower ranks, army	15.7	—	—	2.6	—	—
Retired soldiers, families of lower ranks	60.9	71.6	—	10.1	9.5	—
Foreigners	6.9	10.9	14.7	1.1	1.5	1.3
Others	8.8	18.1	13.7	1.5	2.4	1.1
Total	602.0	753.5	1,174.7			

Source: Rashin, *Naselenie Rossii,* p. 125.

197

Appendix C

Moscow's Population by Occupation, 1902 and 1912

Moscow's Population by Occupation, 1902 (All Numbers in 1,000s)

Category	Men		Women		Total	
	Number	Percent	Number	Percent	Number	Percent
Artisans with hired labor	27.4	5.0	9.0	3.4	36.4	4.5
Artisans without hired labor	38.3	7.0	20.0	7.6	58.3	7.2
Employees in production	54.8	10.0	4.2	1.6	59.0	7.3
Workers and apprentices in production	303.1	55.1	73.4	28.0	376.5	46.3
Administrative employees and aides	37.6	6.9	3.8	1.5	41.4	5.1
Intelligentsia and professions	23.8	4.3	16.7	6.4	40.5	5.0
Rentiers	2.5	0.4	6.4	2.4	8.9	1.1
Persons on public welfare	28.4	5.1	39.4	15.0	67.8	8.3
Domestic servants and day laborers	14.8	2.7	75.7	28.9	90.5	11.1
Other	19.3	3.5	13.7	5.2	33.0	4.1
Total	550.0	100.0	262.3	100.0	812.3	100.0

Source: M. Ia. Vydro, Naselenie Moskvy (po materialam perepisei naseleniia 1871–1970 gg.) (Moscow, 1976), p. 36. The author compiled his material from municipal censuses.

These data are readily comparable with information from 1912, despite slight changes in the categories used by the city.

Moscow's Population by Occupation, 1912

Category	Men		Women		Total	
	Number	*Percent*	*Number*	*Percent*	*Number*	*Percent*
Artisans with hired labor	32.6	4.8	11.6	3.2	44.2	4.2
Artisans without hired labor	48.0	7.0	33.5	9.2	81.5	7.8
Employees in production	81.5	11.9	10.9	3.0	92.4	8.8
Workers and apprentices in production	349.4	51.0	95.6	26.1	445.0	42.3
Administrative employees	32.2	4.7	0.1	0.0	32.3	3.1
Auxiliary personnel outside production	16.4	2.4	6.7	1.8	23.1	2.2
Intelligentsia and professions	31.3	4.6	26.4	7.2	57.7	5.5
Rentiers	5.8	0.8	13.4	3.7	19.2	1.8
Persons on public welfare	43.6	6.4	55.6	15.2	99.2	9.4
Domestic servants	6.8	1.0	92.3	25.2	99.1	9.4
Other	37.4	5.4	20.2	5.4	56.6	5.5
Total	685.0	100.0	366.3	100.0	1,051.3	100.0

Source: Vydro, *Naselenie Moskvy,* p. 38.

Appendix D

Comparison of Workers' Budgets in Moscow and St. Petersburg

A survey of workers' budgets in St. Petersburg can be compared to a similar survey carried out in 1906 in "one large manufacturing factory in the Moscow region":

Workers' Budgets in Moscow and St. Petersburg

	St. Petersburg		Moscow	
Expense	Rubles	Percent Budget	Rubles	Percent Budget
Clothing	90.9	15.5	103.8	24.1
Food	364.3	62.5	236.8	54.8
Games and drink	40.1	7.9	10.8	2.5
Hygiene	24.6	4.2	9.6	2.2
Return to villages	16.2	2.8	23.3	5.4
Other	47.3	8.9	47.2	11.0
Totals	584.0	100.0	432.0	100.0

Source: RV, January 29, 1909. No date was given for the Petersburg study.

Rent was not included in the surveys because St. Petersburg workers had to pay for their rooms, while the Muscovites received their lodging from the factory. This illustrates the lingering tendency of Moscow factories to provide housing for their workers.

Another contemporary survey recorded budget figures that were similar for married textile workers in the two cities but substantially different for single men.

Textile Workers' Budgets by Marital Status, St. Petersburg and
Moscow (Bogorodskii uezd, Just Outside the City of Moscow), 1908

St. Petersburg Workers, Percent Spent on	Married	Single
Food	54.99	39.25
Clothing	15.72	10.60
Housing	14.60	10.16
Money sent to country	1.00	18.18
Moscow Workers, Percent Spent on		
Food	56.77	38.25
Clothing	10.01	9.32
Housing	14.87	3.01
Money sent to country	2.10	40.43

Source: Usloviia byta rabochikh v dorevoliutsionnoi Rossii (Moscow, 1958), p. 107.

Appendix E

Movement of Food Prices in Moscow

Wholesale Price (in Kopecks) of a Pood of Rye Flour in Moscow's Markets, 1900–1913

1900–04 (average)	96.9	1909	144.9
1905	115.8	1910	122.0
1906	132.5	1911	132.1
1907	157.7	1912	144.0
1908	157.4	1913	137.5

Source: Pazhitnov, *Polozhenie,* p. 56.

Average Price of Food Items in Moscow, 1907–1914, in Kopecks

	1907	*1908*	*1909*	*1910*	*1911*	*June 1914*
Best quality white bread, per *pood*	259	310	212	270	270	260
Rye bread, second quality	113	115	101	95	97	106
Beef, first quality per *funt*	19	21	21	22	23	23
Third quality meat	12	12	11	12	11	15

Source: The figures for the years 1907–1911 are taken from Mg uprava, *Svodnyi biulleten' za 1911,* p. 16. The June 1914 figures are from Mg uprava, *Ezhemesiachnyi stat. biulleten',* no. 6 (June, 1915), pp. 13–14.

Appendix F

Wage Trends in Moscow

Daily Pay for Moscow Jobs, 1902–1914, in Kopecks

	1902	1903	1904	1905	1906	1907	1908	1909	1910	1911	4/13	4/14
Carpenters	129	139	125	127	128	133	142	144	143	149	175	190
Joiners	173	183	135	139	152	214	208	190	172	176	180	205
Day labor, male	78	86	86	95	90	94	93	89	86	92	100	110
Day labor, female	64	68	60	63	66	70	72	71	68	70	75	80

Source: The figures for the years 1907–1911 are from Mg uprava, *Svodnyi biulleten' za 1911*, p. 20. The figures for April 1913 and April 1914 are from Mg uprava, *Ezhemesiachnyi stat. biulleten'*, no. 4 (April 1914), p. 15.

Appendix G

The Municipal Budget Before the War

The Municipal Budget in Moscow, 1901 and 1909–1912, in 1,000 Rubles

Income	1901	1909	1910	1911	1912
Taxes and duties:					
Real property	4,269	6,005	6,174	6,409	6,607
From trade and industry	2,372	2,750	2,818	2,913	2,995
On dogs and horses	156	295	298	331	323
Attestation, stamps, etc.	338	327	353	362	350
Hospital tax	666	398	399	345	435
Other	302	372	394	413	435
From city land and property	329	582	614	654	673
Kiosk fees, etc.	402	642	754	810	803
Connecting electricity and sewerage	111	372	433	523	540
Other	212	199	173	191	204
From city enterprises	4,079	15,874	18,517	21,185	24,945
Return on expenses:					
Treasury subsidies	434	638	705	932	1,098
Interest	182	658	557	774	109
Donations	303	445	449	464	489
From Work House	40	107	657	856	857
For paving	59	129	181	447	180
Other	344	857	1,114	1,345	1,479
Other income	374	704	717	851	759
Total	14,973	31,354	35,306	39,805	43,243

Expenses	1901	1909	1910	1911	1912
General state demands:					
State institutions	531	729	726	748	880
Quartering troops	310	478	461	474	468
Police	1,143	1,462	1,568	1,604	1,630
Maintaining city government	950	1,385	1,482	1,576	1,809
Fire department	390	439	441	442	473
External appearance (*blagoustroistvo*)	1,795	1,861	1,939	2,049	2,113
City enterprises	2,563	9,512	10,565	11,231	13,451

The Municipal Budget in Moscow (*Continued*)

Expenses	1901	1909	1910	1911	1912
Education:					
Elementary	881	1,937	2,244	2,681	3,439
Other	427	832	933	1,037	1,097
Welfare	705	1,495	2,222	2,606	2,464
Public health	2,646	5,094	5,459	5,768	5,816
City property	534	325	552	764	574
Debts, principal and interest	1,511	4,817	5,917	7,164	7.169
Deductions for formation of capital	124	480	564	806	1,132
Other	377	518	490	662	727
Total	14,886	31,419	35,564	39,613	43,243

Source: Moskovskaia gorodskaia uprava, *Sovremennoe khoziaistvo goroda Moskvy,* ed. I. A. Verner (M.: 1913), pp. 277–80.

Appendix H

Report of the Council of Ministers to Tsar Nicholas II on the Moscow Mayoral Elections of 1912–1913

The document is valuable not only for the way in which it demonstrates the importance of Moscow city politics to the central government, and the latter's attitudes toward liberalism and opposition in Moscow, but also for its language. An effort has been made to preserve the convoluted and "most humble" Russian of the original.

Confidential

On the original it pleased HIS IMPERIAL MAJESTY to write in his own hand: "Agreed." In Livadia, December 4, 1913.

Signed: President of the Council of Ministers, State Secretary V. Kokovtsov.

Affirmed: Manager of the Council of Ministers

Special Journal of the Council of Ministers
November 27, 1913

Regarding filling the post of Moscow City Mayor

It pleased YOUR IMPERIAL HIGHNESS on November 20, in Livadia, during the most humble [*vsepoddanneishem*] report of the President of the Council of Ministers, to give him the report of the Minister of Internal Affairs [N. A. Maklakov] on the appointment as Moscow City Mayor of the Member of the State Council, Courtmaster Shtiurmer, and accordingly to direct State Secretary Kokovtsov to inform Courtmaster Maklakov, that, in view of the special significance of this matter, the issue should be submitted for the consideration of the State Council, so that the Council's conclusion on this subject be submitted to YOUR MAJESTY's review in the shortest [possible] time.

As a result [of this directive], entering into consideration of the indicated matter, the Council of Ministers first of all noted, independently of the above IMPERIAL command, that the question of filling the post of Moscow City Mayor, as it is undoubtedly linked with extremely important questions of state order, is subject to the review of this Council under articles 15 and 17 of its Statute, which prescribe the introduction for the consideration of the Council of "measures of administration having general significance," and also "consideration (*predpolozhenie*) of heads of administrative bodies belonging to the general ministerial structure and the filling of chief posts of high and local administration." [There followed Minister of the Interior N. A. Maklakov's opinion that this case was not a proper

Source: OZhSM, no. 105, November 27, 1913, pp. 1–6.

206

application of the above statute.] Concerning the question of appointing the City Mayor in its essence, the Minister of Internal Affairs explained in the presence of the Council that in recent years in the Moscow City Duma the number of rightist deputies on the one side and leftist on the other has been almost in a condition of equilibrium, but the city *Uprava* [has been] completely in the hands of the leftist deputies and the so-called third element. Adding its votes to the group of leftist delegates, the *Uprava* gives it superiority over the rightist parties and causes the election of its adherents to municipal positions. As a result, in the elections at the beginning of this year of candidates for Moscow City Mayor, Prince G. E. L'vov and N. I. Guchkov were chosen. Within a few days the latter withdrew his candidacy. But after that in supplementary elections, the deputy S. A. Chaplygin received the largest number of votes. In view of the widely known adherence of Prince L'vov and Chaplygin to the body of public figures who take an antigovernment stance, the Minister of Internal Affairs, agreeing with the conclusion of the Council of Ministers, did not consider it possible to present them for IMPERIAL appointment to the post of City Mayor of the First-throne capital. Following that, by special IMPERIAL order, on the past October 8 new elections for candidates for the post of City Mayor were carried out, in which one candidate was chosen—the hereditary honored citizen L. L. Katuar—a person of foreign origin and not an Orthodox. According to information held by the Ministry of Internal Affairs, this last person, in the same way, is far from meeting those demands that should characterize the person appointed by IMPERIAL authority as Moscow City Mayor. In case of his appointment, he would be only an obedient tool in the hands of the leftist elements in the City Duma. In this situation, foreseeing that in the complicated relationship of forces between the rightist and leftist groups of the Moscow City Duma it is impossible to count on new elections producing a candidate acceptable to the Government, and that to draw out this affair for an undetermined period would be unsatisfactory and harmful, Court-master Maklakov settled on the idea of presenting to YOUR IMPERIAL MAJESTY for appointment as Moscow City Mayor Member of the State Council Courtmaster B. V. Shtiurmer—a person of firm government convictions, extremely tactful, and having wide state experience, obtained in long service in administrative positions and in *zemstvo* affairs. It is the firm conviction of the Minister of Internal Affairs, in which he does not now waver in the slightest, that this appointment would only be for the good of Moscow and would serve for the gradual strengthening and cure [*ozdorovlenie*] of the capital's public self-government. Unfortunately, at the present time the proposal just explained must be considered unrealizable, since leaks to the periodical press have made it a subject of noisy public agitation, directed against the very possibility of appointing anyone as Moscow Mayor who was not chosen as a candidate by the City Duma. In view of these conditions, Courtmaster Shtiurmer considered himself obligated to state that, in the extraordinarily complicated situation, he does not hope for a successful administration of the post suggested for him and considers himself forced to request the withdrawal of his candidacy. On the other hand, the Minister of Internal Affairs definitely does not see the possibility of presenting deputy Katuar for IMPERIAL appointment as City Mayor, because of his political adherence to the progressive party and at the same time, because he does not have, as is generally recognized, the requisite independence and firmness of character so essential for carrying out the obligations of Moscow City Mayor.

In presenting the current question, the Council of Ministers cannot but express its deep conviction that, generally speaking, the appointment of the Moscow City Mayor outside of those chosen by the [city] Duma as candidates, completely allowable by law, represents in its essence an extraordinary measure, one extremely undesirable. It will introduce into the mutual relations of the Government and the publicly elected self-government of the capital harmful bases of distrust, discord, and irritation. In the contemporary circumstances of our government life, when the Supreme Authority considers it necessary to bring public forces even into legislative activity, this point of view takes on greater importance than in former times, and in particular, in relation to Moscow, where there has never been a case of the City Mayor's appointment beyond the choice of the [city] Duma. At the present time it is difficult even to foresee all the complications that would unavoidably arise in the conduct of the city government's affairs, which are founded on the daily and constant mutual action of the City Mayor and the public forces of the city, elected by its population, in case of the filling of the City Mayorship outside of the selection of the Capital Duma. In addition, in view of the information communicated by the Minister of Internal Affairs about the last candidate of the Moscow Duma, Katuar, it would be impossible, in the opinion of the Council, to petition YOUR MAJESTY for his appointment as Moscow Mayor, the more so because the Government's negative attitude toward him has already received wide publicity. Under the evident circumstances of the case under review, the Council of Ministers would consider it more prudent to declare the rejection of deputy Katuar's appointment as Mayor, and to continue the present state of things, that is, to retain the temporary execution of the obligations of Moscow City Mayor by Vice-Mayor Brianskii, and to return again to the present question in more favorable conditions for its resolution. It is fully conceivable that, with the passage of a certain length of time, new elections for Moscow City Mayor, if they are arranged, according to a petition on that point by the City Duma itself, can produce more suitable candidates. In case of new failure in the elections, the Government will have even more weighty bases for selecting someone other than the chosen candidate. In the opinion of the Council of Ministers, this solution would have the advantage of avoiding the inevitable complications foreseen by the Council in the general course of Moscow's municipal life. It would not at all change the existing, although temporary, situation, since Vice-Mayor Brianskii has already been administering the vacant post of City Mayor for a whole year, and would keep his position until the arrival of such circumstances as would secure the possibility of correct and desirable elections for the Government of the Moscow City Mayor.

This its conclusion on the case under review the Council of Ministers most humbly submits for consideration by YOUR IMPERIAL MAJESTY.

The original journal signed by Mssrs. the President and Members of the Council of Ministers and countersigned by the Manager of the Council.

The original affirmed: Head of the Department of the
                       Chancellery of the Council of
                       Ministers

Glossary of Russian Terms

For further information on some of these terms, see S. G. Pushkarev, comp., *Dictionary of Russian Historical Terms from the Eleventh Century to 1917*, ed. George Vernadsky and Ralph Fisher, Jr. (New Haven, 1970).

administratsiia Administration. Refers in this period only to tsarist agencies, that is, aspects of the state apparatus, above all the Ministry of Internal Affairs and the police.

arshin Unit of measure equaling 11.02 centimeters.

blagochinie Literally, good order. Means well-being or commonweal here.

blagoustroistvo Literally, good arrangement. Refers to the external appearance of the city and its physical amenities, from parks and flowers to streets and bridges.

burzhui Russian lower class corruption of bourgeois, a contemptuous term.

chinovniki High tsarist officials, those holding ranks (chiny) in the table of ranks. Vysshie chinovniki: the very highest of such bureaucrats.

duma Council. The State Duma (*Gosudarstvennaia Duma*) was the national parliament that existed from 1906 to 1917. So that the reader will not confuse that body with the Moscow city council (*Moskovskaia gorodskaia duma*), State Duma is always capitalized here, Moscow city duma is never capitalized. Since the word *duma* is used so frequently, it is not italicized and its plural is given as dumas.

dvorianstvo The Russian gentry or nobility, a legal category or estate (*soslovie*). An individual member was a *dvorianin*, plural *dvoriane*.

dvornik Literally, yard man, from *dvor*, court or yard. Plural *dvorniki*. These were janitors and concierges found in every Russian apartment building. They were legally responsible for keeping track of who lived in the building and for aiding police upon request.

funt Unit of measure equivalent in weight to an English or American pound.

gorodovoi Urban policeman, the lowest rank on the force.

gorodskoe obshchestvennoe upravlenie Municipal public administration or government. This was the elected city government in Russian towns after 1870.

gradonachal'nik, pl. gradonachal'niki Literally, city boss or commander. Can be translated as city prefect or governor, for his powers were equivalent within a city to those of a governor in a province. Gradonachal'niki were heads of the *administratsiia* and chiefs of police in several Russian cities before 1917.

gradonachal'stvo (1) The physical urban area administered by a gradonachal'nik; (2) his administration.

intelligent An educated person who is culturally and intellectually active. Plural *intelligenty*. The term connoted liberalism or radicalism before 1917.

Kadets Members of the Constitutional Democratic party, sometimes officially known as the Party of People's Freedom. The word *Kadet* comes from the first letters of the Russian words for constitution and democrat. This party was the most liberal of the major Russian groups; it advocated a constitutional monarchy, full civil liberties and freedoms for all citizens, and compulsory land reform.

kupets, pl. **kuptsy** Merchant, a *soslovie* category dating back to the sixteenth century.

lichnyi or **potomstvennyi pochetnyi grazhdanin** Personal or hereditary honored citizen. A special *soslovie* category for successful businessmen, especially manufacturers, created in 1832.

meshchanin, pl. **meshchane** An estate of city dwellers, a kind of catch-all category for urbanites who were born in towns and did not automatically belong to another *soslovie*.

narod People, but referring particularly to the common people. Adjective: narodnyi, popular, in the sense of something designated above all for the common folk. Contrast to *obshchestvo*.

obshchestvo Society, but referring to Russia's educated, usually progressive elite. The *obshchestvo* did not work with its hands. Obshchestvennost' was often used to mean liberal society, and the obshchestvennoe dvizhenie was the liberal movement, especially before and during 1905.

Okhrana Literally, guard or security. Tsarist secret police. Soviet usage is *Okhranka*.

pood (*pud* in direct transliteration) Unit of measure equal to 16.27 kilograms.

popechitel' Guardian or trustee. **Popechitel'stvo** guardianship, trusteeship, tutelage.

samodeiatel'nyi Literally, self-active. Independent, referring to individuals who did not depend on others for their material support.

sazhen Unit of measure equal to 2.134 meters.

soslovie, pl. **sosloviia** Estate, that is, legal category of society, marked into each citizen's passport.

tsenzovoi Privileged. From *tsenz*, qualification or right. Referred to a qualification such as ownership of a certain amount of property in order to hold the franchise.

uezd, pl. **uezdy** An administrative unit below the level of the province. Often translated as county.

uprava Board, in the sense of executive or administrative body.

upravlenie Administration or government. See *gorodskoe obshchestvennoe upravlenie*.

zemskii sobor Assembly of the land (*zemskii*, adjective from *zemlia*, land; *sobor*, assembly or collection). A tsarist institution of the sixteenth and seventeenth centuries, it was a national assembly of representatives from the *sosloviia* that met infrequently to consider legislation and advise the tsar. Its powers were never formally specified, and it never became permanent.

zemstvo, pl. **zemstva** Organ of rural self-government, elected on the basis of *sosloviia* and property ownership, established 1864. There were two levels, provincial and *uezd*.

zvanie, pl. **zvaniia** Literally, calling. One's *zvanie* was the term one used to identify one's status. It could be *soslovie*, level of education, occupation, or profession.

Notes

Abbreviations Used in Notes

GD   *Gorodskoe Delo* (St. Petersburg, monthly, 1908–1917).

GDSO   Gosudarstvennaia Duma, *Stenograficheskie Otchety* (St. Petersburg, various years). These records are arranged by the number of the Duma itself (I–IV), by chast', sessiia, zasedanie, and column. Citations will be given in the following manner, for example: GDSO III, ch. 1, s. 1, z. 7, col. 308–309.

GSSO   Gosudarstvennyi Sovet, *Stenograficheskie Otchety* (St. Petersburg, various years). These are arranged by sessiia, zasedanie, and column, and will be cited, for example, as GSSO s. 5, z. 45, col. 2765–2767.

IMgd   *Izvestiia Moskovskoe gorodskoi dumy* (Moscow, monthly).

MgdSO   Moskovskaia gorodskaia duma, *Stenograficheskie otchety o sobraniiakh* (Moscow, various years). These were published and bound at one- or two-month intervals and will be cited in that fashion or by date, with page number.

Mgu, *Doklady*   Moskovskaia gorodskaia uprava, *Doklady Moskovskoi gorodskoi upravy i komissii* (Moscow, various years).

Mgu, SKh   Moskovskaia gorodskaia uprava, *Sovremennoe khoziaistvo goroda Moskvy*, ed. I. A. Verner (Moscow, 1913).

MV   *Moskovskie Vedomosti* (Moscow, daily).

OZhSM   *Osobyi Zhurnal Soveta Ministrov* (St. Petersburg, various years). There were two separate sets of this journal, one for matters referred to the tsar for decision and one for questions decided by the ministers themselves; each set was numbered separately. The latter set will be cited as OZhSM, sobstvennoiu vlast'iu.

PSZ   *Polnoe sobranie zakonov Rossiiskoi imperii* (St. Petersburg, various years). These were issued in collections and will be cited by collection number, volume, and page, for example, PSZ-III, 38, pp. 984–985.

RV   *Russkie Vedomosti* (Moscow, daily).

SZ   *Svod Zakonov Rossiiskoi Imperii* (St. Petersburg, various years). These collections of laws by topic will be cited by volume and page.

TsGAgM   *Tsentral'nyi Gosudarstvennyi Arkhiv goroda Moskvy*. These materials are arranged by *fond, opis', delo*, and *list*, and will be cited as, for example, TsGAgM, f. 178, o. 12, d. 73, ll. 12–15.

ZhMNP   *Zhurnal Ministerstva Narodnogo Prosveshcheniia* (St. Petersburg, monthly).

Introduction

1. On the uprising, see A. M. Pankratova, *Pervaia russkaia revoliutsiia 1905–1907 gg.*, izd. vtoroe, dopolnennoe (Moscow, 1951), who gives figures of 922 men and 137 women killed in the "fighting and repression," p. 182. See also Laura Engelstein, *Moscow, 1905*:

Working Class Organization and Political Conflict (Stanford, 1982), pp. 202–221; and G. M. Derenkovskii, et al., *Revoliutsiia 1905–1907 godov v Rossii* (Moscow, 1975), pp. 250–260.

2. Hans Rogger has emphasized this point in his excellent review of the Old Regime's final decades; see his *Russia in the Age of Modernization and Revolution 1881–1917* (London, 1983), p. 132.

3. See, for example, Roberta Thompson Manning, *The Crisis of the Old Order in Russia: Gentry and Government* (Princeton, 1982), p. 165. About the peasant disturbances of 1905 in the right bank Ukraine, Robert Edelman writes that "the turmoil in the cities provided a signal for the settling of old grievances." In his "Rural Proletarians and Peasant Disturbances: The Right Bank Ukraine in the Revolution of 1905," *Journal of Modern History* 57 (1985), 264.

4. Hermann Lerche, (G. G. Lerkhe), "State Credit for Town and County Councils," *Russian Review* (London) 1, no. 3 (1912), 45–48.

5. See Michael F. Hamm, "Continuity and Change in Late Imperial Kiev," in *The City in Late Imperial Russia,* ed. Michael F. Hamm (Bloomington, Indiana, 1986), pp. 90–91, 102. This work appeared too late to permit more than this reference.

6. Leopold Haimson, "The Problem of Social Stability in Urban Russia, 1905–1917," *Slavic Review* 23, no. 4 (1964), 629. Hans Rogger has also written of the "apathy and indifference on the part of much of society" and the gulf of "hostility, fear, or incomprehension which divided the political opposition of the educated from the anger of the urban masses" in 1914. In his "The Question Remains Open," in Robert H. McNeal, ed., *Russia in Transition 1905–1914: Evolution or Revolution?* (New York, 1970), p. 106.

7. Michael F. Hamm, "The Breakdown of Urban Modernization: A Prelude to the Revolutions of 1917," in *The City in Russian History*, ed. Michael F. Hamm (Lexington, Kentucky, 1976), p. 197. However, in recent work Hamm has begun to emphasize the great concern of urban liberals in some cities for local conditions. See his "Riga's 1913 City Election: A Study in Baltic Urban Politics," *Russian Review* 39, no. 4 (1980), particularly p. 448; and his "Kharkov's Progressive Duma, 1910–1914: A Study in Russian Municipal Reform," *Slavic Review* 40, no. 1 (1981), especially p. 19.

8. MgdSO, October 15, 1905, pp. 646–647.

9. For a good example of this kind of statement, see *Pravo*, no. 4 (1905), col. 260–265.

10. There was an avalanche of memoranda, declarations, and reports by business groups after late January 1905, stressing the need for political reform. Only this could pacify labor, in the eyes of many businessmen. Ruth Amende Roosa, "Russian Industrialists, Politics, and Labor Reform in 1905," *Russian History* 2, part 2 (1975), 130–131; and her "The Association of Industry and Trade, 1906–1914: An Examination of the Economic Views of Organized Industrialists in Prerevolutionary Russia," dissertation, Columbia University, 1967, pp. 39–54.

11. For a general discussion of the crucial role of these laws, see Richard Pipes, *Russia Under the Old Regime* (New York, 1974), pp. 305–312; an examination of their application in Moscow is Robert W. Thurston, "Police and People in Moscow, 1906–1914," *Russian Review* 39, no. 3 (1980), pp. 320–338.

12. Alfred J. Rieber, *Merchants and Entrepreneurs in Imperial Russia* (Chapel Hill, NC, 1982), pp. 332 and 373; and James L. West, "The Search for a Middle Class Identity: Two Views of the Russian Bourgeoisie 1905–1914," paper delivered to the Sixteenth National Convention of the American Association for the Advancement of Slavic Studies, New York, October 1984, pp. 3 and 16.

13. A convenient review of this program may be found in V. S. Diakin, *Samoderzhavie, burzhuaziia i dvorianstvo v 1907–1911 gg.*, pp. 38–47. For Stolypin's speech outlining his plans, see GDSO II, ch. 1, s. 2, z. 5, col. 106–120.

14. GDSO III, ch. 1, s. 1, z. 7, col. 308–309. In the Council of Ministers in November

1909, Stolypin again spoke of improving the peasants' way of life, but mentioned no other group. OZhSM, sobstvennoiu vlast'iu, no. 249, November 25, 1909, p. 5.

15. GSSO, s. 2, z. 4, cols. 32–35.

16. GSSO, April 27, 1906, before p. 1 of the records.

17. On the reforms and their passage, see Geroid T. Robinson, *Rural Russia Under the Old Regime: A History of the Landlord-Peasant World and a Prologue to the Peasant Revolution of 1917* (Berkeley, 1960), pp. 208–242.

18. Neil Weissman, *Reform in Tsarist Russia: the State Bureaucracy and Local Government, 1900–1914* (New Brunswick, NJ, 1981), especially p. 181.

19. Sam Bass Warner, Jr., *The Private City: Philadelphia in Three Periods of Its Growth* (Philadelphia, 1968), p. 202.

20. Enid Gauldie, *Cruel Habitations: A History of Working-Class Housing, 1870–1918* (London, 1974), p. 122.

21. Ippolit Verner, *Gorodskoe samoupravlenie v Rossii* (Moscow, 1906), p. 18.

22. Mgu, SKh.

23. Nikolai Ivanovich Astrov, *Vospominaniia* (Paris, 1940), v. 1, p. 268. However, Astrov had an extra bias at work; the Kadets advocated *nadklassnost'*, or "above-class-ness," the idea that the party stood above narrow class interests and worked for the good of all Russians, so that his statement fit his party's platform perhaps too neatly.

24. Veniamin Iakovlevich Kanel', *Gorodskoe khoziaistvo i samoupravlenie* (Moscow, 1917), pp. 18–19.

25. B. V. Zlatoustovskii, "Gorodskoe samoupravlenie," in *Istoriia Moskvy v shesti tomakh* (Moscow, 1952–1955), v. 4, pp. 461–462.

26. *Istoriia Moskvy; kratkii ocherk*, ed. S. S. Khromov, izd. tret'e (Moscow, 1978), pp. 182–186. And see L. F. Pisar'kova, *Moskovskoe gorodskoe obshchestvennoe upravlenie*, Avtoreferat (Moscow, 1980).

27. See, for example, William G. Rosenberg, *Liberals in the Russian Revolution: The Constitutional Democratic Party, 1917–1921* (Princeton, 1974), pp. 5–6. For a provocative discussion and definition of liberalism see Marc Raeff, "Some Reflections on Russian Liberalism," *Russian Review* 18, no. 3 (1959), 218–230. Raeff also concentrates on legal and political aspects of liberalism.

28. See Charles E. Timberlake, "Introduction: The Concept of Liberalism in Russia," in *Essays on Russian Liberalism*, ed. Charles E. Timberlake (Columbia, MO, 1972), pp. 7–13.

29. Raeff, "Some Reflections," pp. 221–222. For the original platforms of the major liberal parties, the Kadets and Octobrists, see Sidney Harcave, *First Blood: The Russian Revolution of 1905* (New York, 1964), pp. 292–300, who gives the Kadet program; and Ben-Cion Pinchuk, *The Octobrists in the Third Duma, 1907–1912* (Seattle, 1974), who discusses the Octobrists' platform on pp. 11–13. The Octobrists had "no all-embracing ideology" and displayed "an almost inherent resistance to the development of a definitive philosophy." They differed "from their former allies, the Kadets, mainly in tactics and priorities." *Ibid.*, pp. 11 and 13. The two parties' leaders, A. I. Guchkov and P. N. Miliukov, also had serious personal differences.

30. Pinchuk writes in *ibid.*, p. 6 that "the right wing [of the Russian liberal movement] founded the Union of October 17." See also pp. 194 and 197. Michael C. Brainerd, in "The Octobrists and the Gentry in the Russian Social Crisis of 1913–1914," *Russian Review* 38, no. 2 (1979), p. 163, terms the Octobrist leader A. I. Guchkov a conservative. William Gleason, *Alexander Guchkov and the End of the Russian Empire*, Transactions of the American Philosophical Society, v. 73, part 3 (Philadelphia, 1983), calls Guchkov a conservative on pp. 56–57 but stresses his liberalism on pp. 70 and 82. Ernst Birth points to an important criterion for the Octobrists' understanding of themselves: "the cult of the middle." In his *Die Oktobristen (1905–1913); Zielvorstellungen und Struktur. Ein Beitrag*

zur russischen Parteiengeschichte (Stuttgart, 1974), p. 17. All writers agree that the Octobrists were roughly in the center of Russian politics; it is also entirely clear that within the party there was a very wide range of opinion, which helped produce a three-way split of its membership by 1913.

31. MgdSO, December 13, 1905, pp. 1007–1008, and December 15, 1905, p. 1054.

32. Marion J. Levy, Jr., *Modernization and the Structure of Societies: A Setting for International Affairs* (Princeton, 1966), p. 11.

33. Cyril Black, *The Dynamics of Modernization: A Study in Comparative History* (New York, 1966), p. 7.

34. *Ibid.*, p. 7.

35. Cyril E. Black, Marius B. Jansen, Herbert S. Levine, Marion J. Levy, Jr., Henry Rosovsky, Gilbert Rozman, Henry D. Smith II, and S. Frederick Starr, *The Modernization of Japan and Russia: A Comparative Study* (New York, 1975), p. 3.

36. On peasants in the city see Joseph Crane Bradley, Jr., *Muzhik and Muscovite: Urbanization in Late Imperial Russia* (Berkeley, 1985). See also his "The Moscow Workhouse and Urban Welfare Reform in Russia," *Russian Review* 41, no. 4 (1982), and "Patterns of Peasant Migration to Late Nineteenth-Century Moscow: How Much Should We Read into Literacy Rates?" *Russian History* 6, part 1 (1979). Also Robert Eugene Johnson, *Peasant and Proletarian: The Working Class of Moscow in the Late Nineteenth Century* (New Brunswick, NJ, 1979). On the workers, see Engelstein, *Moscow*, and Victoria Bonnell, *Roots of Rebellion: Workers' Politics and Organizations in St. Petersburg and Moscow, 1900–1914* (Berkeley, 1983); and on the bourgeoisie, V. Ia. Laverychev, *Po tu storonu barrikad* (*Iz istorii bor'by Moskovskoi burzhuazii s revoliutsiei*) (Moscow, 1967).

Chapter 1

1. Menshikov wrote for the conservative newspaper *Novoe Vremia*; his words were quoted in *Rech'*, October 11, 1907. Menshikov was writing of St. Petersburg, but there is every reason to think he had Moscow in mind as well, for the Revolution of 1905 had reached its peak there. Moscow and St. Petersburg were often referred to collectively as *the capitals*, and Moscow was sometimes called the *first-throne capital* in honor of its status as Russia's capital for centuries before the founding of St. Petersburg in 1703.

2. Samuel N. Harper, *The Russia I Believe in: The Memoirs of Samuel N. Harper, 1902–1941*, ed. Paul V. Harper (Chicago, 1945), p. 17.

3. Karl Baedeker, *Russia with Teheran, Port Arthur, and Peking: Handbook for Travellers* (Leipzig, 1914), pp. 304–305.

4. *Ibid.*, p. 276.

5. Stepan Karapetovich Alaverdian, *Zhilishchnyi vopros v Moskve; ocherki predrevoliutsionnogo perioda* (Erevan, USSR, 1961), p. 27.

6. RV, June 29, 1911.

7. For brief discussions of Moscow's economic history in this period, see Diane Koenker, *Moscow Workers and the 1917 Revolution* (Princeton, 1981), pp. 21–42; and *Istoriia Moskvy: kratkii ocherk*, pp. 137–142.

8. From a report to the *gradonachal'nik* from the city government for the year 1910. TsGAgM, f. 46, o. 14, d. 1212, l. 11.

9. RV, June 6, 1912.

10. V. Mikhailov, "Iz dokladnoi zapiski o novykh raskhodakh po g. Moskve, sostavlennoi V. Mikhailovym po porucheniiu glasnykh Moskovskoi gorodskoi dumy," [TsGAgM?] fond Mosk. gor. upravy, in "Iz dorevoliutsionnogo proshlogo Moskvy," *Krasnyi Arkhiv*, 5 (84) (1937), p. 235.

11. Mikhailov, "Iz dokladnoi zapiski," p. 223.

12. See Bradley, "Patterns of Peasant Migration."

13. E. O. Kabo, *Ocherki rabochego byta* (Moscow, 1928), pp. 157–158.

14. RV, April 27, 1913.

15. Mgu, SKh, p. 16.

16. Kabo, *Ocherki*, p. 158.

17. William Doyle argues that the separation of Parisians in 1789 into fairly distinct areas according to wealth helped produce "the sort of [social] hostility that burst out . . . and was to keep resurfacing throughout the Revolution." In his *Origins of the French Revolution* (London, 1980), pp. 178–179.

18. Alaverdian, *Zhilishchnyi vopros*, p. 36.

19. N. Karzhanskii, *Kak izbiralas' i rabotala Moskovskaia gorodskaia duma*, 2nd ed. (Moscow, 1950), p. 30.

20. The figures on persons per apartment are, for St. Petersburg, from P. V. Sytin, *Kommunal'noe khoziaistvo. Blagoustroistvo Moskvy v sravnenii s blagoustroistvom drugikh bol'shikh gorodov* (Moscow, 1926), p. 70. For other cities, from Alaverdian, *Zhilishchnyi vopros*, p. 34. The number staying in Khitrov is in D. E. Gorokhov, "Nastoiashchee sostoianie i blizhaishie zadachi vrachebno-sanitarnogo dela v Moskve," *Vestnik obshchestvennoi gigieny* 9 (1912), 1353.

21. Sytin, *Kommunal'noe khoziaistvo*, p. 72.

22. See E. A. Oliunina, "The Tailoring Trade in Moscow and the Villages of Moscow and Riazan' Provinces: Material on the History of the Domestic Industry in Russia," excerpts in *The Russian Worker: Life and Labor Under the Tsarist Regime*, ed. Victoria Bonnell (Berkeley, 1983), p. 170.

23. RV, February 15, 1912.

24. A. Lositskii, "Moskva," in *Entsiklopedicheskii slovar' tovarichestva B. A. i I. Granat i ko.* 7–0e, sovershenno pererabotanoe izdanie (Moscow, n.d.), v. 29, p. 367'.

25. A. G-man, "Soobshcheniia s mest. Moskva. Bor'ba s tuberkulezom," GD, no. 18 (1911), 1326.

26. M. N. Petrov, "Naselenie i territoriia Moskvy v kontse XIX v. i nachale XX v.," in *Istoriia Moskvy v shesti tomakh*, v. 5, p. 15.

27. Mgu, SKh, pp. 5–6.

28. *The World Almanac and Encyclopedia 1912* (New York, 1911), p. 610.

29. Moskovakaia gorodskaia uprava. Statisticheskii otdel, *Trudy statisticheskogo otdela za 1913* [hereafter Mg uprava, Trudy stat. otdela za ————], p. 6. For discussions of the nature and causes of peasant migration to Moscow see Johnson, *Peasant and Proletarian*, pp. 32–55, and Bradley, *Muzhik and Muscovite*, pp. 103–41.

30. Johnson, *Peasant and Proletarian*, p. 44.

31. Mgu, SKh, pp. 14–15. Figures from the 1912 census were not yet available.

32. RV, July 2, 1914.

33. Johnson, *Peasant and Proletarian*, pp. 41–42.

34. A. G. Rashin, *Naselenie Rossii za 100 let* (Moscow, 1956), p. 138.

35. Moskovskoe gorodskoe upravlenie, *Vedomosti o Moskovskikh gorodskikh nachal'nykh uchilishchakh za 1905 god* (Moscow, 1906), p. IV.

36. Mgu, SKh, p. 10. Robert Johnson argues that many women who came to Moscow did not stay long; those who did tended to be past family-rearing age, widows, or spinsters and thus did not have a great effect on family life. Johnson, *Peasant and Proletarian*, pp. 55–56. Yet the increase in the absolute and relative numbers of women in the city from 1871 to 1912 is so large that some of them must have stayed for long periods. Of these, some either accompanied their husbands to Moscow or married there. In any case, the point is not that the population was already completely entrenched in the city in 1912, only that there was a clear, albeit slow, trend in that direction.

37. Zakh. Frenkel', "Narodnoe zdorov'e v gorodakh Rossii po poslednym ofitsial'nym dannym," GD, no. 5 (1910), 276.

38. Mg uprava, *Trudy stat. otdela za 1913*, p. 13.

39. Mgu, SKh, p. 11.

40. *Ibid.*, p. 11.

41. A. S. Chebarin, *Moskva v revoliutsii 1905–1907 godov* (Moscow, 1955), p. 14.

42. M. Ia. Vydro, *Naselenie Moskvy (po materialam perepisei naseleniia 1871–1970 gg.)*, Statistika dlia vsekh (Moscow, 1976), p. 37.

43. Rashin, *Naselenie Rossii*, p. 334.

44. M. N. Gernet, *Detoubiistvo* (Moscow, 1911), pp. 130–131.

45. RV, July 2, 1906. On Russian working conditions in general during this period see E. E. Kruze, *Polozhenie rabochego klassa Rossii v 1900–1914 godakh* (Leningrad, 1976).

46. Ministerstvo torgovli i promyshlennosti. Otdel promyshlennosti, *Sbornik postanovlenii glavnogo po fabrichnym i goronozavodskim delam prisutstvie za 1899 po 1915 gg.* (Petrograd, 1915), pp. 612–613.

47. K. A. Pazhitnov, *Polozhenie rabochego klassa v Rossii* (Leningrad, 1924), v. 1, p. 106.

48. RV, January 10, 1910.

49. RV, August 10, 1911.

50. S. G. Strumilin, *Zarabotnaia plata i proizvoditel'nost' truda v russkoi promyshlennosti za 1913–1922 gg.* (Moscow, 1923), p. 22. For a recent discussion of pay in this period, see Iu. I. Kirianov, *Zhiznennyi uroven' rabochikh Rossii, konets XIX-nachalo XX v.* (Moscow, 1979).

51. See Johnson, *Peasant and Proletarian*, pp. 11–27, and Bradley, *Muzhik and Muscovite*, pp. 70–99, for the economic character of Moscow to 1900.

52. V. Iakovlev, "Biudzhet russkogo rabochego," *Obshchestvennyi Vrach*, no. 8 (1911), p. 72.

53. A. Svavitskii and V. Sher, *Ocherk polozheniia rabochikh pechatnogo dela v Moskve* (St. Petersburg, 1909), p. 42.

54. V. Iakovlev, "Vzdorozhanie zhizni i rabochii biudzhet," *Obshchestvennyi Vrach*, no. 8 (1911), p. 72.

55. RV, January 29, 1909, and *Usloviia byta rabochikh v dorevoliutsionnoi Rossii (po dannym biudzhetnykh obsledovanii)* (Moscow, 1958), p. 107.

56. *Ibid.*, pp. 133–134.

57. Kabo, *Ocherki*, p. 167.

58. Svavitskii and Sher, *Ocherk polozheniia*, pp. 34–35.

59. A. M. fon Gibshman, "Munitsipal'noe obozrenie," GD, no. 22 (1913), 1525–1528.

60. *Istoriia Moskvy; kratkii ocherk*, p. 187. Kirianov reports that pay for Russian workers increased an average of 29.9 percent from 1901 to 1913; most (15.2 percent) of the rise came in the years 1905–1907. *Zhiznennyi uroven'*, p. 111.

61. See, for example, Robert E. Park and Ernest W. Burgess, *The City* (Chicago, 1925), p. 54. For a review of similar literature see Wayne Cornelius, "Urbanization as an Agent in Latin American Political Instability: the Case of Mexico," *American Political Science Review* 63, no. 3 (1969), 833–836.

62. For two such views see *ibid.*, pp. 833–857, and Charles Tilly and C. Harold Brown, "On Uprooting, Kinship, and the Auspices of Migration," in *An Urban World*, ed. Charles Tilly (Boston, Toronto, 1974), especially p. 30.

63. Quoted in Gauldie, *Cruel Habitations*, p. 107. See also Joan Nelson, "The Urban Poor: Disruption or Political Integration in Third World Cities?" *World Politics* 22, no. 3 (1970), 401.

64. Engelstein, *Moscow*, pp. 6, 153–154. The "most militant and craft-conscious groups in the working class were artisanal trades undergoing the change from traditional to factory-type production," p. 153. See also Bonnell, *Roots of Rebellion*, pp. 143, 304, 365. Leopold Haimson has argued that it was often new, young workers who displayed a spirit

of rebellion (*buntarstvo*): "Social Stability," 23, pp. 633–635. But the detailed studies just cited suggest the opposite.

65. On this problem and the regime's attitude toward it in the nineteenth century, see Reginald E. Zelnik, *Labor and Society in Tsarist Russia: The Factory Workers of St. Petersburg, 1855–1870* (Stanford, 1971), especially p. 380.

Chapter 2

1. GDSO III, ch. 1, s. 1, z. 7, col. 350.

2. A. Shingarev, "The Reform of Local Finance in Russia," *Russian Review* 1, no. 1 (1912), 42.

3. See William C. Fuller, Jr., *Civil-Military Conflict in Imperial Russia, 1881–1914* (Princeton, 1985), especially chapters 4–7.

4. The standard treatment of Official Nationality is Nicholas V. Riasanovsky, *Nicholas I and Official Nationality in Russia, 1825–1855* (Berkeley, 1969).

5. *Ibid.*, p. 124.

6. Zelnik, *Labor and Society*, pp. 10–11 and 18.

7. Konstantin P. Pobedonostsev, *Reflections of a Russian Statesman*, new foreword by Murray Polner, trans. Robert Crozier Long (Ann Arbor, 1965), p. 121. On Pobedonostsev in general see Robert F. Byrnes, *Pobedonostsev: His Life and Thought* (Bloomington, IN, 1968).

8. Byrnes, *Pobedonostsev*, p. 297.

9. Pobedonostsev, *Reflections*, pp. 96–97; Byrnes, *Pobedonostsev*, p. 312.

10. Byrnes, *Pobedonostsev*, p. 314.

11. Manning, *Crisis of the Old Order*, pp. 282, 301, 309.

12. Manfred Hagen, *Die Entfaltung Politischer Öffentlichkeit in Russland 1906–1914* (Wiesbaden, 1982), p. 237.

13. Manning, *Crisis of the Old Order*, p. 112.

14. Without going into the complex background of the French Revolution, it is worth pointing out that in many respects the Old Regime in France also depended on a hierarchical organization of society in *états* (estates was one meaning of the word) presided over by the king. And by 1789 serious divergence between ideology and reality had developed in France. See the persuasive treatment of these issues in William H. Sewell, Jr., *Work and Revolution in France: The Language of Labor from the Old Regime to 1848* (Cambridge, England, 1980), pp. 24, 35, 37, and 62–91.

15. On the history of Russian urban government see J. Michael Hittle, *The Service City: State and Townsmen in Russia, 1600–1800* (Cambridge, Massachusetts, 1979); and N. I. Astrov, "Iz istorii gorodskikh samoupravlenii v Rossii," *Mestnoe samoupravlenie: Trudy obshchestva dlia izucheniia gorodskogo samoupravleniia v Chekhoslovatskoi respublike* (Prague, 1925), II, pp. 9–38.

16. "Privilege" (*tsenzovoi*) is a term denoting legal qualification, though one usually related to wealth or status.

17. The preceding section is based on Walter Hanchett, "Tsarist Statutory Regulation of Municipal Government in the Nineteenth Century," in *City in Russian History*, pp. 99–101.

18. See Hanchett, "Tsarist Statutory Regulation," and on government in Moscow 1870–1892 see his "Moscow in the Late Nineteenth Century: A Study in Municipal Self-government," dissertation, University of Chicago, 1965.

The new municipal franchise was similar in some respects to the curial system used for the institutions of rural self-government, the *zemstva*. The law of 1864 that created these bodies divided electors for the *uezd* (county) *zemstva* into three curiae: individual land owners in the countryside, regardless of *soslovie*; urban dwellers who owned a certain amount of property, which varied from *uezd* to *uezd*; and delegates previously elected by village communes. Once the *uezd* electors had chosen their *zemstvo*, it in turn elected a provincial body. Thus in contrast to the direct urban elections, the rural peasants were removed from direct voting for their lawmakers by one step at the *uezd* level and two at the provincial level.

19. Hanchett, "Tsarist Statutory Regulation," p. 103. The phrase "golden words" was originally used in GD, 16 (1909), 834, quoted in Hanchett, "Tsarist Statutory Regulation," p. 113n.

Most of the instances in which the administration could intervene in city affairs related only to checking on their legality. Other articles in the law defined the role of the Provincial Office on City Affairs in settling disputes between the administration and towns. Mayors had to be confirmed, and police could change the layout of streets in towns, but the latter could protest to the aforesaid Office. PSZ-II, 1870, st. 6–158.

20. *Zakony o politsii*, comp. N. T. Volkov (Moscow, 1910), p. 248.

21. *Ibid.*, pp. 250–251.

22. SZ, vtoroe izdanie, III, Obshchee uchrezhdenie gubernskoe, st. 421, p. 658.

23. OZhSM, sobstvennoiu vlast'iu, no. 356, December 7 and 8, 1907, p. 6.

24. *Utro Rossii*, no. 1, 1912, quoted in *Pravo*, 1912, no. 27, col. 1440n.

25. A. A. Lopukhin, *Nastoiashchee i budushchee russkoi politsii* (Moscow, 1907), pp. 26–27, quoted in Richard Pipes, *Russia Under the Old Regime* (New York, 1974), p. 307.

26. For a discussion of the crucial role of these laws see Pipes, *Russia*, pp. 305–312.

27. The best treatment of the tsarist government at this critical juncture is Peter A. Zaionchkovsky, *The Russian Autocracy in Crisis, 1878–1882*, ed. and trans. Gary Hamburg (Gulf Breeze, Florida, 1979). On antecedents to the Extraordinary Measures from 1878 on, see *ibid.*, pp. 42–48. For a discussion of views within the government on potential unrest among urban workers see Zelnik, *Labor and Society*. The government recognized that the growth of an urban factory labor force was the most important aspect of urban growth in terms of possible unrest but was unable to adopt a coherent policy toward either question. Zelnik concludes that in the period 1855–1870, government policy led to the "exclusion of the peasant-workers and the otkhodniki [literally "going-away peasants," those who left their villages to find work] in general from all aspects of municipal life that would identify them as urban citizens as distinct from errant countrymen," (p. 43). It was precisely the problem of this identification—and integration—that the Moscow city government was working on from 1906 to 1914.

28. Paul P. Gronsky and Nicholas J. Astrov, *The War and the Russian Government* (New Haven, 1929), p. 134.

29. Arthur Benoit Eklof, "Spreading the Word: Primary Education and the *Zemstvo* in Moscow Province, 1864–1910," dissertation, Princeton University, 1977, p. 18, gives information on the reduction of eligible voters in Moscow Province under the law of 1890.

30. SZ, vtoroe izdanie, II, st. 83, p. 952.

31. *Ibid.*, st. 2, pp. 931–932.

32. *Ibid.*, p. 932.

33. Alaverdian, *Zhilishchnyi vopros*, pp. 49–50.

34. TsGAgM, f. 16, o. 140, d. 12 t.1, l. 54 (1906).

35. OZhSM, sobstvennoiu vlast'iu, no. 30, March 28, 1913, p. 1.

36. SZ, vtoroe izdanie, II, st. 79, primechanie 1, p. 951.

37. OZhSM, number 8, February 22, 1911, p. 1, and number 86, May 3, 1910, p. 1.

38. GDSO III, ch. 2, s. 1, z. 56, col. 2429–2431.

39. *Ibid.*, col. 2393–2397. The Octobrists as a party opposed the Extraordinary Measures as a permanent feature of Russian life; Pinchuk, *Octobrists*, pp. 53–54. However, they could accept such laws in time of actual revolution. The Kadets, of course, vehemently opposed such statutes. Probably only about 138 of 422 deputies to the Third State Duma,

the Nationalists and the Extreme Right, approved of such laws in the absence of massive unrest.

40. GDSO III, ch. 1, s. 2, z. 32, col. 2813–2816.

41. On the State Council's powers and role in legislation, see Alexandra Deborah Shecket, "The Russian Imperial State Council and the Policies of P. A. Stolypin, 1906–1911: Bureaucratic and Soslovie Interests versus Reform," dissertation, Columbia University, 1974.

42. L. Iasnopolskii, "Biudzhetnaia tsentralizatsiia," *Moskovskii Ezhenedel'nik*, no. 9, 1908, pp. 19 and 29, quoted in A. P. Pogrebinskii, *Gosudarstvennye finansy tsarskoi Rossii v epokhu imperializma* (Moscow, 1968), p. 29.

43. Gronsky and Astrov, *War and the Russian Government*, p. 146.

44. SZ, vtoroe izdanie, II, st. 131, p. 964, and Astrov, "Iz istorii," p. 90.

45. SZ, vtoroe izdanie, II, st. 129, p. 964.

46. M. Avs, "Otkaz ot oblozheniia po stoimosti nedvizhimykh imushchestv v Moskve," GD, no. 21 (1911), 1504.

47. N. Karzhanskii, *Kak izbiralas'*, p. 17.

48. MV, March 5, 1909.

49. RV, February 28, 1914.

50. See RV, December 31, 1908, and MV, May 5, 1909.

51. Gronsky and Astrov, *War and the Russian Government*, pp. 145–146.

52. Avs, "Otkaz ot oblozheniia," 1504–1507.

53. A. Mikhailovskii, "Deiatel'nost' Moskovskogo gorodskogo upravleniia v 1913–1916 gg.," IMgd 9 (1916), 6.

54. Astrov, "Iz istorii," p. 96, noted merely that the new assessments "strengthened taxes" on private homes.

55. Avsarkisov, "Finansy," p. 277.

56. *Ibid.*, pp. 249–250.

57. Quoted in Karzhanskii, *Kak izbiralas'*, p. 19.

58. This occurred in 1910, 1912, and 1913. See M. A. Shtromberg, *Gorodskie dorogi v Moskve i drugikh bol'shikh dorogakh i ikh sotsial'noe znachenie* (Moscow, 1913), pp. 346 and 356.

59. Mikhailovskii, "Deiatel'nost'," pp. 10–11.

60. SZ, vtoroe izdanie, II, st. 63, p. 945.

61. OZhSM, sobstvennoiu vlast'iu, no. 121, May 21, 1911, p. 4.

62. Gronsky and Astrov, *War and the Russian Government*, p. 148.

63. Avsarkisov, "Finansy," p. 283.

64. Lerche, "State Credit," pp. 45–48.

65. Avsarkisov, "Finansy," p. 270.

66. *Ibid.*, p. 261. Compare this data with the figures in the table in the same source, pp. 277–280 (see appendix 1). Such discrepancies, though never large, appear at several points in this article.

67. Shtromberg, *Gorodskie dorogi*, p. 349.

68. See *ibid.*, p. 349, and Karzhanskii, *Kak izbiralas'*, p. 18.

69. RV, April 16, 1914.

70. Mikhailovskii, "Deiatel'nost'," p. 18.

71. A. G-man, "Soobshcheniia s mest. Moskva (Neskol'ko slov o gorodskom khoziaistve g. Moskvy)," GD, 1 (1911), 47.

72. "Soobshcheniia s mest," GD, 15–16 (1912), 968.

73. Lerche, "State Credit," p. 48.

74. According to Michael Hamm, most Russian towns operated no enterprises. Hamm, "Breakdown," p. 186.

75. Riga and Kharkov may also have had exceptionally "progressive" city govern-

ments, but they were not able to accomplish as much as Moscow's did. See Hamm, "Riga's 1913 City Election," and "Kharkov's Progressive Duma."

76. Avsarkisov, "Finansy," p. 283.

77. *Ibid.*, p. 254.

78. *Ibid.*, p. 279.

79. A. G-man, "Soobshcheniia," p. 44.

80. *Gazeta Kopeika*, January 1, 1910.

81. Avsarkisov, "Finansy," p. 259.

82. *Ibid.*, p. 279.

83. PSZ-III, v. 32, p. 1634.

84. RV, April 2, 1913.

85. A. M-skogo, "Deiatel'nost' Moskovskogo gorodskogo upravleniia," IMgd 8 (1913), 12.

86. Hamm, "Breakdown," p. 185.

87. Avsarkisov, "Finansy," p. 285.

88. GSSO, s. 2, z. 4, col. 42.

89. Tsentral'nyi Gosudarstvennyi Istoricheskii Arkhiv, f. 1276, v. 2, d. 213, ll. 70–71, quoted in Robert Henry Gorlin, "State Politics and the Imperial Russian Budget, 1905–1912," dissertation, University of Michigan, 1973, p. 128.

90. *Golos Moskvy*, November 4, 1908.

91. N. I. Astrov, "Sud'ba russkikh gorodov," GD, 2 (1911), 148.

92. GSSO, s. 5, z. 20, col. 841.

93. Alfred Levin, "Russian Bureaucratic Opinion in the Wake of the 1905 Revolution," *Jahrbücher für Geschichte Osteuropas*, neue folge, Band 11 (1963), p. 8n.

94. Sergei S. Oldenburg, *Last Tsar: Nicholas II, his Reign and his Russia*, trans. Leonid Mihalap and Patrick Rollins (Gulf Breeze, Florida, 1977), v. 3, p. 66.

95. Michael Ivanovich Bogolepov, *Finansy, pravitel'stvo i obshchestvennye interesy* (St. Petersburg, 1907), p. 97.

96. Albrecht Martiny, *Parlament, Staatshaushalt und Finanzen in Russland vor dem ersten Weltkrieg: Der Einfluss der Duma auf die russische Finanz und Haushaltspolitik (1907–1914)* (Bochum, 1977), p. 217.

97. See Bradley, *Muzhik and Muscovite*, for a discussion of elite Muscovites' concerns for a "stable and disciplined citizenry," appearing by the 1890s at the latest; p. 2 and Chapters 7 and 8. These concerns grew, Bradley argues, out of Russia's "new urban and industrial social order" itself. And see Adele Lindenmeyr, "A Russian Experiment in Voluntarism: The Municipal Guardianships of the Poor, 1894–1914," *Jahrbücher für Geschichte Osteuropas* 30 (1982), 429–451, where she makes an argument similar to the one expressed in this study on the response of "society" to urban poverty.

98. *Istoriia Moskvy; kratkii ocherk*, p. 187. The duma member is not identified.

99. OZhSM, sobstvennoiu vlast'iu, no. 249, November 25, 1909, pp. 1–2.

100. Lerche, "State Credit," p. 45.

101. PSZ-III, v. 32, p. 973.

102. OZhSM, no. 110, May 21, 1911, pp. 1–2.

103. OZhSM, sobstvennoiu vlast'iu, no. 249, November 25, 1909, p. 3.

104. Lerche, "State Credit," p. 48.

105. A. G-man, "Soobshcheniia," p. 46.

106. RV, December 18, 1907.

107. Avsarkisov, "Finansy," p. 279.

108. RV, March 9, 1914.

109. Shingarev, "Reform," p. 41.

110. Quoted in Dumskii, "Chto sdelala tret'ia Gosudarstvennaia Duma po voprosam gorodskogo samoupravleniia," GD, nos. 15–16 (1912), 927.

111. OZhSM, sobstvennoiu vlast'iu, no. 249, November 25, 1909, pp. 2, 5.

112. Robert H. Gorlin, "Problems of Tax Reform in Imperial Russia," *Journal of Modern History* 49, no. 2 (June 1977), 261–262.

113. For a brief review of these programs see Martiny, *Parlament*, pp. 216–217.

114. Gorlin claimed such willingness existed on financial questions in "State Politics," pp. 347–348.

115. As Gorlin suggested in *ibid.*, pp. 347–48.

116. Quoted in *ibid.*, p. 120.

117. *Ibid.*, pp. 125–126.

118. Shingarev, "Reform," p. 48.

119. Gorlin, "Problems of Tax Reform," 250–252.

120. Arkadii Lavrovich Sidorov, *Ekonomicheskoe polozhenie Rossii v gody pervoi mirovoi voiny* (Moscow, 1973), p. 42; see also the table in Shingarev, "Reform," p. 41.

121. See John Shelton Curtiss, *Church and State in Russia: The Last Years of the Empire, 1900–1917* (New York, 1940), p. 350.

122. Shingarev, "Reform," p. 48; his emphasis.

123. Weissman, *Reform in Tsarist Russia*, p. 48.

124. Conroy, *Stolypin*, p. 67, and Weissman, *Reform in Tsarist Russia*, pp. 131–142.

125. Quoted in Weissman, *Reform in Tsarist Russia*, p. 135.

126. OZhSM, sobstvennoiu vlast'iu, no. 356, Dec. 7 and 18, 1907, p. 6.

127. Harcave, *First Blood*, p. 295.

128. James R. Scobie, *Buenos Aires: Plaza to Suburb, 1870–1910* (New York, 1974), p. 110.

129. *Ibid.*, p. 12.

130. Derek Fraser, *Power and Authority in the Victorian City* (London, 1979), pp. 165–166.

131. From a letter from Nicholas to Stolypin, July 1906, in "Perepiska N. A. Romanova i P. A. Stolypina," *Krasnyi Arkhiv*, 5 (1924), 102. In fairness, it should be noted that Guchkov claimed in his memoirs that in a 1905 audience with the tsar, Nicholas had talked to him for two and a half hours and had agreed with him. At a conference in December 1905, Nicholas had spoken "tender words" to him. A. I. Guchkov, "Iz vospominanii A. I. Guchkova," *Posledniia Novosti*, August 9, 1936. But clearly Nicholas felt differently by mid-1906.

132. Pinchuk, *Octobrists*, pp. 105–106. The tsar's treatment of Guchkov might be contrasted with the government's approach to the St. Petersburg industrialist and financier A. I. Putilov. He had a favorable audience with the tsar in May 1905 and in February had been a member of a special commission called to work out the details of a newly decreed consultative parliament. E. D. Chermenskii, *Burzhuaziia i tsarizm v pervoi russkoi revoliutsii*, izdanie vtoroe (Moscow, 1970), pp. 60 and 67. The differences in the treatment of the two men are indicative of general differences between relations with the central government of Moscow's and Petersburg's elites, which will be explored later.

Chapter 3

1. I. I. Ditiatin, *Ustroistvo i upravlenie gorodov Rossii* (St. Petersburg, 1875, and Iaroslavl, 1877), v. 2, p. 246.

2. OZhSM, no. 105, November 27, 1913, pp. 1–2.

3. C. Vann Woodward, *The Strange Career of Jim Crow*, third revised edition (New York, 1974), p. 56.

4. Warner, *Private City*, passim and especially pp. 194 and 202–223.

5. SZ, vtoroe izdanie, II, p. 943.

6. *Ibid.*, pp. 937–938.

7. "Zametka po povodu minuvshikh vyborov v gorodskuiu dumu na chetyrekhletie 1913–1916 gg.," "Iz doklada v gorodskuiu dumu," [TsGAgM?], f. kants. mosk. gor. dumy 1912 g., d. 25, t. 1, ll. 409–17. In "Iz dorevoliutsionnogo proshlogo Moskvy," p. 210.

8. N. P. Eroshkin, "Administrativno-politseiskii apparat," in *Istoriia Moskvy*, v. 5, p. 677.

9. Astrov, *Vospominaniia*, v. 1, p. 257.

10. OZhSM, sobstvennoiu vlast'iu, no. 356, December 7 and 18, 1907, p. 39.

11. MgdSO, January 14, 1905, p. 441.

12. "Tsarskosel'skie soveshchaniia, neizdannye protokoly sekretnogo soveshchaniia pod presedatel'stvom byvshego imperatora po voprosu o rasshirenii izbiratel'nogo prava, s vvedeniem V. V. Vodovozova," *Byloe*, no. 3 (25), September 1917, p. 241.

13. Quoted in Hutchinson, "Octobrists in Russian Politics," p. 19.

14. See Weissman, *Reform*, pp. 120–121; Geoffrey A. Hosking, *The Russian Constitutional Experiment: Government and Duma, 1907–1914* (Cambridge, England, 1973), pp. 45 and 182–188; and Robert Edelman, *Gentry Politics on the Eve of the Russian Revolution: The Nationalist Party 1907–1917* (New Brunswick, NJ, 1980), p. 100. Specialists on the Octobrists differ over whether or not the split was largely along rural-urban lines. Hutchinson, "Octobrists in Russian Politics," pp. 374–379, specifically denies that this was the basis for the division. He cites the fact that the Moscow Central Committee of the party, replete with urban bourgeois, was quite conservative. The quarrel was over "the extent to which their common interest, private property, was threatened by a new upsurge of revolutionary violence." But Hutchinson missed the point that the extent of this threat had been very different in 1905 in city and in country, and thus people of property in each area had different perceptions of how to fend off revolution. Moreover, the Octobrists in general had lost a great deal of ground in the cities by 1913, especially in Moscow. Thus the existence of a group of conservative urbanites in the party certainly does not indicate widespread urban support for conservative Octobrism. On the contrary, the elections of 1912 to the State Duma revealed a marked shift in favor of the Kadets among the towns' upper strata. The argument of Brainerd, "The Octobrists and the Gentry," is more convincing. He finds that "[A. I.] Guchkov's militancy was the product of a social and political crisis that was primarily urban; and . . . the Zemstvo Octobrists [the more conservative faction] were more representative of the rural gentry's mood than . . . the Left Octobrists [Guchkov's followers]." *Ibid.*, p. 168. After all, the name *Zemstvo* Octobrists had to refer to men of the countryside, not urbanites.

15. RV, January 1, 1914.

16. See, among many other days, RV, March 9 and March 24, 1917.

17. This happened in Odessa, for example. See Frederick W. Skinner, "City Planning in Russia: The Development of Odessa, 1789–1892," dissertation, Princeton University, 1973, pp. 333–335.

18. Eklof, "Spreading the Word," p. 18, mentions low voter turnout for elections to the Moscow provincial *zemstvo* after the law of 1890 was adopted.

19. This point is implicit in the work of Schneiderman, *Sergei Zubatov*, and of Walter Sablinsky, *The Road to Bloody Sunday: Father Gapon and the St. Petersburg Massacre of 1905* (Princeton, 1976). This contention is supported by the fact that Zubatov and Gapon initially had great success in attracting workers to their movements, despite their limited goals and programs, and by the mildness of the demands presented by the marchers on Bloody Sunday.

20. Over twenty-five different sources were used, ranging from MgdSO, RV, and MV to *Moskovskaia gorodskaia duma, 1897–1900* (Moscow, 1897), and N. I. Astrov, P. N. Miliukov, and V. G. Zeelera, eds., *Pamiati pogibshikh* (Paris, 1929).

21. *Rech'*, December 24, 1908.

22. James H. Bater, *St. Petersburg: Industrialization and Change* (Montreal, 1976), p. 359.

23. Haimson, "Introduction: The Russian Landed Nobility and the System of the 3rd of June," in *The Politics of Rural Russia, 1905–1914*, ed. Leopold Haimson (Bloomington, Indiana, 1979), p. 10.

24. Shecket, "Russian State Council," p. 133.

25. TsGAOR, f. 539, op. 1, d. 983, ll. 1–3, in Davidovich, *Samoderzhavie*, pp. 103–105. The resolution presented to the Trade-Industrial Union came from the St. Petersburg branch "numbering 704 people."

26. For a general discussion of *sosloviia* and their significance, see Gregory L. Freeze, "The *Soslovie* (Estate) Paradigm and Russian Social History," *American Historical Review* 91, no. 1 (1986).

27. Manning, *Crisis of the Old Order*, pp. 325–326.

28. Michael T. Florinsky, *Russia: A History and an Interpretation* (New York, 1947 and 1953), p. 1199n. These figures do not include Siberia, the Caucasus, or the kingdom of Poland.

29. Manning, *Crisis of the Old Order*, p. 326, and Florinsky, *Russia*, p. 1200n.

30. MgdSO, January-February 1906, p. 20.

31. Karzhanskii, *Kak izbiralas'*, p. 62.

32. Eroshkin, "Administrativno-politseiskii apparat," pp. 677–678.

33. *Ibid.*

34. Manning, *Crisis of the Old Order*, pp. 50–51 and 58.

35. For other descriptions of the duma's social composition, none of which is particularly precise, see G. E. Blok and A. Terterian, comps., *V staroi Moskve. Kak khoziaini-chali kuptsy i fabrikanty. Materialy i dokumenty* (Moscow, 1939), pp. 32–33; RV, December 20, 1908; MV, December 30, 1912; and Verner, *Deiatel'nost'*, p. 2.

36. Buryshkin, *Moskva*, p. 111.

37. See the discussion of rising cultural, educational, and political levels among the "second" and "third" generations of Moscow's merchants in Rieber, *Merchants and Entre-preneurs*, pp. 285–332. Rieber concludes that these younger and more energetic *kuptsy* were highly ineffective in politics. That is so on the national level, but they accomplished a great deal in Moscow. Jo Ann Ruckman has also written a valuable study of Moscow's business leaders: *The Moscow Business Elite: A Social and Cultural Portrait of Two Generations, 1840–1905* (Dekalb, Illinois, 1984). Thomas C. Owen, *Capitalism and Politics in Russia: A Social History of the Moscow Merchants, 1855–1905* (Cambridge, 1981), p. 4, lists various reasons why even successful merchants left the business world earlier in the nineteenth century; above all, the very high risks of Russian business were responsible.

38. Buryshkin, *Moskva*, p. 276.

39. Leon Trotsky, *History of the Russian Revolution*, trans. Max Eastman (New York, 1932), v. 1, p. 71.

40. Pares, *My Russian Memoirs*, p. 168.

41. Menashe, "Liberal," p. 45.

42. Buryshkin, *Moskva*, pp. 274–275.

43. Owen, *Capitalism and Politics*, ix, remarks that "the Moscow merchant estate was in fact neither a genuine class nor a bearer of liberalism before 1905, but achieved a rather comfortable place within the Russian old regime." Ruckman, *Moscow Business Elite*, pp. 209–10, finds that in 1905 the Moscow *kuptsy* were just beginning to break out of the old *soslovie* mentality and did not yet really think or behave in class terms.

44. This passage is based partly on James West, "The Moscow Progressists: Russian Industrialists in Liberal Politics, 1905–1914," dissertation, Princeton University, 1975, pp. 118–123.

45. Owen, *Capitalism and Politics*, p. 104.

46. TsGAOR, f. 539, op. 1, d. 983, ll, 1–3, in Davidovich, *Samoderzhavie*, pp. 103–104.

47. Louis Menashe, "Industrialists in Politics: Russia in 1905," *Government and Opposition* 3, no. 3 (1968), 356.

48. MgdSO, January 14, 1905, p. 12.

49. MgdSO, December 13, 1905, pp. 1007–1008, and December 15, 1905, p. 1054.

50. Engelstein, *Moscow*, p. 211.

51. MgdSO, December 13, 1905, pp. 1005–1006.

52. Engelstein, *Moscow*, pp. 211–222. "Everybody wanted to help the *druzhinniki*," recalled Vladimir Zenzinov, who was there at the time. See his *Perezhitoe* (New York, 1953), p. 240.

53. RV, January 13, 1906. The incident may not have been a misunderstanding at all, as Chetverikov was a prominent critic of the government in 1905.

54. RV, January 15, 1906. The protesting groups were not specified.

55. Laverychev, *Po tu storonu*, p. 47.

56. TsGAOR, f. 875 (N. P. Vishniakov), op. 1, d. 10, l. 146, quoted in Laverychev, "Rossiiskie," p. 260.

57. A. Ermanskii, "Krupnaia burzhuaziia v 1905–1907 gg.," *Obshchestvennoe dvizhenie v Rossii v nachale XX-go veka*, ed. L. Martov et al., 4 vols. (St. Petersburg, 1914), tom II, chast' 2, pp. 69–70.

58. West, "Moscow Progressists," p. 181. It was difficult for businessmen to shake off the feeling, transmitted to them in many overt and subtle ways, that status in Russia depended either on level of culture or on nobility, but not on amassing wealth through entrepreneurship. The teachings of the Orthodox Church did not help much in this respect.

59. *Ibid.*, pp. 61–69.

60. Owen, *Capitalism and Politics*, pp. 26, 153.

61. Gindin, "Russkaia burzhuaziia," II, p. 47.

62. On Putilov's connections see Chermenskii, *Burzhuaziia i tsarizm*, pp. 60 and 67.

63. Laverychev, *Po tu storonu*, p. 46.

64. Robert Wiebe, *The Search for Order, 1877–1920* (New York, 1967), pp. 115–160.

65. William E. Gleason, "The All-Russian Union of Towns and the Politics of Urban Reform in Tsarist Russia," *Russian Review* 35 (1976), 292. See also Astrov, *Vospominaniia*, v. 1, pp. 258, 270.

66. Astrov, *Vospominaniia*, v. 1, p. 257.

67. Paul Miliukov, *Political Memoirs 1905–1917*, ed. Arthur P. Mendel, trans. Carl Goldberg (Ann Arbor, 1967), p. 14.

68. *Utro Rossii*, January 18, 1912.

69. Buryshkin, *Moskva*, p. 278.

70. Quoted in Laverychev, *Po tu storonu*, p. 213.

71. *Pravda*, January 21 (8), 1918.

72. Oldenburg, *Last Tsar*, v. 3, p. 131.

73. RV, December 20, 1908.

74. *Rech'*, December 24, 1908.

75. Moskovskaia gorodskaia duma. Komitet gruppy progressivnykh glasnykh, *Moskovskaia gorodskaia duma, 1913–1916 gg.* (Moscow, 1916) [hereafter M.g.d. Komitet progressivnykh, *M.g.d. 1913–1916*], p. 4.

76. RV, October 20, 1912.

77. Buryshkin, *Moskva*, p. 277.

78. Hutchinson, "Octobrists in Russian Politics," pp. 203–204.

79. Rosenberg, *Liberals*, p. 28.

80. Buryshkin, *Moskva*, p. 274.

81. *Golos Moskvy*, November 15, 1908, p. 2.

82. TsGAOR, f. 579, o. 1, d. 613, ll. 2, 3, 12, in Diakin, *Samoderzhavie*, p. 110.

83. *Golos Moskvy*, November 14, 1908.

84. *Rannee Utro*, February 20, 1909.

85. GD, 4 (1909), 158–159.

86. RV, December 16, 1908.

87. Gruppa bezpartiinykh i umerennykh izbiratelei, *O deiatel'nosti gorodskoi dumy sostava 1909–1912 gg.* (Moscow, 1912), passim and p. 32 on the three-story question.

88. Mikailovskii, "Deiatel'nost'," p. 12.

89. RV, November 24, 1912.

90. See, for example, Karzhanskii, *Kak izbiralas'*, p. 27.

91. RV, December 16, 1908.

92. SZ, vtoroe izdanie, V. II, p. 954.

93. SZ, izdanie 1915 g., v. 2, p. 54.

94. RV, March 5, 1913.

95. Laverychev, *Po tu storonu*, pp. 96–97.

96. RV, November 14, 1906.

97. See Hosking, *Russian Constitutional Experiment*, pp. 119–145. The western *zemstvo* bill ensured the dominance of ethnic Russians in the affected provinces; it angered conservatives because it violated the principle of landlord domination. Conservatives considered that a very dangerous precedent.

98. On this point, see Edelman, *Gentry Politics*, passim and especially pp. 73–127.

99. MgdSO, April, 1913, pp. 383–385.

100. Laverychev, *Po tu storonu*, pp. 96–97.

101. V. N. Kokovtsov, *Out of My Past* (Stanford, 1939), pp. 396–399.

102. OZhSM, no. 105, November 27, 1913, pp. 1–6.

103. Owen, *Capitalism and Politics*, p. 84.

104. Buryshkin, *Moskva*, p. 277.

105. MgdSO, April, 1913, pp. 383–385.

106. Thomas Riha, "Constitutional Developments in Russia," in Theofanis George Stavrou, ed., *Russia Under the Last Tsar* (Minneapolis, 1969), p. 89.

107. "Svedeniia iz Moskvy," GD, 20 (1911), 1458–1459.

108. Bater, *St. Petersburg*, pp. 367 and 408–409.

Chapter 4

1. Bernard Pares, "Conversations with Mr. Stolypin," *Russian Review* (London), v. 2, no. 1 (1913), 105.

2. OZhSM, January 31, 1912, p. 1, and see no. 6, July 12, 1911.

3. For a discussion of police functions in the eighteenth century, see John Le Donne, "The Provincial and Local Police under Catherine the Great, 1775–1796," *Canadian Slavic Studies*, v. 4 (1970), 513–528. On the regular police in the twentieth century, see Neil Weissman, "Regular Police in Tsarist Russia, 1900–1914," *Russian Review* 44, no. 1 (1985).

4. Don Karl Rowney, "Higher Civil Servants in the Russian Ministry of Internal Affairs: Some Demographic and Career Characteristics, 1905–1916," *Slavic Review*, v. 31, no. 1 (1972), 101.

5. Tsuyoshi Hasegawa, "The Formation of the Militia in the February Revolution: An Aspect of the Origins of Dual Power," *Slavic Review*, v. 32, no. 2 (1973), 303.

6. *Sankt Peterburgskaia stolichnaia politsiia i gradonachal'stvo (1703–1903). Kratkii istoricheskii ocherk* (St. Petersburg, 1903), p. 215; and "Gradonachal'nik," *Entsiklopedicheskii Slovar' Brokgauz i Efron* (St. Petersburg, 1893), v. 9, p. 492.

7. Eroshkin, "Administrativno-politseiskii apparat," p. 669.

8. "Proekt, predlozhennyi moskovskimi fabrikantami, o preobrazovanii moskovskoi politsii," December 2, 1905. In *Iz istorii revoliutsii 1905 goda v Moskve i moskovskoi gubernii; materialy i dokumenty* (Moscow, 1931), p. 298.

9. The ratios for cities other than Moscow are derived from figures on police strength and population given in Raymond B. Fosdick, *European Police Systems* (New York, 1915), pp. 401–402. Fosdick gives no dates for his data, which he compiled during visits to these and other cities in 1913–1914.

10. OZhSM, no. 6, July 12, 1911, and January 31, 1912, p. 23.

11. Bradley, *Muzhik and Muscovite*, p. 187, and *Russkoe Slovo*, March 21, 1906.

12. A. P. Martynov, *Moia sluzhba v Otdel'nom Korpuse zhandarmov; Vospominaniia*, ed. Richard Wraga (Stanford, 1972), p. 225.

13. *Ibid.*, editor's notes, p. 331.

14. TsGAgM, f. 46, o. 14, d. 1212, l. 26.

15. Eroshkin, "Administrativno-politseiskii apparat," p. 671.

16. See, for example, RV, April 12, 1912.

17. Letter to the Moscow governor-general from the Ministry of Internal Affairs, Glavnoe Upravlenie po delam pechati, no. 345. TsGAgM, f. 46, o. 14, d. 3374, l. 21.

18. TsGAgM, f. 131, o. 79, d. 35, l. 12.

19. TsGAgM, f. 131, o. 81, d. 88, l. 7.

20. That is, nine months of research at TsGAgM did not uncover systematic evidence on this point.

21. See Samuel Kucherov, *Courts, Lawyers and Trials under the Last Three Tsars* (New York, 1953), pp. 212–225, 233, 235, 264, and 270.

22. *Golos Moskvy*, April 18, 1907.

23. Hagen, *Entfaltung Politischer Öffentlichkeit*, pp. 95–130. A number of the same points were made earlier in Jacob Walkin, "Government Controls over the Press in Russia, 1905–1914," *Russian Review* 13, no. 3 (1954). Hagen may well underestimate repression of the workers' press. According to *Kratkaia istoriia rabochego dvizheniia v Rossii (1861–1917 gody)* (Moscow, 1962), p. 455, the Bolshevik paper *Pravda* was closed eight times in its two and a half years of existence in 1912–1914. Thirty-six issues were confiscated and sixteen fined in its first year; 116 such actions took place in its second. Fines of 14,200 rubles were levied on the paper in that span, and its workers were frequently arrested. Such repression does not constitute full freedom of expression.

24. Walkin, "Government Controls," p. 204, writes that the government continued to remain an "irritating deterrent to full freedom of expression" even though "the situation had materially improved."

25. RV, October 16, 1913.

26. RV, July 25, 1913.

27. MgdSO, April 1914, p. 420.

28. Astrov, "Iz istorii," v. 2, pp. 111–112.

29. RV, January 4, 1914.

30. "Pokazanie M. V. Chelnokova," *Padenie tsarskogo rezhima. Stenograficheskie otchety doprosov i pokazanii, dannykh v Chrezvychainoi Sledstvennoi komissii Vremennogo Pravitel'stva (v 1917 g.)* v semi tomakh. Redaktsiia P. E. Shcheglova (Moscow-Leningrad, 1926), v. 5, p. 295.

31. Levin, "Russian Bureaucratic Opinion," pp. 10–11.

32. MgdSO, November-December 1913, pp. 1317–1318.

33. The incident may be followed in MgdSO, March 1911, pp. 240 and 279; May-June 1911, pp. 666–667; and September 1911, p. 879.

34. MV, February 20, 1913.

35. Conroy, *Stolypin*, pp. 99–110.

36. See GSSO, sessiia IX, Zas.6, November 29, 1913, col. 172. There the head of the Main Administration on Local Affairs remarked that the City Statute of 1892 had as its chief goal the "unification of government and public forces." However, one is reminded of Marx's phrase about the merger of a hungry man with a piece of bread.

37. Crime figures for Moscow are in Moskovskaia gorodskaia uprava, *Obzor po gorodu Moskve za ——— god* (Moscow, 1908–1911) hereafter Mgu, *Obzor po gorodu*. The cites are: *1907*, p. 109; *1908*, p. 121; *1909*; p. 142, *1910*, p. 124. Crime statistics in general for this period in Russia are very scanty. Statistics on court cases, partly because so many trials were removed to military courts or decided administratively under the Extraordinary Measures, are unreliable; see S. S. Ostroumov, *Ocherki po istorii ugolovnoi statistiki dorevoliutsionnoi Rossii* (Moscow, 1961), p. 241. For crime statistics in Paris and Berlin, see Prefecture de la Seine. Direction des affaires municipales. Service de la statistique municipale, *Annuaire statistique de la ville de Paris*. XXXIe année, 1910 (Paris, 1912), p. 600, and *Statistisches Jahrbuch der Stadt Berlin*, 33. Jahrgang (Berlin, 1916), p. 737.

38. "Khronika," *Pravo*, 12 (1911), 766.

39. Ministerstvo Iustitsii, *Svod statisticheskikh svedenii o podsudimykh, opravdannykh i osuzhdaemykh po prigovoram obshchikh sudebnykh mest, sudebno-mirovykh ustanovlenii i uchrezhdenii, obrazovannykh po zakonopolozheniiam 12 iuliia 1889 goda* (St. Petersburg, 1911), chast' I, p. 50.

40. The figures were compiled largely from RV and MV; some accounts are from *Golos Moskvy* and *Russkoe Slovo*. Care has been taken to see that each case has been counted only once. It would be useful to have figures for 1905 as a comparison, but strikes closed Moscow's newspapers in that year at various times and thus their information on police attacks is inadequate. Official police publications mentioned only a very few attacks in these years; the police materials in TsGAgM had almost no such information.

41. The months of January, April, June, and October were checked in RV and MV.

42. Tsentral'nyi Gosudarstvennyi Arkhiv Oktiabr'skoi Revoliutsii [hereafter TsGAOR], fond 102, 4 d-vo, ed. khr. 108, t. 28, list 7.

43. RV, August 17, 1906.

44. "Khronika," *Pravo* 33 (1906), col. 2659–2662, and "Perechen' naibolee vydaiushchikh proiavlenii revoliutsionnogo dvizheniia za 1906 god," *Pravo* 34 (1906), col. 2701–2704 have the lists for August, 1906. "Khronika," *Pravo* 32 (1907), col. 2170–2171, has the list for July, 1907.

45. Great Britain, Public Record Office, Foreign Office 371, v. 726, no. 21149, June 3, 1909, and *ibid.*, v. 732, no. 23026, June 15, 1909, p. 5. Reprinted from *Pravitel'stvennyi Vestnik* [no date given], cited in Conroy, *Stolypin*, p. 91.

46. RV, January 16, 1906.

47. MV, June 6, 1906.

48. *Russkoe Slovo*, June 18 and June 20, 1906.

49. RV, August 9, 1906.

50. MV, July 6, 1906.

51. RV, July 30, 1906.

52. The newspapers list only twenty-three attacks on police during the course of arrests or following police action in the years 1908–1914.

53. G. Matveev, "Moskovskii soiuz rabochikh-metallistov v 1906–07 gg. (Po lichnym vospominaniiam)," in *Materialy po istorii professional'nogo dvizheniia v Rossii* [hereafter *Materialy po istorii p.d.*] (Moscow, 1924–27), sbornik II, p. 251.

54. Kiselev (*sic*), "Vospominaniia 1905–1907 gg. v Butyrskom raione," Arkhiv Institut Istorii partii MK KPSS, quoted in G. D. Kostomarov, "Revoliutsionnaia bor'ba moskovskikh rabochikh v period otstupleniia revoliutsii" in *Istoriia Moskvy*, v. 5, p. 144.

55. "O dvizhenii sredi moskovskikh rabochikh metallistov," *Materialy po istorii p.d.*, sbornik I, pp. 137, 141, and 183.

56. RV, April 22, 1908.

57. RV, October 8, 1908.

58. RV, October 9, 1908.

59. RV, October 22, 1908.

60. Moskovskoe gradonachal'stvo, *Prikazy po Moskovskomu gradonachal'stvu i stolichoi politsii. Ianvar' 1908–noiabr' 1914* (Moscow, 1908–1914). See, among many other days, May 4, 1908, October 18, 1908, May 5, 1909, and September 4, 1909.

61. Moskovskoe gradonachal'stvo, *Alfavitnyi sbornik rukovodiashchikh prikazov i tsirkuliarnykh rasporiazhenii po moskovskomu gradonachal'stvu i stolichnoi politsii s 1881 g. po 1 iuliia 1910 g.* (Moscow, 1911) [hereafter M. gradonachal'stvo, *Alfavitnyi sbornik*], chast' II, p. 630.

62. N. P. Garin, *Pravitel'stvuiushchemu senatu, po pervomu departamentu, senatora revizuiushchego po vysochaishemu poveleniiu Moskovskoe gradonachal'stvo, Donoshenie 13 noiabria 1908 g.* No. 364 (n.p., n.d.), pp. 2–3, 31–33, and 41–44.

63. RV, May 18, 1911.

64. Martynov, *Moia sluzhba*, editor's notes, p. 339.

65. *Ibid.*, p. 337.

66. *Golos Moskvy*, May 31 and June 6, 1908.

67. Mgu, *Doklady*, no. 285, October 15, 1908, p. 1.

68. RV, April 4, 1909.

69. See, for example, *Vedomosti Moskovskogo gradonachal'stva i stolichnoi politsii*, no. 50, March 4, 1906, p. 1.

70. Mgu, *Obzor po gorodu za 1908*, p. 85.

71. MV, October 5, 1912, RV, October 4, 1912, and on other similar incidents, RV, April 5, 1909, MV, October 8, 1913, and RV, October 11, 1913.

72. V. Vishnevskii in *Kino*, March 11, 1936, quoted in Jay Leyda, *Kino: A History of the Russian and Soviet Film* (New York, 1960), p. 68. Leyda provides no further information on the circular, but it undoubtedly reached the Moscow *gradonachal'nik*.

73. GDSO III, ch. 1, s. 2, z. 32, col. 2813.

74. *Ibid.*, col. 2820.

75. *Ibid.*, col. 2813. See also the statement by G. G. Zamyslovskii, quoted in the previous chapter, in *ibid.*, cols. 2813–2816.

76. RV, December 17, 1908.

77. RV, January 12, 1907. There is also a report that at approximately the same time the Gradonachal'nik threatened P. K. Verkholantsev and his son with exile because they had supposedly fired workers for *refusal* to join a political strike. Verkholantsev denied the charge. D. G. Reder, "Sorok vosem' let," in *Krasnaia presnia; ocherki po istorii zavodov* (Moscow, 1934), pp. 17–18. A V. P. Verkholantsev, probably the son, was elected to the Moscow duma in 1912. If he was the same man as in the 1907 case, he may well have harbored doubts or resentment about the administration's power.

78. RV, April 3, 1909.

79. "Protokol pokazanii E. K. Klimovicha," in *Soiuz russkogo naroda. Po materialam chrezvychainoi sledstvennoi komissii vremennogo pravitel'stva 1917 g.*, sost. A. Chernovskii (Moscow, Petrograd, 1919), pp. 71–73.

80. RV, July 25, 1913.

81. RV, January 12, 1914.

82. RV, November 5, 1913.

83. *Utro Rossii*, May 16, 1910, quoted in Diakin, *Samoderzhavie*, p. 186.

84. OZhSM, no. 6, July 12, 1911, and January 31, 1912, pp. 4–5.

85. G. B. Sliuzberg (Sliozberg), *Dorevoliutsionnoi stroi Rossii* (Paris, 1933), p. 179.

Chapter 5

1. Sapronov, *Iz istorii*, p. 9.

2. *Utro Rossii*, April 10, 1912.

3. Among the local studies we do have are Victoria Bonnell, "Radical Politics and Organized Labor in Pre-Revolutionary Moscow, 1905–1914," *Journal of Social History*, no. 2 (1978), and Heather Jeanne Hogan, "Labor and Management in Conflict: The St. Petersburg Metal-Working Industry, 1900–1914," dissertation, University of Michigan, 1981.

4. G. A. Arutiunov, *Rabochee dvizhenie v Rossii v period novogo revoliutsionnogo pod"ema 1910–1914 gg.* (Moscow, 1975), p. 315.

5. See Bonnell, *Roots of Rebellion*, p. 452; and Reginald Zelnik, "Russian Workers and the Revolutionary Movement," *Journal of Social History* 6, no. 2 (1972–73), 223.

6. V. I. Lenin, *What Is To Be Done? Burning Questions of Our Movement* (New York, 1929), pp. 54 and 76. Bonnell, *Roots of Rebellion*, pp. 257–58, reports that Social Democratic activists in Moscow feared the influence of trade unionism.

7. A. Kats, "Iz istorii Moskovskogo Obshchestva vzaimopomoshchi ofitsiantov (1902–1916 gg.)," in *Materialy po istorii*, sbornik I, pp. 44–45.

8. "O dvizhenii sredi Moskovskikh rabochikh metallistov," *Materialy po istorii p.d.*, sbornik I, p. 133.

9. Engelstein, *Moscow*, p. 60.

10. Schneiderman, *Sergei Zubatov*, pp. 139, 145, and 366.

11. *Profsoiuzy SSSR: Dokumenty i materialy v chetyrekh tomakh. Tom I. Profsoiuzy v bor'be za sverzhenie samoderzhaviia i ustanovlenie diktatury proletariata (1905–1917 gg.)* (Moscow, 1963), pp. 37–38.

12. *Ibid.*, pp. 74–75.

13. Engelstein, *Moscow*, pp. 62 and 78.

14. *Ibid.*, p. 97.

15. *Listovki moskovskikh bol'shevikov v period pervoi russkoi revoliutsii* (Moscow, 1955), pp. 314–15.

16. See, for example, Nicholas Riasanovsky, *A History of Russia*, fourth edition (New York, 1984), p. 408; and Leon Trotsky, *1905*, trans. Anya Bostock (New York, 1972), pp. 159–61.

17. *Profsoiuzy*, I, 79. The meeting took place on November 7, 1905.

18. Engelstein, *Moscow*, pp. 174–201.

19. *Listovki*, pp. 510–512.

20. SZ, vtoroe izdanie, v. 14, p. 52.

21. M. gradonachal'stvo, *Alfavitnyi sbornik*, chast'II p. 603.

22. A. F. Kuzovatkin, "Posledam minuvshego," in *Moskovskie bol'sheviki v ogne revoliutsionnykh boev* (Moscow, 1976), pp. 204–205; and Sapronov, *Iz istorii*, pp. 19–20.

23. Matveev, "Moskovskii soiuz rabochikh-metallistov," sbornik II, p. 263.

24. Quoted in A. Aluf, *Bol'shevizm i men'shevizm v professional'nom dvizhenii* (Moscow, 1926), pp. 33–34.

25. *Profsoiuzy*, I, p. 109.

26. Mikhail S. Balabanov, *Ot 1905 k 1917 godu: massovoe rabochee dvizhenie* (Moscow, 1927), pp. 107–8; K. Komarovskii, "Rabochii rynok v 1909 godu," *Promyshlennost' i Torgovlia*, no. 5, March 1, 1910, p. 298; and RV, September 12, 1907.

27. Bonnell, "Radical Politics," 284–87. In her *Roots of Rebellion*, p. 319, she writes that the coup d'état "inaugurated a government campaign to destroy the trade unions."

28. K. Dmitriev (P. Kolokol'nikev), *Professional'nye soiuzy v Moskve* (St. Petersburg, 1913?). Judging by its contents, the book was written in early 1906, before the "temporary rules" on unions were issued.

29. MV, July 1 and July 2, 1906. A similar case is in *Russkoe Slovo*, June 29, 1906.

230

Notes

30. *Golos Moskvy*, May 16, 1907.

31. *Ibid.*, February 14, 1907.

32. RV, August 18, 1906.

33. V. Ia. Laverychev, *Tsarizm i rabochii vopros v Rossii 1861–1917 gg.* (Moscow, 1972), p. 234.

34. *Rannee Utro*, May 23, 1909.

35. N. Shevkov, "Ekonomicheskaia bor'ba Shveinikov v 1911–12 gg.," *Materialy po istorii p.d.*, sbornik III, p. 359.

36. RV, July 25, 1913.

37. TsGAgM, f. 46, o. 14, ed. khr. 1169, ll. 1, 2, 9, 13; ed. khr. 1171, ll. 1, 5. See also RV, November 12, 1906.

38. RV, August 28, 1907.

39. MV, July 2, 1906. See also M. Nikitin, "Moskovskoe stachechnoe dvizhenie v 1905–07 gg.," in Iu. K. Milonov, ed., *Moskovskoe professional'noe dvizhenie v gody pervoi revoliutsii* (Moscow, 1925?), p. 144.

40. On "political strikes" see Haimson, "Social Stability," 23, 628.

41. RV, August 12, 1907.

42. MV, August 12, 1907.

43. RV, September 12, 1907.

44. Bonnell, "Radical Politics," 284–287, and her *Roots of Rebellion*, pp. 202–319.

45. Arkh. b. dep. pol., 4 delopr., 1910, d. no. 42, ch. 2, ll. 50–52, quoted in Balabanov, *Ot 1905 k 1917*, p. 136.

46. TsGAOR, f. 102, 4 d-vo ed. khr. 108, t. 28, ll. 7–47; f. 102 D-4 1910, 42, 2, l. 51. In November 1907, the *gradonachal'nik* claimed that penetration of the unions by revolutionaries drove workers away, because repression inevitably followed: f. 102, 4 d-vo, ed. khr. 108, t. 28, l. 17.

47. Tsentral'nyi Gosudarstvennyi Istoricheskii Arkhiv, f. 1284, op. 187, d. 298 1906 l. 1, quoted in Bonnell, *Roots of Rebellion*, p. 278.

48. Levin, "Russian Bureaucratic Opinion," p. 3.

49. MV, July 7 and July 8, 1906.

50. *Leninskii Zakaz: sto let tipografii "Krasnyi Proletarii"* (Moscow, 1969), pp. 66–67.

51. *Vedomosti Moskovskogo gradonachal'stva i stolichnoi politsii*, no. 141, July 4, 1906, p. 2.

52. RV, April 15, 1907. A clipping of the report is in TsGAOR, f. 102, 4–dvo 42, t. 2, l. 95, which shows that the authorities were at least keeping track of such incidents; these were the Department of Police's files.

53. *Birzhevye Vedomosti*, February 18, 1911, p. 2. Clipping in TsGAOR, 4–dvo, 1911, g. 42, t. 1, l. 1. A police report on l. 2 of the 4–dvo stated that four workers were arrested at first, then thirteen more after the strike began. All were exiled to their villages.

54. Sapronov, *Iz istorii*, p. 9.

55. OZhSM, sobstvennoiu vlast'iu, no. 55, August 8, 1913, pp. 1–5. The document is marked "Secret." For a translation of it, see Appendix H.

56. For accounts of the strike see RV, September 21 and 25–27, 1913.

57. TsGAgM, f. 179, d. 4367, ll. 32–33.

58. Balabanov, *Ot 1905 k 1917*, p. 245.

59. TsGAgM, f. 179, d. 4367, ll. 34–35.

60. Balabanov, *Ot 1905 k 1917*, p. 243.

61. I. A. Menitskii, *Russkoe rabochee dvizhenie i R.S.D.R.P. nakanune voiny* (Moscow, 1923), pp. 12–13.

62. *Sotsial-demokrat*, no. 30, 1913 [no date given], cited in G. G. Morekhin, "Novyi revoliutsionnyi pod"em (1912–1914)," in *Istoriia Moskvy*, v. 5, p. 259.

63. *Sokol'niki* (Moscow, 1967), p. 31.

64. Bonnell, *Roots of Rebellion*, p. 372.

65. Oldenburg, *Last Tsar*, vol. 3, p. 115.

66. Arutiunov, *Rabochee dvizhenie*, p. 253; P. Kabanov, R. Erman, N. Kuznetsov, and A. Ushakov, *Ocherki istorii rossiiskogo proletariata (1861–1917)* (Moscow, 1963), p. 287. These sources give the figure of thirteen unions in the city altogether, whereas Bonnell states that there were about thirty in 1912. See note 44 above.

67. Arutiunov, *Rabochee dvizhenie*, p. 312.

68. Bonnell, "Radical Politics," pp. 290–292, argues that government vacillation toward labor unions in the years 1907–1914 increased workers' radicalism.

69. On the background of the workhouse, see Bradley, "Workhouse," pp. 427–436; and Adele Lindenmeyr, "Charity and the Problem of Unemployment: Industrial Homes in Late Imperial Russia," *Russian Review* 45, no. 1 (1986).

70. Staryi Moskvich, "Prisutstvie po razboru nishchikh," RV, March 15, 1914, p. 6.

71. M. gradonachal'stvo, *Alfavitnyi sbornik*, chast' 3, pp. 178–179.

72. Shvittau, *Trudovaia pomoshch'*, p. 112.

73. Mgu, *Doklady*, "O merakh bor'by s ulichnym nishchestvom v Moskve," January 10, 1906, p. 6.

74. RV, August 3, 1908.

75. Studenetskii, "Obshchestvennoe prizrenie," p. 164.

76. Shvittau, *Trudovaia pomoshch'*, pp. 127–128.

77. MV, August 3, 1908.

78. Mgu, *Doklady*, "O vozvedenii zdanii Doma Trudoliubiia i Rabotnogo Doma v gorodskom vladenii po Furmannomu i Bol'shomu Khariton'evskomu pereulkam," May 21, 1913, pp. 4–5, 28.

79. MgdSO, May–June 1906, pp. 278–279. Zimin's party affiliation is unknown.

80. A. S. Chebarin, *Moskva v revoliutsii 1905–1907 godov* (Moscow, 1955), pp. 221–222.

81. S. Ainzaft, *Pervyi etap professional'nogo dvizheniia v Rossii (1905–1907 gg.)* (Moscow, 1924–25), p. 110, and *Sokol'niki*, p. 16, have the two estimates respectively. The last figure must be a misprint.

82. Mosk. oblastnoe arkhivnoe upravlenie. Ist. arkhiv no. 1, f. M. gor. dumy, kants., arkh. no. 69, sv. 27, ll. 39–40. Quoted in Blok and Terterian, *V staroi Moskve*, pp. 201–202.

83. MgdSO, May–June 1906, pp. 301–302.

84. MV, May 18 and 19, 1906.

85. "Khronika," *Pravo*, no. 21 (1906), col. 1954.

86. MgdSO, May–June 1906, pp. 420–421.

87. *Ibid.*, pp. 421–426.

88. Mgu, *Doklady*, "Otchet po okazaniiu pomoshchi bezrabotnym (s 14 maia po 11 avgusta 1906 g.), (1906), pp. 2–4.

89. Mgu, *Doklady*, "Otchet po okazaniiu," p. 9.

90. RV, August 2, 1907.

91. This account is based on Studenetskii, "Obshchestvennoe prizrenie," pp. 170–73, and Mgu, *Doklady*, "Ob otkrytii posrednicheskoi kontory dlia okazaniia raboty v g. Moskve," no. 213 (1906), pp. 1–2.

92. The figures from 1908 to 1910 are from TsGAgM, f. 46, o. 14, d. 1212, l. 42. The 1911 figures are from Shvittau, *Trudovaia pomoshch'*, pp. 132–133.

93. M. N., "Moskovskie birzhi truda," RV, November 19, 1909, p. 5.

94. TsGAgM, f. 179, o. 21, d. 3001, l. 45.

95. RV, July 16, 1914.

96. MV, February 3, 1906.

97. RV, December 15, 1906.
98. *Rannee Utro*, October 18, 1909.
99. RV, May 31, 1906.
100. MgdSO, November 1, 1905, p. 784.
101. RV, February 25, 1907.
102. MgdSO, January–February 1907, 120–21.
103. *Rech'*, March 6, 1907, clipping in TsGAOR f. 102, 4 d-vo, 1907, 42 t. 2.
104. MgdSO, January–February 1907, p. 129; the quotation is in RV, March 7, 1907.
105. MgdSO, January–February 1907, p. 129.
106. *Ibid.*, pp. 130–31.
107. RV, March 7, 1907.
108. RV, September 21, 1913.
109. RV, September 25, 1913.
110. RV, September 26, 1913.
111. RV, September 21, 1913.
112. RV, September 26 and 27, 1913.
113. See note 19 above.
114. *Rabochii klass i rabochee dvizhenie v Rossii. 1861–1917 gg.* (Moscow, 1966), 266–67.
115. RV, April 28, 1912, and see Sapronov, *Iz istorii*, p. 8, for the same opinion.
116. Arutiunov, *Rabochee dvizhenie*, p. 147.
117. *Ibid.*, p. 180.
118. *Utro Rossii*, April 7, 1912.
119. On the "young group," see Laverychev, *Po tu storonu*, pp. 36–74; Rieber, *Merchants and Entrepreneurs*, pp. 285–332; and West, "Moscow Progressists," pp. 248–352.
120. *Utro Rossii*, January 18, 1912.
121. *Ibid.*, April 10, 1912.
122. *Ibid.*, January 1, 1912; and see West, "Search for a Middle Class Identity," passim and p. 9.
123. RV, January 1, 1912.
124. *Rabochii klass i rabochee dvizhenie*, p. 272.
125. Quoted in *Proletarskaia Pravda* (*Pravda* by another name; such changes were frequent, as the government forced a cat and mouse game with the radical press, which was frequently closed but could reopen immediately under a new name), January 12, 1914. The bill is discussed in RV, June 10, 1914, and Bonnell, *Roots of Rebellion*, pp. 377–78.
126. On Moscow industrialists' attitudes toward unions in 1907, see *ibid.*, p. 294 and Laverychev, *Po tu storonu*, pp. 56–57. Even then, the prominent liberal S. I. Chetverikov maintained, "Many representatives of our industry clearly recognize that you can't get away from the workers' movement with various forms of 'repression.'" He urged winning the trust of workers "through broad satisfaction of the actual needs of the working class," for which purpose capital should unite. *Slovo*, August 25, 1907, quoted in Balabanov, *Ot 1905*, p. 39.
127. Bonnell, *Roots of Rebellion*, p. 382.
128. "Iz zapisnoi knizhki arkhivista. O lokalizatsii prazdnovaniia 1 maia na fabrikakh i zavodakh. Soobshchil N. Dmitriev," *Krasnyi Arkhiv*, 3 (16), 1926, pp. 205–9.
129. *Ibid.*, pp. 205–6.
130. Arutiunov, *Rabochee dvizhenie*, p. 315.
131. Haimson, "Problem of Social Stability," 24, no. 1, pp. 4–8; and I. S. Rosental', "Russkii liberalizm nakanune pervoi mirovoi voiny i taktika bol'shevikov," *Istoriia SSSR*, 6 (1971), pp. 52–64.
132. *Listovki*, p. 455.
133. Aluf, *Bol'shevizm*, pp. 45–46.

134. E. Ignatov, "Iz istorii obshchestva povarov moskovskogo promyshlennogo raiona. Ocherk vtoroi," in *Materialy po istorii p.d.*, sbornik III, p. 141.

135. *Ibid.*, pp. 146–47.

136. *Ibid.*, p. 158.

137. RV, September 25, 1913.

138. "O dvizhenii sredi moskovskikh rabochikh metallistov," p. 144.

139. Novikov, *Ot Moskvy*, p. 149.

140. *Pravda*, May 25, 1912.

141. *Ibid.*, April 22, 1912.

142. *Put' Pravdy [Pravda]*, February 14, 1914.

143. *Proletarskaia Pravda [Pravda]*, January 8, 1914.

144. *Put' Pravdy*, January 30, 1914. See also a quotation from *Pravda*, June 11, 1912, in L. M. Ivanov, "Ideologicheskoe vozdeistvie na proletariat tsarizma i burzhuazii," in *Rossiiskii proletariat: oblik, bor'ba, gegemoniia*, ed. L. M. Ivanov (Moscow, 1970), p. 325. *Pravda* spoke of how the societies for sobriety, sponsored by the *obshchestvo*, were "capturing simple people," who would then "obediently bear any oppression of the capitalists."

145. *Rabochee klass i rabochee dvizhenie*, pp. 266–68. However, at the same time, the Moscow Society of Mill and Factory Owners refused to pay workers for the days they were out in protest against Lena and urged its members to levy fines for May 1 absences. The latter call also received mixed results.

146. Zelnik, "Russian Workers," 223.

147. *Ibid.*, 223.

148. Bonnell, *Roots of Rebellion*, p. 378.

149. G. W. Phillips, "Urban Proletarian Politics in Tsarist Russia: Petersburg and Moscow, 1912–1914," *Comparative Urban Research* 3, no. 3 (1976), 14. Phillips compiled his estimates from "secret reports of the Moscow security police (their estimates are probably low); estimates of Soviet historians (often high); estimates in *Pravda* (often high); and estimates from the publication of the Moscow Society of Factory and Plant Owners (*Izvestiia Obshchestva Zavodchikov i Fabrikantov Moskovskogo Promyshlennogo Raiona*) (probably low)." Phillips, "Urban Proletarian Politics," p. 19.

Chapter 6

1. Lenin, PSS, v. 24, p. 270; his emphasis.

2. Johnson, *Peasant and Proletarian*, pp. 93–94.

3. G. Vasil'ich, "Ulitsy i liudi sovremennoi Moskvy," in *Moskva v eia proshlom i nastoiashchem* (Moscow, 1910–1912), v. 12, p. 9.

4. *Vsia Moskva 1906*, col. 818–830.

5. MV, March 19, 1910.

6. RV, March 16, 1913.

7. MV, July 20, 1913.

8. Mikhailovskii, "Deiatel'nost'," pp. 32–33.

9. Koenker, *Moscow Workers*, p. 163.

10. See the memoir accounts in Bonnell, *Russian Worker*, pp. 62–64, 110, and 170.

11. Moskovskaia gorodskaia uprava, *Otchet gorodskoi upravy za 1908 g.* (Moscow, 1909), p. 297.

12. *Ezhegodnik vneshkol'nogo obrazovaniia*, ed. V. I. Charnoluskii, vyp. II (St. Petersburg, 1910), p. 219.

13. RV, February 11, 1911.

14. Sytin, *Kommunal'noe khoziaistvo*, p. 79.

15. RV, November 11, 1912.

16. MV, July 19, 1913.

17. *Ibid.*

18. Mosoblarkhiv, 1914 g., op. 121, d. no. 77, 1. 44 ob., quoted in "Iz dorevoliutsion-nogo proshlogo," pp. 225–226.

19. Moskovskoe gorodskoe obshchestvennoe upravlenie, *Organizatsiia, kul'turnaia rabota i tekhnika Moskovskikh gorodskikh bibliotek-chitatelen*, izd, 2–e, isprav. i dop. (Moscow, 1916) [hereafter M.g.o.u., *Organizatsiia, kul'turnaia rabota*], p. 4.

20. *Ibid.*, pp. 5–12.

21. Skh, p. 97.

22. M.g.o.u., *Organizatsiia, kul'turnaia rabota*, p. 4.

23. Skh, p. 98.

24. M.g.u., *Doklady*, no. 16 (1914), pp. 2–3.

25. Moskovskaia gorodskaia uprava, *Vedomosti o Moskovskikh gorodskikh nachal'nykh uchilishchakh za 1912 g.* (Moscow, 1913), p. VI.

26. M.g.o.u., *Organizatsiia, kul'turnaia rabota*, p. 4.

27. K. I. Abramov and V. E. Vasil'chenko, *Istoriia bibliotechnogo dela v SSSR*, izd. 2–e, pererabot. i dop. (Moscow, 1970), p. 181.

28. *Ibid.*, p. 173.

29. *Ibid.*, pp. 188–189.

30. *Ibid.*, pp. 174–178, and A. A. Gromova, *Bibliotechnoe delo v Rossii (v 1908–1914 godakh)* (Moscow, 1955), p. 5.

31. Gromova, *Bibliotechnoe*, p. 13.

32. *Ibid.*, p. 37.

33. Abramov and Vasil'chenko, *Istoriia*, p. 178.

34. *Ibid.*, p. 177.

35. As expressed in Skh, p. 28.

36. Alaverdian, *Zhilishchnyi vopros*, pp. 99–100.

37. K. V. Karaffa-Korbut, "Nochlezhnye doma v bol'shikh russkikh gorodakh," GD, no. 10 (1912), 628–632.

38. M.g.u., *Doklady*, no. 4 (1911), pp. 1–2.

39. A. Studenetskii, "Obshchestvennoe prizrenie," p. 182.

40. Alaverdian, *Zhilishchnyi vopros*, pp. 55–56.

41. MV, March 12, 1906, pp. 3–4; and Alaverdian, *Zhilishchnyi vopros*, pp. 55–56.

42. Alaverdian, *Zhilishnyi vopros*, p. 29.

43. The number of registered prostitutes was compiled from figures in TsGAgM, f. 16, o. 144, d. 12, t. 1, l. 18, and Ministerstvo vnutrennikh del. Glavnoe upravlenie po delam mestnogo khoziaistva, *Vrachebno-politseiskii nadzor za prostitutsiei* (St. Petersburg, 1910), chast' vtoraia, p. 14. The estimate of the actual number of all prostitutes is from *Rannee Utro*, June 16, 1911, quoted in Blok and Terterian, *V staroi Moskve*, p. 223.

44. M.g.u., *Doklady*, no. 4 (1911), p. 4.

45. MgdSO, March 1911, pp. 376–377.

46. Studenetskii, "Obshchestvennoe prizrenie," p. 176.

47. Quoted in *ibid.*, p. 176.

48. M.g.u., *Doklady*, no. 110 (1910), pp. 7 and 9.

49. RV, March 18, 1912.

50. Studenetskii, "Obshchestvennoe prizrenie," p. 181.

51. Mikhailovskii, "Deiatel'nost'," p. 43.

52. Studenetskii, "Obshchestvennoe prizrenie," p. 180.

53. Kir'ianov, *Zhiznennyi uroven'*, p. 268.

54. MV, June 2, 1910.

55. TsGAgM, f. 16, o. 140, d. 184, ll. 9–10.

56. Moskovskaia gorodskaia duma, *Sbornik obiazatel'nykh dlia zhitelei goroda Moskvy postanovlenii Moskovskoi gorodskoi dumy* (Moscow, 1913), p. 5.

57. MV, February 3, 1906.

58. MgdSO, May–June 1911, pp. 684–685.

59. MgdSO, March–April 1910, pp. 177–178.

60. Studenetskii, "Obshchestvennoe prizrenie," p. 188.

61. RV, March 28, 1908.

62. N. S. Kudriukov, "Doma deshevykh kvartir G. G. Solodovnikova v Moskve," *GD*, no. 16 (1909), p. 109.

63. RV, June 3, 1909.

64. Studenetskii, "Obshchestvennoe prizrenie," p. 187.

65. RV, February 18, 1912.

66. M.g.d. komitet progressivnykh, *M.g.d. 1913–1916*, p. 34.

67. Studenetskii, "Obshchestvennoe prizrenie," p. 191.

68. For the 1912 plan see *ibid.*, p. 191; for the 1914 plan see Mikhailovskii, "Deiatel'-nost'," pp. 42–43.

69. RV, February 1, 1914.

70. Shtromberg, *Gorodskie zheleznye dorogi*, pp. 234–238.

71. "Soobshcheniia s mest," GD, nos. 15–16 (1912), 966–967.

72. John P. McKay, *Tramways and Trolleys: The Rise of Urban Mass Transport in Europe* (Princeton, 1976), p. 218.

73. MV, March 27, 1906.

74. N. I. Sushkin and A. D. Pudalovyi, "Gorodskie zheleznye dorogi," in Mgu, Skh, p. 420.

75. Mgu, *Doklady*, no. 213 (1910), p. 17; Shtromberg, *Gorodskie zheleznyi dorogi*, p. 312.

76. McKay, *Tramways*, p. 116.

77. Mgu, *Doklady*, no. 71 (1912), pp. 2–3.

78. Kuzovatkin, "Po sledam minuvshego," p. 203.

79. Baedeker, *Russia*, p. 310.

80. McKay, *Tramways*, p. 138.

81. V. Vladimirtsev, "Soobshcheniia s mest. Moskva," GD, no. 3 (1914), 164.

82. M.g.d. Komitet progressivnykh, *M.g.d. 1913–1916*, p. 11.

83. Moskovskaia gorodskaia uprava, *Osnovnye polozheniia proekta sooruzheniia v g. Moskve vneulichnykh dorog bol'shoi skorosti i elektrifikatsii magistral'nykh zheleznykh dorog v raione prigorodnogo soobshcheniia* (Moscow, 1913), p. 13 and passim.

84. For the background of welfare institutions in Russia see Adele Lindenmeyr, "Public Poor Relief and Private Charity in Late Imperial Russia," dissertation, Princeton University, 1980, pp. 18–45. *Ibid.*, p. 44, has Maklakov's position on welfare in 1914. See also her "Russian Experiment."

85. Gruppa bezpartiinykh i umerennykh izbiratelei, *O deiatel'nosti*, p. 16.

86. Lindenmeyr, "Public Poor Relief," pp. 1–56.

87. Studenetskii, "Obshchestvennoe prizrenie," pp. 156 and 214.

88. Lindenmeyr, "Public Poor Relief," p. 96.

89. Studenetskii, "Obshchestvennoe prizrenie," p. 209.

90. *Ibid.*, p. 159.

91. Komissiia po voprosu o prizrenii bezpriiutnykh detei, *Doklad* (Moscow, 1906), pp. 7–8.

92. *Ibid.*, p. 12.

93. Mgu, *Doklady*, no. 225 (1914), p. 37.

94. Lindenmeyr, "Public Poor Relief," pp. 89–90.

95. V. F. Deriuzhinskii, *Politseiskoe pravo*, 3-'e izdanie (St. Petersburg, 1911), pp. 505–509.

96. Lindenmeyr, "Public Poor Relief," p. 92.

97. Bradley, "Moscow Workhouse," 443.

98. *Ibid.*, 432 and 443.

99. RV, August 9, 1906.

100. G. G. Shvittau, *Trudovaia pomoshch' v Rossii* (Petrograd, 1915), p. 145.

101. *Ibid.*, pp. 143–144.

102. Studenetskii, "Obshchestvennoe prizrenie," pp. 218, 240.

103. *Ibid.*, p. 217.

104. Sergei Speranskii, "Gorodskie popechitel'stva," RV, November 27, 1912, pp. 5–6.

105. GDSO III, ch. 2, s. 4, z. 40, col. 105.

Chapter 7

1. OZhSM, no. 127, April 10 and 13, 1907, p. 11. This kind of suspicion toward universities and students among high state officials had appeared at numerous earlier points in Russian history. On the period 1878–1881, for example, see Zaionchkovsky, *Russian Autocracy*, pp. 34, 62, 66, and 73.

2. Manning, *Crisis of the Old Order*, p. 347.

3. A. P. Borodin, "Gosudarstvennyi sovet i stolypinskaia programma preobrazovanii v oblasti mestnogo upravleniia, suda i nachal'nogo obrazovaniia," Kandidat dissertation, Moskovskii Gosudarstvennyi Universitet, 1977, pp. 159 and 173.

4. An exception is Eklof's study of Moscow province and its *zemstvo* schools, "Spreading the Word."

5. Dmitry M. Odinetz, "Russian Primary and Secondary Schools Prior to and During the War," in Paul N. Ignatiev, Dmitry M. Odinetz, and Paul J. Novgorodtsev, *Russian Schools and Universities in the World War* (New Haven, 1929), p. 26. On this same point see also Patrick L. Alston, *Education and the State in Tsarist Russia* (Stanford, 1969), pp. 217, 220; Nicholas Hans, *History of Russian Educational Policy, 1701–1917* (New York, 1964), pp. 220–221; William H. E. Johnson, *Russia's Educational Heritage* (Pittsburgh, 1950), pp. 197–198; V. A. Kumanev, *Revoliutsiia i prosveshcheniia mass* (Moscow, 1973), p. 70; James C. McClelland, *Autocrats and Academics: Education, Culture, and Society in Tsarist Russia* (Chicago and London, 1979), pp. 29–55.

6. Alston, *Education and the State*, pp. 95–104.

7. Hans, *History of Russian Educational Policy*, p. 223.

8. See, for example, Maklakov, *Iz vospominanii*, p. 7.

9. Mgu, *Doklady*, no. 76 (1906), 5.

10. Ol'ga Vladimirovna Kaidanova, *Ocherki po istorii narodnogo obrazovaniia v Rossii i SSSR na osnove lichnogo opyta i nabliudenii* (Berlin, 1938–1939), v. 1, p. 131.

11. I. I. Orlov, "Moskovskie gorodskie letnie kolonii," *Vestnik Obshchestvennoi Gigieny*, 46 (1910), 1300–1302.

12. Mgu, SKh, p. 61.

13. *Ibid.*, pp. 69–70. The impression of widespread drinking among Moscow's youth is supported by a report of a survey in 1908–1909 that showed that 18 percent of minors who committed crimes in the city were drunk at the time of their acts. M. N. Gernet, *Izbrannye proizvedeniia* (Moscow, 1974), p. 385.

14. Mikhailov, "Iz dokladnoi zapiski," p. 220. However, this analysis may well have exaggerated the extent of illiteracy among immigrating adults. See Gregory Guroff and S. Frederick Starr, "A Note on Urban Literacy in Russia, 1890–1914," *Jahrbücher für Geschichte Osteuropas*, Band 14, heft 4 (1971). The authors suggest that *zemstvo* schools may have been providing literacy to many migrants before they reached Russian cities. As shown below, demand for elementary-level courses declined among Moscow's adults in this period, while demand for higher level courses rose. More recently, Joseph Bradley, Jr.,

has suggested that increased literacy in the countryside may not have played a great role in attracting migrants to Russian cities. His view tends to support Mikhailov's statement, for he argues that the literacy rate in Moscow "may actually have been kept *down* by illiterate newcomers." See his "Patterns of Peasant Migration," especially pp. 33–34.

15. Mikhailovskii, "Deiatel'nost' v 1913–1916," p. 30.

16. Moscow industrialists may have been exposed as early as 1895 to the concept that improved education enhanced workers' productivity. In 1895–96 the Second Conference on Technical and Professional Education was held in their city. The papers presented there were published in 1896 as the collection *Ekonomicheskaia otsenka narodnogo obrazovaniia*. Cited in Kumanev, *Revoliutsiia*, p. 48. See also a statement by St. Petersburg industrialists in early 1905 lauding the role of education in developing the country's capacities, in Roosa, "Russian Industrialists," p. 138.

17. Mgu, SKh, p. 26.

18. The figures up to 1913 (except 1905) are from Mgu, SKh, p. 34. The 1905 data are from Hans, *History of Russian Educational Policy*, p. 216, and the 1913 data are from Mikhailovskii, "Deiatel'nost' v 1913–1916," p. 29.

19. Hans, *History of Russian Educational Policy*, p. 216.

20. The number of elementary school pupils in Philadelphia is derived from data in Vincent P. Franklin, *The Education of Black Philadelphia: The Social and Educational History of a Minority Community, 1900–1950* (Philadelphia, 1979), p. 44.

21. Moskovskaia gorodskaia uprava, *Vedomosti o nachal'nykh uchilishchakh*, p. VIII.

22. Mikhailovskii, "Deiatel'nost' v 1913–1916," p. 29.

23. Mgu, SKh, pp. 277–280.

24. I. A. Verner, *Deiatel'nost' Moskovskoi gorodskoi dumy v 1909–1912 godakh* (Moscow, 1912), p. 6. The relevant laws were dated May 3, 1908, June 10, 1909, and July 7, 1913.

25. Quoted in Conroy, *Stolypin*, pp. 78–79.

26. Philip Santa Maria, "The Question of Elementary Education in the Third Russian State Duma, 1907–1912," dissertation, Kent State University, 1977, p. 154.

27. These percentages are calculated from data in A. P. Pogrebinskii, *Gosudarstvennye finansy tsarskoi Rossii v epokhu imperializma* (Moscow, 1968), pp. 70–71.

28. Kumanev, *Revoliutsiia*, p. 70.

29. N. Krasnoperov, "Vvedenie vseobshchego obucheniia v gorodakh Rossiiskoi Imperii," ZhMNP, v. 52 (July 1914), 56–62.

30. Mgu, SKh, p. 36.

31. Orlov, "Moskovskie kolonii," 1300–1302.

32. RV, July 31, 1912.

33. RV, October 19, 1913.

34. N. Krasnoperov, "Resul'taty odnodnevnoi perepisi narodnykh shkol v Rossii 18-go ianvaria 1911 g.," ZhMNP, v. 52 (July 1914), 36, shows that in the Moscow, St. Petersburg, and Kiev educational districts, between 41 and 47.5 percent of all teachers stayed in their positions less than five years. Patrick Alston notes, "The flight of urban pedagogues from their profession was a recognized social phenomenon." Alston, *Education and the State*, p. 227.

35. OZhSM, no. 42, August 8, 1906, pp. 18–19.

36. See Alston, *Education and the State*, pp. 174–199, on unrest among school teachers in 1905.

37. A. Tolstov, "Nachal'nye shkoly," in *Istoriia Moskvy v shesti tomakh*, v. 5, p. 365.

38. Mgu, SKh, p. 35.

39. *Ibid.*, p. 27. In 1908 a law requiring primary education for all children in the empire was adopted by the government, but it was not scheduled for full implementation until 1922.

40. Report no. 36 of the city's Financial Commission, January 3, 1905, quoted in Blok and Terterian, *V staroi Moskve*, p. 243.

41. Mgu, *Doklady*, no. 76 (1906), 3–4.

42. RV, October 4, 1909.

43. Mgu, SKh, p. 27.

44. *Ibid.*, p. 80. This desire of Moscow's parents to have their children receive broad academic education stands in contrast to James McClelland's arguments that the liberals were not in touch with the needs of the industrializing society. The liberals retained a preference, he says, for Western educational models and academic courses. McClelland, *Autocrats and Academics*, p. 39. In the case of Moscow, the liberal city government was attempting to respond to the wishes of a broad segment of the population rather than following a foreign model.

45. Verner, *Deiatel'nost'*, p. 9.

46. On the "urban schools," see Alston, *Education and the State*, pp. 102 and 212.

47. OZhSM, no. 221, December 9, 1908, pp. 1–2.

48. Mgu, SKh, p. 28.

49. E. M. Chemodanova, "Za dvadtsat' let (1897–1917 gody)," in *Prechistenskie rabochie kursy; pervyi rabochii universitet v Moskve. Sbornik statei i vospominaniia. K piatidesiatiletiiu kursov (1897–1947)*. (Moscow, 1948), p. 15.

50. "Vechernye klassy, kursy i lektsii dlia rabochikh," IMGD, otdel Narodnoe Obrazovanie, no. 9–10 (1912), pp. 53–55. The courses were set up by "a group of progressive *intelligenty* of the Prechistenskii district." *Prechistenskie rabochie kursy*, p. 15.

51. RV, March 16, 1913.

52. Mgu, SKh, pp. 76–77.

53. "Vechernye klassy," p. 57.

54. A. A. Kizevetter, *Na rubezhe dvukh stoletii* (Prague, 1929), pp. 486–493.

55. The first figure is from Gorodskoi narodnyi universitet imeni A. L. Shaniavskogo, *Otchet Moskovskogo gorodskogo narodnogo universiteta imeni A. L. Shaniavskogo za 1909–1910 akademicheskii god* (Moscow, 1911), p. 10. The second figure is from A. Mikhailovskii, "Munitsipal'naia Moskva," in *Po Moskve. Progulki po Moskve i ee khudozhestvennym i prosvetitel'nym uchrezhedeniiam* (Moscow, 1917), p. 157.

56. A. O-va, "Moskovskii gorodskoi narodnyi universitet," IMGD (October, 1911), p. 12.

57. Kizevetter, *Na rubezhe*, pp. 489–491.

58. TsGAgM, f. 635, op. 3, d. 10, ll. 60–61.

59. Quoted in Ivanov, "Ideologicheskoe vozdeistvie," p. 350.

60. "Samarskii Narodnyi Universitet," *Vestnik Narodnykh Universitetov*, no. 1 (May 15, 1910), p. 63.

61. Richard Stites, *The Women's Liberation Movement in Russia: Feminism, Nihilism, and Bolshevism 1860–1930* (Princeton, 1978), p. 169.

62. The assertion of A. S. Tolstov that the Moscow duma deputies were "enemies" of any expansion or improvements in public education is contrary to the available evidence. "Nachal'nye shkoly," p. 368.

63. RV, November 27, 1912.

64. N. V. Chekhov, *Narodnoe obrazovanie v Rossii s 60-kh godov XIX veka* (Moscow, 1912), pp. 84–85.

65. Mgu, *Doklady*, "Zaiavlenie A. L. Shaniavskogo v Mos. Gor. Dumu ot 15 sentiabria 1905 g." prilozh. k dokladu no. 7–9, April 2, 1908, p. 20. For a discussion of the background of the people's university idea in Russia, see M. Gran, "Ocherednye voprosy russkogo narodno-universitetskogo dela." part 2, *Vestnik Narodnogo Universiteta*, 7 (1911), 306–308.

66. MgdSO, May 1910, p. 611.

67. GDSO II, ch. 1, s. 2, z. 5, col. 118.

68. See, for example, a statement by Shvarts to the State Duma in June 1908, GDSO III, ch. 3, s. 1, z. 82, col. 2745.

69. OZhSM, no. 42, August 8, 1906, p. 28.

70. GDSO III, ch. 3, s. 1, z. 82, cols. 2744 and 2739.

71. GDSO III, ch. 3, s. 1, z. 83, col. 2759.

72. GDSO III, ch. 4, s. 1, z. 5, col. 320.

73. See Edelman, *Gentry Politics,* passim and especially pp. 73–127. For a recent analysis of the government's increasing conservatism and its social basis in this period, see Roberta Thompson Manning, "The Zemstvo and Politics, 1864–1914," in *The Zemstvo in Russia,* ed. Terence Emmons and Wayne S. Vucinich (London, 1982), especially pp. 166–167.

74. Richard Charques, *The Twilight of Imperial Russia* (Oxford, 1958), p. 207.

75. GDSO III, ch. 4, s. 1, z. 6, col. 404.

76. GDSO III, ch. 1, s. 4, z. 5, col. 357.

77. Quoted in Evgrav Kovalevsky, "The Duma and Public Instruction," *Russian Review* (London), v. 1, no. 3 (1912), 71. I have not been able to locate the original statement.

78. GDSO III, ch. 3, s. 1, z. 80, col. 2401.

79. These were Shvarts' words to the Council of Ministers, OZhSM, no. 77, April 13, 1910, p. 5. See Avrekh, *Stolypin i tret'ia duma,* pp. 27–28, on the agreement of the Rightists and Nationalists with Shvarts on this point.

80. Harcave, *First Blood,* p. 257.

81. See James T. Flynn, "Tuition and Social Class in the Russian Universities: S. S. Uvarov and 'Reaction' in the Russia of Nicholas I," *Slavic Review* 35, no. 2 (1976); Riasanovsky, *Nicholas I,* pp. 216–217; and McClelland, *Autocrats and Academics,* pp. 9–55.

82. The laws on elementary education are found most easily in ZhMNP, v. 123 (July 1964), pp. 39–47, and v. 174 (August 1874), pp. 227–237.

83. For a concise review of this point in the nineteenth and early twentieth centuries, see McClelland, *Autocrats and Academics,* pp. 9–17.

84. Pobedonostsev, *Reflections of a Russian Statesman,* pp. 1, 23, 78, and 157.

85. McClelland, *Autocrats and Academics,* p. 14.

86. A. V. Ososkov, *Voprosy istorii nachal'nogo obrazovanii v Rossii (II. pol. XIX-nach. XX vv.) Uchebnoe posobie.* (Moscow, 1975), Chast' pervaia, p. 20.

87. In Bertram D. Wolfe, *Three Who Made a Revolution: A Biographical History* (New York, 1960), p. 48.

88. This remark was by an Octobrist, K. N. Timirev of Novgorod province. GDSO III, ch. 1, s. 4, z. 5, col. 325. But there were many shades of opinion within the Octobrist party; here Timirev was echoing the conservative viewpoint, for his words drew shouts of "That's right, correct," from the right.

89. Diakin, *Samoderzhavie,* p. 104.

90. GDSO III, ch. 3, s. 1, z. 81, cols. 2503–2504.

91. Conroy, *Stolypin,* p. 10.

92. GDSO III, ch. 3, s. 1, z. 82, cols. 2749–2750.

93. GDSO III, ch. 3, s. 1, z. 77, col. 1967.

94. Levin, *Third Duma,* p. 10.

95. OZhSM, no. 127, April 10 and 13, 1907, p. 10.

96. *Ibid.,* p. 13.

97. Quoted in Alston, *Education and the State,* viii.

98. GDSO III, ch. 2, s. 1, z. 38, col. 414.

99. Mgu, *Doklady,* "Zaiavlenie A. L. Shaniavskogo," p. 20. The academic section of Shaniavskii University survived until August 1919, when it was absorbed by Moscow Uni-

versity. The scientific-popular section lasted until November 1920, when it merged with the *rabfak* (workers' faculty) of Communist (later Sverdlov) University. "Shaniavskogo Universiteta," *Moskva Entsiklopediia* (Moscow, 1980), p. 662. Before its demise, Shaniavskii University performed one service for the Bolshevik regime. M. N. Pokrovskii, then deputy commissar of the Commissariat of Education, attended several sessions of the university's board of trustees in August 1918. At one he indicated general approval of the institution's work and said, "Shaniavskii University by its work and its statute has helped in the preparation of a normal type of Higher School." He then announced that the new reform of higher education would have much in common with the university's statute. TsGAgM, f. 635, d. 3, o. 119, ll. 58–59. Indeed, the reform had several similarities to Shaniavskii University's rules: anyone over the age of sixteen would be admitted to the universities, regardless of sex, national origin, or prior education. Thus, more than thirteen years after his death, the Polish nobleman and tsarist general A. L. Shaniavskii had a substantial impact on early Soviet educational policy.

100. Shecket, "Russian Imperial State Council," pp. 100 and 124.

101. "Iz perepiski P. A. Stolypina s Nikolaem Romanovym," *Krasnyi Arkhiv* 30 (1928), 81.

102. "Perepiska N. A. Romanova i P. A. Stolypina," *Krasnyi Arkhiv* 5 (1924), 117.

103. *Rannee Utro*, March 27, 1908.

104. Moskovskii gorodskoi narodnyi universitet imeni A. L. Shaniavskogo, *Tekst zakona s stenograficheskim otchetom Gosudarstvennoi Dumy i biografiei A. L. Shaniavskogo* (Moscow, 1908), pp. 11–40. Or see GDSO III, ch. 3, s. 1, z. 77, cols. 1949–2057.

105. This was the *Tekst zakona* of the previous note.

106. *Moskovskie Vedomosti*, November 13, 1908.

107. Similar events happened at Kiev Polytechnical Institute in 1911. Institut istorii Akademii nauk SSSR, *Istoriia Kieva* v. 2, p. 588.

108. PSZ-III, v. 12, 1892, p. 433.

109. OZhSM, no. 42, August 8, 1906, p. 7.

110. This apparatus and its duties are specified in the laws on elementary education of 1864 and 1874. ZhMNP, v. 123 (July 1864), and v. 174 (August 1874).

111. RV, March 1, 1912.

112. N. A. Konstantinov, *Ocherki po istorii srednei shkoly; gimnasii i real'nye uchilishcha s kontsa XIX v. do Fevral'skoi revoliutsii 1917 goda*, 2nd ed. (Moscow, 1956), pp. 109–110.

113. Mgu, SKh, p. 45.

114. RV, June 27, 1913.

115. TsGAgM, f. 16, o. 147, d. 12, t. 1, l. 9.

116. Mgu, SKh, p. 82.

117. RV, September 19, 1912.

118. Moskovskoe gorodskoe obshchestvennoe upravlenie, *Otchet o sostoianii gorodskikh nachal'nykh uchilishch i drugikh uchebnykh i prosvetitel'nykh uchrezhdenii 1913–1914 gg.* (Moscow, 1915), I chast', pp. 83–84.

119. RV, November 25, 1912.

120. Blok and Terterian, *V staroi Moskve*, p. 250.

121. *Ezhegodnik Vneskhol'nogo obrazovaniia*, vypusk vtoroi (St. Petersburg, 1910), p. 223.

122. *Ezhegodnik Vneshkol'nogo Obrazovaniia*, vypusk pervyi (St. Petersburg, 1908), pp. 30–31.

123. GDSO III, ch. 2, s. 1, z. 38, col. 423.

124. GDSO III, ch. 3, s. 1, z. 80, col. 2338.

125. GDSO III, ch. 1, s. 4, z. 5, cols. 327–328.

126. GDSO III, ch. 2, s. 1, z. 38, cols. 429–430. For emphases by other conservative

deputies on the necessity of keeping religion as a basis of education, see *ibid.*, III, ch. 1, z. 5, cols. 341 and 357.

127. *Prechistenskie rabochie kursy*, p. 198; see also pp. 233, 265 for similar recollections by other listeners.

128. Konstantin Lemberg, "Dorogoe proshloe," in Kaidanova, *Ocherki po istorii*, v. 2, p. 119.

129. *Ibid.*, p. 119. For the same phenomenon in an evening school for adults in 1914 in the Khamovnicheskii district, see N. A. Vantorina-Stogova, "Moi put' k revoliutsii," in *Moskovskie bol'sheviki*, pp. 389–390; she reports that the police soon closed this school.

130. Quoted in Kruze, *Polozhenie rabochego klassa*, p. 124.

131. RV, February 11, 1911; also in Buryshkin, *Moskva*, pp. 296–297, in slightly different form.

132. Alston, *Education and the State*, p. 242.

133. Oskar Anweiler, *Geschichte der Schule und Pädagogik in Russland, vom Ende des Zarenreiches bis zum Beginn der Stalin-Ära* (Berlin, 1964), p. 28.

134. GDSO III, ch. 3, s. 2, z. 96, col. 2334.

135. OZhSM, no. 28, February 5 and March 3, 1909, p. 5.

Conclusion

1. *Pravo*, no. 4 (1905), cols. 260–265.

2. "Khronika," *Zapiski Moskovskogo Otdeleniia Imperatorskogo Russkogo Tekhnicheskogo Obshchestva*, 35, no. 4 (1911), 148. The table was compiled "on the basis of official data." It is reproduced here in part; as published in the journal it included data on lighting, slaughterhouses, and telephone and (private) telegraph systems. That information would not alter the picture presented here of services in the towns.

3. Zelnik, *Labor and Society*, p. 23.

4. GSSO, s. 2, z. 4, col. 28.

5. Quoted in John T. Alexander, *Autocratic Politics in a National Crisis: The Imperial Russian Government and Pugachev's Revolt, 1773–1775* (Bloomington, IN, 1969), p. 89.

6. Boris V. Anan'ich, "The Economic Policy of the Tsarist Government and Enterprise in Russia from the End of the Nineteenth through the Beginning of the Twentieth Century," in *Entrepreneurship in Imperial Russia and the Soviet Union*, ed. Gregory Guroff and Fred V. Carstensen (Princeton, 1983), p. 136.

7. Manning, *Crisis of the Old Order*, p. 201.

8. Byrnes, *Pobedonostsev*, pp. 241–242. Pobedonostsev scorned all forms of politics and legislatures: *Reflections*, pp. 45–49.

9. S. Iu. Witte, *Samoderzhavie i zemstvo. Konfidentsial'naia zapiska Ministra Finansov Stats-Sekretaria S. Iu. Witte (1899 g.)*, vtoroe izdanie, s dvumia predisloviiami Petra Struve (Stuttgart, 1903), pp. 18–19, 21, and 92.

10. RV, January 1, 1914.

11. RV, May 18, 1911.

12. Novikov, *Ot Moskvy do N'iu-Iorka*, pp. 137–138.

13. Lev Tikhomirov, "Iz dnevnika Lva Tikhomirova," *Krasnyi Arkhiv*, 1 (74), 1936, pp. 184, 188–189.

14. A. I. Guchkov, "The General Political Situation and the Octobrist Party," *Russian Review* (London) 3, no. 1 (1914), 151. This was a speech given to an Octobrist party conference, November 21, 1913. See also Kizevetter on his feeling in the summer of 1914 that "toward all of us, the Russian people, something terrible, evil, and gigantic was approaching." Kizevetter, *Na rubezhe*, 523. Rogger, *Russia*, pp. 23–35, reports similar anxiety by A. I. Putilov and Count Witte.

15. GDSO, III, ch. 1, s. 1, z. 7, col. 344.

16. Novikov, *Ot Moskvy*, pp. 156–57. He reports that the police closed the conference at this point.

17. Quoted in Hutchinson, "Octobrists in Russian Politics," p. 215.

18. Novikov, *Ot Moskvy*, pp. 156–57; and see Kizevetter, *Na rubezhe*, pp. 517–18.

19. Kizevetter, *Na rubezhe*, 517–18.

20. Quoted in Buryshkin, *Moskva*, p. 291. Diakin, *Samoderzhavie*, p. 186, says the article appeared in *Utro Rossii* [Riabushinskii's progressist newspaper], May 18, 1910.

21. Buryshkin, *Moskva*, p. 246. Thomas Owen also noted the same tendency of Moscow merchants and industrialists to remain silent about politics; *Capitalism*, pp. 70, 152, and 200.

22. Pares, *Russia*, p. 318.

23. Manning, "Zemstvo and Politics, 1864–1914," argues that there were "relatively few times when the zemstvos did engage in overt oppositional activities" and that those "coincided with major political crises." After 1905 the *zemstva* became increasingly conservative. Pp. 135 and 139–168.

24. Ivanov, "Ideologicheskoe vozdeistvie," pp. 343 and 349.

25. Florinsky, *Russia*, vol. 2, p. 1143.

26. For a recent restatement of this view and references to Soviet works taking the same position, see Rosental', "Russkii liberalizm," pp. 52–53; also Laverychev, *Po tu storonu*, p. 108; and Diakin, *Samoderzhavie*, p. 7. Elsewhere, however, Diakin puts more emphasis on the "bourgeoisie's move to the left" on the eve of the war. V. S. Diakin, *Russkaia burzhuaziia i tsarizm v gody pervoi mirovoi voiny (1914–1917 gg.)* (Leningrad, 1967), pp. 41–44.

27. V. I. Lenin, *Polnoe Sobranie Sochinenii* (Moscow, 1958–1965), Vol. 21, p. 220. However, in May 1914 Lenin did perceive "clear dissatisfaction with the government, a clearly oppositional mood" among the Russian bourgeoisie. Quoted in Arutiunov, *Rabochee dvizhenie*, p. 308.

28. To be sure, "bourgeois" and "liberal" are not synonyms. Yet, as this study has consistently argued, Russian liberalism grew much better in the urban, industrial milieu than in the agrarian setting after 1906. Professionals, also often liberals, found urban life, particularly Moscow's, more congenial in this span.

29. Allan K. Wildman, *The End of the Russian Imperial Army: The Old Army and the Soldiers' Revolt (March–April 1917)* (Princeton, 1980), p. 76.

30. One of the figures Wildman mentions as a key part of the loyal opposition, Paul Miliukov, noted that after 1912 "two opposing camps stood openly against each other." These were "society" and the government. He also spoke of "the complete hopelessness of the [Fourth] Duma's legislative work." Miliukov, *Political Memoirs*, pp. 278 and 286. These descriptions are far from the situation of the contemporary loyal opposition in Britain or America. The feelings of Miliukov and many others went well beyond such opposition, to a position of rejection of the very political basis of the regime.

31. Charques, *Twilight*, p. 250.

Epilogue

1. Gronsky and Astrov, *War and the Russian Government*, p. 165, lists a number of projects in Moscow cut off by the war.

2. On the contributions during World War I, see Hamm, "Breakdown," pp. 191–192; on earlier contributions see Owen, *Capitalism*, pp. 30, 32, 93.

3. MgdSO, July–August 1914, p. 802.

4. Thomas Fallows, "Politics and the War Effort in Russia: The Union of Zemstvos and the Organization of the Food Supply, 1914–1916," *Slavic Review* 37, no. 1 (1978), 71–87.

5. See Lewis H. Siegelbaum, *The Politics of Industrial Mobilization in Russia, 1914–1917: A Study of the War-Industries Committees* (New York, 1983), pp. 44–45, 73–75, 183–184, and 192–194.

6. Buryshkin, *Moskva*, p. 325.

7. Martynov, *Moia sluzhba*, p. 288.

8. Quoted in Owen, *Capitalism*, p. 210.

9. RV, March 10, 1917.

10. Aleksandr Ivanovich Grunt, *Moskva 1917-i: revoliutsiia i kontrrevoliutsiia* (Moscow, 1976), p. 58.

11. *Ibid.*, p. 44.

12. Koenker, *Moscow Workers*, p. 106.

13. Institut istorii partii MK i MGK KPSS, *Moskva v dvukh revoliutsiiakh; fevral' - oktiabr' 1917 g.* (Moscow, 1958), pp. 205–206; see also the statement along the same lines of a Bolshevik, made in March 1917, in Aleksandr Ivanovich Grunt, *Pobeda oktiabr'skoi revoliutsii v Moskve, fevral'-oktiabr' 1917 g.* (Moscow, 1961), p. 58.

14. Institut istorii partii MK i MGK KPSS, *Moskva*, p. 209.

15. A. N. Voznesenskii, *Moskva v 1917 godu* (Moscow, 1928), p. 98.

16. See a recent review of this literature in Ronald Grigor Suny, "Toward a Social History of the October Revolution," *American Historical Review* 88, no. 1 (1983), 31–52. On Moscow in 1917 see especially Koenker, *Moscow Workers*.

17. Institut istorii partii MK i MGK KPSS, *Moskva*, p. 219.

18. On this fighting, see Robert Daniels, *Red October: The Bolshevik Revolution of 1917* (New York, 1967), pp. 205–209.

19. Rex A. Wade, *Red Guards and Workers' Militias in the Russian Revolution* (Stanford, 1984), pp. 307–8.

20. On Moscow's situation in the 1920s, see William John Chase, "Moscow and Its Working Class, 1918–1928: A Social Analysis," dissertation, Boston College, 1979.

Bibliography

Unpublished Materials

Archival Materials

Tsentral'nyi Gosudarstvennyi Arkhiv goroda Moskvy [TsGAgM] fond 16, Kantseliariia moskovskogo general-gubernatora.

    o. 16, d. 147, 12 t. l.   Circular from P. A. Stolypin as head of the Ministry of Internal Affairs, January 1908.

    o. 140, d. 12 t. 1.   Circular from Main Factory Office of Ministry of Internal Affairs to military governors, governors, and *gradonachal'niki.*

    o. 144, d. 12 t. 1.   Circulars of the Ministry of Internal Affairs concerning prostitution.

    o. 140, d. 184.   Rules on sleeping quarters for workers issued by the *gradonachal'nik,* 1906.

fond 46, Kantseliariia moskovskogo gradonachal'nika.

    o. 14, d. 1169.   Letter from a worker to the *gradonachal'nik* about poor living and working conditions, police action taken, 1909.

    o. 14, d. 1171.   Inspection of a workshop by police, threat of a fine, 1909.

    o. 14, d. 1212.   Report from the city to the *gradonachal'nik,* 1910.

    o. 14, d. 3374.   Protocols of court cases of press arrests.

fond 131, Moskovskii komitet po delam pechati.

    o. 81, d. 88.   Court rejection of arrest of *Utro Rossii,* 1912.

    o. 79, d. 35.   Court rejection of arrest of *Gazeta-kopeika,* 1911.

fond 179, Moskovskaia gorodskaia duma i Moskovskaia gorodskaia uprava.

    o. 21, d. 4367.   Statements given to *uprava* by city transport workers, 1913.

fond 635, Moskovskii gorodskoi narodnyi universitet im. A. L. Shaniavskogo.

    o. 3, d. 10.   Surveys of Shaniavskii University listeners, 1909–11.

    o. 3, d. 111.   Trustees' meetings, 1918.

Tsentral'nyi Gosudarstvennyi Arkhiv Oktiabr'skoi Revoliutsii [TsGAOR].

fond 102, Department politsii.

    Deloproiz. 4, 1911 g., 42 t. l.   Clipping of *Birzhevye Vedomosti* and report of 4–oe deloproizvodstvo on arrests at the Bromley factory.

    4 d-vo ed. khr. 108, t. 28, ll. 7–47; D-4 1910, 42, l. 51; 4 d-vo ed. khr. 108, t. 28, l. 17.   Reports from the *gradonachal'nik* to the *Departament politsii* on workers' politics and organizations.

Dissertations

Borodin, A. P. "Gosudarstvennyi sovet i stolypinskaia programma preobrazovanii v oblasti mestnogo upravleniia, suda i nachal'nogo obrazovaniia." Kandidat diss., Moskovskii Gosudarstvennyi Universitet, 1977.

Chase, William John. "Moscow and its Working Class, 1918–1928: A Social Analysis." Boston College, 1979.

Eklof, Arthur Benoit. "Spreading the Word: Primary Education and the Zemstvo in Moscow Province, 1864–1910." Princeton University, 1977.

Gorlin, Robert Henry. "State Politics and the Imperial Russian Budget, 1905–1912." University of Michigan, 1973.

Hanchett, Walter. "Moscow in the Late Nineteenth Century: A Study in Municipal Self-government." The University of Chicago, 1965.

Hogan, Heather Jeanne. "Labor and Management in Conflict: The St. Petersburg Metal-Working Industry, 1900–1914." University of Michigan, 1981.

Hutchinson, John Franklin. "The Octobrists in Russian Politics, 1905–1907." University of London, 1966.

Lindenmeyr, Adele. "Public Poor Relief and Private Charity in Late Imperial Russia." Princeton University, 1980.

Roosa, Ruth Amende. "The Association of Industry and Trade, 1906–1914: An Examination of the Economic Views of Organized Industrialists in Prerevolutionary Russia." Columbia University, 1967.

Santa Maria, Phillip. "The Question of Elementary Education in the Third Russian State Duma, 1907–1912." Kent State University, 1977.

Shecket, Alexandra Deborah. "The Russian Imperial State Council and the Policies of P. A. Stolypin, 1906–1911: Bureaucratic and Soslovie Interests versus Reform." Columbia University, 1974.

Skinner, Frederick W. "City Planning in Russia: The Development of Odessa, 1789–1892." Princeton University, 1973.

West, James Lawrence. "The Moscow Progressists: Russian Industrialists in Liberal Politics, 1905–1914." Princeton University, 1975.

Published Materials

Newspapers

Birzhevye Vedomosti
Gazeta Kopeika
Golos Moskvy
Moskovskie Vedomosti
Posledniia Novosti
Pravda, 1912–14 and 1918
Rannee Utro
Rech'
Russkoe Slovo
Russkie Vedomosti
Utro Rossii
Vedomosti Moskovskogo Gradonachal'stva i Stolichnoi Politsii

Periodicals

American Historical Review
American Political Science Review
Byloe. Zhurnal posviashchennyi istorii osvoboditel'nogo dvizheniia
Canadian Slavic Studies/Revue Canadienne d'Etudes Slaves
Comparative Urban Research
Ezhegodnik vneshkol'nogo obrazovaniia

Ezhemesiachnyi zhurnal literatury, nauki i obshchestvennoi zhizni
Gorodskoe delo
Government and Opposition
Jahrbücher für Geschichte Osteuropas
Journal of Modern History
Journal of Social History
Krasnyi arkhiv
Moskovskaia Gorodskaia Duma. *Izvestiia Moskovskoi gorodskoi dumy*
————. *Izvestiia. Otdel Narodnoe obrazovanie*
Moskovskaia Gorodskaia Uprava. *Ezhegodnik*
————. *Ezhenedel'nik Gorodskoi Upravy*
Moskovskaia Gorodskaia Uprava. Statisticheskii Otdel *Ezhemesiachnyi biulleten' po gorodu Moskve. Bulletin statistique mensuel de la ville de Moscou*
————. *Ezhenedel'nyi biulleten' po gorodu Moskve*
————. *Statisticheskii atlas goroda Moskvy.* Moscow, 1887–1890
————. *Statisticheskii ezhegodnik goroda Moskvy. Annuaire statistique de la ville de Moscou. l'année 1906–07.* Moscow, 1908
————. *Trudy.* Statisticheskogo dela za [various years]. Moscow, 1882–
Moskva. Statisticheskii Otdel. *Statisticheskii ezhegodnik goroda Moskvy i Moskovskoe gubernii.* Moscow, 1907–1910
Obshchestvennyi Vrach
Pravo; ezhenedel'naia iuridicheskaia gazeta
Russian History
Russian Review
Russian Review (London)
Slavic Review
Slavonic and East European Review
Trudovaia pomoshch'
Vestnik Narodnykh Universitetov. Zhurnal, izdavaemykh sovetom S. Petersburgskogo obshchestva narodnykh universitetov. St. Petersburg, 1910–11
Vestnik obshchestvennoi gigieny, sudebnoi i prakticheskoi meditsiny
World Politics
Zapiski Moskovskogo Otdeleniia Imperatorskogo Russkogo Tekhnicheskogo Obshchestva
Zhurnal Ministerstva Narodnogo Prosveshcheniia

Memoirs

Astrov, Nikolai Ivanovich. *Vospominaniia.* Paris, 1940. Only the first volume of a projected two-volume work was published.
Belousov, Ivan Alekseevich. *Ushedshaia Moskva. Zapiski po lichnym vospominaniiam s nachala 1870 godov.* Moscow, 1927.
Buryshkin, P. A. *Moskva kupecheskaia.* New York, 1954.
Chemodanova, E. M. "Za dvadtsat' let (1897–1917 gody)." In *Prechistenskie rabochie kursy; pervyi rabochii universitet v Moskve. Sbornik statei i vospominanii. K piatidesiatiletiiu kursov (1897–1947).* Moscow, 1948.
Chicherin, Boris Nikolaevich. *Vospominaniia Borisa Nikolaevicha Chicherina.* Vol. 4: *Zemstvo i moskovskaia duma.* Moscow, 1934.
Guchkov, A. I. "Iz vospominanii A. I. Guchkova." *Posledniia Novosti,* August 9–September 30, 1936.
Harper, Samuel N. *The Russia I Believe In: The Memoirs of Samuel N. Harper, 1902–1941.* Ed. Paul V. Harper. Chicago, 1945.

Kaidanova, Ol'ga Vladimirovna. *Ocherki po istorii narodnogo obrazovaniia v Rossii i SSSR na osnove lichnogo opyta i nabliudenii.* 2 vols. Berlin, 1938–39

Kats, A. "Iz istorii Moskovskogo obshchestva vzaimopomoshchi ofitsiantov (1902–1916 gg.)." In *Materialy po istorii professional'nogo dvizheniia v Rossii,* sbornik 1. Moscow, 1924.

Kizevetter, A. A. *Na rubezhe dvukh stoletii.* Prague, 1929.

Kokovtsov, V. N. *Out of My Past.* Stanford, 1935.

Kuzovatkin, A. F. "Po sledam minuvshego." In *Moskovskie bol'sheviki v ogne revoliutsionnykh boev* (vospominaniia). Moscow, 1976.

Lemberg, Konstantin. "Dorogoe proshloe." In Kaidanova, *Ocherki po istorii.* Vol. 2, vypusk 2-oi.

Maklakov, Vasilii Alekseevich. *Iz vospominanii.* New York, 1954.

Martinov, A. P. *Moia sluzhba v Otdel'nom Korpuse zhandarmov; Vospominaniia.* Ed. Richard Wraga. Stanford, 1972.

Matveev, G. "Moskovskii soiuz rabochikh-metallistov v 1906–07 gg. (Po lichnym vospominaniiam)." In *Materialy po istorii professional'nogo dvizheniia v Rossii,* sbornik 2. Moscow, 1924.

Miliukov, Paul. *Political Memoirs 1905–1917.* Ed. Arthur P. Mendel. Trans. Carl Goldberg. Ann Arbor, 1967.

Moskovskie bol'sheviki v ogne revoliutsionnykh boev. Moscow, 1976.

Novikov, Mikhail Mikhailovich. *Ot Moskvy do N'iu-Iorka.* New York, 1952.

Pares, Bernard. *My Russian Memoirs.* London, 1931.

"Pokazanie M. V. Chelnokova." *Padenie tsarskogo rezhima. Stenograficheskie otchety doprosov i pokazanii, dannykh v Chrezvychainoi Sledstvennoi komissii Vremennogo Pravitel'stva (v 1917 g.) v semi tomakh.* Redaktsiia P. E. Shcheglova. Moscow-Leningrad, 1926.

Prechistenskie rabochie kursy. *Sbornik statei i vospominaniia k piatidesiatiletiiu kursov (1897–1947).* Moscow, 1948.

Reder, D. G. "Sorok vosem' let." In *Krasnaia presnia; ocherki po istorii zavodov.* Moscow, 1934.

Sapronov, T. *Iz istorii rabochego dvizheniia (po lichnym vospominaniiam).* Moscow-Leningrad, 1925.

Sokol'niki. Moscow, 1967.

Ushedshaia Moskva; vospominaniia sovremennikov o Moskve vtoroi poloviny XIX veka. Ed. Nikolai Sergeevich Ashukin. Moscow, 1964.

Vantorina-Stogova, N. A. "Moi put' k revoliutsii." In *Moskovskie bol'sheviki v ogne revoliutsionnykh boev (Vospominaniia).* Moscow, 1976.

Zenzinov, Vladimir. *Perezhitoe.* New York, 1953.

Documents and Other Primary Sources

Astrov, N. I. "Sud'ba russkikh gorodov." *Gorodskoe Delo,* no. 2 (1911).

Avs, M. "Otkaz ot oblozheniia po stoimosti nedvizhimykh imushchestv v Moskve," *Gorodskoe Delo,* no. 21 (1911).

Avsarkisov, M. P. "Finansy goroda Moskvy." In Moskovskaia gorodskaia uprava, *Sovremennoe khoziaistvo goroda Moskvy.* Ed. I. A. Verner. Moscow, 1913.

Blok, G. E., and A. Terterian, comp. *V staroi Moskve. Kak khoziainichali kuptsy i fabrikanty. Materialy i dokumenty.* Moscow, 1939.

Budget of the Empire for 1914. N.p., n.d.

Ditiatin, I. I. *Ustroistvo i upravlenie gorodov Rossii.* 2 vols. St. Petersburg, 1875, and Iaroslavl, 1877.

Dmitriev, K. (P. Kolokol'nikev). *Professional'nye soiuzy v Moskve.* St. Petersburg, 1913 (?).

Dumskii, "Chto sdelala tret'ia Gosudarstvennaia Duma po voprosam gorodskogo samou-pravleniia." *Gorodskoe Delo,* no. 15–16 (August 1–15, 1912).

Entsiklopedicheskii Slovar' Brokgauz i Efron. St. Petersburg, 1893.

Entsiklopedicheskii Slovar tovarishchestva B. A. i I. Granat i ko. 7–oe sovershenno perer-abotanoe izdanie. Moscow, n.d.

Ezhegodnik vneshkol'nogo obrazovaniia. Ed. V. I. Charnoluskii. St. Petersburg, 1910.

fon Gibshman, A. M. "Munitsipal'noe obozrenie." *Gorodskoe Delo,* no. 22 (1913).

Frenkel', Zakh. "Narodnoe zdorov'e v gorodakh Rossii po poslednim offitsial'nym dan-nym." *Gorodskoe Delo,* no. 5 (March 1, 1910), 275–282.

Garin, Nikolai Pavlovich. *Pravitel'stvuiushchemu senatu, po pervomu departmentu, sena-tora revizuiushchego po vysochaishemu poveleniiu Moskovskoe gradonachal'stvo, Donoshenie. 13 Noiabria 1908 g.* No. 364. N.p., n.d.

G-man, A. "Soobshcheniia s mest. Moskva. Bor'ba s tuberkulezom." *Gorodskoe Delo,* no. 18 (1911).

————. "Soobshcheniia s mest. Moskva. (Neskol'ko slov o gorodskom khoziaistve g. Moskvy)." *Gorodskoe Delo,* no. 1 (January 1911).

Gorokhov, D. E. "Nastoiashchee sostoianie i blizhaishie zadachi vrachebno-sanitarnogo dela v Moskve." *Vestnik Obshchestvennoi Gigieny,* 48, no. 9 (September 1912).

Gosudarstvennaia Duma. *Stenograficheskie otchety.* St. Petersburg, various years.

Gosudarstvennaia rospis' dokhodov i raskhodov na 1908 g. N.p., n.d.

Gosudarstvennyi Sovet. *Stenograficheskie otchety.* St. Petersburg, various years.

"Gradonachal'nik." *Entsiklopedicheskii Slovar' Brokgauz i Efron.* St. Petersburg, 1893.

Gran, M. "Ocherednye voprosy russkogo narodno-universitetskogo dela" part 2. *Vestnik Narodnogo Universiteta,* 7 (1911).

Granovskii, L. B. "Strakhovanie rabochikh na sluchai bolezni i gorodskoe samouprav-lenie." *Obshchestvennyi Vrach,* 4, no. 3 (1913), 299–329.

Gruppa bezpartiinykh i umerennykh izbiratelei. *O deiatel'nosti gorodskoi dumy sostava 1909–1912 gg.* Moscow, 1912.

Guchkov, A. I. "The General Political Situation and the Octobrist Party." *Russian Review* (London) 3, no. 1 (1914), 141–158.

Iakovlev, V. "Biudzhet russkogo rabochego." *Obshchestvennyi Vrach,* no. 9 (1911).

"Iz dorevoliutsionnogo proshlogo Moskvy." *Krasnyi Arkhiv,* 5 (84), (1937).

"Iz perepiski P. A. Stolypina s Nikolaem Romanovym." *Krasnyi Arkhiv,* 30 (1928), 80–88.

"Iz zapisnoi knizhki arkhivista. O lokalizatsii prazdnovanii 1 maia na fabrikakh i zavo-dakh. Soobshchil N. Dmitriev." *Krasnyi Arkhiv,* 3 (16), 1926.

Kalendar'-Spravochnik Gorodskogo Deiatelia na 1917 god. St. Petersburg, 1912–1917.

Kalendar'-Spravochnik Gorodskogo i Zemskogo Deiatelia na 1911 god. St Petersburg, 1911.

Karaffa-Korbut, K. V. "Nochlezhnye doma v bol'shikh russkikh gorodakh. *Gorodskoe Delo,* 10 (1912).

Kovalevsky, Evgrav. "The Duma and Public Instruction." *Russian Review* 1, no. 3 (1912), 64–79.

Krasnoperov, N. "Resul'taty odnodnevnoi perepisi narodnykh shkol v Rossii 18–go ian-varia 1911 g. *Zhurnal Ministerstva Narodnogo Prosveshcheniia,* chast' LII (July 1914).

————. "Vvedenie vseobshchego obycheniia v gorodakh Rossisskoi Imperii." *Zhurnal Ministerstva Narodnogo Prosveshcheniia,* chast' LII (July 1914).

Kudriukov, N. S. "Doma deshevykh kvartir G. G. Solodovnikova v Moskve." *Gorodskoe Delo,* no. 16 (August 15, 1909), 105–111.

Lenin, V. I. *Polnoe Sobranie Sochinenii.* Moscow, 1958–1965.
————. *What Is To Be Done? Burning Questions of Our Movement.* New York, 1929.
Lerche, Hermann (G. G. Lerkhe). "State Credit for Town and County Councils." *Russian Review* (London) 1, no. 3 (1912).
Listovki moskovskikh bol'shevikov v period pervoi russkoi revoliutsii. Moscow, 1955.
Lopukhin, A. A. *Nastoiashchee i budushchee russkoi politsii.* Moscow, 1907.
Lvov, Nicholas. "The Place of Local Government under the Constitution." *Russian Review* (London) 3, no. 2 (1914), 122–133.
M. "Voprosy gorodskoi zhizni." *Russkie Vedomosti,* May 22, 1908.
Materialy po istorii professional'nogo dvizheniia v Rossii. Moscow, 1924–27.
Mikhailov, V. "Iz dokladnoi zapiski o novykh raskhodakh po g. Moskve, postavlennoi V. Mikhailovym po porucheniiu glasnykh Moskovskoi gorodskoi dumy," "Iz dorevoliutsionnogo proshlogo." *Krasnyi Arkhiv,* 5 (84) (1937).
Mikhailovskii, A. "Deiatel'nost' Moskovskogo gorodskogo upravleniia v 1907 g." *Izvestiia Moskovskoi gorodskoi dumy,* no. 1 (1908).
Mikhailovskii, A. G. *Deiatel'nost' Moskovskogo gorodskogo upravleniia v 1913–1916 gg.* Moscow, 1916.
————. "Deiatel'nost' Moskovskogo gorodskogo upravleniia v 1913–1916 gg." *Izvestiia Moskovskaia Gorodskaia Duma otdel obshchii,* 40, no. 9 (September 1916).
————. "Munitsipal'naia Moskva." In *Po Moskve: progulki po Moskve,* pp. 121–158.
Ministerstvo iustitsii. *Svod statisticheskikh svedenii o podsudimykh, opravdannykh i osuzhdennykh po prigovoram obshchikh sudebnykh mest, sudebno-mirovykh ustanovlenii i uchrezhdenii, obrazovannykh po zakonopolozheniiam iz iiulia 1889 g.* St. Petersburg, 1905–1912.
Ministerstvo torgovli i promyshlennosti. Otdel promyshlennosti. *Sbornik postanovlenii glavnogo po fabrichnym i gornozavodskim delam prisutstvie za 1899 po 1914 g.* Petrograd, 1915.
————. *Vrachebnaia pomoshch' fabrichnozavodskim rabochim v 1907 godu.* St. Petersburg, 1909.
Ministerstvo vnutrennykh del. Glavnoe upravlenie po delam mestnogo khoziaistva. *Vrachebno-politseiskii nadzor za gorodskoi prostitutsiei.* St. Petersburg, 1910.
Moskovskaia gorodskaia duma, 1897–1900. Ed. Aleksandr Odintsov. Moscow, 1897.
Moskovskaia gorodskaia duma. *Sbornik obiazatel'nykh dlia zhitelei goroda Moskvy postanovlenii Moskovskoi gorodskoi dumy.* Moscow, 1913.
————. *Stenograficheskie otchety o sobraniiakh Moskovskoi gorodskoi dumy.* Moscow, 1900–1908.
————. komitet gruppy progressivnykh glasnykh. *Moskovskaia gorodskaia duma, 1913–1916 gg.* Moscow, 1916.
Moskovskaia gorodskaia uprava. *Doklady Moskovskoi gorodskoi upravy i komissii.* Moscow, various years.
————. *Obzor po gorody Moskva za* [various years] *god.* Moscow, 1906–1910.
————. *Osnovnye polozheniia proekta sooruzheniia v g. Moskve vneulichnykh dorog bol'shoi skorosti i elektrifikatsii magistral'nykh zheleznykh dorog v raione prigorodnogo soobshcheniia.* Moscow, 1913.
————. *Otchet o deiatel'nosti Moskovskoi gorodskoi upravy za* [various years]. Moscow, 1900–1909.
————. *Sovremennoe khoziaistvo goroda Moskvy.* Ed. I. A. Verner. Moscow, 1913.
————. *Vedomost' o Moskovskikh gorodskikh nachal'nykh uchilishchakh i drugikh uchebnykh, uchebno-vospitatel'nykh i prosvetitel'nykh uchrezhdeniiakh, soderzhimykh na sredstva Moskovskogo gorodskogo upravleniia, na 1 ianvaria 1912 g.* Moscow, 1912.
Moskovskaia Gorodskaia Uprava. Spravochnoe otdelenie po delam blagotvoritel'nosti pri

Moskovskoi Gorodskoi Uprave. *Sbornik spravochnik svedenii o blagotvoritel'nosti v Moskve.* Moscow, 1901.

Moskovskaia Gorodskaia uprava. Statisticheskii otdel'. *Ezhemesiachnyi statisticheskii biulleten' goroda Moskvy.* Moscow, various years.

―――. *Svodnyi Biulleten' po gorodu Moskve. Bulletin récapitulatif de la ville de Moscou.* Moscow, 1913.

―――. *Trudy Statisticheskogo Otdela Moskovskoi Gorodskoi Upravy. Vypusk 1. Glavneishie predvaritel'nye dannye perepisi g. Moskvy 6 marta 1912 goda.* Moscow, 1913.

Moskovskoe Gorodskoe Obshchestvennoe Upravlenie. *Organizatsiia, kul'turnaia rabota i tekhnika Moskovskikh Gorodskikh bibliotek-chitatelen.* Moscow, 1916.

―――. *Otchet o sostoianii gorodskikh nachal'nykh uchilishch i drugikh uchebnykh i prosvetitel'nykh uchrezhdenii. 1913–14 gg.* Moscow, 1915–1916.

Moskovskoe gorodskoe upravlenie. *Vedomosti o Moskovskikh gorodskikh nachal'nykh uchilishchakh za 1905 god.* Moscow, 1906.

Moskovskii gorodskoi narodnyi universitet imeni A. L. Shaniavskogo. *Otchet Moskovskogo Gorodskogo Narodnogo Universiteta imeni A. L. Shaniavskogo za* [various years] *akademicheskii god.* Moscow, various years.

―――. *Tekst zakona s stenograficheskim otchetem Gosudarstvennoi Dumy i biografiei A. L. Shaniavskogo.* Moscow, 1908.

Moskovskoe gradonachal'stvo. *Alfavitnyi sbornik rukovodiashchikh prikazov i tsirkuliarnykh rasporiazhenii po moskovskomu gradonachal'stvu i stolichnoi politsii s 1881 g. po 1 iulia 1910 g.* Moscow, 1911.

―――. *Prikazy po Moskovskomu Gradonachal'stvu i Stolichnoi Politsii. Ianvar' 1908–noiabr' 1914.* Moscow, 1908–1914.

Moskva-entsiklopediia. Moscow, 1980.

Moskva v eia proshlom i nastoiashchem. 12 vols. Moscow, 1910–1912.

M-skogo, A. "Deiatel'nost' Moskovskogo gorodskogo upravleniia." *Izvestiia Moskovskoe gorodskoi dumy,* 8 (1913).

N., M. "Moskovskie birzhi truda." *Russkie Vedomosti,* November 19, 1905.

Nikitin, A. A. "Kanalizatsiia gor. Moskvy." In Moskovskaia gorodskaia uprava, *Sovremennoe khoziaistvo goroda Moskvy.* Ed. I. A. Verner. Moscow, 1913.

"O dvizhenii sredi Moskovskikh rabochikh metallistov." In *Materialy po istorii professional'nogo dvizheniia v Rossii,* sbornik 1. Moscow, 1924.

Orlov, I. I. "Moskovskie gorodskie letnie kolonii." *Vestnik obshchestvennoi gigieny, sud. i prak. med.,* 46, nos. 8 and 9 (August 1910).

Osobyi zhurnal soveta ministrov. St. Petersburg, various years.

Padenie tsarskogo rezhima. Stenograficheskie otchety doprosov i pokazanii, dannykh v Chrezvychainoi Sledstvennoi komissii Vremennogo Pravitel'stva (v 1917 g.) v semi tomakh. Redaktsiia P. E. Shcheglova. Moscow-Leningrad, 1926.

Pares, Bernard. "Conversations with Mr. Stolypin." *Russian Review* 2, no. 1 (1913), 101–110.

"Perechen' naibolee vydaiushchikh proiavlenii revoliutsionnogo dvizheniia za 1906 god." *Pravo,* 34 (1906).

"Perepiska N. A. Romanova i P. A. Stolypina." *Krasnyi Arkhiv,* 5 (1924), 102–128.

Po Moskve. Progulki po Moskve i ee khudozhestvennym i prosvetitel'nym uchrezhdeniiam. Ed. N. A. Geinike. Moscow, 1917.

Pobedonostsev, Konstantin P. *Reflections of a Russian Statesman.* With a new foreword by Murray Polner. Trans. Robert Crozier Long. Ann Arbor, 1965. Originally published as *Moskovskii Sbornik.* Moscow, 1896.

Polnoe sobranie zakonov Rossiiskoi imperii. *Sobranie tret'e.* St. Petersburg, various years.

―――. *Sobranie vtoroe.* St. Petersburg, various years.

Préfecture de la Seine. Direction des affaires municipales. Service de la statistique municipale. *Annuaire statistique de la ville de Paris XXXIe année 1910.* Paris, 1912.

——. *Annuaire statistique de la ville de Paris XXXIIIe année—1912.* Paris, 1915.

Profsoiuzy SSSR: Dokumenty i materialy v chetyrekh tomakh. Tom I. *Profsoiuzy v bor'be za sverzhenie samoderzhaviia i ustanovlenie diktatury proletariata (1905–1917 gg.).* Moscow, 1963.

"Protokol pokazanii E. K. Klimovicha." In *Soiuz russkogo naroda. Po materialam chrezvychainoi sledstvennoi komissii vremennogo pravitel'stva 1917.* Ed. A. Chernovskii. Moscow-Leningrad, 1929.

Put' k Oktiabriu: sbornik statei, vospominanii i dokumentov. Ed. S. I. Chernomordik. 5 vols. Moscow, 1923–1926.

"Samarskii narodnyi universitet." *Vestnik narodnykh universitetov*, no. 1 (May 15, 1910).

Shevkov, N. "Ekonomicheskaia bor'ba moskovskikh shveinikov v 1911–12 g.g." In *Materialy po istorii professional'nogo dvizheniia v Rossii*, sbornik 3. Moscow, 1925.

Shingarev, A. "The Reform of Local Finance in Russia." *Russian Review* 1, no. 1 (1912), 41–55.

Shiskii, N. "Moskovskie ocherki. V gorodskikh rodil'nykh priiutakh." *Gazeta-Kopeika*, May 5, 1909.

S-N, K. "Moskva. Rasshirenie raiona kanalizatsii. Uporiadochenie Khitrova Rynka." *Gorodskoe Delo*, no. 9 (1911).

"Soobshcheniia s mest." *Gorodskoe Delo*, 15–16 (1912).

Soiuz russkogo naroda. Po materialam chrezvychainoi sledstvennoi komissii vremennogo pravitel'stva 1917. Ed. A. Chernovskii. Moscow-Leningrad, 1929.

Speranskii, Sergei. "Gorodskie popechitel'stva." *Russkie Vedomosti*, November 27, 1912.

Staryi Moskvich. "Organizatsiia upravleniia gorodskim khoziaistvom v Moskve." *Russkie Vedomosti*, November 1, 1911.

——. "Prisutstvie po razboru nishchikh." *Russkie Vedomosti*, March 15, 1914.

Statistisches Jahrbuch der Stadt Berlin 33. Jahrgang. Berlin, 1916.

Statistisches Jahrbuch der Stadt Wien für das Jahr 1913. Wien, 1916.

Studenetskii, S. A. "Obshchestvennoe prizrenie." In Moskovskaia gorodskaia uprava, *Sovremennoe khoziaistvo goroda Moskvy.* Ed. I. A. Verner. Moscow, 1913.

Sushkin, N. I., and A. D. Pudalovyi. "Gorodskie zheleznye dorogi." In Moskovskaia gorodskaia uprava, *Sovremennoe khoziaistvo goroda Moskvy.* Ed. I. A. Verner. Moscow, 1913.

"Svedeniia iz Moskvy." *Gorodskoe Delo*, 20 (1911).

Svod zakonov Rossiiskoi Imperii, vtoroe izdanie. St. Petersburg, various years.

Tikhomirov, Lev. "Iz dnevnika Lva Tikhomirova." *Krasnyi Arkhiv*, 1 (74), 1936.

"Tsarkosel'skie soveshchaniia, neizdannye protokoly sekretnogo soveshchaniia pod predsedatel'stvom byvshego imperatora po voprosu o rasshirenii izbiratel'nogo prava, s vvedeniem V. V. Vodovozova." *Byloe; zhurnal posviashchennyi istorii osvoboditel'nogo dvizheniia*, 25, no. 3 (September 1917), 217–265.

Uspenskii, V. V. "Vrachebno-sanitarnaia organizatsiia." In Moskovskaia gorodskaia uprava, *Sovremennoe khoziaistvo goroda Moskvy.* Ed. I. A. Verner. Moscow, 1913.

Vasil'ich, G. "Ulitsy i liudi sovremennoi Moskvy." *Moskva v eia proshlom i nastoiashchem.* Vol. 12. Moscow, 1910–1912.

"Vechernie klassy, kursy i lektsii dlia rabochikh." In Moskovskaia Gorodskaia Duma, *Izvestiia Moskovskoi gorodskoi dumy, otdel Narodnoe Obrazovanie*, nos. 9–10 (1912), 49–59.

Vedomost' o Moskovskikh gorodskikh nachal'nikh uchilishchakh s prilozheniem svedenii. Moscow, 1908.

Verner, Ippolit Antonovich. *Deiatel'nost' Moskovskoi Gorodskoi Dumy v 1909–1912 godakh.* Moscow, 1912.

————. *Gorodskoe samoupravlenie v Rossii.* Moscow, 1906.

Vladimirtsev. V. "Soobshcheniia s mest. Moskva." *Gorodskoe Delo,* no. 3 (1914).

Vsia Moskva; adresnaia i spravochnaia kniga g. Moscow, various years.

Witte, S. Iu. *Samoderzhavie i zemstvo. Konfidentsial'naia zapiska Ministra finansov Stats-Sekretaria S. Iu. Witte (1889 g.).* Vtoroe izdanie. S dvumia predisloviiami Petra Struve. Stuttgart, 1903.

The World Almanac and Encyclopedia 1912. New York, 1911.

Zakony o politsii. N. T. Volkov, comp. Moscow, 1910.

Zviagintsev, Evgenii Alekseevich. *Moskva; putevoditel'.* Moscow, 1915.

Secondary Sources

Abramov, K. I., and V. E. Vasil'chenko. *Istoriia bibliotechnogo dela v SSSR.* Izdanie vtoroe. Moscow, 1970.

Ainzaft, S. *Pervyi etap professional'nogo dvizheniia v Rossii (1905–1907 gg.).* Moscow, 1924–1925.

Alaverdian, Stepan Karapetovich. *Zhilishchnyi vopros v Moskve; ocherki predrevoliutsionnogo perioda.* Erevan, 1961.

Alexander, John T. *Autocratic Politics in a National Crisis: The Imperial Russian Government and Pugachev's Revolt, 1773–1775.* Bloomington, IN, 1969.

Alston, Patrick L. *Education and the State in Tsarist Russia.* Stanford, 1969.

Aluf, A. *Bol'shevizm i men'shevizm v professional'nom dvizhenii.* Moscow, 1926.

Anan'ich, Boris V. "The Economic Policy of the Tsarist Government and Enterprise in Russia from the End of the Nineteenth through the Beginning of the Twentieth Century." In *Entrepreneurship in Imperial Russia and the Soviet Union.* Eds. Gregory Guroff and Fred V. Carstensen. Princeton, 1983.

Anweiler, Oskar. *Geschichte der Schule und Pädagogik in Russland, vom Ende des Zarenreiches bis zum Beginn der Stalin-Ära.* Berlin, 1964.

Arutiunov, G. A. *Rabochee dvizhenie v Rossii v period novogo revoliutsionnogo pod″ema 1910–1914 gg.* Moscow, 1975.

Astrov, N. I. "Iz istorii gorodskikh samoupravlenii v Rossii." *Mestnoe samoupravlenie: Trudy obshchestva dlia izucheniia gorodskogo samoupravleniia v Chekhoslovatskoi respublike.* Prague, 1925.

Astrov, Nikolai Ivanovich, V. F. Zeelera, and P. N. Miliukov, eds. *Pamiati pogibshikh.* Paris, 1929.

Avrekh, A. Ia. *Stolypin i tret'ia duma.* Moscow, 1968.

————. *Tsarizm i tret'eiunskaia sistema.* Moscow, 1966.

Balabanov, Mikhail Solomonovich. *Ot 1905 k 1917 godu: massovoe rabochee dvizhenie.* Moscow, 1927.

Bater, James H. *St. Petersburg: Industrialization and Change.* Montreal, 1976.

Birth, Ernst. *Die Oktobristen (1905–1913); Zielvorstellungen und Struktur. Ein Beitrag zur russischen parteiengeschichte.* Kieler Historische Studien, Band 19. Stuttgart, 1974.

Black, Cyril E. *The Dynamics of Modernization: A Study in Comparative History.* New York, 1966.

Black, Cyril E., Marius B. Jansen, Herbert S. Levine, Marion J. Levy, Jr., Henry Rosovsky, Gilbert Rozman, Henry D. Smith II, and S. Frederick Starr. *The Modernization of Japan and Russia: A Comparative Study.* New York, 1975.

Bogolepov, Mikhail Ivanovich. *Finansy, pravitel'stvo i obshchestvennye interesy.* St. Petersburg, 1907.

Bonnell, Victoria E. *Roots of Rebellion: Workers, Politics, and Organizations in St. Petersburg and Moscow, 1900–1914.* Berkeley, 1983.

————. "Radical Politics and Organized Labor in Pre-Revolutionary Moscow 1905–1914." *Journal of Social History*, no. 2 (1978), 282–300.

————, ed. *The Russian Worker: Life and Labor Under the Tsarist Regime*. Berkeley, 1983.

Bradley, Joseph. "The Moscow Workhouse and Urban Welfare Reform in Russia." *Russian Review* 41, no. 4 (October 1982), 427–444.

————. *Muzhik and Muscovite: Urbanization in Late Imperial Russia*. Berkeley, 1985.

————. "Patterns of Peasant Migration to Late Nineteenth-Century Moscow: How much should we read into Literacy Rates?" *Russian History* 6, part 1 (1979).

Byrnes, Robert F. *Pobedonostsev: His Life and Thought*. Bloomington, IN, 1968.

Charques, Richard. *The Twilight of Imperial Russia*. Oxford, 1958.

Chebarin, A. S. *Moskva v revoliutsii 1905–1907 godov*. Moscow, 1955.

Chekhov, N. V. *Narodnoe obrazovanie v Rossii s 60–kh godov XIX veka*. Moscow, 1912.

Chermenskii, E. D. *Burzhuaziia i tsarizm v pervoi russkoi revoliutsii*. Izdanie vtoroe, pererabotannoe i dopolnennoe. Moscow, 1970.

Conroy, Mary Schaeffer. *Peter Arkad'evich Stolypin: Practical Politics in Late Tsarist Russia*. Boulder, 1976.

Cornelius, Wayne. "Urbanization as an Agent in Latin American Political Instability: The Case of Mexico." *American Political Science Review* 63, no. 3 (1969), 833–857.

Curtiss, John Shelton. *Church and State in Russia: The Last Years of the Empire, 1900–1917*. New York, 1940.

Daniels, Robert V. *Red October: The Bolshevik Revolution of 1917*. New York, 1967.

Davidovich, A. M. *Samoderzhavie v epokhu imperializma*. Moscow, 1975.

Derenkovskii, G. M., et al. *Revoliutsiia 1905–1907 godov v Rossii*. Moscow, 1975.

Deriuzhinskii, V. F. *Politseiskoe pravo*. Izd. 3–e, dopol. St. Petersburg, 1911.

Diakin, V. S. *Samoderzhavie, burzhuaziia i dvorianstvo v 1907–1911 gg*. Leningrad, 1978.

————. *Russkaia burzhuaziia i tsarizm v gody pervoi mirovoi voiny (1914–1917 gg.)*. Leningrad, 1967.

Doyle, William. *Origins of the French Revolution*. London, 1980.

Edelman, Robert. *Gentry Politics on the Eve of the Russian Revolution: The Nationalist Party 1907–1917*. New Brunswick, NJ, 1980.

————. "Rural Proletarians and Peasant Disturbances: The Right Bank Ukraine in the Revolution of 1905." *Journal of Modern History* 57 (1985).

Emmons, Terence, and Wayne S. Vucinich, eds. *The Zemstvo in Russia*. Cambridge, 1982.

Engelstein, Laura. *Moscow, 1905: Working Class Organization and Political Conflict*. Stanford, 1982.

Entsiklopedicheskii slovar' russkogo bibliograficheskogo instituta Granat. 7th edition.

Ermanskii, A. "Krupnaia burzhuaziia v 1905–1907 gg." In *Obshchestvennoe dvizhenie v Rossii v nachale xx-go veka*. Ed. L. Martov et al. 4 vols. St. Petersburg, 1914.

Eroshkin, N. P. "Administrativno-politseiskii apparat." In *Istoriia Moskvy v shesti tomakh*.

Fallows, Thomas. "Politics and the War Effort in Russia: The Union of Zemstvos and the Organization of the Food Supply, 1914–1916." *Slavic Review* 37, no. 1 (1978).

Florinsky, Michael T. *Russia: A History and an Interpretation*. 2 vols. New York, 1953.

Fosdick, Raymond B. *European Police Systems*. Montclair, NJ, 1969.

Franklin, Vincent P. *The Education of Black Philadelphia: The Social and Educational History of a Minority, 1900–1950*. Philadelphia, 1979.

Fraser, Derek. *Power and Authority in the Victorian City*. London, 1979.

Freeze, Gregory L. "The *Soslovie* (Estate) Paradigm and Russian Social History." *American Historical Review* 91, no. 1 (1986).

Fuller, William C., Jr. *Civil-Military Conflict in Imperial Russia, 1881–1914*. Princeton, 1985.

Gauldie, Enid. *Cruel Habitations: A History of Working-Class Housing, 1870–1918*. New York and London, 1974.

Gernet, Mikhail Nikolaevich. *Detoubiistvo; sotsiologicheskoe i sravnitel'no-iuridicheskoe izsledovanie*. Moscow, 1911.

———. *Izbrannye proizvedeniia*. Moscow, 1974.

Gindin, I. F. "Russkaia burzhuaziia v period kapitalizma, ee razvitie i osobennosti." *Istoriia SSSR*, no. 2 (1963), 97–80 and no. 3 (1963), 37–60.

Gleason, William E. *Alexander Guchkov and the End of the Russian Empire*. Transactions of the American Philosophical Society, v. 73, part 3. Philadelphia, 1983.

———. "The All-Russian Union of Towns and the Politics of Urban Reform in Tsarist Russia." *Russian Review* 35, no. 3 (1976), 190–202.

Gorlin, Robert H. "Problems of Tax Reform in Imperial Russia." *Journal of Modern History* 49, no. 2 (June 1977), 246–265.

Gromova, A. A. *Bibliotechnoe delo v Rossii (v 1908–1914 godakh)*. Moscow, 1955.

Gronsky, Paul P., and Nicholas I. Astrov. *The War and the Russian Government*. New Haven, 1929.

Grunt, Aleksandr Ivanovich. *Moskva 1917-i: revoliutsiia i kontrrevoliutsiia*. Moscow, 1976.

———. *Pobeda oktiabr'skoi revoliutsii v Moskve, fevral'-oktiabr' 1917 g*. Moscow, 1961.

———, and Vera Nikolaevna Firstova. *Rossiia v epokhu imperializma, 1907–1917 gg*. Moscow, 1960.

Guroff, Gregory, and Fred V. Carstensen, eds. *Entrepreneurship in Imperial Russia and the Soviet Union*. Princeton, 1983.

Guroff, Gregory, and S. Frederick Starr. "A Note on Urban Literacy in Russia, 1890–1914." *Jahrbücher für Geschichte Osteuropas*, Band 19, heft 4 (1971), 520–531.

Hagen, Manfred. *Entfaltung Politischer Öffentlichkeit in Russland 1906–1914*. Wiesbaden, 1982.

Haimson, Leopold. "Introduction: The Russian Landed Nobility and the System of the 3rd of June." In *The Politics of Rural Russia, 1905–1914*. Ed. Leopold Haimson. Bloomington, IN, 1979.

———. "The Problem of Social Stability in Urban Russia, 1905–1917." *Slavic Review* 23, no. 4 (1964), and 24, no. 1 (1965).

———, ed. *The Politics of Rural Russia, 1905–1914*. Bloomington, IN, 1979.

Hamm, Michael F. "The Breakdown of Urban Modernization: A Prelude to the Revolutions of 1917." In *The City in Russian History*. Ed. Michael F. Hamm. Lexington, KY, 1976.

———. "Continuity and change in late Imperial Kiev," in *The City in Late Imperial Russia*, ed. Michael F. Hamm. Bloomington, IN, 1986.

———. "Kharkov's Progressive Duma, 1910–1914: A Study in Russian Municipal Reform." *Slavic Review* 40, no. 1 (1981).

———. "Riga's 1913 City Election: A Study in Baltic Urban Politics." *Russian Review* 39, no. 4 (1980).

———, ed. *The City in Late Imperial Russia*. Bloomington, IN, 1986.

———, ed. *The City in Russian History*. Lexington, KY, 1976.

Hanchett, Walter. "Tsarist Statutory Regulation of Municipal Government in the Nineteenth Century." In *The City in Russian History*. Ed. Michael F. Hamm. Lexington, KY, 1976.

Hans, Nicholas A. *History of Russian Educational Policy, 1701–1917*. New York, 1964.

Harcave, Sydney. *First Blood: The Russian Revolution of 1905*. New York, 1964.

Hasegawa, Tsuyoshi. "The Formation of the Militia in the February Revolution: An Aspect of the Origins of Dual Power." *Slavic Review* 32, no. 2 (1973).

Hittle, J. Michael. *The Service City: State and Townsmen in Russia, 1600–1800.* Cambridge, MA, 1979.

Hosking, Geoffrey A. *The Russian Constitutional Experiment: Government and Duma, 1907–1914.* Cambridge, England, 1973.

Hutchinson, J. F. "The Octobrists and the Future of Imperial Russia as a Great Power." *Slavonic and East European Review* 50, no. 119 (April 1972), 220–237.

Ignatiev, Paul N., Dimitry M. Odinetz, and Paul J. Novgorodtsev, *Russian Schools and Universities in the World War.* New Haven, 1929.

Ignatov, E. "Iz istorii obshchestva povarov moskovskogo promyshlennogo raiona. Ocherk vtoroi." In *Materialy po istorii professional'nogo dvizheniia v Rossii,* sbornik 2. Moscow, 1924.

Institut istorii Akademii nauk USSR. *Istoriia Kieva.* 2 vols. Kiev, 1963.

Institut istorii partii MK i MGK KPSS—Filial Instituta Marksizma-Leninizma pri Tsk KPSS. *Moskva v dvukh revoliutsiiakh; fevral'-oktiabr' 1917 g.* Moscow, 1958.

Istoriia Moskvy; kratkii ocherk. Izd. tret'e. Ed. S. S. Khromov. Moscow, 1978.

Istoriia Moskvy v shesti tomakh. Moscow, 1952–1955.

Ivanov, L. M. "Ideologicheskoe vozdeistvie na proletariat tsarizma i burzhuazii." In *Rossiiskii proletariat: oblik, bor'ba, gegrmoniia.* L. M. Ivanov, ed. Moscow, 1970.

"Iz dorevoliutsionnogo proshlogo Moskvy." *Krasnyi Arkhiv,* 5 (84) 1937.

Iz istorii revoliutsii 1905 goda v Moskve i moskovskoi gubernii; materialy i dokumenty. Moscow, 1931.

Johnson, Robert Eugene. *Peasant and Proletarian: The Working Class in Moscow in the Late Nineteenth Century.* New Brunswick, NJ, 1979.

Johnson, William Herman Eckart. *Russia's Educational Heritage.* Pittsburgh, 1950.

Kabanov, P., R. Erman, N. Kuznetsov, and A. Ushakov. *Ocherki istorii rossiiskogo proletariata (1861–1917).* Moscow, 1963.

Kabo, E. O. *Ocherki rabochego byta; opyt monograficheskogo issledovaniia domashnego rabochego byta.* Moscow, 1928—.

Karpovich, Michael. *Imperial Russia 1801–1917.* New York, 1932.

Kanel', Veniamin Iakovlevich. *Gorodskoe khoziaistvo i samoupravlenie.* Moscow, 1917.

Karzhanskii, N. *Kak izbiralas' i rabotala Moskovskaia gorodskaia duma.* Izd. 2, perer. i dop. Moscow, 1950.

Katz, Michael B. *Class, Bureaucracy, and Schools: The Illusion of Educational Change in America.* New York, 1971.

Kir'ianov, Iu. I. *Zhiznennyi uroven' rabochikh Rossii, konets XIX-nachalno XXV.* Moscow, 1979.

Koenker, Diane. *Moscow Workers and the 1917 Revolution.* Princeton, 1981.

Konstantinov, N. A. *Ocherki po istorii srednei shkoly; gimnasii i real'nye uchilishcha s kontsa xix v. do Fevral'skoi revoliutsii 1917 goda.* 2nd ed. Moscow, 1956.

Krasnaia presnia; ocherki po istorii zavodov. Moscow, 1934.

Kratkaia istoriia rabochego dvizheniia v Rossii (1861–1917 gody). Moscow, 1962.

Krupskaia, N. K. *Reminiscences of Lenin.* Trans. Bernard Pares. New York, 1970.

Kruze, E. E. *Polozhenie rabochego klassa Rossii v 1900–1914 godakh.* Leningrad, 1976.

Kucherov, Samuel. *Courts, Lawyers and Trials under the Last Three Tsars.* New York, 1953.

Kumanev, V. A. *Revoliutsiia i prosveshchenie mass.* Moscow, 1973.

Laverychev, V. Ia. *Po tu storonu barrikad; iz istorii bor'by moskovskoi burzhuazii s revoliutsiei.* Moscow, 1967.

LeDonne, John P. "The Provincial and Local Police under Catherine the Great, 1775–1796." *Canadian Slavic Studies/Revue Canadienne d'Etudes Slaves* 4, no. 3 (Fall 1970), 513–528.

Leninskii zakaz: *sto let tipografii "krasnyi proletarii"*. Moscow, 1969.

Levin, Alfred. "Peter Arkad'evich Stolypin: A Political Appraisal." *Journal of Modern History* 37, no. 4 (December 1965), 445–463.

———. "Russian Bureaucratic Opinion in the Wake of the 1905 Revolution." *Jahrbücher für Geschichte Osteuropas*, neue folge, Band 11 (1963), 1–12.

———. *The Third Duma, Election and Profile*. Hamden, CT, 1973.

Levy, Marion J., Jr. *Modernization and the Structure of Societies: A Setting for International Affairs*. Princeton, 1966.

Leyda, Jay. *Kino: A History of the Russian and Soviet Film*. New York, 1960.

Lindenmeyr, Adele. "Charity and the Problem of Unemployment: Industrial Homes in Late Imperial Russia." *Russian Review* 45, no. 1 (1986).

———. "A Russian Experiment in Voluntarism: The Municipal Guardianships of the Poor, 1884–1914." *Jahrbücher für Geschichte Osteuropas*, 30 (1982).

Lositskii, A. "Moskva." In *Entsiklopedicheskii slovar' tovarichestva B. A. i I. Granat i ko.* 7-oe, sovershenno pererabotanoe izdanie. Moscow, n.d.

McClelland, James C. *Autocrats and Academics: Education, Culture and Society in Tsarist Russia*. Chicago and London, 1979.

McKay, John P. *Tramways and Trolleys: The Rise of Urban Mass Transport in Europe*. Princeton, 1976.

McNeal, Robert H., ed. *Russia in Transition 1905–1914: Evolution or Revolution?* New York, 1970.

Manning, Roberta Thompson. *The Crisis of the Old Order in Russia: Gentry and Government*. Princeton, 1982.

———. "The zemstvo and politics, 1864–1914." In *The Zemstvo in Russia*. Ed. Terence Emmons and Wayne S. Vucinich. Cambridge, MA, 1982.

Menashe, Louis. "Industrialists in Politics: Russia in 1905." *Government and Opposition* 3, no. 3 (1968), 352–368.

———. "A Liberal with Spurs: Alexander Guchkov, a Russian Bourgeois in Politics." *Russian Review* 16, no. 1 (January 1967).

Menitskii, I. A. *Russkoe rabochee dvizhenie i R.S.D.R.P. nakanune voiny*. Moscow, 1923.

Milonov, Iu. K., ed. *Moskovskoe professional'noe dvizhenie v gody pervoi revoliutsii*. Moscow, 1925 (?).

Morekhin, G. G. "Novyi revoliutsionnyi pod"em (1912–1914)." In *Istoriia Moskvy v shesti tomakh*, pp. 256–276.

Nelson, Joan. "The Urban Poor: Disruption or Political Integration in Third World Cities?" *World Politics* 22, no. 3 (1970), 393–414.

Nikitin, M. "Moskovskoe stachechnoe dvizhenie v 1905–1907 gg." In Iu. K. Milonov, ed., *Moskovskoe professional'noe dvizhenie v gody pervoi revoliutsii*. Moscow, 1925 (?).

Obshchestvennoe dvizhenie v Rossii v nachale xx-go veka. Ed. L. Martov et al. 4 vols. St. Petersburg, 1914.

Odinetz, Dmitry M. "Russian Primary and Secondary Schools Prior to and During the War." In *Russian Schools and Universities in the World War*. Ed. Paul N. Ignatiev, Dmitry M. Odinetz, and Paul J. Novgorodtsev. New Haven, 1929.

Oldenburg, Sergei S. *Last Tsar: Nicholas II, his Reign and his Russia*. Trans. of *Tsarstvovanie Imperatora Nikolaia II* by Leonid Mihalap and Patrick Rollins. 4 vols. Gulf Breeze, FL, 1977.

Ososkov, A. V. *Voprosy istorii nachal'nogo obrazovaniia v Rossii (II. pol. XIX-nach. XXVV.) Uchebnoe posobie*. chast' pervaia. Moscow, 1975.

Ostroumov, Sergei Sergeevich. *Ocherki po istorii ugolovnoi statistiki dorevoliutsionnoi Rossii*. Moscow, 1961.

Owen, Thomas C. *Capitalism and Politics in Russia: A Social History of the Moscow Merchants, 1855–1905*. Cambridge, MA, 1981.

Pankratova, A. M. *Pervaia russkaia revoliutsiia 1905–1907 gg.* Izd. vtoroe, dopolnennoe. Moscow, 1951.

Pares, Bernard. *Russia: Between Reform and Revolution.* New York, 1962.

Park, Robert E., and Ernest W. Burgess. *The City.* Chicago, 1925.

Pazhitnov, Konstantin Alekseevich. *Polozhenie rabochego klassa v Rossii.* 3 vols. Leningrad, 1924.

Petrov, M. N. "Naselenie i territoriia Moskvy v kontse XIX V i nachale XX V." In *Istoriia Moskvy v shesti tomakh.*

Phillips, G. W. "Urban Proletarian Politics in Tsarist Russia: Petersburg and Moscow, 1912–1914." *Comparative Urban Research* 3, no. 3 (1976).

Pinchuk, Ben-Cion. *The Octobrists in the Third Duma, 1907–1912.* Seattle, 1974.

Pipes, Richard. *Russia Under the Old Regime.* New York, 1974.

Pisar'kova, L. F. *Moskovskoe gorodskoe obshchestvennoe upravlenie.* Avtoreferat. Moscow, 1980.

Pogrebinskii, Aleksandr Petrovich. *Gosudarstvennye finansy tsarskoi Rossii v epokhu imperializma.* Moscow, 1968.

Rabochii klass i rabochee dvizhenie v Rossii. 1861–1917 gg. Moscow, 1966.

Raeff, Marc. "Some Reflections on Russian Liberalism." *Russian Review* 18, no. 3 (1959).

Rashin, A. G. *Naselenie Rossii za 100 let, 1811–1913 gg.; statisticheskie ocherki.* Ed. S. G. Strumilin. Moscow, 1956.

Rieber, Alfred J. *Merchants and Entrepreneurs in Imperial Russia.* Chapel Hill, NC, 1982.

Riha, Thomas. "Constitutional Developments in Russia." In *Russia Under the Last Tsar.* Ed. George Stavrou. Minneapolis, 1969.

Robinson, Geroid T. *Rural Russia Under the Old Regime: A History of the Landlord-Peasant World and Prologue to the Peasant Revolution of 1917.* Berkeley, 1960.

Rogger, Hans. "The Question Remains Open." In *Russia in Transition 1905–1914: Evolution or Revolution?* Ed. Robert H. McNeal. New York, 1970.

————. *Russia in the Age of Modernization and Revolution 1881–1917.* London, 1983.

Roosa, Ruth Amende. "Russian Industrialists, Politics, and Labor Reform in 1905." *Russian History* 11, part 2 (1975), 124–148.

————. "Workers' Insurance Legislation and the Role of the Industrialists in the Period of the Third State Duma." *Russian Review* 34, no. 4 (October 1975), 410–452.

Rosenberg, William G. *Liberals in the Russian Revolution: The Constitutional Democratic Party, 1917–1921.* Princeton, 1974.

Rosental', I. S. "Russkii liberalizm nakanune pervoi mirovoi voiny i taktika bol'shevikov." *Istoriia SSSR,* 6 (1971).

Rossiiskii proletariat: oblik, bor'ba, gegemoniia. Ed. L. M. Ivanov. Moscow, 1970.

Rowney, Don Karl. "Higher Civil Servants in the Russian Ministry of Internal Affairs: Some Demographic and Career Characteristics, 1905–1916." *Slavic Review* 31, no. 1 (March 1972), 101–110.

Rubinov, Anatolii Zakharovich. *Otsy goroda.* Moscow, 1966.

Ruckman, Jo Ann. *The Moscow Business Elite: A Social and Cultural Portrait of Two Generations, 1840–1905.* DeKalb, IL, 1984.

Sablinsky, Walter. *The Road to Bloody Sunday: Father Gapon and the St. Petersburg Massacre of 1905.* Princeton, 1976.

Sankt Peterburgskaia stolichnaia politsiia i gradonachal'stvo (1703–1903). Kratkii istoricheskii ocherk. St. Petersburg, 1903.

Schneiderman, Jeremiah. *Sergei Zubatov and Revolutionary Marxism: The Struggle for the Working Class in Tsarist Russia.* Ithaca, NY, 1976.

Scobie, James R. *Buenos Aires: Plaza to Suburb, 1870–1910.* New York, 1974.

Sewell, William H., Jr. *Work and Revolution in France: The Language of Labor from the Old Regime to 1848.* Cambridge, England, 1980.

Shtromberg, M. A. *Gorodskie zheleznie dorogi v Moskve i drugikh bol'shikh gorodakh i ikh sotsial'noe znachenie.* Moscow, 1913.

Shvittau, Georgii Georgievich. *Trudovaia pomoshch' v Rossii.* Petrograd, 1915.

Sidorov, Arkadii Lavrovich. *Ekonomicheskoe polozhenie Rossii v gody pervoi mirovoi voiny.* Moscow, 1973.

Siegelbaum, Lewis H. *The Politics of Industrial Mobilization in Russia, 1914–1917: A Study of the War-Industries Committees.* New York, 1983.

Sliuzberg (Sliozberg), G. B. *Dorevoliutsionnoi stroi Rossii.* Paris, 1933.

Stavrou, Theofanis George, ed. *Russia Under the Last Tsar.* Minneapolis, 1969.

Stites, Richard. *The Women's Liberation Movement in Russia: Feminism, Nihilism, and Bolshevism 1860–1930.* Princeton, 1978.

Strumilin, Stanislav Gustatovich. *Zarabotnaia plata i proizvoditel'nost' truda v russkoi promyshlennosti za 1913–1922 g.* Moscow, 1923.

Suny, Ronald Grigor. "Toward a Social History of the October Revolution." *American Historical Review* 88, no. 1 (1983).

Svavitskii, A., and V. Sher. *Ocherk polozheniia rabochikh pechatnogo dela v Moskve.* St. Petersburg, 1909.

Sysin, A. N. "Sanitarno-lechebnoe delo." In *Istoriia Moskvy v shesti tomakh,* vol. 5.

Sytin, Petr Vasil'evich. *Kommunal'noe khoziaistvo. Blagoustroistvo Moskvy v sravnenii s blagoustroistvom drugikh bol'shikh gorodov.* Moscow, 1926.

Tilly, Charles, and C. Harold Brown. "On Uprooting, Kinship, and the Auspices of Migration." In *An Urban World.* Ed. Charles Tilly. Boston and Toronto, 1974.

Tilly, Charles, ed. *An Urban World.* Boston and Toronto, 1974.

Timberlake, Charles E. "Introduction: The Concept of Liberalism in Russia." In *Essays on Russian Liberalism.* Ed. Charles E. Timberlake. Columbia, MO, 1972.

————, ed. *Essays on Russian Liberalism.* Columbia, MO, 1972.

Tolstov, A. S. "Nachal'nye shkoly." In *Istoriia Moskvy v shesti tomakh,* vol. 5.

Trotsky, Leon. *History of the Russian Revolution.* 3 vols. Trans. Max Eastman. New York, 1932.

————. *1905.* Trans. Anya Bostock. New York, 1972.

Usloviia byta rabochikh v dorevoliutsionnoi Rossii (po dannym biudzhetnykh obsledovanii). Gen. ed. N. K. Druzhinin. Ed. L. Speranskaia. Moscow, 1958.

Von Laue, Theodore H. "The Chances for Liberal Constitutionalism." *Slavic Review* 24, no. 1 (1965).

Voznesenskii, A. N. *Moskva v 1917 godu.* Moscow and Leningrad, 1928.

Vydro, M. Ia. *Naselenie Moskvy (po materialam perepisei naseleniia 1871–1970 gg.).* Moscow, 1976.

Wade, Rex A. *Red Guards and Workers' Militias in the Russian Revolution.* Stanford, 1984.

Walkin, Jacob. "Government Controls over the Press in Russia, 1905–1914." *Russian Review* 13, no. 3 (1954).

————. *The Rise of Democracy in Pre-revolutionary Russia: Political and Social Institutions Under the Last Three Czars.* New York, 1962.

Warner, Sam Bass, Jr. *The Private City: Philadelphia in Three Periods of Its Growth.* Philadelphia, 1968.

Weissman, Neil. *Reform in Tsarist Russia: The State Bureaucracy and Local Government, 1900–1914.* New Brunswick, NJ, 1981.

————. "Regular Police in Tsarist Russia, 1900–1914." *Russian Review* 44, no. 1 (1985).

West, James L. "The Search for a Middle Class Identity: Two Views of the Russian Bourgeoisie 1905–1914." Paper presented to the 16th National Convention of the American Association for the Advancement of Slavic Studies, New York, 1984.

Wiebe, Robert. *The Search for Order, 1877–1920.* New York, 1967.

Wildman, Allan K. *The End of the Russian Imperial Army: The Old Army and the Soldiers' Revolt (March–April 1917)*. Princeton, 1980.

Wolfe, Bertram D. *Three Who Made a Revolution: A Biographical History*. New York, 1960.

Woodward, C. Vann. *The Strange Career of Jim Crow*. 3rd rev. ed. New York, 1974.

Woytinsky, Vladimir S., and Emma S. Woytinsky. *World Population and Production: Trends and Outlooks*. New York, 1953.

Zaionchkovsky, Peter A. *The Russian Autocracy in Crisis, 1878–1882*. Ed. and trans. Gary Hamburg. Gulf Breeze, FL, 1979.

Zelnik, Reginald E. *Labor and Society in Tsarist Russia: The Factory Workers of St. Petersburg, 1855–1870*. Stanford, 1971.

————. "Russian Workers and the Revolutionary Movement." *Journal of Social History* 6, no. 2 (1972–73).

Zlatoustovskii, B. V. "Gorodskoe samoupravlenie." In *Istoriia Moskvy v shesti tomakh*. Moscow, 1952–1955.

Index

261